SECOND EDITION

Essential CVS

Jennifer Vesperman

O'REILLY®

Beijing · Cambridge · Farnham · Köln · Paris · Sebastopol · Taipei · Tokyo

Essential CVS, Second Edition

by Jennifer Vesperman

Copyright © 2007, 2003 O'Reilly Media, Inc. All rights reserved.
Printed in the United States of America.

Published by O'Reilly Media, Inc., 1005 Gravenstein Highway North, Sebastopol, CA 95472.

O'Reilly books may be purchased for educational, business, or sales promotional use. Online editions are also available for most titles (*safari.oreilly.com*). For more information, contact our corporate/institutional sales department: (800) 998-9938 or *corporate@oreilly.com*.

Editor: Brian Jepson	**Indexer:** John Bickelhaupt
Executive Editor: Mary O'Brien	**Cover Designer:** Karen Montgomery
Production Editor: Lydia Onofrei	**Interior Designer:** David Futato
Copyeditor: Nancy Kotary	**Illustrators:** Robert Romano and Jessamyn Read
Proofreader: Lydia Onofrei	

Printing History:

June 2003:	First Edition.
November 2006:	Second Edition.

 This book uses RepKover™, a durable and flexible lay-flat binding.

ISBN-10: 0-596-52703-9
ISBN-13: 978-0-596-52703-7

[M]

Essential CVS

Other resources from O'Reilly

To my grandmother, Emilie Carrick.
Born 1907, died 2002.

Nan,
You lived through changes and troubles and rose
above them. You saw the best in everyone you
met, and helped them see it as well. You loved
everyone, and helped us learn to love.

I miss you. I love you.

Table of Contents

Part II. Using CVS

Part III. CVS Administration

Part IV.   Reference

Part V.   Appendixes

Preface

CVS (Concurrent Versions System) is a tool that enables you to track changes to a set of files over time. CVS is commonly used in software development, for instance, to allow multiple developers to coordinate changes, track versions, and permit simultaneous development of different versions of the same code.

This book is not just for software developers. It is for anyone who produces things that change. CVS can manage versions of anything that can be stored in files, so it is useful for programmers, system administrators, software architects, writers, graphic artists, and user-interface (UI) specialists. Outside the computing field, it can be used by authors, poets, managers, architects, engineers, accountants, and other people running their everyday lives.

Changes for the Second Edition

First, *Essential CVS*, Second Edition, is current for both the stable and feature tracks of CVS. Feature releases contain new CVS features as well as current bug fixes. At the time I'm writing this, the current versions are stable CVS 1.11.22, and feature CVS 1.12.13; the book is up to date for these versions. Most CVS features are available in both the stable and the feature versions of CVS. Where there is a difference, it is mentioned in the book.

Second, I've added and expanded the examples in general, and specifically added screenshots and examples of using graphical CVS clients to run CVS commands.

Another feature of the second edition that I'm excited about is the sidebars—I've provided chatty sidebars explaining how I've used CVS in the past, or how a command could be used. I've also provided sidebars that discuss aspects or features of Unix that you need to know.

There's a new appendix—a FAQ. I went through the CVS mailing list and grabbed the questions that kept being repeated. They're now answered in the FAQ appendix of *Essential CVS*!

Finally, the text is tightened up in general. I've clarified things more, and added explanations and cross-references.

I'd like to thank all my reviewers and every reader who wrote to me or to O'Reilly. I've learned a lot about writing from all of you, and a lot about what makes the difference between a good book and a great book.

I believe that the second edition of this book is a lot closer to the Great Australian Technical Book than the first edition was.

Structure of the Book

This book can be read out of sequence, so you can learn about any aspect of CVS at the time you need it. However, the concepts are presented in a logical order, and they might be more easily understood if you read the chapters in order. The book is organized into five parts.

Part I explains the basic concepts of CVS and includes a quickstart guide. If you don't already know CVS, read the quickstart guide before going on to the rest of the book. Part I includes the following chapters:

Chapter 1, *What Is CVS?*
    This chapter is an overview of CVS, versioning systems, and the practical uses of CVS.

Chapter 2, *CVS Quickstart Guide*
    If you need to get up to speed rapidly, this is the chapter for you. It explains how to build and use a basic CVS repository with the default settings and a minimum of extras.

Part II explains the core concepts behind CVS and describes the commands that most people use on a day-to-day basis. Part II consists of the following chapters:

Chapter 3, *Basic Use of CVS*
    This chapter explains the everyday CVS commands and concepts—the ones that almost everyone who uses CVS will need. Each command is accompanied by an example and a description of the most commonly used options to the command.

    Commands in this chapter include *add*, *remove*, *commit*, and *update*. Concepts covered include the CVS repository and sandboxes, conflicts and merges, using CVS with binary files, and switching repositories.

Chapter 4, *Tagging and Branching*
    Tagging, branching, and merging branches back to the trunk are closely related topics. This chapter explains tagging and branching, including why and when to tag or branch your project, tagging before releases, and using branching to create a bugfix version of a project.

Chapter 5, *Multiple Users*

This chapter explains the systems used in CVS to permit multiple developers to work on the same project without loss of data. For example, it discusses the commands available for displaying changes to files.

Part III is for project managers and repository administrators. The chapters can be read in any order, but later chapters assume familiarity with commands explained in earlier chapters. Part III includes the following chapters:

Chapter 6, *Repository Management*

This chapter discusses repository management and the modules in the repository. It covers creating a repository and estimating disk space, the structure of the CVS repository, configuration and permissions, repository security, and hand-editing a repository.

Chapter 7, *Project Management*

This chapter covers the tools used by project administrators. Topics include importing and exporting projects, using the *cvs admin* command, reading the output of the logging commands, and using the *info* configuration files to interact with bug-tracking systems or to enforce log-message formats.

Chapter 8, *Remote Repositories*

Most projects involve a repository on a different machine from the client. This chapter discusses security considerations, methods of remote access, and how to set up each method.

Chapter 9, *Troubleshooting*

Every tool has its caveats and gotchas. This chapter provides examples of things that can go wrong when using CVS and how to fix them.

Part IV is designed to be used as a reference manual. It includes the following chapters:

Chapter 10, *Command Reference*

This chapter provides a list of CVS commands, including the syntax and options for each command.

Chapter 11, *Miscellaneous Topics Reference*

This chapter covers CVS administrative files, environment variables that affect CVS, date formats, pattern matching, and repository access methods, in reference form.

Part V contains brief information on and pointers to various third-party tools that work with CVS. It includes the following appendixes:

Appendix A, *Clients and Operating Systems*

This appendix discusses third-party CVS clients for the Windows, Unix, GNU/ Linux, and Macintosh operating systems. It also discusses the tools that integrate CVS with programmers' integrated development environments (IDEs).

Appendix B, *Administrators' Tools*

Because CVS is a useful open source tool, people have written third-party tools for it. This appendix explains some of the useful third-party tools available for CVS.

Appendix C, *Frequently Asked Questions*

This appendix is a collection of frequently asked questions from the *info-cvs* mailing lists, and the answers to those questions.

In addition to the five parts just described, this book also contains a pull-out CVS quick-reference card for when you need a quick reminder of command syntax.

Conventions Used in This Book

The following typographical conventions are used in this book:

Italic

Used to indicate CVS commands and their options, CVS configuration file keywords, filenames and directory names, emphasis, and the first use of technical terms.

Constant width

Used in code examples and to show the contents of files.

Constant width italic

Used in syntax descriptions to indicate user-defined items.

Constant width bold

Used to indicate user input in examples that show both input and output.

[ ]

Square brackets enclose optional elements in syntax diagrams.

{ }

Braces enclose lists of elements from which you are required to make one choice.

|

Vertical bars separate elements in lists that are enclosed by square brackets ([...]) or braces ({...}).

. . .

Ellipses are used within syntax diagrams to indicate repetition. Ellipses are also used in code examples to indicate nonessential command output that has been eliminated for the sake of clarity and space.

(tab)

In some syntax diagrams, (tab) is used to indicate a point at which you must type a tab character.

SSH, *ssh*

I use SSH (uppercase, regular text) as an acronym when referring to the *Secure Shell* protocol. I use *ssh* (lowercase, italic text) to refer to the Unix command often used to invoke an SSH program.

Learning More About CVS

In addition to this book, there are a number of other helpful CVS resources that you should know about. CVS has an active user community, and additional resources may become available over time.

Web Site and Manpages

The CVS home page is at *http://cvs.nongnu.org*. This site provides a copy of the *info cvs* manual by Per Cederqvist et al.; a CVS FAQ; and links to most of the available third-party tools for CVS.

The official web site for the book (*http://www.oreilly.com/catalog/essentialcvs2/*) and my personal web site (*http://essential-cvs.vesperman.id.au*) will have extra information added to them over time that may prove useful or interesting.

On Unix and Linux systems, the *man cvs* and *info cvs* commands provide documentation for the server and the command-line client.

Related Books

The *CVS Pocket Reference*, by Gregor N. Purdy (O'Reilly), is a useful take-anywhere book.

Applying RCS and SCCS, by Don Bolinger and Tan Bronson (O'Reilly), explains RCS, which is the tool that CVS calls to manage individual files within its database.

Pragmatic Version Control Using CVS, by Dave Thomas and Andy Hunt (The Pragmatic Programmers), is an example-based book about using CVS.

Open Source Development with CVS, by Moshe Bar and Karl Franz Fogel (Paraglyph Press) contains a guide to CVS and a guide to open source project management. It is available online at *http://cvsbook.red-bean.com*.

Version Management with CVS, by Per Cederqvist et al. (Network Theory Ltd.), is published online at *http://ximbiot.com/cvs/manual/* and is also available as *info cvs*.

Linux Server Hacks, by Rob Flickenger (O'Reilly), contains 11 hacks for using CVS as a system administrator.

Support

CVS is an open source project. Although there's no one company backing CVS and providing support for it, you can get a wealth of support from your fellow CVS users. The official CVS mailing lists are available at *http://savannah.nongnu.org/mail/ ?group=cvs*. The most important lists are *info-cvs@nongnu.org* for discussion and support and *bugs-cvs@nongnu.org* for bug reports.

Using Code Examples

This book is here to help you get your job done. In general, you may use the code in this book in your programs and documentation. You do not need to contact us for permission unless you're reproducing a significant portion of the code. For example, writing a program that uses several chunks of code from this book does not require permission. Selling or distributing a CD-ROM of examples from O'Reilly books *does* require permission. Answering a question by citing this book and quoting example code does not require permission. Incorporating a significant amount of example code from this book into your product's documentation *does* require permission.

We appreciate, but do not require, attribution. An attribution usually includes the title, author, publisher, and ISBN. For example: "*Essential CVS,* Second Edition, by Jennifer Vesperman. Copyright 2007 O'Reilly Media, Inc., 978-0-596-52703-7."

If you feel your use of code examples falls outside fair use or the permission given above, feel free to contact us at *permissions@oreilly.com*.

How To Contact Us

Please address comments and questions concerning this book to the publisher:

> O'Reilly Media, Inc.
> 1005 Gravenstein Highway North
> Sebastopol, CA 95472
> 800-998-9938 (in the United States or Canada)
> 707-829-0515 (international or local)
> 707-829-0104 (fax)

We have a web page for this book, where we list errata, code examples, and any additional information. Corresponding files for code examples are mentioned on the first line of the example. You can access this page at:

> *http://www.oreilly.com/catalog/essentialcvs2/*

To comment or ask technical questions about this book, send email to:

> *bookquestions@oreilly.com*

For more information about our books, conferences, Resource Centers, and the O'Reilly Network, see our web site at:

> *http://www.oreilly.com*

Safari® Enabled

 When you see a Safari® Enabled icon on the cover of your favorite technology book, that means the book is available online through the O'Reilly Network Safari Bookshelf.

Safari offers a solution that's better than e-books. It's a virtual library that lets you easily search thousands of top tech books, cut and paste code samples, download chapters, and find quick answers when you need the most accurate, current information. Try it for free at *http://safari.oreilly.com*.

Acknowledgments for the First Edition

No book is written in isolation, and I have had a lot of help with this one. My family and friends have been very encouraging and helpful, and the women and men of LinuxChix were there to keep me going when things were hard. Thank you all!

I would like to thank Chris Klint and David North for the donation of a laptop and a laptop hard drive when I had to travel while preparing the book. Thanks to Sonja Krause-Harder and Rebecca Walter Pedersen for SuSE information, Alan Cox and Telsa Gwynne for Red Hat information, and Akkana Peck for Red Hat testing. Thanks also go to Mia Ridge for Macintosh information and Michelle Peglar for the use of a Macintosh.

I am grateful to my editor, Jonathan Gennick. I thought I was a pretty good writer when I started, but I'm a much, much better writer now. Thank you, Jonathan.

Thank you to Derek Price for technical review. Your comments have ensured that the book is accurate and that it reflects the recommendations of the CVS developers.

Many thanks to Ellie Volckhausen, Betsy Waliszewski, Bonnie Sheehan, and all the others at O'Reilly who have worked hard to make this book happen.

To Dr. Anne Small and her team of dedicated medical professionals and support staff—thank you. Without you, I would be an invalid, not an author, and I am eternally grateful.

I want to thank my dear friends Mike Whitaker and Richard Gencks for general encouragement and emotional support, especially when my wonderful grandmother died while I was reviewing the book. (I love you, Nan.)

And to my husband, Dancer Vesperman, and our housemate and friend Karen Hall—thank you. There is no way I could have done this without you.

Acknowledgments for the Second Edition

Once again, I owe a great debt of thanks to many people for this book. Among the most important are family, friends, the LinuxChix members, and the Free Software/ Open Source community in Melbourne, Australia.

Specific thanks go to Jonathan Gennick, Mary O'Brien, and Brian Jepson, my editors at O'Reilly. I would also like to thank the many people at O'Reilly who will work and have worked on this book and whose names I don't know. There is a great deal of effort involved in producing a book: please look on the copyright in this book. It wouldn't be in your hands if it weren't for the people listed there.

Thank you to Maria Blackmore, Tom Sgouros, and Christina Zeeh for technical editing. Your comments provided both technical corrections and clarifications. There are many places where I've reworded a phrase or expanded on a paragraph thanks to your advice, and the book is much improved for your efforts.

Christina Zeeh also provided information and screenshots specific to Macintosh computers, and Maria Blackmore and Brian Jepson assisted with examples on various distributions of Linux.

Carla Schroder is an invaluable support and a good friend, and would have also been doing technical editing if she were not busy writing her own book. Look for her books!

Once again, I am grateful to my medical team. Dedicated medical professionals and their support staff make a huge difference in life. Thank you, Dr. Small.

And finally, to Dancer Vesperman, Anastasia Vesperman, and Richard Gencks: I love you.

## PART I

Introduction

This part of the book explains the basic concepts of CVS and includes a quickstart guide that you can use if you're new to CVS and need to get CVS installed, configured, and operational in a hurry. Part I includes the following chapters:

Chapter 1, *What Is CVS?*
> This chapter is an overview of CVS, versioning systems, and the practical uses of CVS.

Chapter 2, *CVS Quickstart Guide*
> If you need to get up to speed rapidly, this is the chapter for you. It explains how to build and use a basic CVS repository with default settings and a minimum of extras.

What Is CVS?

CVS is a version tracking system. It maintains records of files throughout their development, allows retrieval of any stored version of a file, and supports production of multiple versions of a file. CVS enables multiple developers to work simultaneously on a single file without loss of data. Each developer works on her own copy of a file, and all changes are later merged into a single master copy. CVS can be integrated with bug-tracking and feature-tracking systems, and it provides features that can assist a project manager by tracking changes to a project over time.

CVS can be used in many environments for many purposes: maintaining configuration files, mail aliases, source code, FAQ files, art, music, articles, essays, and books. Some system administrators keep the contents of their */etc* directory under CVS in order to track system configuration changes over time. CVS is also used to store and automatically publish content to web sites and FTP servers.

CVS follows the Unix ethos of small programs doing what they do well. The RCS (Revision Control System) program handles revision control of single files, so CVS uses RCS to store file data. CVS adds features to RCS—most notably, the abilities to work on collections of files and to work out of a repository that may be local or remote.

What Is a Versioning System?

Version control is the process of recording and being able to retrieve changes to a project. Computer scientists define version control, source control, and change management as different but overlapping tasks; version control is the most accurate term for the aspects of the field that apply to CVS. A version control system lets you retrieve an old version to fix bugs or update features, to *branch* development to allow the project to progress along multiple tracks simultaneously, and to generate reports that show the differences between any two arbitrary stages of a project.

Most version control systems store notes with each change, and many provide tools that allow a project leader to analyze the changes. Most also include the ability to retrieve differences between arbitrary versions of files, which makes it easier to create patches or locate bugs.

The benefits of a version control system such as CVS include:

- Any stored revision of a file can be retrieved, viewed, and changed.
- The differences between any two revisions can be displayed.
- Patches can be created automatically.
- Multiple developers can work simultaneously on the same project or file without overwriting one another's changes.
- The project can be branched to allow simultaneous development along varied tracks. These branches can be merged back into the main line of development.
- Distributed development is supported across large or small networks. (CVS offers a variety of authentication mechanisms.)

Using version control for a project requires some extra work on an ongoing basis. In addition, previous versions of files, or records of changes to the various files in a project, occupy disk space that you might otherwise use for something else. However, the features that a good version control system makes available are well worth the investment of time and disk space. For example, without version control, project backups typically are timestamped copies of an entire project, hopefully stored together in a logical fashion. Version control provides organized storage and retrieval of the complete record of project changes, rather than whichever copies someone might remember to make.

Version control systems store files as the files are created and updated, in a way that allows any saved version of a file, or related versions of a set of files, to be retrieved at any given time. Many version control systems, including CVS, encourage a project's files to be stored together, which means that backups are easy to produce.

The ability to recover any earlier version of a given file allows you to roll back to support feature requests for previous releases and is critical when you create a bugfix branch of the project. CVS (as do some other version control systems) allows simultaneous storage of the bugfix branch of a project and its main trunk code.

Many version control systems, including CVS, can display the differences between versions in a computer-readable format. The format CVS uses produces a file that allows the Unix *patch* program to automatically convert one version of a file (or set of files) to another.

Version control often allows multiple projects to use the same files, which helps divide a larger project among smaller teams. You can give each team a version-controlled copy of the section it's working on, as well as the latest stable version of the files it needs to use to test its section.

Sometimes, two or more developers may make changes to the same file. Those changes may be in different parts of the file, and they may be made in such a way as not to conflict with each other. Other times, two or more developers may make conflicting changes to the same portion of a file. In such a case, CVS does its best to merge conflicting changes, but it only knows which lines of a file have been changed. It doesn't know what the changes mean. CVS provides tools to display changes between arbitrary revisions, which can help locate and resolve problems.

Version control is not a substitute for communication between team members. File updates should be passed through CVS, but the meaning of the changes must be passed to other team members by actually discussing them. If one developer needs to change the arguments to a function or the chapter numbering of a book, that must somehow be communicated to the other developers.

Versioning systems are most commonly used for programming, but they are also useful for writing (I used CVS to write this book), system administration (configuration files), and anything else that involves files that change, where you might want to retrieve older versions of those files, or for situations where several people may be working on the same files. One family I know uses CVS to store its shopping list, to keep family members from overwriting each other's entries.

Why CVS?

With all the version control systems available, why choose CVS? If you work with files that change over time, the most important thing is to have some kind of version control: after the first time it's saved your bacon, you'll never want to work without it. If it's your first time with a version control system, choose one with good documentation and the features you think you'll need for the first year or two. Read the available tutorials and quickstart guides, and use a system that you feel you can understand. As you're already taking a look at this book, CVS is a fine choice: it will get you through that first year or two, and beyond.

 Any version control is better than no version control.

Once you're used to working with version control, you can make a more informed decision about the features you'll want long term, and choose a system with those features in mind. Changing systems is not something to fear, as there are tools for conversion between many version control systems. At worst, you can use one system for the old data and another for the new, or write a script that checks out each revision in turn from the old system and commits it to the new.

Features of Version Control Systems

Every version control system that I'm familiar with records the changes in a document, enables you to retrieve older versions of the document, and enables you to display the differences between versions. (The first two features are what defines a version control system.) Some systems do little more than that, but most have additional features. You should choose a system based on the features that are most important to your project and working style.

One of the most important features a version control system can provide is support for multiple developers. There are two common models for this support; choose the model that works best for you. The easiest to understand is *exclusive development*: the version control system permits only one developer at a time to work on any individual file. A system may have strict exclusive development and make it nearly impossible for a developer to work on a file he hasn't reserved, or it may have advisory exclusive development and simply warn the developer before allowing access to a file that another developer is editing. The alternative to exclusive development is *simultaneous development*, where multiple developers can work on the same file and the version control system attempts to merge the respective changes seamlessly. CVS supports both modes, which are more fully explained in Chapter 5.

Traditional version control systems have *central repositories*, but some of the newer ones have *distributed repositories*, and many systems have central repositories but support *proxying*. If you are a single developer, this issue won't affect you, but managers of projects with multiple developers should think about whether a central or distributed repository better suits their needs. See the sidebar "Central, Distributed, or Proxied" later in this chapter for more information.

Systems should support *remote access* to the repository, or remote connection among distributed repositories. Most projects will need the ability to access the repository from outside the local network. The remote repository support in CVS is explained in Chapter 8.

Another important feature is *data export*. An exported set of data should not contain administrative files or data for the version control system. Most version control systems provide some form of export. CVS's *export* command is explained in Chapter 7.

Customization is also important to many users. For example, some project managers want every change exported immediately to a test area. Some want committed changes reviewed to ensure they meet project standards. A proxy repository may need to initialize or finalize a connection when it communicates with the master repository. To achieve all these (and other) special tasks, a version control system needs *hooks*. A *hook* is a place to hang a script, such that the script is run at a specific stage of the version control process—perhaps before or after a change is committed, when a log message is stored, or when a file is checked out for exclusive development. CVS has hooks in the form of scripting files, explained in Chapters 6 and 7.

Internally, revision control systems usually keep numeric identifiers for each revision. One very useful feature is the *tag*—a symbolic name applied by the user. It's much easier to remember that alpha_0-1 is your first alpha test than to remember that it's revision 1.17. Most systems that provide tags allow you to apply the same tag to either the files you specify or to a full project with one command. Tags are explained in Chapter 4.

Branches enable you to run two simultaneous lines of development on the same project, stored in the same repository. The most common use is to separate out a bugfix branch independent of the main development branch. Some version control systems also have a *vendor branch* feature, a special branch that lets you store data provided by a third party. Branches are explained in Chapter 4, and vendor branches in Chapter 7.

A feature that CVS *doesn't* have, and that many teams like, is *atomic commits*. This feature ensures that while one person is committing changes to the repository, no one else can. Thus, each commit is a separate process, and the repository is never in a state where it has mismatched files—e.g., one directory with Bill's latest changes, and one with Sally's. CVS has atomic commits on a directory-by-directory basis, but not true project-by-project or repository-by-repository atomic committing.

You may need data encryption, user authentication, and other security features. You need to be able to back up the repository and restore it to a fully working repository easily. To learn about CVS's security and backup capabilities, see Chapter 6.

If you use a particular development suite, your choice of version control may be affected by whether the suite supports the version control system. Another factor might be the availability of programs such as web (HTTP/HTML) viewers or project management tools. Lists of some of the tools available to CVS and development suites that support CVS are in Appendixes A and B.

Comparing Version Control Systems

Table 1-1 compares the features of various version control systems. This table is based on the information provided in their web sites and other available documentation at the time of writing, and on discussion with friends who have used the systems (in cases where I haven't).

Central, Distributed, or Proxied

CVS and other traditional version control systems use a *central repository*. This means that the historic data about project changes is stored in a single place. Typically, developers have a *sandbox*, or working area, on their local computer, which contains the version that they are currently working on and which they update from the central repository.

Bitkeeper, Arch, and some other new systems use *distributed repositories*. Each developer has a personal repository, and the repositories update from their peers. In some cases, the system treats each repository as equal, and whether a project has a master repository is up to the project's lead developers. In others, there is a master repository that has children, each of which may have children, which in turn may have children, and so on recursively.

Proxied repositories are an intermediate form. There is a *central repository*, which holds the changes data, and *proxy repositories*, which are used for read requests and which refer write requests to the central repository. Some systems support only reading from proxies, and some projects choose to use only read proxies and have all writing done directly to the central repository.

Each style has advantages and disadvantages. Proponents of *distributed repositories* say that they're easier to use in very large projects, as access to the central repository can become congested. You can also *stage* work, keeping a section of work in a secondary repository until it's been thoroughly tested and only then committing it to the master repository.

Something that I consider a disadvantage of using distributed repositories is that it encourages large merges—it's very easy to keep committing to a local repository for a long time, then try to commit an entire feature set to the main development strand at once. If this is taken into account at the project management stage, it's not a problem. If it isn't taken into account, trying to blend the changes seamlessly can require a lot of unexpected work.

In a *central repository* system, your data is all in one place, which makes it easier to secure it and plan backups. If you choose to, you can stage work through branches. Congestion can be a problem in very large projects.

Using *proxies* reduces congestion in a central repository system. The proxies take the load caused by read requests off the central repository (save for the read requests used to update the proxy repositories) and, depending on how the proxy system is implemented, may also be able to reduce the write load.

Table 1-1. Version control systems compared

VCS	Development model	Repository type	Atomic commits	URL
CVS	Simultaneous or exclusive	Central and proxied	No	*http://cvs.nongnu.org*
Bitkeeper	Simultaneous	Distributed	Yes	*http://www.bitkeeper.com*

Table 1-1. Version control systems compared (continued)

VCS	Development model	Repository type	Atomic commits	URL
ClearCase	Simultaneous or exclusive	Central or distributed	N/A	*http://www-306.ibm.com/ software/awdtools/clearcase*
Git	Simultaneous	Distributed	Yes	*http://git.or.cz*
GNU Arch	Simultaneous	Distributed	Yes	*http://www.gnu.org/ software/gnu-arch/*
Perforce	Simultaneous or exclusive	Central	Yes	*http://www.perforce.com*
Subversion	Simultaneous or exclusive	Central	Yes	*http://subversion.tigris.org*
Visual Source Safe	Exclusive	Central	No	*http://msdn.microsoft.com/ ssafe/*

It's well worth it to read the Wikipedia articles on revision control systems. Wikipedia has a more complete list of available programs, as well as links to their home pages and to other peoples' comparisons of systems they have worked with. The main article is available at *http://en.wikipedia.org/wiki/Revision_control*.

CVS Versus Subversion

Subversion is designed to be "CVS, only better." It has support for binary files built into the design, permits versioning of directories as well as files, allows you to rename files with a simple command and to maintain their history, and has atomic commits. It works just like CVS does. So why not change to Subversion?

I've been looking at Subversion, and it's not quite true that it's "CVS, only better." It's "CVS, only different." It uses a different repository structure, different methods of remote access, different administrative commands, and different hooks. It currently doesn't support proxying or GSSAPI (Generic Security Services API, a client-server authentication system), and many of its commands, such as *diff*, have fewer features than CVS's versions of those commands.

I like Subversion, and I think it has potential, but it's not a direct replacement for CVS. It's similar, but it's different enough that some people prefer to use CVS for its feature set, and others prefer Subversion for its feature set.

CVS and CVSNT

CVSNT is a different system; it split off from CVS around version 1.10. Both projects have changed significantly since then. CVSNT can merge binary files, and has several Windows-specific bonuses such as use of DLLs (dynamic link libraries) for sophisticated trigger actions when a change is committed. CVS has gone in a different direction, and has added support for *PAM* (pluggable authentication modules), created proxying, and provided more scripting file hooks.

Why I Prefer CVS

CVS is free. That's a really good start for small projects, free software projects, and small businesses, and most of my work has been in at least one of those fields. I've also been able to use existing servers for all the CVS repositories I've administered, and to use sites like Sourceforge or other open source hosting sites for CVS repositories for open source work. The total cost of the CVS system has been trivial, for me.

CVS is a mature system. It's solid and reliable, and I've seen it fail only when I misunderstood how it worked—which happened only when I was first learning it. That's one reason I wrote this book: by explaining the things I've learned, hopefully I can prevent other people from facing the problems I faced.

CVS has all the functionality I need. Most of that is built in, but because it's such a mature system, there are third-party tools that do most of the things it doesn't. For instance, if you want strict exclusive development, you can use the *rcslock* program. If you need finer-grained security, there's the *cvs_acls* script. Web browsing of your repository? *ViewCVS*.

CVS is familiar. It's widespread and has a huge user base. In my experience, members of my team have usually used CVS before, which saves time spent on training.

CVS in the Field

CVS records file changes during a project's development. Project files are added to the repository as they are created, and developers check out a personal *sandbox*—a personal copy of the project's files—to work from. Each developer works in his own sandbox and regularly commits his changes to the repository. Developers also update the contents of their sandboxes regularly to ensure that changes to the repository are reflected in each sandbox.

The term *project* can take on many different meanings. The stereotypical CVS project is a programming project in which files contain source code for the various programs written as part of the project. But that's a narrow view of what a CVS project can be. CVS can be used in many other settings as well, as the next few sections demonstrate.

System Administration

CVS can store configuration files, mail aliases, domain records, and other files for which changes should be tracked. Import the files (or all of */etc*) into a repository and require administrators to check them out into a sandbox to make changes. Commit the files back to the repository and export the changes to the server. If the changes fail, rolling back to the previous state is easy.

Multiple servers with varied but similar configurations can be maintained using different branches of the same files. Changes to any given branch can be merged into other branches selectively.

Every change made through CVS is recorded in a file history, along with the username of the person making the change, the date the change was made, and any notes recorded with the change. All this information can help, for example, when trying to spot which change to which configuration file broke the mail server.

Both the CVS server and the client run on all Unix and Linux operating systems, including modern Macintosh environments. Third-party graphical clients are available for Unix, Linux, Windows, and Macintosh systems, and for the Java runtime environment. The CVSNT CVS server is available for Windows NT or later. This makes CVS particularly useful for cross-platform environments. See Appendix A for more information.

Software Development

Program development is perhaps the most common use for version control systems. After the initial release of a program, two versions usually need to be maintained: the new version that will eventually be the next release and the bugfix version for the current release. CVS allows you to split the development into two or more parts, called a *trunk* and a *branch*. Typically, the branch is used for bug fixes, and the main trunk is used for new feature development. Both versions of the program, the bugfix branch and the main trunk, are stored in the same repository. This approach allows the changes from the bugfix branch to ultimately be merged into the main trunk, ensuring that all bugfixes get rolled into the next release of the program.

A CVS repository can be hosted on the machine that most developers will be using, or you can host the repository on a machine that developers access via a local or wide-area network. A repository can be accessed simultaneously by multiple computers. If you need to authenticate your CVS users, there are a variety of authentication mechanisms available.

When multiple developers are trying to work on the same project, it's likely that two or more developers will eventually want to work with the same file at the same time. Without version control, this would lead to problems, as developers would soon find themselves overwriting one another's changes. One way that some version control systems prevent such conflicts is to enable developers to lock whatever files they are working on, so that no one else can make changes at the same time.

Instead of locking files to prevent conflicts, CVS allows multiple developers to work on the same file. CVS's file-merging feature then allows you to merge all changes into one file. File merging aids development across remote time zones, as developers can work on different sections of the same file, regardless of the lock status. In fact, there is no lock status, because there is no locking. With a file-locking system, a developer may have to email someone and then wait until that person wakes up, reads her email, and unlocks the needed file. The CVS approach prevents one developer from blocking another, thus increasing productivity. However, if your project team needs file locking, you can use the *cvs watch* command (discussed in Chapter 5) to emulate it.

The *cvs diff* command (also discussed in Chapter 5) displays the differences between any two revisions of a file (or set of files) in the repository. A variation of the command creates a Unix standard patch file to update one revision to another, which is useful when sending patches or updates to customers.

CVS can be configured to record commit messages in bug-tracking systems. Chapter 7 explains how to use the administrative files to provide message templates and run scripts automatically during commits. This step does not necessarily record the stage of each change (completed, tested, etc.). Unless you rigorously enforce a requirement to write meaningful commit messages, you should maintain a separate change log.

Store your build and installation scripts in CVS to maintain a record of changes and to ensure that such scripts are kept with the project files. Releases should always be built from a freshly checked-out sandbox and tagged with a human-friendly name.

CVS does not include build or installation tools, though *cvs export* (see Chapter 7) should be part of the installation process for your project. I use *make* for build and installation scripts.

Content-Controlled Publishing

Many people use CVS to maintain web sites and other file servers, and use scripts to automatically publish updates to those servers. Some people use scripts to distribute and apply patch files on remote machines, saving bandwidth by distributing only the changes. A variety of such scripts are available at *http://www.cvshome.org*, and some are discussed in Appendix B.

Other Uses for CVS

CVS is also useful for managing any other type of file, from book chapters or blueprints, to music, art, mailing lists, or shopping lists. The features that make it useful to programmers are also useful to anyone who produces something that can be stored as a computer file, or that can be generated from a computer file. A friend of mine, Maria Blackmore, uses CVS to store router configurations by using a script to retrieve and commit copies of the configuration.

## CHAPTER 2

CVS Quickstart Guide

To help you get up to speed quickly using CVS, this chapter explains the most common CVS operations. The commands and examples in this chapter are based on standard situations and cover only the most common options. Future chapters go into more depth on each topic covered in this chapter.

Most of the examples and instructions in this chapter are based on the Unix/Linux command-line CVS client, though I also provide examples using multiplatform clients. Most graphical clients use the CVS command names for their menu options and buttons, so if you're using a graphical client other than one of the ones I provide examples for, you should be able to follow this chapter reasonably easily. Those using Mac OS X can use CVS from the command line, and people using Windows who want to use the command line can use Cygwin (available from *http://www. cygwin.com*). CVS is available via the Cygwin installer. Graphical clients and clients for operating systems other than Unix/Linux are described in Appendix A.

You may not need to read all of this chapter:

- If CVS is installed, and you're working on an existing project that is already stored in CVS, skip the early sections and start at "Checking Out Files." You may need your system administrator (or the person who installed your repository and existing project) to tell you the *repository path* and *project name*.

- If CVS is already installed and running, with a repository available for your project, go straight to "Importing Projects." You may need your system administrator to tell you the repository path.

- If CVS is installed but there is no repository, go to "Building Your First Repository."

- For information on installing graphic clients, see Appendix A.

If you're not sure whether CVS is already installed and running, read the first part of "Installing CVS," which tells you how to check. If you're uncertain about having a repository, try searching for the directory *CVSROOT*. The *repository root* is the first directory in the repository and is the directory that contains *CVSROOT*. The *repository path* is the full pathname of the repository root, along with any remote access information needed; see "Accessing Remote Repositories" later in this chapter. The directories in the repository root, other than *CVSROOT*, are CVS projects.

Installing CVS

CVS is client/server software that runs on Unix and Linux platforms, including Mac OS X. The CVSNT program is a CVS-like server that runs on Windows, and there are CVS clients for Windows, Mac (including pre-OS X Macintosh), Linux, and Unix. When you install CVS on a Unix/Linux server, you automatically get both server and client software. To access CVS across the network from any Unix/Linux machine, install CVS on the machine in question. The server and (command-line) client software are one and the same.

CVS is available from *http://cvs.nongnu.org*. It is also available as an installation package with many GNU/Linux distributions, including Debian, Red Hat, and SUSE.

A Windows-compatible CVS server is available at *http://www.cvsnt.org*. This server is not identical to the Unix server, but the differences are clearly listed in the CVS NT FAQ, and an installation guide is available on its web site.

Is CVS Installed?

If you are running Mac OS X, Cygwin, Unix, or Linux, you may already have CVS installed. If it's installed and in your path, typing *cvs* at the command line produces the results shown in Example 2-1.

Example 2-1. CVS help display

```
$ cvs
Usage: cvs [cvs-options] command [command-options-and-arguments]
  where cvs-options are -q, -n, etc.
    (specify --help-options for a list of options)
  where command is add, admin, etc.
    (specify --help-commands for a list of commands
     or --help-synonyms for a list of command synonyms)
  where command-options-and-arguments depend on the specific command
    (specify -H followed by a command name for command-specific help)
  Specify --help to receive this message

The Concurrent Versions System (CVS) is a tool for version control.
For CVS updates and additional information, see
  the CVS home page at http://www.cvshome.org/ or
  Pascal Molli's CVS site at http://www.loria.fr/~molli/cvs-index.html
```

If you already have CVS installed, you can skip this section and jump ahead to "Building Your First Repository."

Graphic User Interfaces

If you prefer GUI clients, I recommend a visit to *http://www.wincvs.org*. There you'll find gCVS, WinCVS, and MacCVS, which are GUI clients for Unix and GNU/Linux, Windows, and Macintosh (pre-OS X), respectively.

 If you are a Macintosh user running OS X, you can use the command-line version of CVS that comes with Mac OS X and can be downloaded from *http://developer.apple.com*, or you can install the latest version of the standard Unix CVS server and client. To get a shell prompt in Mac OS X, open the Terminal application (which is located in */Applications/Utilities*).

To compile and install the latest version of CVS, you need the free Xcode install (*http://developer.apple.com/tools/xcode/*) for Mac OS X, which includes the GNU C compiler and other tools needed to compile source code.

A list of additional GUI clients is available in the CVS Wiki (*http://ximbiot.com/cvs/wiki/index.php?title=CVS_Clients*).

Secure Shell

If you plan to use CVS over a network, I recommend using the Secure Shell (SSH) protocol to establish secure connections between clients and server. You must install compatible versions of SSH on your client and server machines. For clients, you may need to find a version of SSH that can be used from the command line. See "Accessing Remote Repositories" later in this chapter for more information on this topic.

The OpenSSH web site (*http://www.openssh.com*) is a good starting point for information on SSH and SSH clients. You may also want to read *SSH, The Secure Shell: The Definitive Guide*, by Daniel J. Barrett et al. (O'Reilly). For more than you ever wanted to know about SSH, see the FAQ at *http://www.openssh.org/faq.html*. The Google list of SSH documentation is at *http://directory.google.com/Top/Computers/Internet/Protocols/SSH/Documentation/*.

Most Unix and Linux systems have an SSH client installed as part of the standard set of programs. Mac OS X also comes with an SSH client preinstalled. If it is not installed automatically, an SSH client is usually available in your distribution as an optional program.

The web site for MacCVS has a useful article on SSH for pre-OS X Macintosh users at *http://www.heilancoo.net/MacCVSClient/MacCVSClientDoc/ssh-classic.html*. The instructions are useful regardless of which Macintosh CVS client you use.

To find an SSH client for Windows, start from the OpenSSH web site on Windows clients (*http://www.openssh.com/windows.html*).

Once you have installed SSH on both the server and the client computers, generate keys for the clients and add their public keys to the server. This step lets your users run CVS without needing to give their password for every command.

Installing CVS with a Package Manager

The easiest way to install CVS under GNU/Linux is with a package manager such as YaST, GnoRPM, Kpackage, or Synaptic. In all of the package managers that I'm familiar with, the package name is either *cvs* or *cvs* followed by some punctuation and a version number. Figures 2-1 and 2-2 are screenshots of the installation with package managers, and show which menu CVS can be found in. Find and select CVS, and then click on the Install or OK button, as appropriate.

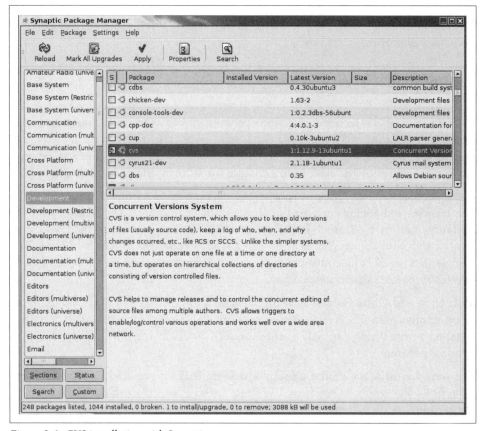

Figure 2-1. CVS installation with Synaptic

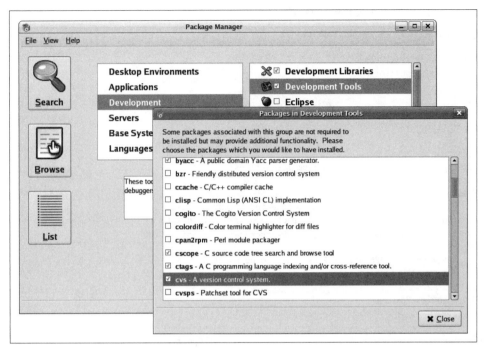

Figure 2-2. CVS installation with Fedora

The second easiest way to install CVS on GNU/Linux is using a command-line package manager. If you're using *apt* (Debian, Ubuntu, and Mac OS X users who are running Fink), log in as root and use the command *apt-get install cvs*. apt will find the most recent version in its sources list. If using *yum*, the command is *yum install cvs*. Examples 2-2 and 2-3 show an *apt* and a *yum* installation.

Example 2-2. CVS installation with apt

```
root@pharaoh:/home# apt-get install cvs
Reading package lists... Done
Building dependency tree... Done
The following NEW packages will be installed:
  cvs
0 upgraded, 1 newly installed, 0 to remove and 30 not upgraded.
Need to get 1441kB of archives.
After unpacking 3088kB of additional disk space will be used.
Get:1 http://au.archive.ubuntu.com breezy/main cvs 1:1.12.9-13ubuntu1 [1441kB]
Fetched 1441kB in 0s (2519kB/s)

Preconfiguring packages ...
Selecting previously deselected package cvs.
(Reading database ... 64166 files and directories currently installed.)
Unpacking cvs (from .../cvs_1%3a1.12.9-13ubuntu1_i386.deb) ...
Setting up cvs (1.12.9-13ubuntu1) ...
```

Example 2-3. CVS installation with yum

```
[root@localhost ~]# yum install cvs
Loading "installonlyn" plugin
Setting up Install Process
Setting up repositories
core
[1/3]
updates
[2/3]
extras
[3/3]
Reading repository metadata in from local files
Parsing package install arguments
Resolving Dependencies
--> Populating transaction set with selected packages. Please wait.
---> Downloading header for cvs to pack into transaction set.
cvs-1.11.21-3.2.i386.rpm   100% |=========================|  18 kB
00:00
---> Package cvs.i386 0:1.11.21-3.2 set to be updated
--> Running transaction check

Dependencies Resolved


=============================================================================
Package                  Arch      Version         Repository    Size
=============================================================================
Installing:
cvs                      i386      1.11.21-3.2     core          732 k

Transaction Summary
=============================================================================
Install      1 Package(s)
Update       0 Package(s)
Remove       0 Package(s)
Total download size: 732 k
Is this ok [y/N]: y
Downloading Packages:
(1/1): cvs-1.11.21-3.2.i3 100% |=========================| 732 kB
00:03
Running Transaction Test
Finished Transaction Test
Transaction Test Succeeded
Running Transaction
   Installing: cvs                          #########################
[1/1]

Installed: cvs.i386 0:1.11.21-3.2
Complete!
```

Installing and Building CVS from Source

Download the compressed *.tar* file from *http://cvs.nongnu.org*. Decompress and unarchive the file. If you intend to keep the source after you compile it, unzip the compressed *.tar* file into */usr/src/cvs*. Otherwise, you can decompress and unarchive it into */tmp*. Next, *cd* into the *cvs* directory, read the *INSTALL* and *README* files, and run the commands there. I recommend that novice users disable *automake* and *autoconf*. (In CVS 1.12.1 and later, *autoconf* and *automake* are disabled by default.)

You should compile CVS as a user without superuser privileges (for security), but you must have superuser privileges when installing CVS (running *make install*) for everyone to use. If you are installing it into your own home directory for your personal use, you don't need superuser privileges, but your choice of remote connection methods is limited.

Example 2-4 shows a sample installation from source. In this example, I decompress and unarchive the *.tar* file into */tmp* and change directory into the top level of the resulting source tree. As I'm using a later version than 1.12.1, I don't need to disable *automake* and *autoconf*. The next steps described in *INSTALL* for CVS 1.12.9 are to run the *configure* script provided and then, if that exits successfully, run *make*, switch to the root user, and run *make install*.

Example 2-4. Installing from source

```
$ ls
cvs-1.12.9.tar.bz2
$ bunzip2 cvs-1.12.9.tar.bz2
$ tar -xpf cvs-1.12.9.tar
$ cd cvs-1.12.9
$ ./configure
checking for a BSD-compatible install... /usr/bin/install -c
checking whether build environment is sane... yes
.
.
.
config.status: executing depfiles commands
config.status: executing default-1 commands
$ make
make  all-recursive
make[1]: Entering directory `/tmp/cvs-1.12.9'
.
.
.
make[2]: Entering directory `/tmp/cvs-1.12.9'
make[2]: Nothing to be done for `all-am'.
make[2]: Leaving directory `/tmp/cvs-1.12.9'
make[1]: Leaving directory `/tmp/cvs-1.12.9'
```

Example 2-4. Installing from source (continued)

```
$ su - root
$ make install
Making install in lib
make[1]: Entering directory `/tmp/cvs-1.12.9/lib'
make  install-am
.
.
.
make[2]: Nothing to be done for `install-data-am'.
make[2]: Leaving directory `/tmp/cvs-1.12.9'
make[1]: Leaving directory `/tmp/cvs-1.12.9'
```

Building Your First Repository

CVS relies on a file-based database called the *CVS repository*. The repository contains all the historic data about your project, including each change that has been committed to the repository, as well as the user making each change. Your developers work from a sandbox which contains working copies of the files in your project. Changes from your sandbox (and other developer's sandboxes) are committed to the repository, and changes in the repository but not in your sandbox are updated from the repository. Figure 2-3 shows a diagram of the relationship between a repository and sandboxes.

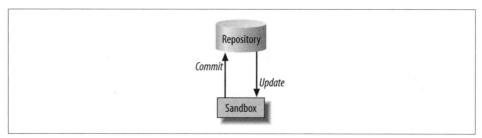

Figure 2-3. Repository/sandbox relationship

The repository must be hosted on a machine with sufficient disk space to store your files and all the change data for your projects. The repository should be accessible to all the users from their workstations. Chapter 6 contains more information on choosing a repository server and setting up a more complex repository.

If the repository is on a remote computer, I recommend that users access the repository via SSH. Ensure that the server is running an SSH server and the workstations have a compatible SSH client. For more information on remote repositories and SSH, see "Accessing Remote Repositories" later in this chapter. Chapter 8 contains a full discussion of remote repositories.

For any one project, ensure there is enough disk space for three times the expected final size of that project. If you intend to store binary files, multiply by at least five. After your first project, you'll have a feel for how much space to allow.

A repository can store many projects. If you are creating a repository that might handle several projects of unknown size, estimate as best you can and ensure that you can add more room later.

Not only can one repository store many projects, but one server can store many repositories. It's usual for a server to have only a single repository, though.

A CVS repository is user data, and it should be on a partition that is backed up and won't shut down the machine if it gets full. Repositories are often stored in */cvsroot*, */var/lib/cvsroot*, */home/cvsroot*, or */usr/local/cvsroot*. According to the Filesystem Hierarchy Standard (available at *http://www.pathname.com/fhs/*), the preferred location for a repository is */var/lib/cvsroot*.

Another possibility is to put the repository in */cvsroot*. This location is easiest for users to remember.

Example 2-5 illustrates the steps involved in creating a repository. First, create the repository root directory on the CVS server. In Example 2-5, I create the */var/lib/ cvsroot* directory, and then install the security measures necessary to allow all users in the *anthill* group to write to the repository directories. (Ubuntu and Debian systems create the initial repository for you when the package is installed. You may need to add users to the default repository group, however.)

You must be root to work in the */var* directory on most Unix, Linux, and Mac OS X systems. You can run a command as root on Ubuntu and Mac OS X by prefixing the command with *sudo*, as in *sudo mkdir /var/lib/cvsroot*. On other Linux and Unix systems, use the command *su -* to get a root shell first. A root shell is indicated with the # prompt.

Example 2-5. Creating a repository

```
$ su -
Password: ******
# mkdir /var/lib/cvsroot
# chgrp anthill /var/lib/cvsroot
# ls -la /var/lib
total 153
drwxr-xr-x    2 root      anthill      4096 Jun 28 16:31 cvsroot
 .
 .
 .
```

Example 2-5. Creating a repository (continued)

```
# chmod g+srwx /var/lib/cvsroot
# ls -la /var/lib
total 153
drwxrwsr-x   2 root     anthill    4096 Jun 28 16:33 cvsroot
.
.
.
# cvs -d /var/lib/cvsroot init
# ls -la /var/lib
total 3
drwxrwsr-x   3 root     anthill    4096 Jun 28 16:56 cvsroot
# ls -la /var/lib/cvsroot
total 12
drwxrwsr-x   3 root     anthill    4096 Jun 28 16:56 .
drwxr-xr-x  10 root     staff      4096 Jun 28 16:35 ..
drwxrwsr-x   3 root     anthill    4096 Jun 28 16:56 CVSROOT
# chown -R cvs /var/lib/cvsroot
```

To allow others to use the repository, create a Unix group for CVS users (*anthill* in the preceding example) and *chgrp* the repository's root directory to that group. You'll need to add users to that group, using the appropriate command for your system (often *gpasswd*). Use *chmod* to set the directory's SGID bit, so that files created in the directory have the same group ID as the directory's group ID (this can prevent trouble later). You should also use *chmod* to set the directory group-writable, -readable, and -executable (you can do all your *chmod* work in one command with *chmod g+srwx,* as shown in Example 2-5).

To minimize security risks, create a user named *cvs* to own the repository and the administrative files. Use the *--system* option to *adduser*, so that *cvs* is created as a user who can never be logged into. *chown* the repository's root directory and administrative files to that username. Chapter 6 explains security.

 In OS X, you can use the *niload* command to add a user:

```
$ sudo niload passwd . <<EOF
> username:*:701:20::0:0:New User:/Users/username:/bin/bash
> EOF
```

Execute the following command to set up your chosen directory as a CVS repository:

```
cvs -d repository_root_directory init
```

CVS commands follow the format:

```
cvs [cvs-options] command [command-options]
```

The CVS options modify the behavior of CVS as a whole, and the command options modify the behavior of a CVS command. This format is explained more fully in Chapter 3.

Example 2-5 illustrates the entire process of creating a directory and then creating a CVS repository within that directory. In this case, the CVS option is *-d repository_ path*, and the command is *init*. There is no command option. *anthill* is the name of the group with access to CVS, and *cvs* is the name of the CVS owner.

Setting up the repository produces a place to store projects and also adds the special *CVSROOT* directory. The *CVSROOT* directory contains configuration and metadata files. Chapter 6 explains this directory in more detail. Projects are stored in subdirectories of the repository root directory, which is */var/lib/cvsroot* in our example.

Importing Projects

When you have created a new repository, you may want to import your first *project*—a related collection of files stored under a single directory. It is possible to store a single file under CVS, but it will also be considered a project and you will need to store it under its own project directory. CVS groups things into projects because it needs to be able to create a subdirectory to store metadata about the project.

> Your repository can hold one project, or it can hold many different projects. CVS scales well: a repository can help a single person with a small job to do, or can be used by a large company to provide version control to hundreds of separate groups.

Before loading a project into CVS, consider the project's structure. If you move a file after it has been created and stored in CVS, CVS treats it as two files: the original in the original location and the new file in the new location. The history of the file is then split into two parts. Decide how you want to structure the source files for a project before you import it into CVS.

If you will eventually want to distribute your project's files across several unrelated directories, it is best to develop the project under a single root directory, then distribute the files as part of the installation script. Chapter 7 describes the issue of project structure in more detail.

> If you have binary files or other files that are not plain text, please see the information on binary files in Chapter 3 before adding them to the repository.
>
> If you have any files or directories named *CVS*, please rename them before you import them—CVS restricts that name for its own purposes.

Create your initial project directory structure, possibly in */tmp*. Once the project is stored in CVS, the repository backed up, and the backup verified, this initial version can be removed (which is one reason to use */tmp*). You won't be using it as a sandbox, and the project is duplicated in CVS, so there's no reason to retain it once you have copies in the repository and its backup.

Once you have your initial structure, add any initial files you want. Change into the root directory of the project. Then, from within that directory, import the project with the command:

```
cvs -d repository_path import name_of_project vendor_tag release_tag
```

If the repository is on the local machine, use the full path of the repository directory for the repository path. If the repository is on a remote server, see "Accessing Remote Repositories" for help on specifying the repository path.

For most cases, you will not need to know about *vendor tags* and *release tags*. CVS requires them to be present, but for now you can use the name of the project as the vendor tag and the current revision name as the release tag. These names must start with a letter and can contain only alphanumeric characters, underscores, and hyphens. See Example 2-6, which illustrates the process of creating a project structure and some project files, and then importing the project into CVS.

The vendor tag and release tag are explained in Chapter 7.

Example 2-6. Importing a project

```
/tmp$ mkdir example
/tmp$ touch example/file1
/tmp$ touch example/file2
/tmp$ cd example
/tmp/example$ cvs -d /var/lib/cvsroot import example example_project ver_0-1
```

After you run the commands in Example 2-6, CVS opens an editor window, shown in Figure 2-4. Enter a message to remind you what you intend this project to be.

The lines in the editor window that start with "CVS:" will not be included in the project's history. The text displayed in the editor is configurable through the *rcsinfo* file described in Chapter 7.

The default editor for most Unix and Linux systems is *vi*. You need to type an *i* before inserting text; push the Esc key to return to the mode in which you can move the cursor around. The movement keys are the arrow keys, or *h, j, k,* and *l*. To save and exit, press the Esc key followed by *:wq*, then press Return. Chapter 3 explains how to change the editor to something other than *vi*.

After exiting from the editor, CVS completes the import, as shown in Example 2-7.

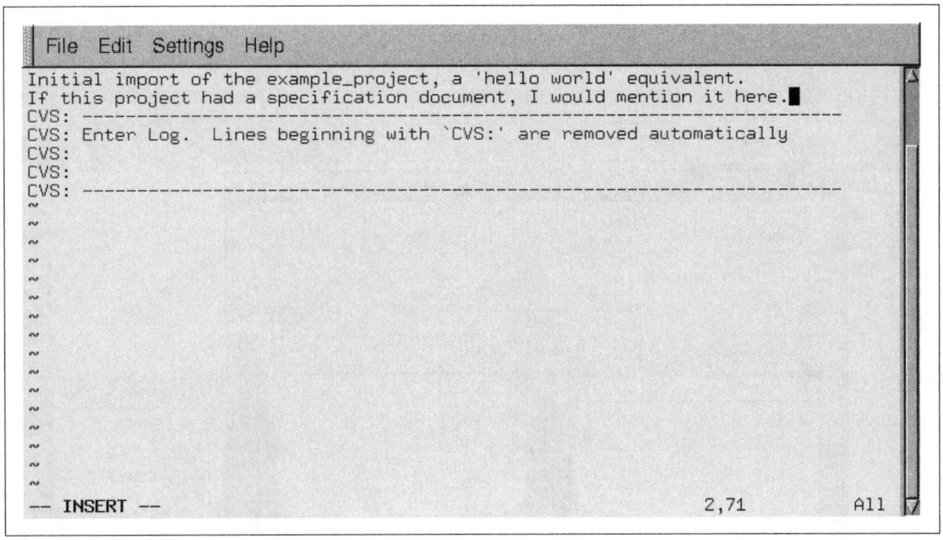

```
Initial import of the example_project, a 'hello world' equivalent.
If this project had a specification document, I would mention it here.█
CVS: ---------------------------------------------------------------
CVS: Enter Log.  Lines beginning with `CVS:' are removed automatically
CVS:
CVS:
CVS: ---------------------------------------------------------------
~
~
~
~
~
~
~
~
~
~
~
~
~
~
~
~
-- INSERT --                                        2,71        All
```

Figure 2-4. Entering an import message

Example 2-7. Completing the import

```
N example/file1
N example/file2

No conflicts created by this import
```

In the repository, the imported project is stored as a collection of RCS format files. Example 2-8 shows the files for the project imported in Example 2-7. Note the *,v* extension to the filenames—it signals that they're RCS format files, and contain not only the file data, but also information about the files' various changes over the life of the project.

Example 2-8. Repository contents

```
$ ls -la /var/lib/cvsroot
total 16
drwxrwsr-x    4 root      anthill     4096 Jun 28 17:06 .
drwxrwsr-x   10 root      staff       4096 Jun 28 16:35 ..
drwxrwsr-x    3 root      anthill     4096 Jun 28 16:56 CVSROOT
drwxrwsr-x    2 jenn      anthill     4096 Jun 28 17:09 example
$ ls -la /var/lib/cvsroot/example
total 16
drwxrwsr-x    2 jenn      anthill     4096 Jun 28 17:09 .
drwxrwsr-x    4 root      anthill     4096 Jun 28 17:06 ..
-r--r--r--    1 jenn      anthill      387 Jun 28 17:06 file1,v
-r--r--r--    1 jenn      anthill      387 Jun 28 17:06 file2,v
```

Figure 2-5 shows the same import done with gCVS.

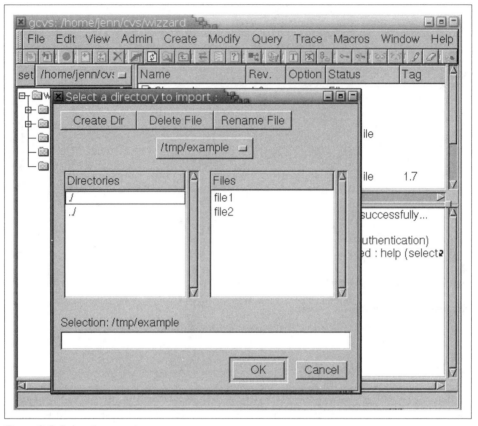

Figure 2-5. Importing a project

Once you've created your project, back up your CVS repository. You should continue to back up the repository periodically during your project's lifetime. Once the repository has been backed up and the project verified, you can remove the original files. You need exclusive use of the repository when you do a backup, so do it at a time when you know other users won't be committing changes.

 Chapter 6 explains how to back up a repository and how to prevent others from making changes while you do so.

Before you do any work on the project, verify that the project is in CVS by checking out a sandbox (see "Checking Out Files" later in this chapter). Don't try to use your original files as a sandbox. You must do any new work in files that you check out to a sandbox, which is why you can safely discard the originals. You should remove the original files to prevent yourself from accidentally modifying them instead of the files in a sandbox.

Accessing Remote Repositories

There are several ways to access a remote repository. This quickstart guide uses the *ext* method with the SSH protocol, but if your system administrator gives you different instructions, follow those. Chapter 8 explains the use of remote repositories in detail. The *ext* and SSH approach uses the *ext* repository access method, with an SSH client as the program that performs the connection. These are also explained in Chapter 8.

Your first step—at least, the first step that I recommend—is to install SSH on the client machine. Make sure that the client-end SSH protocol matches the server's SSH protocol. Set up SSH keys or passwords and test the connection. Using SSH enables you to create a secure connection to the remote repository.

Next, if you're on a Mac OS X, Unix, or Linux system, set the *CVS_RSH* environment variable on your client machine to the name of your SSH program; usually, this is *ssh* or *ssh2*. Graphical clients that support the *ext* and SSH approach may have *ssh* as an authentication type option in the dialog that requests the repository path. Check the documentation for your client.

> In WinCVS and gCVS, call up the Preferences dialog under the Admin menu and select "ssh" as the Authentication method under the General tab. Under the Ports tab, you may need to enter the name of your SSH program in the option "Check for an alternate rsh name."
>
> In MacCVSX (for OS X), *ssh* is one of the authentication method options listed in the Preferences dialog. MacCVS for OS 9 and earlier versions do not support SSH as a standard option. Instead, you can make use of SSH from MacCVS via port tunnelling, as described in Appendix A.

If the repository is on the same machine as the client, the repository path is simply the full path to the repository's root directory. On a remote machine, the repository path takes the form:

```
[:method[;option=arg...]:][[[user][:password]@]hostname[:[port]]]/path
```

The method is the protocol used to connect to the repository. To use SSH, use *ext* as the method. Include the username and the at sign (@) if the username on the server differs from the username on the client. If you don't have an SSH key on the host, the system asks you for a password when you try to log in.

> The *ext* method doesn't use the password or port portions of the repository path, and will ignore them if you include them. A full explanation of the repository path is given in Chapter 8.

Use the following command from your operating system prompt to run a CVS command against the remote repository:

```
cvs -d repository_path command
```

For instance, Example 2-9 shows how to import a project into a remote CVS repository that is located on the host named *cvs_server*.

Example 2-9. Remote repository import

```
bash-2.05a$ cvs -d :ext:cvs_server:/var/lib/cvsroot import example no-vendor release-0
N example/file1
N example/file2
No conflicts created by this import
bash-2.05a$
```

Checking Out Files

CVS stores projects and files in a central repository, but you work from a working copy, the sandbox, in your local directories. You create the sandbox with *cvs checkout*.

CVS creates the sandbox as a subdirectory of your current working directory. I like to create a directory to contain all my CVS sandboxes, and I use *~/cvs*. Run this command from whichever directory you want a sandbox created in:

```
cvs -d repository_path checkout project_name
```

It checks out all files for the named project. If your repository is on the local machine, the repository path is the full pathname of the CVS repository. If your repository is on a remote server, see the preceding section, "Accessing Remote Repositories." Example 2-10 shows a local checkout.

Example 2-10. Local repository checkout

```
$ mkdir ~/cvs
$ cd ~/cvs
$ cvs -d /var/lib/cvsroot checkout example
cvs checkout: Updating example
U example/file1
U example/file2
```

The *checkout* command puts a copy of the project's files and subdirectories into a directory named for the project, created in the current working directory. It also puts some administrative files of its own in a subdirectory of the project directory, called *CVS*.

You can check out an individual file or subdirectory of a project by replacing *project_name* with the pathname to the file or directory, from the project's root directory. See Chapter 3 for more information.

CVS stores the repository path as part of the sandbox, so you should never again need to use *-d repository_path* in commands executed within that sandbox.

Note that the repository paths for local or remote checkout are the same as the repository paths for local and remote import. So if you used *-d /var/lib/cvsroot* for the import, you'd use the same for checkout.

If you are checking out a sandbox from a remote repository, the repository path must follow the remote repository format introduced in "Accessing Remote Repositories," earlier in this chapter. Example 2-11 shows a checkout from a remote repository. Figure 2-6 shows the same checkout with gCVS.

Example 2-11. Remote repository checkout

```
$ cvs -d :ext:cvs_server:/var/lib/cvsroot checkout example
cvs checkout: Updating example
U example/file1
U example/file2
```

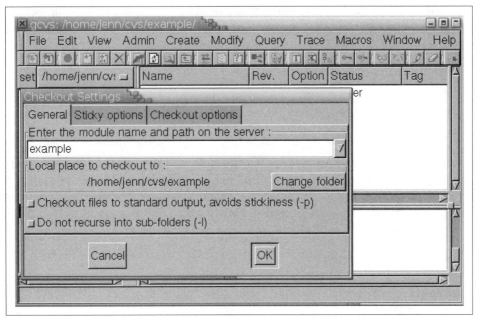

Figure 2-6. Remote repository checkout with gCVS

Editing Files

Once you've checked out your project files into a sandbox, you can edit them with your favorite editor. Your sandbox is an ordinary set of files and directories, with an extra CVS subdirectory in each directory. Ignore the contents of the CVS subdirectory, and edit your project files as you normally would.

Some of CVS's functions will not work properly in files with complex formats, such as image or sound files, and these files should be stored in binary format (see Chapter 3 for more information). The default save file format of editors such as Microsoft Word and OpenOffice.org doesn't react well with the line-based *diff* system that CVS uses, and these files should also be stored in the repository as binary files, using the *-kb* option to *cvs add* (as explained in Chapter 3). However, if you save in plain-text, RTF, XML, or HTML format, you can commit them as normal CVS files.

Committing Changes

Changes to your sandbox files are not synchronized with the repository until you run the *cvs commit* command. This command is best run from the root directory of your sandbox, and it must be run from within the sandbox.

Commit to the repository frequently. Rules of thumb for when to commit include "every time the code compiles cleanly" and "every day before lunch and before you leave." Speak to your project manager about the preferred working style, or read Chapter 7 for ideas.

 In programming projects with several developers, try to avoid committing code that doesn't compile, unless your project manager tells you that your project is using a different working style.

When you commit, CVS examines each directory and subdirectory under the current working directory. It searches for files that it is tracking that have changed, and commits all changes to the repository. See Example 2-12 for an example of committing files. Remember that the repository path is stored in the sandbox, so you don't need to specify the path explicitly in your *cvs commit* command.

Example 2-12. Committing files

```
$ cd ~/cvs/example
$ cvs commit
cvs commit: Examining .
```

If your repository is not on the local machine and your repository server doesn't have your SSH public key, CVS asks for a password for the remote machine. If the server has the public key, your SSH client can use the private key to authenticate you. It's much easier to use CVS if the server has the public key.

Keeping a public key on the server is a security decision: it's much more convenient to use CVS if you don't have to keep typing in your password, but it also means that if an intruder has access to your shell, he can gain access to the data stored in the repository. I keep my desktop's public key on the server, but not my laptop's. It's always possible that I'll lose my laptop, so I don't want it to have password-free access into our network. The desktop computer is a little bit harder to lose.

 SSH is a system of authentication and encryption that relies on a public key and a private key. Only you (or your sandbox computer) should ever know your private key. Anyone (or any computer) can be told your public key, which they use to encrypt messages specifically for you. Your SSH documentation should include instructions for making and storing your private and public keys.

If any files have been changed, CVS opens an editor to allow you to record a change message. By default, the editor is *vi,* just as when importing a project. Chapter 3 gives instructions on changing your editor.

I strongly recommend meaningful change notes. If you're trying to do a rollback and all you have are messages that say "fixed a few bugs," you won't know which revision to roll back to. See Example 2-13 for an example of a good change note.

Example 2-13. Enter a commit message

```
Corrected bug #35. 'hello' was misspelled as 'helo'.
CVS:-------------------------------------------------------------------
CVS: Enter Log.  Lines beginning with 'CVS:' are removed automatically
CVS:
CVS: Committing in .
CVS:
CVS: Modified Files:
CVS:  file1
CVS:-------------------------------------------------------------------
```

After you exit the editor, CVS completes the commit, displaying messages similar to those in Example 2-14.

Example 2-14. Completing the commit

```
Checking in file1;
/var/lib/cvsroot/example/file1,v  <--  file1
new revision: 1.2; previous revision: 1.1
done
```

Figure 2-7 shows the same commit in gCVS.

If a revision in the repository is more recent than the revision the sandbox was based on, *cvs commit* fails. Use the *cvs update* command to merge the changed files; resolve the conflict as shown in the next section, "Updating Sandboxes," then run *cvs commit* again. Example 2-15 shows the response to a failed commit.

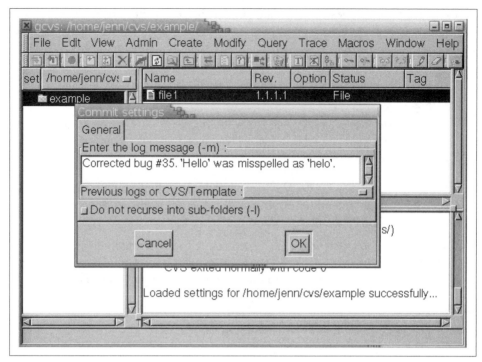

Figure 2-7. Committing files in gCVS

Example 2-15. Failed commit response

```
cvs server: Up-to-date check failed for 'file2'
cvs [server aborted]: correct above errors first!
cvs commit: saving log message in /tmp/cvst7onmJ
```

Updating Sandboxes

The *cvs update* command checks your sandbox against the repository and downloads any changed files to the sandbox. It complements the *cvs commit* command, which uploads changes from the sandbox to the repository. Use the *-d* command option to download new directories as well. Example 2-16 shows the use of *cvs update*.

Example 2-16. Updating the sandbox

```
$ cvs update -d
cvs update: Updating .
U file2
cvs update: Updating directory
$ ls
CVS  directory  file1    file2
```

As with committing, you should not have to specify the repository; it should be stored in the special *CVS* subdirectory in the sandbox. You must run *cvs update* from within the sandbox, and it is best to run it from the root directory of the sandbox to ensure that it checks all the subdirectories.

Note that *-d* means two different things, depending on where it is in the command. Recall that CVS commands take the following form:

```
cvs [cvs-options] command [command-options]
```

As a CVS option, *-d* defines the repository path. As a command option to the *update* command, *-d* downloads directories that were not previously in the sandbox. This is explained in more detail in Chapter 3.

As the *update* command runs, it generates a list of files that are modified. To the immediate left of each filename is a single uppercase letter. Those letters report the status of each file listed, and they have the following meanings:

A filename

> Marked for addition but not yet added to the repository (need to run a *cvs commit*).

C filename

> There was a conflict between the repository copy and your copy. The conflict requires human intervention.

M filename

> Modified in your working directory. The file in the sandbox is more recent than the repository version, or the sandbox and the repository both had changes that the system could safely merge into your sandbox copy (need to run a *cvs commit*).

P filename

> Patched in the sandbox; similar to U (updated successfully), but in this case CVS sent only the changes, not the entire file.

R filename

> Marked for removal but not yet removed from the repository (need to run a *cvs commit*).

U filename

> Updated successfully. A newer version in the repository has replaced your sandbox version.

? filename

> The file is in your working directory but not in the repository. CVS doesn't know what to do with it. It's common to see this marker next to temporary or intermediate files that you haven't cleaned up.

The A, R, and M codes mean that your sandbox contains changes that are not in the repository and it would be a good idea to run a *cvs commit*.

Figure 2-8 shows the update dialog from gCVS. In the background, at the bottom right, you can see the dialog from a successful update, showing that *file1* is modified in the sandbox.

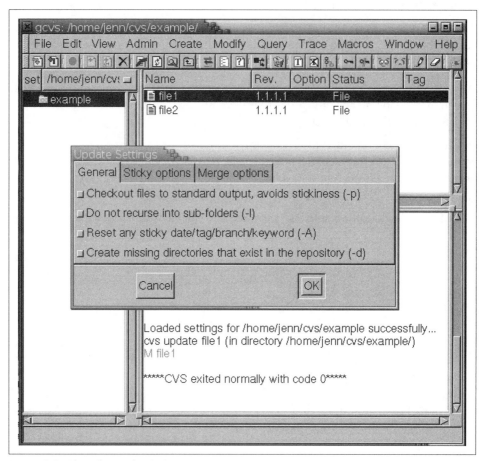

Figure 2-8. File update with gCVS

If CVS can't merge a modified file successfully with the copy in the repository, it announces the conflict in the output of *cvs update*, as shown in Example 2-17. Figure 2-9 shows a conflict in gCVS.

Example 2-17. File conflict

```
cvs/example$ cvs update
cvs server: Updating .
RCS file: /var/lib/cvsroot/example/file1,v
retrieving revision 1.3
retrieving revision 1.4
```

Example 2-17. File conflict (continued)

```
Merging differences between 1.3 and 1.4 into file1
rcsmerge: warning: conflicts during merge
cvs server: conflicts found in file1
C file1
```

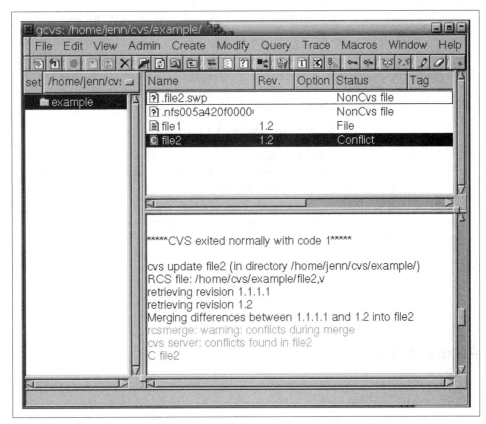

Figure 2-9. File conflict with gCVS

CVS automatically merges files when the changes are on different lines. If a line in the repository copy is different from the corresponding line in the sandbox copy, CVS reports a conflict and creates a file with the two revisions of the line surrounded by special marks, as shown in Example 2-18.

Example 2-18. Conflict marks

```
<<<<<<<file2
This line came from the sandbox.
= = = = = = = =
This line came from the repository.
>>>>>>> 1.4
```

The contents of the original file are stored in *.#file.revision* in the file's working directory, and the results of the merge are stored as the original filename.

To resolve the conflict, search the file with the original filename for the pattern of repeated greater-than or less-than symbols. Study the two options for each set of changes, and discuss the changes with the person who committed the previous version of the file. (Use *cvs log filename* to find out who committed the previous version; see Chapter 5 for information on *cvs log*.)

Once you and the previous author have agreed on how the file needs to be changed, edit the file accordingly and remove the conflict markers. Then commit the changed file.

How I Lost Penny's Changes

The first time I used CVS, I had no idea what I was doing. My coworker sent me to *man cvs*, which is just a summary of the commands, with no tutorial information. Penny, who I was working with, had never used it either.

We struggled through, until we reached our first conflict. We couldn't understand why Penny couldn't commit, and after some time, decided to remove Penny's existing file and update from the repository. I'm sure we thought CVS must have saved it somehow.

If only we'd updated with Penny's file still in her sandbox. But we didn't, and the work she had done was lost.

Penny, if you ever read this, I'm sorry. And now I know what I should have done.

Adding Files

To add a file to a project in the repository, first create the file in your sandbox. Be sure to consider your project's structure and place the file in the correct directory. Then, issue the following command from the sandbox directory containing the file:

```
cvs add filename
```

This command marks the new file for inclusion in the repository. Directories are added with the same command. Files within a directory can't be added until the directory itself is added. A file is only marked for addition when you run *cvs add*; it is actually added to the repository when the next *cvs commit* is run. A directory is added to the repository immediately. Example 2-19 shows a file being created and added to the repository. Remember that the file is not actually stored in the repository until the *cvs commit* command is run. Figure 2-10 shows the same file addition in gCVS.

Example 2-19. Adding files

```
$ touch file3
$ cvs add file3
cvs add: scheduling file `file3' for addition
cvs add: use 'cvs commit' to add this file permanently
$ cvs commit
...
Log message editor opens
...
RCS file: /var/lib/cvsroot/example/file3,v
done
Checking in file3;
/var/lib/cvsroot/example/file3,v  <--  file3
initial revision: 1.1
done
```

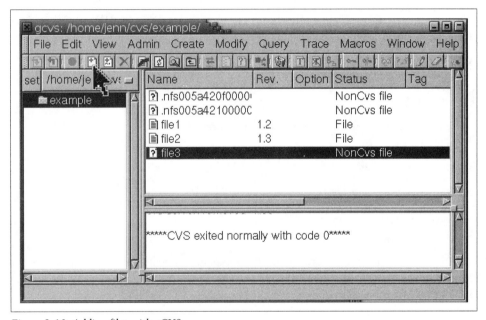

Figure 2-10. Adding files with gCVS

 If you have binary files or other files that are not plain text, please see the section "Binary Files and Wrappers" in Chapter 3 before adding them to the repository. These files should be added with the *-kb* command option.

As with committing for other reasons, an editor window will open asking you to enter a log message describing the files to be added.

Removing Files

To remove a file from the repository, first remove the file from the sandbox directory, then run the following command from the sandbox directory that contained the file:

```
cvs remove filename
```

The deletion does not take effect until the next *cvs commit* command is run; the file remains in the repository until then.

Example 2-20 shows a deletion, and Figure 2-11 shows the same deletion in gCVS. After the *cvs commit* is run, CVS doesn't remove the file entirely; it puts it in a special subdirectory in the repository called *Attic*. This step saves the file history and enables the file to be returned to the repository later.

CVS opens an editor so you can record the reason for the file deletion, as it does when you commit changes.

Example 2-20. Removing a file

```
$ rm file3
$ cvs remove file3
cvs remove: scheduling `file3' for removal
cvs remove: use 'cvs commit' to remove this file permanently
$ cvs commit
...
Log message editor opens
...
Removing file3;" 9L, 308C written
/var/lib/cvsroot/example/file3,v <--  file3
new revision: delete; previous revision: 1.1
done
```

CVS does not remove directories from the repository, because doing so would break the change tracking. Use the -P flag to *cvs checkout* and *cvs update* to avoid empty directories in your sandbox.

Exporting and Building Projects

When you're ready to compile and test a program, to send a book to an editor, or to post a web site to the server, you will want a copy of the project that doesn't have the CVS administrative files. You could use *cvs checkout* and remove the CVS subdirectories, but that's tedious and unnecessary. Use *cvs export* instead. It works exactly the same as *checkout*, but doesn't create the administrative files necessary for a sandbox.

If you need to compile a program, distribute the project's files, or otherwise modify the results of the export, I recommend using a build tool such as *make* on the exported project. Unfortunately, the use of *make* is beyond the scope of this book, but

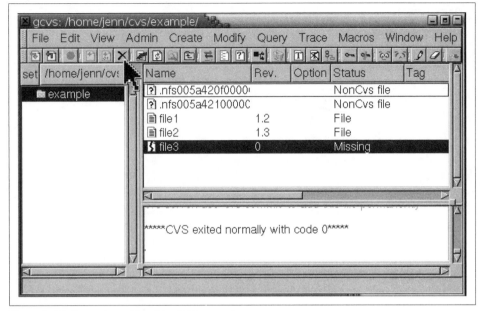

Figure 2-11. Removing a file with gCVS

I recommend the article "Introduction to Make" at *http://www.linuxdevcenter.com/pub/a/linux/2002/01/31/make_intro.html.*

Quick Tips for Success

CVS is a tool for improving project development and system maintenance. Like all tools, there are ways to use it most efficiently:

- Synchronize the clocks of computers sharing a repository to the same universal time. CVS relies on file timestamps to determine which files have changed. NTP (Network Time Protocol) is a very useful tool for time synchronization.

- Give each developer his own sandbox, and communicate all file changes through CVS. This method maintains change tracking and prevents developers from irretrievably overwriting each other's work.

- Update frequently, at least before starting work every day, to keep your sandbox current.

- Commit frequently to keep your repository current. Programmers typically commit every time their code compiles cleanly; other people may commit after completing each block of work.

- Programming teams: use build-management tools and ensure that all files in the build are committed to the repository. Ensure that builds for testing or release come from the repository rather than a sandbox, but allow sandbox builds for programmers to do prealpha tests.

Using CVS

This part of the book explains the core concepts behind CVS and describes the commands most people use on a day-to-day basis. All CVS users should be familiar with the topics covered in this part of the book. Part II consists of the following chapters:

Chapter 3, *Basic Use of CVS*
> This chapter explains the everyday CVS commands and concepts—the ones that almost everyone who uses CVS will need. Each command is accompanied by an example and a description of the most commonly used options to the command.
>
> Commands in this chapter include *add*, *remove*, *commit*, and *update*. Concepts covered include the CVS repository and sandboxes, conflicts and merges, using CVS with binary files, and switching repositories.

Chapter 4, *Tagging and Branching*
> Tagging, branching, and merging branches back to the trunk are closely related topics. This chapter explains tagging and branching, including why and when to tag or branch your project, tagging before releases, and using branching to create a bugfix version of a project.

Chapter 5, *Multiple Users*
> This chapter explains the systems used in CVS to permit multiple developers to work on the same project without loss of data. For example, it discusses the commands available for displaying changes to files.

## CHAPTER 3

Basic Use of CVS

This chapter provides a thorough discussion of the most critical CVS commands and topics. It is designed for end users who do not have to administrate the repository and who do not have to make changes that affect the entire project.

The commands explained in this chapter include *checkout*, *commit*, *update*, *release*, *add*, *remove*, *ls*, and *status*. Other topics explained in this chapter include sandboxes, merging, conflicts, binary and special files, keywords, editing files in CVS, and the CVS command syntax.

This chapter assumes that you have installed CVS, set up a repository, and created a project. Instructions for these tasks are in Chapter 2. Chapter 2 also touches on many of the commands in this chapter, but this chapter provides a full explanation of their uses.

General Information

CVS stores project data in a repository, but you don't work directly from the repository. As mentioned earlier, you work from a *sandbox*. A sandbox may be on the same machine as the repository, on a machine on the same local network, or on a machine connected through the Internet or another wide-area network. Figure 3-1 illustrates some of these possibilities.

The sandbox is a directory on a client machine that contains a copy of a project's files. Sandboxes are usually within a user's home directory. All of a given project's files should be underneath the top directory, but the files may be in any number of subdirectories. Every subdirectory contains a special *CVS* directory, with metadata files.

A typical CVS session would involve the developer updating a sandbox with the latest versions from the repository, editing the files and making changes, perhaps running a build script and testing changes, and then committing those changes to the repository.

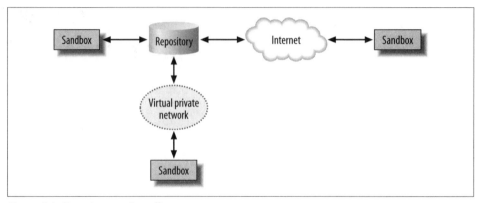

Figure 3-1. Repository and sandboxes

When you are ready to test or install your project, use the *export* command, as explained in Chapter 7. If you want to install your project over several directories or outside of your home directory, that should be part of your build or installation script; the script can include the necessary export commands if desired. The sandbox is a place for making changes; it's not a place for running the project.

Lock Files

Sandboxes and repositories do not exist on a one-to-one basis; many sandboxes may share the same repository. To ensure that the repository does not become unstable, the repository locks files that are being changed while the changes are being committed to the repository. (The locks are actually over entire directories.) Occasionally, a developer will get a warning message that the repository is waiting on a lock, as shown in Example 3-1.

Example 3-1. Lock message

```
cvs server: [23:20:43] waiting for jenn's lock in /var/lib/cvs/wizzard/src
```

This message indicates that CVS is waiting on the other developer's lock in the specified directory—that is, that CVS is in the act of committing the other developer's changes. Depending on the size of the files being changed, and the speed of the network, this process can take as little as a fraction of a second, or as long as 10 minutes. In my experience, it takes CVS less than a second to make text changes on a local LAN, or a minute or two to process a large image file across a dial-up network.

If a CVS process is killed before it's finished tidying up, a lock file may be created and not cleared. If CVS seems to be taking an inordinate amount of time to clear a lock, your repository administrator can clear it manually. Chapter 6 provides instructions and an example of how to do so, including how to determine whether the lock is valid.

CVS Command Syntax

CVS commands follow this syntax:

```
cvs [cvs-options] command [command-options] [arguments]
```

The *cvs-options* modify the behavior of CVS as a whole, and their functions include help, quiet operation, changing the default editor, and changing the CVS root directory.

 All the commands have aliases, which are short versions of the command. For example, *cvs commit* can be run as *cvs ci*. The aliases are in the reference section of this book, and are listed with the command *cvs --help-synonyms*.

The *command-options* modify the command's behavior and can change which parts of the sandbox, or which revisions in the repository, a command will operate on.

Here are the *cvs-options* (left-side options) that you will use most often (see Chapter 10 for a full list):

-H or *--help*
> Displays information about the CVS command but does not execute it.

-Q or *-q*
> Suppresses informational messages. *-q* is quiet; *-Q* is very quiet and prints only warnings.

-d repository_path
> Tells CVS which repository to use to run the command on.

-e editor
> Changes the editor that CVS calls when prompting for messages.

-n Does not change any files. This option is useful when trying to figure out what a command does without risking damage to the repository or the sandbox.

-z compression_level
> Compresses the file transfer over a network.

In this book, the *command-options* (right-side options) are discussed with their commands. Full lists of each set of options are available in Chapter 10.

At the command line, documentation for the CVS options is available with *cvs --help-options*. Command options for each command are available with *cvs -H command*. The list of all available CVS commands is available with *cvs --help-commands*.

Choosing Your Editor

In Unix, Linux, and Mac OS X, CVS invokes the *vi* editor by default when asking for log messages. There are several ways you can change the default editor. Chapter 10 has a more extensive discussion of Unix editors.

CVS checks the command line, the *.cvsrc* file, or your environment variables to see whether you have set an editor. You can use any of the following options to set an editor. These options are in order; the earliest option takes precedence.

1. Call CVS with the *-e editor* option.
2. Set the *cvs -e editor* line in your *.cvsrc* file on the client machine.
3. Set the environment variables *CVSEDITOR*, *EDITOR*, or *VISUAL* on the client machine as the calling user. *CVSEDITOR* is preferred and overrides *EDITOR* and *VISUAL*.

You can avoid calling an editor at all by using the *-m message* command option. This option is available with *add*, *commit*, and *import*.

Sandboxes and Repositories

A sandbox is a local copy of a project's files, used to make changes and to test work. Each developer should work from her own sandbox on a computer that is convenient for her.

The CVS repository contains the master copies of a project's files and their full histories. The repository may be on the same machine as the sandbox or on a remote machine accessed across a network. The repository is explained more fully in Chapter 6.

Every directory in the sandbox contains a *CVS* subdirectory. This directory has several files; the most important are *Root*, *Repository*, and *Entries*. The *Root* file contains the path to the sandbox's repository, the *Repository* file contains the subpath within the repository that leads to the directory in question, and the *Entries* file holds metadata about the files in the directory. The *CVS* subdirectory is explained more fully in Chapter 6. CVS maintains this subdirectory itself, and it is extremely rare for users to need to edit it.

Two commands keep your sandbox synchronized with the repository: *cvs update* and *cvs commit*. An update brings changes from the repository to the sandbox, and a commit sends changes from the sandbox to the repository. See Figure 3-2 and the sections "Committing Changes to the Repository" and "Updating the Sandbox Files from the Repository" later in this chapter.

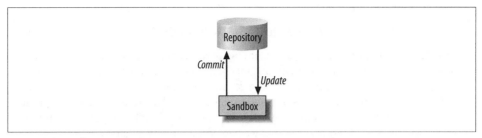

Figure 3-2. Updating and committing

Permissions and Ownership

Files lose their permissions when they are transferred to the repository. CVS normally checks out files with read and write permissions, but it can be configured to check them out as read-only. The person who checks a file out into the sandbox becomes the file's owner within the sandbox.

CVS works on many operating systems, each of which has its own way of recording ownership of files. The repository might not be on the same machine or have the same operating system as the sandbox. These circumstances may cause files to lose their ownerships and group memberships when the files are transferred to the repository, especially if the owning user does not exist on the repository machine. If the sandbox is connected to the repository through a proxy or network tunnel, the existence of appropriate users and groups on intermediate machines can also affect the ownership of files.

This setup would normally cause problems, but CVS relies on the Unix feature called *groups*, which is also used on Mac OS X and Linux. A group of users can have *group ownership* of a file, and CVS will allow any member of the group to access the file and download it to his sandbox. Chapter 6 explains ownership and security issues with CVS in more detail (in this paragraph, I have oversimplified the issue).

If the ownership of files and permissions on files are important to your project, you should set them in build and installation scripts. This issue usually affects projects that are installed for production use. Chapter 7 discusses this topic in more detail.

Repository Paths

When you create a sandbox, you need to specify the repository to which it is connected. You do this by setting the repository path, either by putting it in the *CVSROOT* environment variable on your client computer, or by declaring it with the *-d* command option when you check out the sandbox. CVS stores the repository path in the sandbox.

We Couldn't Get Our Files!

This is another tale of CVS ignorance from my past. My colleagues and I were working on a project, and were connecting to one machine (call it *bechamel*) from our workstations, because it had the necessary build tools and testing tools. So our sandboxes were on *bechamel*. Our repository was on another machine (call it *caramel*), but to get from *bechamel* to *caramel*, we had to go through a tunnel via a third machine. The network admin set it up for us and ensured that we had access to the repository.

However, neither we nor the network admin fully understood CVS security. He ensured that the group existed on both *bechamel* and *caramel*. We ensured that our files were set with read-write-execute for the group, in our sandboxes on *bechamel*, then added them to the repository on *caramel*—but our fellow group members didn't receive the files when they updated.

When we investigated the repository, we found that they'd lost the group membership. I still don't know why. But we fixed it anyway: by setting the *SGID* bit in the repository's project directories, we ensured that the correct group ownership and permission was set for all files in the directory. In fact, I've been doing that ever since, and have never had a recurrence of the problem.

The quickstart guide and Chapter 6 explain how to set the *SGID* bit.

The repository path is the path CVS uses to find the repository. The general format for repository path is:

```
[:method[;option=arg]:][[[user][:password]@]hostname[:[port]]]/path
```

Each access method (*method* in the syntax) has a slightly different syntax. Chapter 8 provides the correct syntax for each method.

These are the access methods:

local
    Connect to the local machine.

ext
    Connect using an externally defined *rsh* or *rsh*-like connection method (such as *ssh*).

server
    Connect using the internal *rsh* server (available only on some operating systems).

pserver
    Connect using the *pserver* (password server) connection method.

gserver
    Connect through the GSS-API (currently used for Kerberos 5.0).

kserver
> Connect through Kerberos 4 and earlier.

fork
> Connect to a local machine as if it were a remote machine, using pipes for communication (useful if you are trying to diagnose problems).

Everything except the path itself may be left out of a repository path definition.

If the method is left out but the host is included, CVS uses either the *server* or the *ext* method, depending on whether an internal RSH server is available. If both the host and the method are left out, CVS uses the *local* access method.

If *user* is left out, CVS uses the current, operating-system login username. If *password* is left out but is required, CVS asks for it.

Chapter 8 explains repository connection methods.

Browsing the Repository

CVS 1.12.8 introduced a pair of wonderful new commands. These commands allow you to browse the repository as if it were your local filesystem. Both the repository and the client must be 1.12.8 or later.

The commands are *cvs ls* and *cvs rls*. Without a parameter, the commands display the contents of the repository equivalent of the local directory (*cvs ls*), or the repository root directory (*cvs rls*). Parameters can be filenames or paths, and should be relative to the default directory the command displays. You must provide a repository path with *cvs rls*.

Creating a Sandbox

The *cvs checkout* command is used to create a sandbox. Once the sandbox is created, *checkout* no longer needs to be used in that sandbox; *update* is the preferred command from that point. However, *checkout* may be called in a sandbox, in which case it is similar to *update -d*.*

checkout is called with the names of files, directories, or modules in the repository. A *module* is a collection of files and directories under one root directory that has been given a module name. Chapter 7 explains modules.

The syntax of *cvs checkout* is:

```
cvs [cvs-options] checkout [command-options] project
```

---

* *checkout* is similar to *update -d* if it is called from the directory in the sandbox that corresponds to the *project* parameter given to *checkout*. If it is called from a different directory, it checks out a new sandbox based in the current working directory.

cvs checkout directory and *cvs checkout directory/* are identical. However, *cvs checkout module* and *cvs checkout directory/* are different, unless the module happens to refer to a directory of the same name at the root level in the repository.

You must provide the path to the repository that contains the module or directory. This can be done with the *CVSROOT* environment variable on the client machine, or with the *-d repository_path* CVS option. If your repository is on a local machine, the repository path is the full path of your CVS repository's root directory. If your repository is on a remote machine, contact your system administrator and request the path for the repository. Once you have created a sandbox, you do not need to specify the repository path for that sandbox again, because it is stored in the *CVS* subdirectory.

"Sandboxes and Repositories," earlier in this chapter, discusses accessing repositories.

 If you expect to use a repository for many sandboxes on the same machine, specify its path using the *CVSROOT* environment variable. If you expect to use it only for one sandbox, use the *-d* CVS option.

checkout creates a new directory in the current working directory. By default, this directory has the name of the module, file, or directory being checked out.

checkout creates a *CVS* subdirectory in every directory of the sandbox. The *CVS* subdirectory was described in the earlier section "Sandboxes and Repositories," and is further described in Chapter 6.

The following command options are commonly used with *cvs checkout* and can also be used with *cvs update:*

-P   Prunes empty directories.

-D date or *-r revision* or *-r tag*
   Checks out a specific revision of the module based on *date*, *revision*, or *tag*.

-f   Forces CVS to check out the latest revision of a file if the date specified with *-D* doesn't match any date of the file or if the revision specified by *-r* doesn't match any revision of the file. *-f* is useful only with *-D* or *-r*. Use this option carefully, as it can cause confusion.

-j revision or *-j revision1 -j revision2*
   Merges revisions. With one *-j*, CVS merges the changes between a common ancestor and the specified revision into the current sandbox. The common ancestor is the most recent revision that predates both the specified revision (found in the repository) and the sandbox revision.

   With two revisions specified, CVS determines the differences between *revision1* and *revision2* and then merges those changes into the sandbox.

Example 3-2 shows the *wizzard* project being checked out of a CVS repository. Figure 3-3 shows the dialog window for the same checkout, from the graphic CVS client Cervisia. The Checkout option is under the Repository menu in Cervisia.

Example 3-2. Using cvs checkout

```
bash-2.05a$ ls
cvsbook   linuxchix newsforge   oreilly
bash-2.05a$ cvs -d cvs_server:/var/lib/cvs checkout wizzard
cvs server: Updating wizzard
U wizzard/Changelog
U wizzard/INSTALL
U wizzard/Makefile
U wizzard/README
U wizzard/TODO
cvs server: Updating wizzard/doc
cvs server: Updating wizzard/lib
cvs server: Updating wizzard/man
cvs server: Updating wizzard/src
U wizzard/src/main.c
U wizzard/src/wizzard.h
bash-2.05a$ ls
cvsbook   linuxchix newsforge  oreilly  wizzard
bash-2.05a$ ls wizzard
Changelog CVS     doc INSTALL lib Makefile man  README src  TODO
```

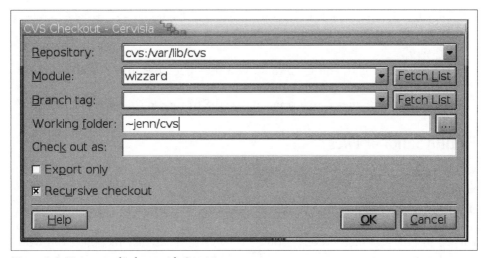

Figure 3-3. Using cvs checkout with Cervisia

The need to retrieve a list of the projects stored in the CVS repository is common. The command *cvs -d repository_path checkout -c* provides a list of the modules registered in the *modules* file in the repository. Unfortunately, this command lists only modules and does not include files and directories that are not part of a module. If you have CVS 1.12.8 or later, you can use the new *cvs rls* command to find the ones which aren't modules. Modules are explained in Chapter 7.

The command *cvs -d repository_path checkout* downloads everything in the repository, which usually is not what you desire. If you have direct access to the repository, listing the root directory of the repository provides a full list of project root directories. Combining this with the list of modules from *checkout -c* provides a complete list of projects.

Checking Out from Multiple Repositories

CVS permits you to check out directories from multiple repositories into the same sandbox directory. You do this by creating the sandbox with checkout, as normal, then changing directory into the sandbox and checking out other sandbox directories from within the first. When you use a recursive command from the top directory of the sandbox, CVS will use the correct repository for each subdirectory.

Versions of CVS prior to 1.10 do not handle this properly—update to a modern version of CVS if you intend to use multiple repositories within the one sandbox.

Changing Repositories

There are two ways to switch the repository that a sandbox is checked out from:

- The official, recommended way is to commit all changes, use *cvs release* to release the sandbox, delete the sandbox, then check out a new sandbox from the new repository.

- The other way is to edit *CVS/Root* in all the directories in the sandbox. Unless you have only one directory, this way actually is more work than the first approach. It also means that some of the CVS history tracking may be lost.

Editing Sandbox Files

Once files are in your sandbox, you can edit them normally. For files saved as text, use your favorite text editor.

If you intend to produce text but prefer an editor that provides page and style formatting, be aware that files from editors that save in a nontext file format must be flagged as binary, which prevents some of CVS's most useful functions from working. File formats such as RTF, TeX, XML, HTML, and LaTeX are text-based and can be used with CVS without needing to be flagged as binary.

If you are producing an image or some other nontext file, these must also be added to the repository as a binary file, as explained in "Adding Files to the Repository" later in this chapter.

Committing Changes to the Repository

Files are edited in the sandbox, but changes to the sandbox have no effect on the repository until they are committed. The *cvs commit* command uploads changes from the sandbox to the repository. After determining which files need to be changed in the repository, *cvs commit* opens an editor and expects you to enter a log message.

> "Choosing Your Editor," earlier in this chapter, explained how to change the default editor.

The syntax of *cvs commit* is:

```
cvs [cvs-options] commit [command-options] [filename]
```

cvs commit has only a few options, the most useful of which are:

-*f* Force a commit even if there are no changes to the file. (This option implies *-l* as well.)

-*l* Perform a local, nonrecursive commit operation on the current working directory only.

-*R* Perform a recursive commit operation on all subdirectories, as well as the current directory (default).

-*m message*
   Provide a log message.

-*F filename*
   Provide a log message from the specified file.

-*r revision*
   Set an updated revision number (not recommended for novice users).

> When you need to record important information in the log for a particular file (or files), use the *-f* option to force CVS to commit those files even if they're unchanged.

Example 3-3 shows a typical *cvs commit*. The vertical ellipsis denotes the point at which CVS normally calls the editor. Example 3-4 shows the default text displayed in the editor and the log message for this commit. Figure 3-4 shows the Pharmacy graphic client just before a commit.

Example 3-3. Using cvs commit

```
/home/jenn/cvs/wizzard$ cvs commit
cvs commit: Examining .
cvs commit: Examining doc
cvs commit: Examining lib
cvs commit: Examining man
```

Example 3-3. Using cvs commit (continued)

```
cvs commit: Examining src
.
.
.
RCS file: /var/lib/cvs/wizzard/src/main.c,v
done
Checking in src/main.c;
/var/lib/cvs/wizzard/src/main.c,v  <--  main.c
initial revision: 1.1
done
RCS file: /var/lib/cvs/wizzard/src/wizzard.h,v
done
Checking in src/wizzard.h;
/var/lib/cvs/wizzard/src/wizzard.h,v  <--  wizzard.h
initial revision: 1.1
done
/home/jenn/cvs/wizzard$
```

Example 3-4. Entering log messages for cvs commit

```
Added main.c: parses parameters and calls functions in other files.
Added wizzard.h: defines compile-time global variables.
CVS: ------------------------------------------------------------------
CVS: Enter Log.  Lines beginning with `CVS:' are removed automatically
CVS:
CVS: Committing in .
CVS:
CVS: Added Files:
CVS:   src/main.c src/wizzard.h
CVS: ------------------------------------------------------------------
```

By default, *cvs commit* operates recursively on the current working directory. It can also take files or directories as parameters and operate recursively on them.

Use either of the following variations of *cvs commit* to avoid having to enter a message during the commit process:

    cvs commit -m *message*

or:

    cvs commit -F *filename*

Examples 3-3 and 3-4 show a recursive commit, which commits files not only in your current working directory, but also in all subdirectories. If you want to commit only the current working directory (sometimes called the *local* directory), use *cvs commit -l*.

 Use *cvs status* or *cvs -n update* to find out which files need to be updated or committed.

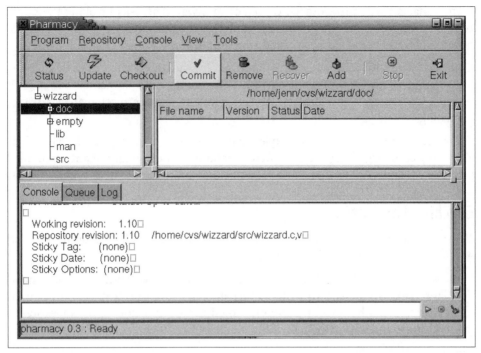

Figure 3-4. Commit with Pharmacy

Setting Revision Numbers

You can use the -r option of *cvs commit* to set every file currently being committed to a specific revision number. This option is not used often; if it is used, it's usually by the project lead. The option changes the most recent revision number on the current line of development of all files being committed, regardless of whether they've changed in the sandbox. The revision number must be higher than any number currently in the repository, and it must be in the same format as the existing revision numbers for the files.

 CVS developers recommend you use tags to track revisions, and leave the internal revision numbers as CVS sets them by default. Chapter 4 explains how to use tags.

When to Commit

If your changes will not affect anyone else, commit frequently. Commit every time you'd hate to have to redo your work. Frequent commits keep your work in a single place for backup. If you are working in a team, frequent commits and updates reduce the chance of having to do a major, difficult merge.

If your changes will affect others, especially in a way that risks breaking the build, commit every time the effect will be negligible. For example, run a test-compile before lunch and before you leave, and commit if it compiles.

Don't ever work for long without committing. If a full day's work doesn't compile, wrap comment tags around your changes and commit the commented-out code or consider committing to a branch. Always speak to your project manager before branching.

There are several different work styles and commit strategies possible with CVS. Your project manager may have a different commit strategy than the one mentioned here; if so, follow that. Chapter 7 discusses commit strategies in more detail.

Checking File Status

The *cvs status* command is a quick way to determine which files are up to date and which need to be committed or merged.

Files that have not been added to the repository are prefixed with a question mark. Files stored in CVS are shown with the filename, the current status, the working (or sandbox) revision, the revision currently stored in the repository and its location in the repository, and the sticky state of the file. Stickiness is explained in Chapter 4.

The syntax of *cvs status* is:

```
cvs [cvs-options] status [command-options] [filename]
```

The *status* command has only three options:

-l   Perform local, nonrecursive operation on this directory only.

-R   Perform recursive operation on all subdirectories, as well as the current directory (default).

-v   Use verbose mode (display information about tags as well).

Example 3-5 shows the CVS status report for the *wizzard.h* file. Figure 3-5 shows the TkCVS graphic client display for this book, at the time I'm writing this, including displays of the status, last modified date, and revision level.

Example 3-5. Output from the cvs status command

```
=======================================================================
File: wizzard.h             Status: Up-to-date

   Working revision:    1.5
   Repository revision: 1.5      /var/lib/cvs/wizzard/src/wizzard.h,v
   Sticky Tag:          (none)
   Sticky Date:         (none)
   Sticky Options:      (none)
```

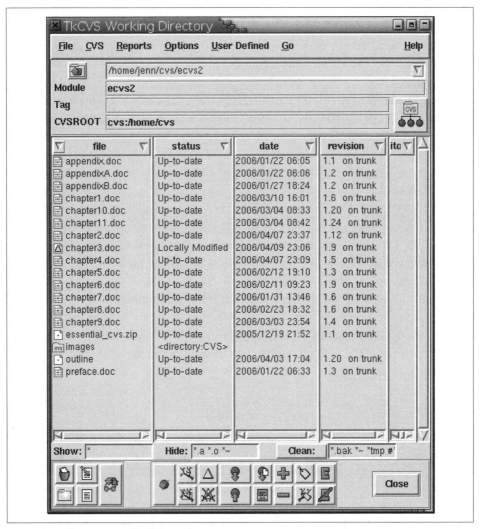

Figure 3-5. TkCVS status display

A file may be in one of the following states:

Up-to-date
The file in the sandbox is synchronized with the file in the repository.

Needs Checkout
The file does not exist in the sandbox; it exists only in the repository.

Needs Patch

> The file in the sandbox has not been modified, and the file in the repository is more recent. The sandbox file needs to be patched using *cvs update* in order to be brought up to date with the repository.

Unresolved Conflict

> The repository copy and the sandbox copy cannot be merged. This status occurs when you have a file in the sandbox with the same name as a file in the repository, but which you did not receive from the repository.

Locally Added

> The file in the sandbox has been added, but the addition has not been committed.

Locally Removed

> The file in the sandbox has been removed, but the removal hasn't been committed.

File had conflicts on merge

> There is a known conflict between the file in the repository and the file in the sandbox.

Locally Modified

> The file in the sandbox has been modified but not committed.

Needs Merge

> The file in the repository does not match the file in the sandbox and both files have new data. The files need to be merged using *cvs merge*.

There are three error states:

Classify Error

> CVS could not determine the state of this file.

Unknown

> This file is not known to CVS. Normally, the *cvs status* command displays unknown files at the start of its sequence with a *?* beside them. If an unknown file does get passed to the *status* command, CVS displays its name in the main body of its display with the status *Unknown*.

> For example, if you run the command *cvs status filename* and the filename refers to a file that is not stored in the repository, CVS reports its status as *Unknown*.

Entry Invalid

> The state of the repository and sandbox files does not match CVS's record keeping. This usually occurs when one of the files has been removed by editing the repository directly, or when a newly added file has been removed from the sandbox without calling *cvs remove*.

Note that the revision number shown in the status (and other places) is the CVS internal revision number; it has nothing to do with the version number that a file or project may have outside of CVS.

Updating the Sandbox Files from the Repository

The *cvs commit* command uploads changes from the sandbox to the repository; *cvs update* downloads changes from the repository to the sandbox. The two commands complement each other, and you need to call both to keep the sandbox synchronized with the repository. Use *cvs commit* when you have changed sandbox files since your last *commit*; use *cvs update* when you know that the repository has been changed since you last updated, or when you wish to check whether it has changed.

cvs update attempts to preserve any changes you have made to your sandbox since you last synchronized it with the repository. These changes will be merged into the files retrieved from the repository. If you intend to overwrite your sandbox files with a clean repository copy, use the *-C* (clean) option in conjunction with any other options. Most often, you will use *-C* when you want to discard changes, but you can also use the *-r* (retrieve by revision), *-D* (retrieve by date), or *-A* (clear sticky tags) options.

Example 3-6 shows output from *cvs update* executed with the *-d* option. The *-d* option instructs CVS to download new directories from the repository to the sandbox. Figure 3-6 shows Cervisia immediately after an update.

Example 3-6. Using cvs update

```
bash-2.05a$ cvs update -d
cvs server: Updating .
cvs server: Updating doc
cvs server: Updating doc/design
U doc/design/Analysis.rtf
U doc/design/Specification.rtf
cvs server: Updating doc/plan
U doc/plan/Schedule.rtf
cvs server: Updating lib
cvs server: Updating man
cvs server: Updating src
M src/wizzard.h
```

cvs update displays symbols next to each file it downloads. The symbols report file status, similar to those reported by *cvs status*. You'll see the following symbols in *cvs update* command output:

A *filename*

> The file has been added to the sandbox, but it has not been committed.

C *filename*

> There is a conflict between the repository copy and the sandbox copy; this conflict requires human intervention to resolve.

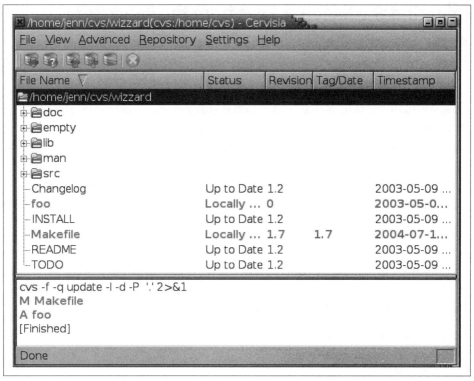

Figure 3-6. Update with Cervisia

M *filename*

The file has been modified in the sandbox. Either the sandbox version had changes that the repository did not, or both the sandbox and the repository had changes that CVS could safely merge together.

P *filename*

The file has been patched in the sandbox. The repository copy changed, but not the sandbox copy, so the repository changes were added to the sandbox.

 U and *P* report the same effect in the sandbox: the file has been updated from the repository. *P* means that CVS downloaded a patch, and *U* means that it downloaded the whole file.

R *filename*

The file has been removed from the sandbox, but it has not been committed.

U *filename*

The file was updated successfully. Either a new revision from the repository has replaced the sandbox copy, or there was no sandbox copy and the repository revision has been checked out.

? filename

The file is in the sandbox but not the repository, and it is not marked for addition to the repository.

 If you don't want CVS to report on certain files, use the *cvsignore* features as described in Chapter 6.

cvs update uses the following syntax:

```
cvs [cvs-options] update [command-options] [filename]
```

If used without a filename, *cvs update* updates the current working directory recursively. The most commonly used update options are:

-d   Pull down new directories.

-P   Avoid pulling down empty directories (not compatible with *-d*).

-j revision or *-j revision1 -j revision2*

Merge revisions. The *revision* parameter can be a revision number or a tag.

With one *-j*, CVS merges the changes between a common ancestor and the specified revision into the current sandbox. The common ancestor is the most recent revision that predates both the specified revision (found in the repository) and the sandbox revision.

With two revisions specified, CVS determines the differences between *revision1* and *revision2* and then merges the changes into the sandbox.

-A   Reset any sticky tags, dates, or keyword options and replace the existing files in the sandbox with the revision at the head of the trunk. CVS merges any changes that you have made to the sandbox with the revision it downloads. Use *-C* as well as *-A* if you want the changes overwritten.

-C   Overwrite files in the sandbox with copies from the repository.

-l   Perform a local, nonrecursive update operation on this directory only.

-R   Perform a recursive operation on all subdirectories, as well as the current directory (default).

-D date or *-r revision* or *-r tag*

Check out a specific revision of the module based on the given date, revision number, or tag. These options retrieve a static revision; they are not intended for undoing changes.

If a *date* is used, CVS selects the latest revision prior to that date. A date can include the time as well.

CVS attempts to preserve your changes since your last *checkout*, *update*, or *commit* and merge them with the revision it is retrieving.

-*f*   Force CVS to update to the latest revision of a file if the date specified with -*D* doesn't match any date of the file, or if the revision specified by -*r* doesn't match any revision of the file. This option is useful only with -*D* or -*r*. Use it carefully, as it can cause confusion.

-*W* "*wrapper string*"
   Use file extensions to determine how to merge the file or files being updated.

Tags and stickiness are explained in Chapter 4. Wrappers and keywords are explained later in this chapter.

Retrieving Past Revisions of a File

You can use CVS to retrieve a past revision of a file. Use the *cvs log* command to find the revision number or tag for the revision you want to retrieve. Tag names or log messages can help you determine which revision has the data you want. Example 3-7 shows a typical *cvs log* message header and one revision message. The tags are listed under the "symbolic names" heading. Figure 3-7 shows a log display from the TkCVS graphic client.

Example 3-7. cvs log output

```
RCS file: /var/lib/cvs/wizzard/src/wizzard.h,v
Working file: src/wizzard.h
head: 1.15
branch:
locks: strict
access list:
symbolic names:
     bugfix_version_branch: 1.14.0.2
     bugfix_branch_root: 1.14
keyword substitution: kv
total revisions: 1;     selected revisions: 1
description:
.
.
.
----------------------------
revision 1.15
date: 2006/04/11 13:33:13;  author: jenn;  state: Exp;
Started the multiple satellite tracking feature.
=================================================================
```

This chapter discusses retrieving past revisions in the context of a single line of development. Chapter 4 describes forking development to produce two or more simultaneous development tracks.

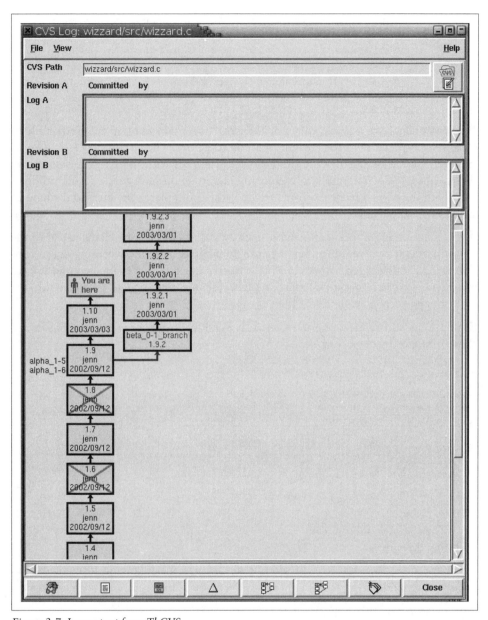

Figure 3-7. Log output from TkCVS

Retrieving a static file

Calling *cvs update* with the *-r* or *-D* options downloads a static, unchangeable copy of the file or files to the sandbox. Such files can be useful to view past data, but changes to these files cannot be committed to the repository.

If the file has changes that haven't yet been committed to the repository, CVS merges those changes with the old revision. To prevent this from happening, use -C in conjunction with -r or -D, as shown in Example 3-8.

If you have any uncommitted changes and you use -C, CVS stores the pre-update file in .#*filename.revision* in the same directory.

The static files have a mark, called a *sticky tag* or a *sticky date*, in the *Entries* file in the *CVS* subdirectory of the current sandbox directory. The command *cvs update -A* removes the sticky tags or dates and replaces the files with the latest revision from the repository. CVS attempts to merge any changes you have made to the sandbox copy with the copy it retrieves from the repository, and places the merged file in your sandbox. See "Conflicts and Merging," later in this chapter.

If you make changes to a static revision and want to commit the changed file to the repository as a new revision (but losing any changes made between the static revision and the current repository revision), create a backup of the changed file, use *cvs update -A* to clear the sticky state, replace the file that *update* created with the backup, and then *cvs commit* the file.

Example 3-8 shows the retrieval of an early version of the *wizzard.h* file. Figure 3-8 shows retrieval by tag in Cervisia.

Example 3-8. Retrieval by revision number

```
bash-2.05a$ cvs update -C -r 1.2 src/wizzard.h
U src/wizzard.h
bash-2.05a$ less src/wizzard.h
/*
 * Wizzard.h
 * Apr 12 2006
 * Developer: Jenn Vesperman
 *
 * Headers, macros and constants file for the Wizzard project.
 */
```

Reverting changes

To revert a sandbox file to a previous revision, use the following form of the *cvs update* command:

```
cvs update -j sandbox_revision -j previous_revision
```

This command calculates the differences from the older revision to the newer revision, then applies the differences to the sandbox. Be careful to get the order right. If you have any changes in the sandbox made since the *sandbox_revision* was last committed, those changes are preserved; if you want to get rid of those changes as well, remove the file before you run this command, or use -C, as explained earlier in this section.

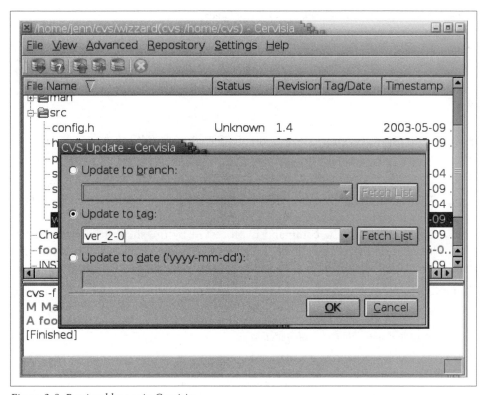

Figure 3-8. Retrieval by tag in Cervisia

Example 3-9 shows reverting a messed-up version (1.3) of *wizzard.h* to the previous revision, using the *-j* option. The less commands are there only to show you the content of the files; they are not part of the process. You can use *cvs log* or *cvs status* to determine which revision is the current version of a file.

Example 3-9. Reverting changes with update -j

```
bash-2.05a$ less wizzard.h
/*
 * Wizzard.h
 * Apr 14 2006
 * Destroyer: Doppel
 *
 * Headaches, messes and constraints file for the Wizbang project.
 */
bash-2.05a$ cvs update -j 1.3 -j 1.2 wizzard.h
RCS file: /var/lib/cvs/wizzard/src/wizzard.h,v
retrieving revision 1.3
retrieving revision 1.2
Merging differences between 1.3 and 1.2 into wizzard.h
bash-2.05a$ less wizzard.h
/*
```

Example 3-9. Reverting changes with update -j (continued)

```
 * Wizzard.h
 * Apr 12 2006
 * Developer: Jenn Vesperman
 *
 * Headers, macros and constants file for the Wizzard project.
 *
 */
```

You can also revert to a previous revision of a file with the following command:

```
    cvs update -r revision -p filename > filename
```

This command uses the *-p* option of *cvs update* to write the specified revision to *stdout*. That output is then redirected to *filename* using the > shell operator. The > operator is a shell redirection operator and may vary depending on the shell you use. The > *filename* part of the command is processed by the shell; it is not passed to CVS. This method overwrites the file in the sandbox: any changes you've made to it that haven't been committed to CVS will be irretrievably gone.

Example 3-10 reverts the corrected revision of *wizzard.h* to the corrupted revision, using the *-p* option. The less command shows the contents of the file after the reversion.

Example 3-10. Reverting changes with update -r -p

```
bash-2.05a$ cvs update -r 1.3 -p > wizzard.h
cvs server: Updating .
= = = = = = = = = = = = = = = = = = = = = = = = = = = = =
Checking out wizzard.h
RCS:  /var/lib/cvs/wizzard/src/wizzard.h,v
VERS: 1.3
***************
bash-2.05a$ less wizzard.h
/*
 * Wizzard.h
 * Apr 14 2006
 * Destroyer: Doppel
 *
 * Headaches, messes and constraints file for the Wizbang project.
 */
```

Using *cvs commit* after retrieving with either method adds the current contents of the sandbox file (identical to the old revision) to the repository as the newest revision.

Retrieving by date

The *-D* option retrieves the most recent revision that precedes the date and time you specify. CVS accepts a wide range of date formats, including ISO 8601, RFC 822, and RFC 1123, as well as certain English terms such as "yesterday." Chapter 11 provides the full range of date formats.

The date formats *YYYY-MM-DD* and *YYYY-MM-DD HH:MM* are acceptable and fairly universal. You can also use the date and time formats from *cvs log* output.

CVS repositories use Coordinated Universal Time (UTC) rather than your local time, so it can be useful to include the time zone at the end of a date string. If you don't specify a time zone, CVS assumes that you intend your time or date string to be in local time.

 Times in *cvs log* output are in UTC. If you copy a time from *cvs log* to use for a -D option, either specify the UTC time zone or modify the time to local time.

If the CVS server is 1.12.9 or later and the client is 1.12.10 or later, the *cvs log* output is in local time.

If the time is not specified along with a date, CVS locates the latest revision that is older than that date—the revision that was active at midnight at the start of the date. Example 3-11 demonstrates retrieving the revision of *wizzard.h* that was current at 2 P.M. on 13 April 2006. Note the use of -C, as for retrieving by revision.

Example 3-11. Retrieving with update -D

```
bash-2.05a$ cvs update -C -D 2006-04-13 14:00 src/wizzard.h
U src/wizzard.h
bash-2.05a$ less wizzard.h
/*
 * Wizzard.h
 * Apr 12 2006
 * Developer: Jenn Vesperman
 *
 * Headers, macros and constants file for the Wizzard project.
 */
```

When to Update

Update frequently. Always update before beginning work—perhaps first thing in the morning and just after lunch. This habit ensures that any changes are merged often. Frequent commits and updates leave little chance of having to do a major, pain-in-the-neck merge.

In programming projects, if people are careful about ensuring that their code compiles before a commit, their commits won't break your code gratuitously. If your code doesn't work after an update, you can check to see who made the change that broke it and speak to that person immediately (see Chapter 5 for commands that show recent changes). Frequent commits and updates catch these problems early.

Conflicts and Merging

CVS attempts to merge files using a line-based merging system. If the changes are on different lines, this system just adds, replaces, or removes lines as appropriate. CVS uses an internal implementation of the *diff* and *patch* programs to merge files.

Merging is done during *cvs update*, but it can also occur when *checkout* is used on an existing sandbox. Example 3-6 showed a merge during an update. Example 3-12 shows both a merge and a conflict.

Example 3-12. File merge and conflict during update

```
bash-2.05a$ cvs update
cvs server: Updating .
RCS file: /var/lib/cvs/wizzard/src/main.c,v
retrieving revision 1.1
retrieving revision 1.2
Merging differences between 1.1 and 1.2 into main.c
rcsmerge: warning: conflicts during merge
cvs server: conflicts found in main.c
C main.c
RCS file: /var/lib/cvs/wizzard/src/wizzard.h,v
retrieving revision 1.3
retrieving revision 1.4
Merging differences between 1.3 and 1.4 into wizzard.h
M wizzard.h
bash-2.05a$
```

If a line in the repository copy is different from the corresponding line in the sandbox copy, CVS reports a conflict and creates a file with the two revisions of the line surrounded by special marks, as shown here:

```
<<<<<<< filename
sandbox content
=======
repository content
>>>>>>> revision
```

The original file is stored in *.#file.revision* in the file's working directory, and the results of the merge are stored as the original filename.

CVS creates a set of conflict marks and content revisions for every conflict in the file. If several neighboring lines have a conflict, CVS produces a single set of conflict marks around the group of lines, as shown in Example 3-13. Figure 3-9 shows the conflict resolution display in TkCVS.

Example 3-13. Conflicts in a file

```
<<<<<<< main.c
/*
 * main.c
 * Apr 12 2006
```

Example 3-13. Conflicts in a file (continued)

```
* Developer: Doppel
*
* Main program file for the Wizbang project.
*/

=======
/*
 * main.c
 * Apr 12 2006
 * Developer: Jenn Vesperman
 *
 * Main program file for the wizzard project.
 */
>>>>>>> 1.2
```

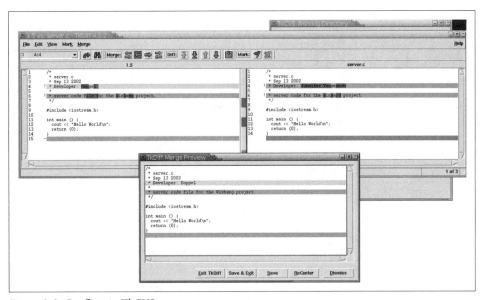

Figure 3-9. Conflicts in TkCVS

To resolve a conflict, search for the conflict marks and edit the file; then commit the changed file to the repository. The sandbox version is always shown first, and the repository version is second. Doppel performed the update shown in Example 3-13 and she needs to resolve the conflict before she commits this file.

Because CVS cannot merge binary files, you'll always get a conflict if a binary file has been changed in the repository and the sandbox copy has also been changed since it was checked out.

More detailed examples of conflict resolution and merging are given in Chapter 4.

Adding Files to the Repository

Use *cvs add* to add a file or directory to the repository. Using *cvs add* on a file marks the file as needing to be added when *cvs commit* is run. Running *cvs add* on a directory adds the directory to the repository and the *CVS* subdirectory to the directory.

The *Attic* and *CVS* directories are special directories that CVS uses for its own purposes. Do not make a file or directory with these names.

> If you attempt to commit and get an error message that includes *PANIC* administration files missing, you may have created a file or directory named *CVS*. This message means that CVS could not find the *Repository* file in the *CVS* subdirectory of the sandbox directory that it is trying to commit.

You can use *cvs remove* to remove a file that has been added but not committed. This command removes the marking in the *CVS* subdirectory and doesn't record the aborted addition in the repository's history. Similarly, you can use *cvs add* to abort a file removal; it resurrects the file without recording the aborted removal.

The file or directory to be added must exist within the sandbox, and a directory must not contain a file or subdirectory named *CVS*.

> Files and directories are case-sensitive in the repository. If you are using a CVS client or operating system that is not case-sensitive, you may encounter problems. Avoid using file or directory names that would be the same if case were not an issue.

In the process of adding a file, CVS strips trailing slashes and any special CVS files from the arguments, then checks for name conflicts (including some case-comparison testing). If CVS detects a name conflict, it notifies the user and does not add the file or directory.

cvs add has the following syntax:

```
cvs [cvs-options] add [command-options] filename
```

The available options are *-k,* followed by any of the keyword flags, and *-m,* followed by an addition message. Keyword flags set default keyword-substitution modes. The most common keyword flag used with *cvs add* is *-kb,* used to add binary files. Any message specified using *-m* becomes the description message for the file (displayed in *cvs log* output) and is stored with the file when the file is committed. At least one filename must be used, and the file or directory to be added must exist.

Keyword modes that are arguments to *cvs add* combine to become the default mode for the file. See "Keywords" and "Binary Files and Wrappers" later in this chapter.

Example 3-14 shows use of *cvs add* to add directories and files. Figure 3-10 shows adding a file in Pharmacy.

Example 3-14. Using cvs add

```
bash-2.05a$ cvs add design plan design/*.rtf plan/*.rtf
Directory /var/lib/cvs/wizzard/doc/design added to the repository
Directory /var/lib/cvs/wizzard/doc/plan added to the repository

cvs server: scheduling file `design/Analysis.rtf' for addition
cvs server: scheduling file `design/Specification.rtf' for addition
cvs server: scheduling file `plan/Schedule.rtf' for addition
cvs server: use 'cvs commit' to add these files permanently
```

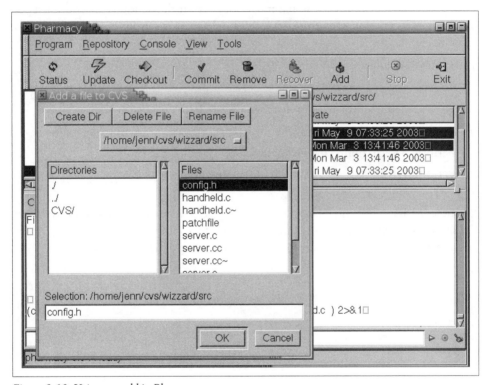

Figure 3-10. Using cvs add in Pharmacy

Removing Files from the Repository

The *cvs remove* command is used to mark a file as removed in the repository. The file isn't actually removed from the repository; it is stored in a special directory called *Attic*, so that its earlier revisions can be recalled. The file is no longer sent to sandboxes, and it is removed from existing sandboxes at the next *cvs update*, which displays the message *cvs server: filename is no longer in the repository*.

A removal must be committed before it affects the repository. If you notice that you accidentally removed a file you need (before you run *cvs commit*), you can use *cvs add* to undo the removal and then use *cvs update* to retrieve the removed file. This process leaves no record in the repository. Similarly, if a file has been added but not committed, *cvs remove* undoes the addition and leaves no record in the repository.

If someone else modifies a removed file before the removal is committed, the commit will fail and report a conflict. Resolve the conflict by unremoving the file with *cvs add*, checking the changes with *cvs update* or *cvs diff*, and removing the file again if desired. I strongly recommend speaking with the person who modified the file before you resolve such a conflict, lest you remove a file that should be retained.

To use *cvs remove* on a file, the file must not exist in the sandbox or you must call the *cvs remove* command with *-f*. Usually, I delete the file from the sandbox before running *cvs remove*.

The syntax for *cvs remove is:*

```
cvs [cvs-options] remove [command-options] filename
```

cvs remove has the following options:

-f Delete the file from the sandbox.

-l Perform a local, nonrecursive operation on this directory only.

-R Perform a recursive operation on all subdirectories as well as the current directory (default).

Example 3-15 shows a file being removed. Notice that the file is first removed from the sandbox using the Unix *rm* command. Only then can you use *cvs remove* (unless you specify the *-f* option). Figure 3-11 shows removing a file in Cervisia.

Example 3-15. Using cvs remove

```
bash-2.05a$ ls
CVS  main.c  wizzard.h
bash-2.05a$ rm main.c
bash-2.05a$ cvs remove main.c
cvs server: scheduling `main.c' for removal
cvs server: use 'cvs commit' to remove this file permanently
```

cvs remove is affected by tags, and CVS cannot remove a file that has a sticky tag or a sticky date. Chapter 4 explains sticky tags and dates in detail. Here we will discuss only how they affect file removal.

When a file is retrieved using a tag name or a date, the file in the sandbox reflects the state of the repository at the time the tag or date occurred. Such files are not intended to be changed: they're only static representations of the past. That they are static implies that such files can't be removed, either.

When you try to remove a nonremovable sticky-tagged file, CVS issues an error message such as the following: *cvs server: cannot remove file `filename' which has a numeric sticky tag of `1.3'.* Correct this error by using *cvs update -A,* then remove the file.

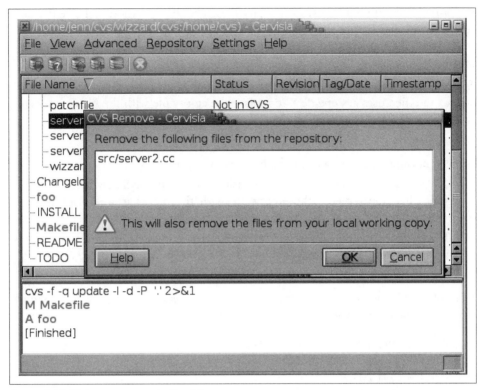

Figure 3-11. Using cvs remove in Cervisia

 If a file has a nonbranch sticky tag, *cvs remove* removes the tag from the file in the sandbox. A comment in the CVS source code implies that this behavior may change in future, so if you wish to remove a sticky tag, use *cvs update -A* instead of *cvs remove*.

Retrieving Removed Files

Retrieving a removed file is similar to retrieving a previous revision of a file. If you need to look at a file without making changes, use either:

```
cvs update -r revision
```

or:

```
cvs checkout -r revision
```

If you need to make changes, you can use any of three methods to bring the removed file back into active service. The methods are explained in the following sections. Methods 1 and 2 are essentially the same, differing mostly in whether the file is added before or after the data is retrieved. Method 3 uses file merging to accomplish the task and should not be used on binary files. The three methods achieve the same result, so you can choose the one that you will remember most easily.

Method 1

Method 1 creates an empty file of the same name, uses *cvs add* to declare the file active, and then uses *cvs update -j* to replace the empty file with the file as it was just prior to the removal. The steps are as follows:

1. Use *touch filename* to create a file of the specified name.

2. Use *cvs add filename* to make the name active again.

3. Use *cvs update -j revision* with the revision number immediately before the deletion. This step replaces the empty file with the file as it was prior to being removed.

   If you choose the revision number that corresponds to the deletion, the following error message is returned: *cvs server: `filename' is no longer in the repository.*

4. Use *cvs commit* to commit the newly restored file to the repository.

Example 3-16 illustrates this method by retrieving *main.c*, which was previously removed using *cvs remove*.

Example 3-16. Retrieving a removed file, method 1

```
bash-2.05a$ touch main.c
bash-2.05a$ cvs add main.c
cvs server: re-adding file main.c (in place of dead revision 1.3)
cvs server: use 'cvs commit' to add this file permanently
bash-2.05a$ cvs update -j 1.2 main.c
A main.c
bash-2.05a$ cvs commit
Checking in main.c;, 307C written
/var/lib/cvs/wizzard/src/main.c,v  <--  main.c
new revision: 1.4; previous revision: 1.3
done
```

Method 2

Method 2 uses *cvs update* to retrieve the file to *stdout*, sends *stdout* to a file of the same name as the removed file, and then uses *cvs add* to restore the file to the repository. The steps are as follows:

1. Use *cvs update -r previous_revision -p filename > filename*, where *previous_ revision* is the revision just before the file was removed.

2. Use *cvs add filename* to make the name active again.

3. Use *cvs commit* to commit the newly restored file to the repository.

Example 3-17 shows this method of retrieving a removed file.

Example 3-17. Retrieving a removed file, method 2

```
bash-2.05a$ cvs update -r 1.5 -p main.c > main.c
= = = = = = = = = = = = = = = = = = = = = = = = = = = = = = = =
Checking out main.c
RCS:  /var/lib/cvs/wizzard/src/Attic/main.c,v
VERS: 1.5
***************
bash-2.05a$ cvs add main.c
cvs server: re-adding file main.c (in place of dead revision 1.6)
cvs server: use 'cvs commit' to add this file permanently
bash-2.05a$ cvs commit
Checking in main.c;, 314C written
/var/lib/cvs/wizzard/src/main.c,v  <--  main.c
new revision: 1.7; previous revision: 1.6
done
```

---

stdin, stdout, stderr

So what is this *stdout* I'm talking about in method 2? To oversimplify the concept, Unix and Linux systems (and several others) have three special *data streams*, which are called *stdin*, *stdout*, and *stderr*. Any command-line program can connect to these data streams, and can expect that any input the user generates will be available from *stdin*, that anything the program sends to *stdout* will go to whatever output device the user has specified, and that anything the program sends to *stderr* will go to wherever the user expects to find errors.

Typically, *stdin* is the keyboard and mouse. *stdout* is usually the monitor screen, and *stderr* is either the monitor screen or an error file. However, one of the other features of Unix and Linux systems is the ability to redirect these data streams.

Method 2 makes use of the ability to redirect *stdout* into a file. The redirection part of the command is > *filename*.

Method 3

Method 3 merges the removed file with the unremoved file just before its removal. The steps are as follows:

1. Use *cvs update -j deletion_revision -j previous_revision filename*. Be aware of the order of the *-j* arguments; it's important to specify the revision number that refers to the deletion first.

2. Use *cvs commit* to commit the newly restored file to the repository.

Example 3-18 shows this method of retrieving a removed file.

Example 3-18. Retrieving a removed file, method 3

```
bash-2.05a$ cvs update -j 1.8 -j 1.7 main.c
U main.c
bash-2.05a$ cvs commit
Checking in main.c;, 323C written
/var/lib/cvs/wizzard/src/main.c,v  <--  main.c
new revision: 1.9; previous revision: 1.8
done
```

Removing Directories

CVS doesn't include any mechanism for removing directories from a repository. Any directory that contained files at a point in a project's history should be retained so that earlier revisions of the project can be retrieved.

If a directory is deprecated and its contents are no longer needed for the project, use *cvs remove* to empty the directory and its subdirectories of files other than the contents of the *CVS* subdirectory. To prevent these empty directories from being added to the sandbox, use the *-P* flag to the *cvs update* and *cvs checkout* commands. The *-P* flag instructs CVS not to download empty directories to the sandbox.

> The *-d* command option to *update* and *checkout* brings down all directories that are in the repository but not the sandbox, including empty directories.

To remove a directory that has never contained any files, or to remove any directory completely, edit the repository, as described in Chapter 6.

Moving Files or Directories

There is no CVS command designed specifically to move a file or file directory. In fact, CVS's design doesn't accommodate such moves. However, you can work around this limitation using a combination of CVS commands, or by altering the repository using operating-system commands. Moving files can make project history difficult to track, because then a file's history is recorded across two different files in different locations. Minimize this potential source of confusion by recording the new and old locations with meaningful log messages.

> To rename a file or directory at the operating-system level, "move" it from the old filename to the new filename. For example, use the *mv* command on Unix, Linux, and Mac OS X; on Windows, you can use the *move* command.

Moving Files

The recommended way to move a file is to use *cvs remove* followed by *cvs add*, with messages that state where the file was moved from and to. This method preserves the file's history and allows reversion to earlier versions of the project in its old location. However, the messages stored with the *add* and *remove* commands are the only record of the move. Example 3-19 shows this method being used to rename the *wizzard.h* file.

Example 3-19. Renaming a file

```
bash-2.05a$ mv wizzard.h config.h
bash-2.05a$ cvs remove wizzard.h
cvs server: scheduling `wizzard.h' for removal
cvs server: use 'cvs commit' to remove this file permanently
bash-2.05a$ cvs add config.h
cvs server: scheduling file `config.h' for addition
cvs server: use 'cvs commit' to add this file permanently
bash-2.05a$ cvs commit
.
.
.
Moving src/wizzard.h to src/config.h
CVS: ----------------------------------------------------------------------
CVS: Enter Log.  Lines beginning with `CVS:' are removed automatically
CVS:
CVS: Committing in .
CVS:
CVS: Added Files:
CVS:   config.h
CVS: Removed Files:
CVS:   wizzard.h
CVS: ----------------------------------------------------------------------
.
.
.
RCS file: /var/lib/cvs/wizzard/src/config.h,v
done
Checking in config.h;
/var/lib/cvs/wizzard/src/config.h,v  <--  config.h
initial revision: 1.1
done
Removing wizzard.h;
/var/lib/cvs/wizzard/src/wizzard.h,v  <--  wizzard.h
new revision: delete; previous revision: 1.5
done
```

Moving Directories

The recommended way to move a directory is to create the destination directory and add it to CVS. Use the technique described in the previous section to move all the files from the original directory to their new location, and use the -P flag for all checkouts and updates. By maintaining the old directory, previous releases of the project can be retrieved and the old copies of files that were in that directory are still stored in the repository.

Another way to move files or directories is to edit the repository directly. See Chapter 6 for editing methods and their advantages and consequences.

Releasing a Sandbox

The *cvs release* command should be used before you delete a sandbox. CVS first checks whether there are any files with uncommitted changes; then, if all is well, CVS runs *cvs unedit* on each file to signal that you no longer intend to edit the files, and writes to the *history* file in the repository to state that the sandbox was released. (The CVS *unedit* command is explained in Chapter 5; the *history* file is explained in Chapter 7.) CVS also reports on files and directories that are not currently stored in the repository.

If there are uncommitted changes, CVS alerts you to the changes and does not release the sandbox. You can either use *cvs commit* to commit the changes, remove the changed files manually, or use *cvs update -A* to revert to a state where you can release the sandbox (and lose the changed data).

It's not strictly necessary to use *cvs release* before deleting a sandbox. You can delete a sandbox with no effect on the repository. However, if you get into the habit of using *cvs release*, you'll remember to use it the one time you do need to run an *unedit* or when you have made an uncommitted but important change.

The syntax for *cvs release is:*

```
cvs [cvs-options] release [-d] directory
```

The only option for *cvs release* is -d, which deletes the sandbox after checking it for uncommitted changes. You can use *cvs release* on an entire sandbox or on a subdirectory within the sandbox.

When you execute *cvs release*, you must specify a directory, but you can use a dot (.) to indicate your current working directory. Example 3-20 shows use of *cvs release* to release the *wizzard* sandbox. Note that a dot is used to specify the current working directory as the sandbox to release.

Example 3-20. Using cvs release

```
bash-2.05a$ cvs release .
cvs server: warning: src/wizzard.h is not (any longer) pertinent
? src/test
? src/test.c
U src/config.h
U src/main.c
You have [0] altered files in this repository.
Are you sure you want to release directory `.': n
** `release' aborted by user choice.
```

As a response to the question, *Are you sure you want to release directory `directory'*, any line starting with *Y* or *y* is considered to be a yes; any other initial character is considered to be a no.

Keywords

CVS recognizes keywords that you can embed in any source file other than a binary file. When CVS finds a keyword in a file that it is checking out, it expands the keyword to provide metadata about the latest revision of the file. CVS keywords take the following form:

> *$Keyword$*

Example 3-21 shows a file that includes CVS keywords.

Example 3-21. CVS keywords

```
# Makefile for the Wizzard project
# First created by J Vesperman, 1 September 2002
#
# Current revision $Revision$
# On branch $Name$
# Latest change by $Author$

# Initial declarations
CC=gcc
SUBDIRS = man doc src lib

# Declaring phony targets
.PHONY: all clean install

all: wizzard
        echo "all: make complete"

clean:
        rm -f src/*.o
        rm -f wizzard
        echo "clean: make complete"
```

Example 3-21. CVS keywords (continued)

.
.
.

```
# Log record for Makefile changes:
# $Log$
```

Example 3-21 shows a makefile. The keywords are expanded when the file is checked out or updated. Example 3-22 shows the resulting expansions.

Example 3-22. Expanded keywords

```
# Current revision $Revision$
# On branch $Name$
# Latest change by $Author$ on $Date$

# Initial declarations
CC=gcc
SUBDIRS = man doc src lib
```

.
.
.

```
# Log record for Makefile changes:
# $Log$
# Revision 1.6  2004/04/16 16:15:52  chodacki
# sfcleanup fixes
#
# Revision 1.5  2003/07/11 20:00:23  madd
# madd final SC edits
#
# Revision 1.4  2003/07/09 21:31:56  madd
# madd SC edits
#
# Revision 1.3  2003/07/07 21:52:50  madd
# madd SC edits
#
# Revision 1.2  2003/06/27 21:47:43  madd
# madd R2 conversion edits
#
# Revision 1.1  2003/06/26 22:22:10  madd
# Initial revision
```

The full list of possible keywords is provided in Chapter 11. These are the most commonly used keywords:

Author
> The username of the user who committed the last revision.

Date
> The date on which the last revision was committed, in UTC.

Header

A header that contains information about the file, including the author, date, and revision number, pathname of the RCS file, file status, and whether the file is locked. See Chapter 5 for information about file locking.

Name

The tag name under which the file was checked out. This keyword can display a branch or provide a more meaningful identification of a revision than the revision number alone. See Chapter 4 for more information about tags and branches.

 In CVS 1.11.5, the *Name* keyword is updated only on a fresh check-out, and displays only static tags. This problem may be corrected in a later version.

Log

Commit messages, dates, and author, recorded in the file itself. Any characters that prefix the keyword are also used to prefix log lines; this feature enables comment markers to be included automatically. Unlike most keywords, existing log expansions are not overwritten with the new ones; the new ones are merely prepended to the list.

 The *cvs log* command displays all the information that the *Log* keyword provides.

The *Log* keyword is best used at the end of a file, to prevent users from having to go through all the log messages to get to the important parts of the file.

The log created by the *Log* keyword does not merge neatly when CVS merges a branch back to the trunk. If it is likely that your file will be branched and remerged, it is better to use the *cvs log* command than to store a log within the file.

Revision

The CVS internal revision number of the file. This number is specific to the individual file and does not identify a stage within the project.

Do not edit keyword expansions. CVS will change them automatically each time a file is checked out. Altering the format or syntax of an expansion may make it unrecognizable to CVS.

 CVS 1.12.2 adds the ability to configure your own local keywords. See Chapter 6 for more information.

Resist the urge to edit the data stored in the *Log* expansion. Doing so means that it will differ from the output of the *cvs log* command, which will create doubt about who actually did what, and when.

Keyword expansion can be modified when using the *admin*, *add*, *checkout*, *export*, and *update* commands. Options to *admin* and *add* modify the default keyword-expansion mode of a file. Options to *checkout*, *export*, and *update* modify the keyword-expansion mode of the current sandbox version of a file, overriding the file's default mode. When *checkout* and *update* create or modify a sandbox, they can set a keyword-expansion mode to apply to the copy of a file in that sandbox. Some commands (such as *diff*) have temporary keyword-expansion modes that apply while the command is running.

Keyword-expansion modes are set with *-k* or *-A* flags to the relevant command. These are the most common modes:

-kb

Inhibits keyword expansion and line-ending conversion. Use this keyword-expansion mode to signal that a file is binary.

 CVS can convert line endings from the form appropriate to the server to the form appropriate to the client. Line-ending conversion can corrupt binary files.

-kk

Generates only the keyword name, not the name and the value. Use this mode when merging different (nonbinary) versions of a file, to prevent keyword substitution from creating spurious merge errors.

-ko

Generates the version of the keyword string that was present just before the file was last committed, rather than as it should be with the modifications of the last commit. This mode is similar to the effect of *-kb*, but with line-ending conversion.

-kv

Generates only the value of the keyword, rather than the name and value. This mode is most useful with *cvs export*, but do not use it for binary files. (Note that once a keyword name is removed from a file, further expansions are not possible unless the word is replaced: don't use this with *cvs checkout*.)

-A

Resets all sandbox-specific dates, tags, and keyword-expansion modes to the file's defaults, and retrieves the latest revision (the revision at the head of the trunk). This mode is used only for *checkout* and *update*.

Binary Files and Wrappers

The default CVS method of handling file conflicts works well for text files, because CVS can determine which lines have changed and add or remove them as appropriate. It doesn't work well on binary files, because such files are not usually built around lines of text separated by carriage returns.

Some files with textual content are not actually text files, as they contain binary formatting codes or nonstandard line endings. Files such as those created by Microsoft Word or OpenOffice.org should be flagged as binary, because line-by-line merging and keyword expansion could damage the saved data.

 CVS doesn't work for device files, symbolic links, or other files that cannot be modified and moved. Rather than trying to store these files in CVS, include the commands to create or connect them in your build scripts.

For binary files, CVS uses a different method of conflict resolution. The two methods CVS has available are *MERGE* and *COPY*. *MERGE* is the default CVS method. *COPY* instructs CVS to provide the user with both versions of the file if there is a conflict, so the user can blend the changes manually and recommit.

Binary files should be added to CVS using the *-kb* command option to *cvs add*. If the expansion mode is not set at the time the file is added, the *-kb* command option to *cvs admin* sets the mode retroactively. This option informs CVS not to expand keywords, not to modify line endings, and to use the COPY method of conflict resolution. Example 3-23 shows the use of these command options. Note the use of *cvs admin* to change the way the *AcceptanceTest.doc* file is stored. This user was lucky enough to have a pristine copy of that file around, because checking it in as a regular, nonbinary file almost certainly rendered the repository version unreadable.

Example 3-23. Setting keyword expansion for binary files

```
bash-2.05a$ cvs add -kb Requirements.doc
cvs server: scheduling file `Requirements.doc' for addition
cvs server: use 'cvs commit' to add this file permanently
bash-2.05a$ cvs add AcceptanceTest.doc
cvs server: scheduling file `AcceptanceTest.doc' for addition
cvs server: use 'cvs commit' to add this file permanently
bash-2.05a$ cvs commit
.
.
.
bash-2.05a$ cvs admin -kb AcceptanceTest.doc
RCS file: /var/lib/cvs/wizzard/doc/design/AcceptanceTest.doc,v
done
```

The flag to *cvs add* works well on a file-by-file basis, but when you need to add or import a large set of files, setting each binary file's expansion mode manually is annoying. CVS *wrappers* allow you to control the merge methodology or keyword-substitution modes used on a file, based on the filename (usually specified by the file extension). When a file matches a wrapper, the merge method or substitution mode in the wrapper is used instead of the method otherwise used in the command.

Wrappers can be specified using the *-W* command option for *update* and *import*, in the *.cvswrappers* file in the user's home directory on the client machine, or in the *cvswrappers* file in the repository's *CVSROOT* subdirectory.

> The *CVSWRAPPERS* environment variable is respected, but comments in the CVS source code imply that its behavior may change. The code currently reads one wrapper from this environment variable. If you are using a version of CVS later than 1.11.2, check the documentation to see whether multiple wrappers are recognized.

To specify a wrapper in a *.cvswrappers* or *cvswrappers* file, use the following syntax:

```
wildcard option 'value' [option 'value'...]
```

Specify a wrapper using the *-W* command option as follows:

```
-W "wildcard option 'value'"
```

In the files, use one wrapper per line.

> When specifying wrappers on the command line, use the shell escape character to escape any symbols that your shell tries to expand.

These are the available wrapper options:

-m Indicates the merge methodology to be used for files that match the pattern. The values for *-m* are *COPY* or *MERGE*, described earlier in this section.

-k 'mode'
    Indicates the keyword-expansion mode to be used for files that match the pattern. The values for *-k* are the keyword-substitution modes explained earlier in this chapter in "Keywords," without the *-k* prefix. For example, the value that indicates the binary-file mode is *b*, not *-kb*.

Replace `wildcard` in the wrapper syntax with a regular expression for pattern matching. Chapter 11 provides a full explanation of CVS pattern matching. These are the most important of the special symbols:

* Matches any string, including the empty string

? Matches any single character

Example 3-24 shows *cvs update* using a wrapper parameter that specifies the *v* mode for all files beginning with "Ma". (Note that I use the shell escape character for the bash shell to escape the asterisk.)

Example 3-24. Using cvs update with wrappers

```
bash-2.05a$ cvs update -W"Ma\* -k 'v'"
cvs server: Updating .
U Makefile
cvs server: Updating doc
cvs server: Updating doc/design
cvs server: Updating doc/plan
cvs server: Updating lib
cvs server: Updating man
cvs server: Updating src
bash-2.05a$ less Makefile
#
# Makefile for the Wizzard project
# First created by J Vesperman, 1 April 2006
#
# Current revision 1.3
# On branch
# Latest change by jenn on 2006/04/12 12:57:40
```

 Upgrade to at least CVS 1.10 before using wrappers to signal binary files. In CVS 1.9 and earlier, the *COPY* option of a wrapper overwrites a file rather than providing two versions.

Specifying Default Command Options

If you find yourself regularly using the same options with a command, you can use the *.cvsrc* file to set default options and minimize your typing. If the *.cvsrc* file is in your home directory on your client machine, CVS reads the file, looks for the CVS command you are currently running, and runs the command with the options specified for that command in the file. To temporarily avoid parsing the *.cvsrc* file, use the *-f* CVS option.

The *.cvsrc* file format is one line per command. Start a line with the command that you want to modify followed by the options you want as the default. You can also specify default CVS options in the *.cvsrc* file. To do so, use *cvs* as the command.

Example 3-25 shows a *.cvsrc* file. This file specifies a default description for adding files, specifies (using *-P*) that update and checkout prune empty directories, and specifies (using *-q*) that CVS run quietly, but not as quietly as it would with the *-Q* option.

Example 3-25. A .cvsrc file

```
add -m "Part of the wizzard project"
update -P
checkout -P
cvs -q
```

CHAPTER 4

Tagging and Branching

One of the most helpful—yet underused—facilities of CVS is the *tag*. CVS's tagging feature allows you to label a revision for later retrieval. This feature also allows you to fork development so that you can work on two or more lines of development of your project simultaneously. The line that has been forked off is called a *branch*, and the original line is called the *trunk*.

 If your project has never been branched, the project is on the *trunk*.

This chapter explains tags, branches, and how to merge branches and trunks. It also discusses why and when to branch and provides strategies and hints for using branches effectively in your project.

Tagging

CVS allows you to retrieve any checked-in revision of a file. Although retrieving revisions of individual files is useful, it's even more useful to be able to retrieve the compatible set of revisions that make up a complete, functional version of a project, such as all the revisions that become release 1.0 of a program, or that become the first edition of a book. This ability is also important for compliance with standards and regulations.

Tagging is a way of marking a group of file revisions as belonging together. You can't use the revision numbers for this purpose, because revision 2.3 of one file might belong with revision 2.17 of another. Figure 4-1 shows a group of file revision numbers, with an imaginary string denoting which revision numbers belong to the same release.

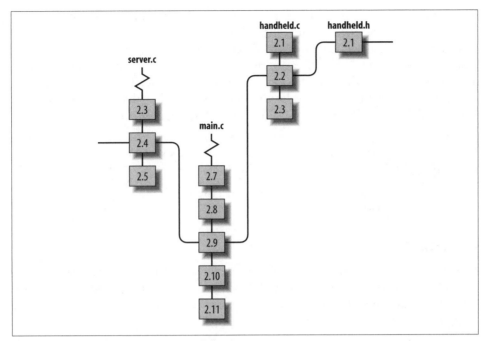

Figure 4-1. File revisions that belong together

CVS allows you to create a single tag that denotes all the file revisions that connect to that virtual string. When you want to look at all the file revisions that belong to a tag, CVS can "pull the string" to locate the tagged revisions. Figure 4-2 shows the same group of files, with the string pulled tight to show which set of revisions belong to that tag.

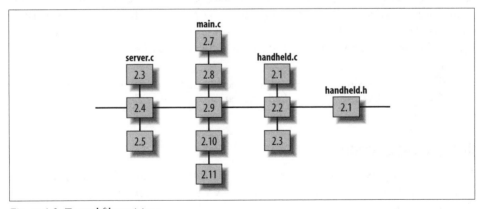

Figure 4-2. Tagged file revisions

A tag can mark a specific revision of a single file or a specific set of revisions of a group of files—in essence, naming the string. The tag then gives you a convenient way to retrieve that revision or matched set of revisions. Remembering the significance of a text string is much easier than remembering a version number, not to mention a handful of different version numbers for each file. Tags are often used to record the version number used by the developers, rather than the CVS revision number, which is used primarily as a CVS internal designation.

An advanced technique is to use *floating* tags, which indicate a current release, such as the current production release in use in a particular department in a university. The tag is moved when the production release is changed. Floating tags are explained later in this chapter in the sidebar "Floating Tags."

Tag Names

Tag names must start with a letter and can contain alphanumeric characters, hyphens (-), and underscores (_). Each tag must be unique within the tagged file. You tag files with the *cvs tag* and *cvs rtag* commands, explained in "Tagging by Sandbox" and "Tagging by Date or Revision" later in this chapter.

I recommend that you use meaningful tag names. Tag names should immediately tell you something about the revisions they tag and, if they tag across several files, why those revisions belong together. For example, *release-1-3-beta*, *release-2-13-patch-5*, *testing-1-5-alpha*, and *release-2-5-stable* are all effective tag names.

Set a standard tag name format for your project and encourage your developers to use it. Assign names that describe versions of the project, using the version-naming convention that your developers are familiar with. Create tag names from which your team can identify revisions, rather than allowing them to rely on the CVS revision numbers. The CVS numbers are intended for internal reference by CVS, and do not map to the way that people typically number software releases.

"The taginfo File" in Chapter 7 includes the first part of a script that can be used to enforce tag name standards automatically.

Reserved Tag Names

There are two reserved tag names. CVS uses the *BASE* tag name for the revision that was last synchronized with the repository. CVS uses the *HEAD* tag name for the most recent revision of the trunk in the repository.[*]

---

[*] The *trunk* is the default line of development. If you are using *branches*, the trunk is the original line of development and the branches are the lines you have added. If you aren't using branches, your development is automatically on the trunk. See "Branching" later in this chapter for a detailed explanation.

If you and your coworker both check out revision 1.23 of the *main.c* file, you both start with a *BASE* of 1.23. If your coworker commits twice, the *BASE* revision for your sandbox is still 1.23, because you haven't synchronized with the changes in the repository. The *HEAD* revision is now 1.25, because your coworker's two commits were given revision numbers 1.24 and 1.25. The *BASE* revision for your coworker's sandbox has become 1.25, because his sandbox copy of *main.c* was synchronized to revision 1.25 when he committed his second change.

Tagging by Sandbox

Use the *cvs tag* command to tag the files in the current sandbox directory and all subdirectories. By default, *cvs tag* adds the tag to the *BASE* revision. You can specify files to tag by providing their filenames as an argument to *cvs tag*.

The syntax for the *cvs tag* command is:

```
cvs [cvs-options] tag [command-options] tagname [filenames]
```

cvs tag determines which files and revisions to mark based on your sandbox, but it marks them based on the revision that was most recently synchronized with the repository. If changes have occurred in the sandbox since the files were last synchronized with the repository, those changes will *not* be reflected in the tagged revisions.

The *-c* command option to *cvs tag* allows you to check whether your sandbox files have been modified and not committed before you tag the files. If *cvs tag -c* finds uncommitted changes, it will stop without tagging any files. If you want to tag the revision in the repository, without the uncommitted changes, omit the *-c* and rerun the *cvs tag* command. If you want to tag the revision in the sandbox, commit your changes before rerunning *cvs tag*.

You can use dates, existing tags, or revision numbers to determine which revisions to tag. Use the *-r revision* or *-r tagname* options of *cvs tag* to specify a revision or an existing tag, and use the *-D date* option to specify a date. If you're using a date, CVS tags the latest revision before the date you specify. See Chapter 11 for more information on dates.

The *-f* option can be used only in combination with *-r* or *-D*. This option instructs CVS to use the *HEAD* revision if no revision can be found to match the revision specified by *-r* or *-D*.

By default, *cvs tag* acts recursively down the sandbox subdirectories. The *-l* option restricts it to the local directory. You can also use *-R* to explicitly instruct CVS to act recursively.

Example 4-1 shows how to use *cvs tag* to tag the files in the current sandbox directory with the tag name *pre_alpha_0-1*. Figure 4-3 shows tagging in the graphic client Cervisia.

Example 4-1. Using cvs tag

```
bash-2.05a$ cvs tag pre_alpha_0-1
cvs server: Tagging .
T Changelog
T INSTALL
T Makefile
T README
T TODO
cvs server: Tagging doc
cvs server: Tagging doc/design
T doc/design/AcceptanceTest.doc
T doc/design/Analysis.rtf
T doc/design/Requirements.doc
T doc/design/Specification.rtf
cvs server: Tagging doc/plan
T doc/plan/Schedule.rtf
cvs server: Tagging lib
cvs server: Tagging man
cvs server: Tagging src
T src/config.h
T src/main.c
```

Figure 4-3. Tagging with Cervisia

Tagging by Date or Revision

The *cvs rtag* command allows you to tag files without referring to a specific sandbox. Instead of using the sandbox to determine which revisions of which files to tag, *rtag* relies on the parameters to the command. You must use either the *-r* or *-D* options to specify which revision of the files in question to tag, and you must specify at least one directory name, filename, or module name. Modules are explained in Chapter 7. If you specify multiple directories, files, or modules, separate them with spaces.

The syntax for the *cvs rtag* command is:

```
cvs [cvs-options] rtag command-options tagname filenames
```

Example 4-2 shows the *cvs rtag* command being used to apply the *pre_alpha_0-2* tag to all files within the *wizzard* directory and its subdirectories. The *-r HEAD* option specifies that the *pre_alpha_0-2* tag be applied to the *HEAD* revision of all files (the *HEAD* is the most recent revision on the trunk; see "Reserved Tag Names," earlier in this chapter). Figure 4-4 shows tagging in TkCVS.

Example 4-2. Using cvs rtag

```
bash-2.05a$ cvs -d cvs_server:/var/lib/cvs rtag -r HEAD pre_alpha_0-2 wizzard
cvs rtag: Tagging wizzard
cvs rtag: Tagging wizzard/doc
cvs rtag: Tagging wizzard/doc/design
cvs rtag: Tagging wizzard/doc/plan
cvs rtag: Tagging wizzard/lib
cvs rtag: Tagging wizzard/man
cvs rtag: Tagging wizzard/src
```

If you are in a sandbox when you use the *cvs rtag* command, CVS can use the repository referenced in that sandbox's *CVS* directory as the repository to search for the files to be tagged. If you are in a sandbox that is connected to a repository other than the one you want to act on, leave the sandbox using the *cd* command or use the *-d repository_path* CVS option, as I've done in Example 4-2.

If your current working directory is not a sandbox, you can specify the repository with either the *CVSROOT* environment variable on the client machine or the *-d repository_path* CVS option.

When you want to tag the most recent revision of any file in the repository, use *-r HEAD*. Be aware that CVS operations are not atomic, so if someone commits while you are tagging and you use *-r HEAD*, you may find that one directory has been tagged at the point before your coworker's commit and another has been tagged after it. To avoid this problem, tag the sandbox with *cvs tag*, or use a date. In some cases, you can also use *-r* with a preexisting tag name (such as when creating a branch, explained later in this chapter).

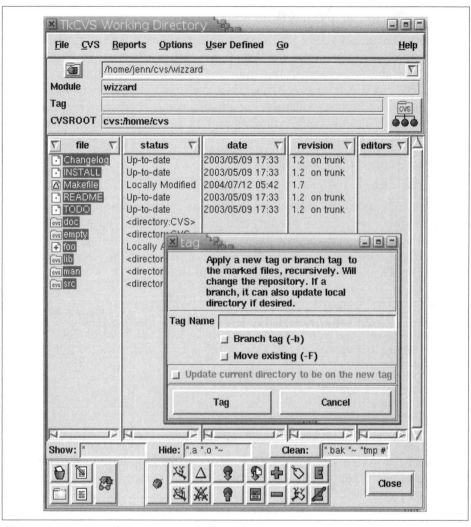

Figure 4-4. Tagging in TkCVS

When using the -D option, be aware that unless a time has been specified, CVS tags the most recent revision at midnight on the day in question. This means that if you use -D 12 Feb 2002, CVS tags the file revisions as they were at 12:00 A.M. on 12 February 2002, local time. Date formats are listed in Chapter 11.

Most of the options to *cvs tag* can be used the same way with *cvs rtag*. The -l and -R options control recursion, and the -r, -D, and -f options specify revisions as they do with *cvs tag*. The -c option to *cvs tag* is not used with *cvs rtag*.

Retrieving Tagged Files

To list the tags on a file, use *cvs status -v* in a sandbox that includes the file. This command also provides information, such as the current sandbox (or *working*) revision, the current repository revision, and any sticky information in the current sandbox. The tags are listed at the bottom of the report. You may note that some tags have the word *branch* beside the revision number; these are the tags at the base of a branch, as explained in "Branching" later in this chapter. Example 4-3 shows the use of *cvs status* to show tags for *main.c*. Figure 4-5 shows the tag list in TkCVS.

Example 4-3. Listing file tags

```
bash-2.05a$ cvs status -v src/main.c
===============================
File: main.c                  Status: Up-to-date

    Working revision:    1.9
    Repository revision: 1.9      /var/lib/cvs/wizzard/src/main.c,v
    Sticky Tag:          (none)
    Sticky Date:         (none)
    Sticky Options:      (none)

    Existing Tags:
        pre_alpha_0-2             (revision: 1.9)
        pre_alpha_0-1             (revision: 1.9)
```

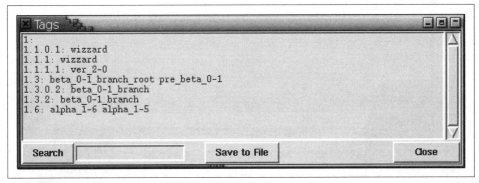

Figure 4-5. Listing file tags in TkCVS

To retrieve a tagged file or set of files, use the *-r tagname* option to *cvs checkout* or *cvs update*. Use *checkout* to create a new sandbox, and *update* to modify an existing sandbox. If you retrieve a set of tagged files into an existing sandbox, any existing files will be overwritten with the tagged revisions, but changes you have made since the files were last synchronized with the sandbox will be merged forward into the new revisions.

If you want a copy of the specified revision that doesn't include any new changes, use *cvs update -C -r tagname*. If you have any unsynchronized changes, CVS will store them in *.#filename.revision* in the same directory.

Example 4-4 shows a checkout of a tagged sandbox, and Figure 4-6 shows checking out a tagged sandbox in Cervisia.

Example 4-4. Checking out a tagged sandbox

```
bash-2.05a$ cvs -d cvs_server:/var/lib/cvs checkout -r pre_alpha_0-2 wizzard
cvs server: Updating wizzard
U wizzard/Changelog
U wizzard/INSTALL
U wizzard/Makefile
U wizzard/README
U wizzard/TODO
cvs server: Updating wizzard/doc
cvs server: Updating wizzard/doc/design
U wizzard/doc/design/AcceptanceTest.doc
U wizzard/doc/design/Analysis.rtf
U wizzard/doc/design/Requirements.doc
U wizzard/doc/design/Specification.rtf
cvs server: Updating wizzard/doc/plan
U wizzard/doc/plan/Schedule.rtf
cvs server: Updating wizzard/lib
cvs server: Updating wizzard/man
cvs server: Updating wizzard/src
U wizzard/src/config.h
U wizzard/src/main.c
```

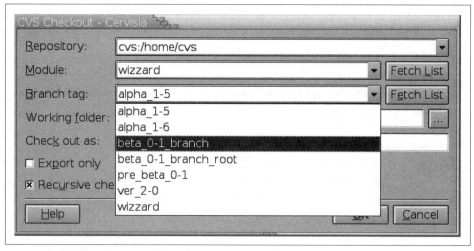

Figure 4-6. Checking out a tagged sandbox in Cervisia

When you check out or update a sandbox via a nonbranch tag or a date (branches are explained later in this chapter), the tag or date is *sticky* on the files in that sandbox. A sandbox checked out with a date or a nonbranch tag is a static representation of the project at that point. You cannot commit changes to a file that was checked out as static. Stickiness applies only to the sandbox copy of a file and does not affect the repository. See the "Stickiness" section later in this chapter for more details.

Removing and Moving Tags

Normally, tags are intended to remain fixed, to mark a specific moment in time. Sometimes, you do need to remove, rename, or move a tag. Do this with caution, as these actions may discard historical information and may be impossible to undo.

There are special tags called *branch tags*, explained in "Branching," later in this chapter. If you try to remove or move a branch tag, CVS returns an error message and does not delete or move the tag, though you can force CVS to remove or move the branch tag with the *-B* option.

 Do not delete, move, or rename a branch tag without an extremely good reason and a very recent backup of the repository, as doing so can cause data loss.

Removing a tag

There usually is no need to remove a correctly placed tag from a file. However, if you make an error when tagging, you may want to remove the tag and try again.

To remove a tag, use the *-d* option:

```
cvs tag -d tagname [filename]
```

or:

```
cvs rtag -d tagname filename
```

If you use the *rtag* command outside a sandbox, you need to specify the repository path. If you use *rtag* inside a sandbox, CVS searches the *CVS* subdirectory to determine the repository.

The *tag* command must be issued from within a sandbox, and by default acts on the files in the current sandbox directory and its subdirectories. CVS searches the *CVS* subdirectory to determine the repository.

Example 4-5 shows the use of *cvs tag* to remove a tag. The user is in the top level of the project's sandbox. Figure 4-7 shows tag removal in Cervisia.

Example 4-5. Removing tags

```
bash-2.05a$ cvs tag -d pre_alpha_0-2
cvs server: Untagging .
cvs server: Untagging doc
cvs server: Untagging doc/design
cvs server: Untagging doc/plan
cvs server: Untagging src
```

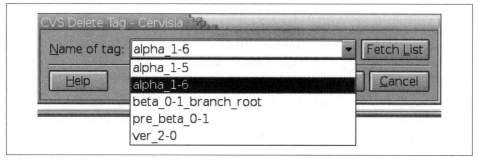

Figure 4-7. Removing a tag in Cervisia

Moving a tag

The most common reason to move a tag is to correct a tagging mistake. Some project teams also like to have a mobile tag that marks the most recent version that is ready for release or the current bugfix version of the project, and they move that tag when they finish a new version.

To move a tag from one revision to another revision in the same file or set of files, use the *-F* option to *cvs tag* and *cvs rtag*. Use *-r* to designate the revision to move the tag to and *-F* to designate the tag to move. Example 4-6 shows the use of *cvs rtag* to move a tag, from within a sandbox. The status report for the file is shown before and after the move. Because I am using *rtag* rather than *tag*, I need to specify the full path from the repository root directory to *main.c*, including the project name. I don't need to specify the full path with *cvs status*, because I'm in the sandbox.

Example 4-6. Moving a tag

```
bash-2.05a$ cvs status -v src/main.c
===============================
File: main.c            Status: Up-to-date

   Working revision:    1.9
   Repository revision: 1.9    /var/lib/cvs/wizzard/src/main.c,v
   Sticky Tag:          (none)
   Sticky Date:         (none)
   Sticky Options:      (none)
```

Example 4-6. Moving a tag (continued)

```
    Existing Tags:
        pre_alpha_0-1              (revision: 1.9)
bash-2.05a$ cvs rtag -r 1.8 -F pre_alpha_0-1 wizzard/src/main.c
bash-2.05a$ cvs status -v src/main.c
===============================
File: main.c                Status: Up-to-date

    Working revision:    1.9
    Repository revision: 1.9       /var/lib/cvs/wizzard/src/main.c,v
    Sticky Tag:          (none)
    Sticky Date:         (none)
    Sticky Options:      (none)

    Existing Tags:
        pre_alpha_0-1    (revision: 1.8)
```

Moving or removing tags from Attic files

Files that have been removed from the main trunk using *cvs remove*, or that were never on the trunk, are stored in an *Attic* subdirectory in the repository. These files may be associated with old tags that should be removed, moved, or renamed. There is no easy way to perform these tasks for files in the *Attic* directory using *cvs tag*, but *cvs rtag* provides the *-a* option, which applies *-d* and *-F* to tags in removed files (i.e., in the *Attic*) from the appropriate module or directory.

If you are using the *-r revision* option with *tag* or *rtag*, CVS searches *Attic* files to determine whether the revision existed in those files. The *-a* option is unnecessary if *-r* is specified.

Renaming a tag

If you or one of your development team has added a tag that does not conform to your tag name standards, or that is inaccurately named, you can rename it.

CVS does not include a command to rename a tag, but the *-r* option to *tag* and *rtag* makes it easy to add a new tag to the revisions that were tagged with an existing tag. Then you can remove the old tag. (Do not try to use this approach with branches.)

Example 4-7 shows how to rename a tag. The goal is to rename *pre_alpha_0-1* to *pre_beta_0-1*. First, *cvs tag -r* is used to tag all the *pre_alpha_0-1* files with *pre_beta_0-1*. Next, the unwanted *pre_alpha_0-1* tag is deleted via a *cvs tag -d* command. The effect is the same as renaming *pre_alpha_0-1* to *pre_beta_0-1*.

Example 4-7. Renaming a tag

```
bash-2.05a$ cvs tag -r pre_alpha_0-1 pre_beta_0-1
cvs server: Tagging .
T Changelog
```

Example 4-7. Renaming a tag (continued)

```
T INSTALL
T Makefile
.
.
.
cvs server: Tagging src
T src/config.h
T src/main.c
bash-2.05a$ cvs tag -d pre_alpha_0-1
cvs server: Untagging .
D Changelog
D INSTALL
D Makefile
.
.
.
cvs server: Untagging src
D src/config.h
D src/main.c
```

Floating Tags

A couple of years ago I consulted for a university's internal IT department, which wanted to improve its use of CVS. It had very strict requirements for standards compliance, and frequent change requests to answer.

We developed a range of potential solutions together, and the one thing all the solutions had in common was floating tags. The current production release would always be tagged with a specific tag—for the purposes of this discussion, I'll call it *current_production*.

At every release, the person in charge of the release would check out a sandbox for testing. Once it was found satisfactory, the sandbox would be tagged with the release number via *cvs tag -c*. Then the developer running the release would run *cvs rtag* to move *current_production* to the current release number.

The commands would be something like:

```
$ cvs tag -c prod_3-5
$ cvs rtag -r prod_3-5 -F current_production projectname
```

They planned to use the tag *current_production* for a variety of automated scripts, including the script that distributed the current release to the production servers. This also ensured that no one had to remember which release number was current—they could simply use the floating tag to get the most current production version of the project.

Removed Files

If a file has been removed from the project in the revisions you're tagging, the file will not be tagged. If the file is not added again, this won't matter.

If a file has been removed and then added again, there is no simple way to show whether the tag doesn't exist in that file because the tag was created between the remove and the second addition, or because the tag is older than the file. You can use dates to determine which is the case, or you can issue the command *cvs rdiff -s -r tagname project*. The *-s* option to *rdiff* provides a summary report that lists files that have been changed, added, or removed.

To tag a removed file as well as existing files, use the *-r* option to *cvs tag* and *cvs rtag*. Using *-r HEAD* is typical, as this refers to the most recent revision (of the trunk) in the repository.

If you are tagging against the *HEAD*, you may want to find a way to prevent others from changing the repository between the time you decide the files are ready to be tagged and the time you actually tag them. Some suggestions for doing this are included in "Freezing a Repository" in Chapter 6.

Tagging Strategies

Tagging makes it easier to retrieve snapshots of a project. The basic rule is to tag every time you reach a significant stage of a project. At an absolute minimum, tag every time you branch and tag on completion of each release of a project.

Devise your own in-house tagging strategy. The following list of times to consider tagging is heavily biased toward programmers:

- On completion of each major feature
- At each milestone or each major phase of a project
- Just before dropping an existing feature
- Just before testing begins
- Before making changes that might break working code
- Just before splitting off a branch
- Just after merging a branch

Use meaningful tag names in a fixed format, including all the essential information in the tag name. This is one possible, but very detailed, format for tag names:

```
version-[alpha-|beta-][test-|final-|patch-][patch#-][pub|priv]
```

When you need to check out an older version of the code to test it or create a patch, you need an easy way to identify the exact version you're after. This tag name format lists the version number, whether the tagged release is a test or final release, the release's stage of testing, and whether it is an internal or external release.

Remember, this format is just an example. Use your own format, based on your own project team's needs. Most project teams prefer a shorter format than the one shown here.

Stickiness

Stickiness is an important concept in CVS, especially when talking about tagging and branching. Stickiness is primarily internal to CVS, but it affects what can be done in a sandbox.

When a file in a sandbox has a persistent state that is not the default state in the repository, the persistent state is said to be *sticky*. A sandbox copy of a file can be set to a specific revision, belong to a branch, or have specific keyword options. Any of these things can cause a file to be sticky.

A file can be set to a specific revision by being retrieved from the repository with a tag, revision number, or date. If the file is retrieved with a date, it is said to have a *sticky date*. If it is retrieved with a tag, it is said to have a *sticky tag*, and if it is retrieved with a revision number, it is said to have a *sticky revision*.

Along the same lines, a sandbox file that belongs to a branch is said to have a *sticky branch*, and a sandbox file with sandbox-specific keywords has *sticky keywords*.

A sticky state applies to all commands run on the file. A file with a sticky date, revision, or nonbranch tag will not be updated to a more recent copy; nor can such files be committed. A file with a sticky branch is always committed to or updated from the branch in question.

Sticky states on a file can be viewed with *cvs status*. For example, use the command *cvs status index.htm* to see the status for the *index.htm* file. Example 4-8 shows a *cvs status* report that lists a sticky branch.

Example 4-8. Viewing a sticky file

```
bash-2.05a$ cvs status main.c
===============================
File: main.c                Status: Up-to-date

   Working revision:    1.9
   Repository revision: 1.9    /var/lib/cvs/wizzard/src/main.c,v
   Sticky Tag:          beta_0-1_branch (branch: 1.9.2)
   Sticky Date:         (none)
   Sticky Options:      (none)
```

Sandbox directories can also have sticky states, and a directory with a sticky state applies that state as the default to any file added to that directory. Sticky states in a directory can be seen in the *Tag* file in the *CVS* subdirectory of that directory. Example 4-9 shows a *Tag* file.

Example 4-9. Stickiness in the Tag file

```
bash-2.05a$ less CVS/Tag
Tbeta_0-1_branch
```

Stickiness is created or changed using the *-k*, *-D*, or *-r* options to *cvs checkout* or *cvs update*. It can be removed with *cvs update -A*, which retrieves the current *HEAD* revision from the trunk of the repository, resets the state to the default for the appropriate files, and clears any directory stickiness.

To clear stickiness from a directory, you must run *cvs update -A* on the directory. Using *cvs update -A files*, where *files* refers to a file or files, does not clear directory stickiness or affect other files in the directory.

Branching

In the introduction to this chapter, I defined a branch as a forked line of development in your project, with the line that has been forked off called the branch, and the main line the trunk. CVS builds the branch and the trunk from the same source data, up until the point at which they diverge, which is called the *base* of the branch. From that point, CVS stores the changes made to the branch separately from the changes in the trunk. Revisions on the branch are given their own revision numbers, based on the revision number of the base of the branch.

You can branch a single file, any group of files, or a whole project, just as you can tag individual files or any group of them. I usually recommend branching a project. In my experience, if you branch one file, you will eventually need to branch others in the project for the same reason. It is much easier to keep track of a single branch over the whole project than a group of unrelated branches of individual files.

A tag marks a specific revision of each tagged file, and a sandbox checked out with that tag cannot be changed (you can edit the files, but when you try to check them in, you'll get the error *sticky tag `tag' for file `file' is not a branch*). In contrast, a branch creates revisions that can be edited, committed, checked out, updated, and tagged independently of the revisions on the trunk. In many ways, a branch can be treated as an independent development line of a project.

You can tag a file with any number of tags, as long as each tag name in that file is unique, including any tags on the branch. CVS relies on each tag and branch name to be unique within each file, so it considers the branch name to be a tag name when determining tag uniqueness.

A branch is an ongoing line of development, and any tags on the branch are used to mark the specific revisions when significant events occur. Though branches are created with the *cvs tag* command, branches and tags are different things. A branch represents multiple revisions and a tag represents a single revision.

For some commands, such as *cvs diff*, CVS needs a branch to resolve to a single revision. In these cases, CVS resolves to the most recent revision on the branch.

Branches are often used when a public release of a project is due, to allow testers to work on the release candidate while new development goes on independently of the testing. Branches can also keep major changes or experimental work, such as a complete rewrite of a code library, separate from the main line of development.

Ideally, you will know you want a branch before you start modifying your sandbox copies of a project's files. You can then create a branch from the sandbox, as shown in "Making a Branch," later in this section.

Sometimes you realize after making changes that your work is experimental or will require a section of the project to be redesigned. At such times, you might create a branch to allow you to keep your revision under version control without affecting the rest of the project's development. See "Retroactive Branching," later in this chapter, for instructions on how to do so. Retroactive branching can be more difficult than standard branching, so try to plan branches in advance.

Figure 4-8 shows how a branch is developed from a trunk. Revision 2.6 is the base of the branch, and the branch itself is represented by the revision number 2.6.2. The branch has independent revisions from the trunk, starting with revision 2.6.2.1. The trunk continues with revision 2.7.

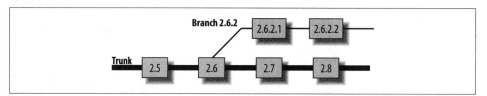

Figure 4-8. A branch

The branch is dependent on the main trunk. However, the trunk and the branch are stored in the same file in the repository, and commands that operate on that file at the repository level can affect both trunk and branch. For example, the same tag cannot be used twice in the same file, even if one use is on the trunk and the other is on the branch. Also, the *cvs status* and *cvs log* commands show the overall state of the file, including the trunk and the branch.

Changes from the trunk can be merged onto a branch, and changes from a branch can be merged back into the main trunk. The branch can either be abandoned or continued, depending on the purpose for the merge.

Uses for Branches

Branching has many uses. A project's trunk is usually used for the main line of development, and branches are usually used for variations on that line.

In programming projects and content management, branches are often used for experimental work, candidates for product releases to the users, refactoring code or content, or bug fixes. For configuration management, the trunk can be used for the default configuration, and branches can be the standard variants—one branch for web servers, one for mail servers, and so on.

The following list describes some common uses for different types of branches (branch types are explained in detail in "Branching Strategies," later in this chapter):

Variations on a theme, such as stored configurations for similar servers
> Use long branches, and occasionally nested branches, for variations on similar themes. Make changes on the trunk and merge them to the branch if the branch needs those changes.

Bugfix management
> Use long branches for bug fixes, and merge the changes to the trunk.

Experimental work, such as experimental code or a new web page design
> Use short branches, and merge changes back to the trunk.

Major changes, such as a complete code rewrite
> Depending on how major the rewrite is, you can use long branches merged to the trunk, long branches merged in both directions, or short branches.

Release candidates for testing
> Use long branches, and merge changes to the trunk. You can convert the branch to a bugfix-management branch after release.

Standards compliance
> Some development standards require that the production line of a project be kept separate from ongoing development. Branching the project complies with all of such standards that I am aware of.

Making a Branch

You can make a branch with the *-b* option to the *cvs tag* or *cvs rtag* commands. This option can be combined with any of the other tag-creation options of those commands. You can use a date, existing tag, or revision number to specify the revision to be branched from.

If you use *cvs tag,* you can also make a branch from the most recently synchronized sandbox revision. Doing so acts like tagging from the sandbox revision, as shown earlier in this chapter, under "Tagging by Sandbox."

Example 4-10 demonstrates the creation of a branch from an existing tag using *cvs tag*. The *cvs update* command ensures that all files in *pre_beta_0.1* are present in the sandbox. The output from the *cvs update* command can be used to confirm that no files have changed. Figure 4-9 shows branch creation in Cervisia.

Example 4-10. Creating a branch

```
bash-2.05a$ cvs update -d -r pre_beta_0-1
.
.
.
bash-2.05a$ cvs tag -r pre_beta_0-1 -b pre_beta_0-1_branch
cvs server: Tagging .
T Changelog
T INSTALL
T Makefile
T README
T TODO
cvs server: Tagging doc
cvs server: Tagging doc/design
T doc/design/AcceptanceTest.doc
T doc/design/Analysis.rtf
T doc/design/Requirements.doc
T doc/design/Specification.rtf
cvs server: Tagging doc/plan
T doc/plan/Schedule.rtf
cvs server: Tagging src
T src/config.h
T src/main.c
```

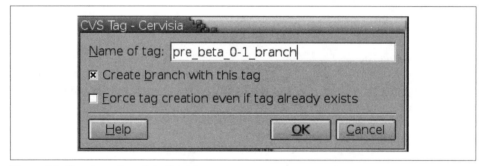

Figure 4-9. Creating a branch in Cervisia

Branch creation occurs in the repository, not the sandbox. To edit the branch revisions of the files, check out a branch sandbox or use *update* to alter the current sandbox to the branch.

It is good practice to tag the trunk just before splitting off a branch, because this makes it easier to merge the changes back later. To be absolutely certain that the revisions tagged with the *prebranch tag* (the tag you are basing the branch on) are the revisions used as the base of the branch, use *cvs rtag -r prebranch-tag -b branch-tag project* to create the branch. This command uses the prebranch tag to specify the revisions the branch is created from.

Example 4-11 shows how to create a prebranch tag and then the branch. Then, *cvs status* is run to show the tag status of one of the files.

Example 4-11. Tagging before branching

```
bash-2.05a$ cvs tag beta_0-1_branch_root
cvs server: Tagging .
T Changelog
T INSTALL
.
.
.
cvs server: Tagging src
T src/config.h
T src/main.c
bash-2.05a$ cvs rtag -r beta_0-1_branch_root -b beta_0-1_branch wizzard
cvs rtag: Tagging wizzard
cvs rtag: Tagging wizzard/doc
cvs rtag: Tagging wizzard/doc/design
cvs rtag: Tagging wizzard/doc/plan
cvs rtag: Tagging wizzard/lib
cvs rtag: Tagging wizzard/man
cvs rtag: Tagging wizzard/src
bash-2.05a$ cvs status -v src/main.c
===============================
File: main.c                    Status: Up-to-date

    Working revision:    1.9
    Repository revision: 1.9      /var/lib/cvs/wizzard/src/main.c,v
    Sticky Tag:          (none)
    Sticky Date:         (none)
    Sticky Options:      (none)

    Existing Tags:
      beta_0-1_branch              (branch: 1.9.2)
      beta_0-1_branch_root         (revision: 1.9)
      pre_beta_0-1                 (revision: 1.8)
```

Retroactive Branching

If you make changes and realize at the time you're ready to commit that you want to make a branch, you need to try to make a branch from the revisions before the changes. If you have not committed any of the changes, you can retroactively create a branch from the current sandbox using the following process:

1. Do not commit your changes until after you have made the branch. This is important, because you are using a feature of the *tag* command to make the branch point before the latest set of changes.

Because you can't commit your changes before starting, it is a good idea to back up the changed files with your operating system's *copy* command. Copy the whole sandbox to a temporary directory until after the changes have been successfully committed into CVS.

2. Use the command *cvs tag -b branchname* to create the branch. The *tag* command tags the last revisions that were committed to the repository or updated from the repository, which hopefully are the revisions before the changes you want to branch off of. The *cvs tag* command does not modify your sandbox.

3. Use the command *cvs update -r branchname* to change your sandbox to a branch sandbox. This command causes CVS to try to merge the branch revisions into the files currently in the sandbox, but because the sandbox files are based on the branch revisions, this merge results in unchanged files. CVS sets sticky branch tags on the files in the sandbox, marking them as belonging to the branch.

4. Issue *cvs commit* to upload your changes in the files to the repository as the next revision on the branch.

5. Confirm that the files are correct, then delete the temporary backup copy.

This technique relies on the fact that *cvs tag* marks the repository at the point when the sandbox was last synchronized with the repository. The branch is created at that time, so when you update the sandbox to your branch, CVS tries to merge the base files your sandbox was created from with the files in the sandbox, leaving your sandbox unchanged.

Example 4-12 shows an example of retroactive branching.

Example 4-12. Retroactive branching

```
bash-2.05a$ cvs tag -b test_0-1_branch
cvs server: Tagging .
T config.h
T main.c
bash-2.05a$ cvs update -r test_0-1_branch
cvs server: Updating .
M config.h
bash-2.05a$ cvs commit
```

If you have committed changes, you can retroactively make a branch from a date with the method shown in Example 4-12, but use the *-D date* command option to the *cvs tag* command.

If you copy and paste the times from *cvs log* output, include the UTC time zone (+0000) with your *-D date* option.

If the log contains date 2006-05-12 06:08:24 +0000, ensure that you paste **2006-05-12 06:08:24 +0000**.

Creating a Branch Sandbox

To change the files in a branch, check out a sandbox that is based on the branch you want to change. In a branch sandbox, *cvs commit* commits the changes to the branch in the repository and *cvs update* brings down changes from the repository copy of the branch to the sandbox.

Create a branch sandbox with the *-r branch-tag-name* argument to *cvs checkout* or *cvs update*. Figure 4-10 illustrates the results of checking out a branch sandbox. Figure 4-6, in the "Tagging" section of this chapter, shows how to check out a branch sandbox in Cervisia. The only difference is that you select a branch tag rather than a static tag.

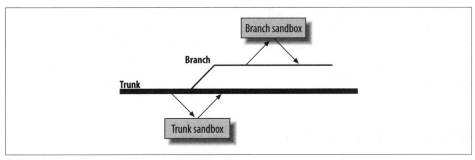

Figure 4-10. Branch sandboxes

CVS marks the sandbox copies of files in a branch sandbox with a sticky tag to record that those files belong to the branch. See Example 4-13 for an example of creating a branch sandbox and a status report of one of the files with a sticky branch tag.

Example 4-13. Creating a branch sandbox

```
bash-2.05a$ cvs -d cvs_server:/var/lib/cvs checkout -r beta_0-1_branch wizzard
cvs server: Updating wizzard
U wizzard/Changelog
U wizzard/INSTALL
.
.
.
cvs server: Updating wizzard/src
U wizzard/src/config.h
U wizzard/src/main.c
bash-2.05a$ cd wizzard/src/
bash-2.05a$ cvs status main.c
==============================
File: main.c                Status: Up-to-date

   Working revision:    1.9
   Repository revision: 1.9      /var/lib/cvs/wizzard/src/main.c,v
   Sticky Tag:          beta_0-1_branch (branch: 1.9.2)
   Sticky Date:         (none)
   Sticky Options:      (none)
```

You can also retrieve individual branch files to a normal sandbox, but I do not recommend allowing yourself to have a sandbox of mixed branch and trunk files. Use *checkout* from a nonsandbox directory if you want to check out individual files that do not belong to the same branch or trunk as the current sandbox.

 The -*A* flag with *update* allows you to revert from a branch sandbox to a trunk. It removes the sticky flags and retrieves the most recent trunk versions of the files. Any changes in your sandbox since the revision that the sandbox files are based on (the *BASE* revision) are merged into the retrieved files.

Use a branch sandbox like a normal sandbox. Actions based on revisions of a file affect the branch rather than the trunk. Actions based on the repository copy of the file as a whole reflect the full file. For instance, running *cvs status* in a branch sandbox reports the status of the local copy of the files, the trunk revision numbers for the working and repository revisions, and the current branch tag and revision as the sticky tag.

Adding and Removing Files

When *cvs add* or *cvs remove* are applied to files in a branch sandbox, the addition or removal applies only to the branch and does not affect the trunk. Example 4-14 shows the response from CVS after adding a file to a branch.

Example 4-14. Adding a file to a branch

```
bash-2.05a$ cvs add handheld.c
cvs server: scheduling file `handheld.c' for addition on branch `beta_0-1_branch'
cvs server: use 'cvs commit' to add this file permanently
```

Merging Branches

Merging a branch to the trunk applies the differences created during the life of the branch to the most recent revisions of the trunk code. Whether this is desirable depends on the reason for the branch; you may want to apply bug fixes to the main code, or an experimental branch may have content you want to merge into the main code. It is also possible to merge changes from the trunk to the branch, or to merge the contents of two branches together.

When you merge a branch, it is good practice to tag the branch at the merge point. Such tags on the branch act as markers to show you when you did each merge.

Graphic tools such as TkCVS often include branch merging tools, and some automatically apply a tag at the merge point. Figure 4-11 shows the TkCVS branch merging tool.

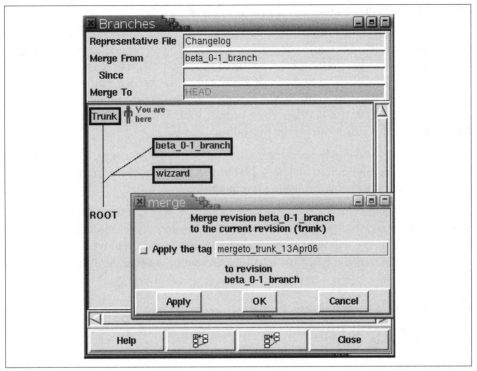

Figure 4-11. Branch merging with TkCVS

Once you have merged two branches, or a branch and a trunk, usually you are left with one unchanged and one changed. If you merge the changes from a branch to the trunk and commit the changed sandbox, the next revision of the trunk will include those changes. If you want to have a copy of the trunk to work from that doesn't have those changes, you may want to consider merging the trunk to the branch instead, or creating another branch to hold both the current trunk and branch data.

 Remember that *HEAD* is a special tag that signifies the most recent revision on the trunk (see "Reserved Tag Names" earlier in this chapter). You will use the *HEAD* tag during branch merging.

When you finish with a branch, it can seem logical to remove it or somehow close it. However, CVS does not expect you to delete branches. Instead, it keeps them as part of the record of the project. There is no command to mark a branch as no longer to be used. Use a log message to mark the end point of the branch.

 Use the *-f* flag to *cvs commit* to force CVS to commit unchanged files, thus storing the fact that you have just merged into the log messages for those files.

Merging from branch to trunk

To merge changes from a branch to the trunk (for example, when you want to merge the development line back into the production line), check out a current sandbox of the trunk and run *cvs update -j branchbasetag -j branchname*, where *branchbasetag* is the root of the branch, and *branchname* is the tag of the branch you need to merge into the root. Resolve any conflicts the merge creates and commit the changes. If the changes are complex, the developers or project leads who manage the branch and the trunk should perform this conflict resolution.

If the branch has previously been merged to the trunk and you tagged the branch at that point, the command *cvs update -j lastmergetag -j branchname* in the same sandbox merges only the changes since the last merge tag.

Example 4-15 demonstrates merging a branch to a trunk. Here, CVS refuses to remove a file that was changed in the trunk but removed in the branch. The developer doing the merge will have to decide whether to keep or remove the file: in this example, he removed the file. This example also shows an update of the *handheld.c* file.

Example 4-15. Merging a branch to the trunk

```
bash-2.05a$ cvs checkout wizzard
cvs server: Updating wizzard
U wizzard/Changelog
U wizzard/INSTALL
.
.
.
cvs server: Updating wizzard/src
U wizzard/src/config.h
U wizzard/src/main.c
bash-2.05a$ cd wizzard
bash-2.05a$ cvs update -j beta_0-1_branch_root -j beta_0-1_branch
cvs server: Updating .
cvs server: file config.h has been modified, but has been removed in revision beta_0-1_
branch
U handheld.c
bash-2.05a$ rm config.h
bash-2.05a$ cvs remove config.h
cvs remove: scheduling `config.h' for removal
cvs remove: use `cvs commit' to remove this file permanently
bash-2.05a$ cvs commit
cvs commit: Examining .
/home/cvs/wizzard/src/config.h,v  <--  config.h
new revision: delete; previous revision: 1.4
/home/cvs/wizzard/src/handheld.c,v  <--  handheld.c
new revision: 1.4; previous revision 1.3
```

Merging from trunk to branch

To merge changes from the trunk to a branch (for example, when you want to merge the most recent bugfixes from the production line into the development line), check out a current sandbox of the branch and run *cvs update -j branchbasetag -j HEAD* from that sandbox. Resolve any conflicts the merge creates and commit the changes. If the changes are complex, the developers or project leads who manage the branch and the trunk should perform this conflict resolution.

If the trunk has previously been merged to the branch and you tagged the trunk at that point, the command *cvs update -j lastmergetag -j HEAD* in the same sandbox merges only the changes since the last merge tag.

Example 4-16 shows the result and error messages caused by attempting to merge a trunk to a branch. The *config.h* file has been removed from the branch but is still active in the trunk. This issue needs to be resolved, probably by reverting the removal. The *handheld.c* file did not previously exist in the trunk but was added to the trunk when the branch was merged to it; the related error message can be ignored.

Example 4-16. Merging the trunk to a branch

```
bash-2.05a$ cvs checkout -r beta_0-1_branch wizzard
cvs server: Updating wizzard
U wizzard/Changelog
U wizzard/INSTALL
.
.
.
cvs server: Updating wizzard/src
U wizzard/src/handheld.c
U wizzard/src/main.c
bash-2.05a$ cd wizzard
bash-2.05a$ cvs update -j beta_0-1_branch_root -j HEAD
cvs server: Updating .
cvs server: file config.h does not exist, but is present in revision HEAD
cvs server: file handheld.c exists, but has been added in revision HEAD
U server.c
```

Merging from branch to branch

To merge changes from one branch to another branch, check out a sandbox of the target branch and run *cvs update -j branchbasetag -j otherbranch*, merging from the other branch to the checked-out branch's sandbox.

If the branches have been previously merged and you tagged the source branch at the time of the merge, the command *cvs update -j lastmergetag -j branchname* in the sandbox of the target branch merges the changes since the last merge.

Keyword issues when merging branches

Keyword expansion (see Chapter 3) can cause conflicts when merging two different revisions of files together. The *Revision* keyword is the most obvious cause of conflicts, because it expands to display the current revision of a file. Avoid these conflicts by using the *-kk* keyword-expansion mode, which prevents keywords from being replaced by their associated values.

 The *-kk* mode can damage binary files if they contain a string that CVS recognizes as a keyword name and value, because CVS will replace the name and value with just the keyword name.

Merging binary and special files

Changes to binary files and other nonmergeable files cannot be merged from the branch to the trunk automatically. If there are utilities similar to *diff* and *patch* for the file type in question, it may be possible to merge such files using those utilities. Otherwise, you'll need to merge changes manually. You should consider this issue when deciding whether to branch development of such files.

Branch Revision Numbers

An ordinary file's revision numbers consist of a prefix and an incrementing revision identifier; thus, revision 1.1 is succeeded by 1.2, 1.3, and 1.4 as each change is committed.

A branched file's branch number is based on the revision from which it is branched. So, a branch based on revision 1.4 of a file may be branch 1.4.2. Each revision within that branch uses the branch number as its base number and then adds its own number to the end. So, revision numbers for branch 1.4.2 would be 1.4.2.*x*, where *x* is the incrementing revision identifier. Remember that a branch is not a single revision; a branch is a line of revisions.

Figure 4-12 shows a branched file and its revision numbers.

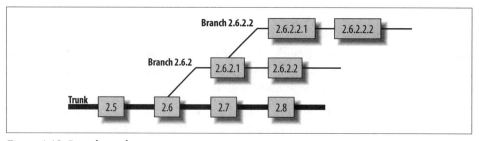

Figure 4-12. Branch numbers

CVS never gives a user-created branch the branch number 1.1.1; this number is used for a special branch called the *vendor branch*.

Magic Branch Numbers

CVS sometimes inserts a 0 in the second-rightmost position of a branch number to make internal code more efficient. This sometimes shows up in *cvs log* and may affect *cvs admin* commands on that branch, but it is otherwise hidden by CVS. If this happened to branch 1.4.2, the branch number would be displayed as 1.4.0.2. Revisions on the branch would not have the 0, so the first revision on branch 1.4.0.2 would be 1.4.2.1 and the second would be 1.4.2.2.

This vagary with respect to zeros in branch numbers does not affect how you use CVS; you can refer to a branch without the 0. For example, the commands *cvs update -r 1.4.2* and *cvs update -r 1.4.0.2* retrieve the same revisions of the same files.

Deleting or Moving a Branch

Deleting or moving a branch is done with the *-d* or *-F* command options to *cvs tag* and *cvs rtag*, in the same way you delete or move any other tag. CVS also requires the *-B* option in the command as a way of indicating that you know the tag denotes a branch and that you really mean to move or delete it.

Unless the branch has just been created and no work has been done on it, I recommend against deleting or moving a branch. (Even with a newly created branch, be careful and have a backup.) Most tags can be deleted or moved without affecting a project's history, but changes on a branch become part of the change record of each file in the branch.

Example 4-17 shows how to delete a just-created branch. (You may also want to delete the branch root tag.)

Example 4-17. Deleting a branch

```
bash-2.05a$ cvs tag -d -B pre_beta_0-1_branch
cvs server: Untagging .
D Changelog
D INSTALL
D Makefile
D README
D TODO
cvs server: Untagging doc
cvs server: Untagging doc/design
D doc/design/AcceptanceTest.doc
D doc/design/Analysis.rtf
D doc/design/Requirements.doc
D doc/design/Specification.rtf
cvs server: Untagging doc/plan
D doc/plan/Schedule.rtf
cvs server: Untagging src
D src/config.h
D src/main.c
```

Branching Strategies

This section explains the basis of branching strategies and the two main philosophies of branching. It also provides some answers to the question of when and why you should branch on a project.

Branching Philosophies

The general rule of thumb for branching is that you should keep the main line of development on the trunk; everything else can be branched. The problem is determining the main line of development. Should the trunk contain stable code or unstable code? Should each release be branched when it goes to be tested? Should new features be developed on the trunk or on a branch?

These decisions all stem from two distinct definitions of "the main line of development." These two definitions result in two different branching philosophies, distinguished here as *basically stable* and *basically unstable*.

Basically stable

The basically stable branching philosophy states that the trunk should contain project data that is always close to being ready for release. Branches are used for development, bug fixes, prerelease quality assurance (QA), and refactoring. Branches are also used for experimental code.

The strictest variation of this philosophy states that nothing should be merged to the trunk until it has been through QA. This ensures that at any time a release candidate can be taken from the trunk, put through a small amount of QA, and then published or sold.

More lenient variations of this philosophy allow anything that passes developer unit-testing to be merged into the trunk. Such a relaxed approach requires a release candidate to be branched off and put through a full QA analysis before publication.

Advantages of the basically stable method include the following:

- You can take a snapshot of the trunk at any time, run it through QA, and publish it.
- Because the trunk contains stable code that changes slowly, you can perform experimental work on a branch with little likelihood of causing errors in someone else's work when the branch is merged back into the trunk.

The greatest disadvantage of the basically stable philosophy is that merging usually gets done by a QA tester rather than by a person who understands the semantics of the code being merged. Also, the trunk may change significantly between the original time a branch was split from it and the time the branch is merged back. Both of these problems can be reduced by having the developer merge the trunk to the branch periodically, or by using a less strict variation.

Basically unstable

The basically unstable philosophy states that the trunk should contain the latest code, regardless of its stability, and that release candidates should be branched off for QA.

The strictest variation states that all development takes place on the trunk and that branches are used only for release candidates, bugfix branches, and releases.

More lenient variations also allow branching for experimental code, refactoring, and other special-case code. Merging of a branch back into the trunk is done by the managers of the branch.

The advantage of this philosophy is that merging doesn't happen often and is easier to do, because it is usually done by people familiar with the code.

The disadvantage of this philosophy, especially when applied in its strictest form, is that the main trunk often contains buggy code, experimental work, and sometimes code that doesn't compile at all. Frequent tagging can reduce this disadvantage, so tag every time there's good code or whenever someone starts to experiment or refactor. More lenient variations keep the buggiest code and the code most likely to cause significant breakage off the trunk, reducing the time it takes to prepare a release for publication.

Branch Styles

CVS includes code to create and use branches, but it doesn't enforce any particular technique for using them. This section explains several styles for using branches.

In this section, the term *long branch* means either ongoing branches or branches that merge several times and then are no longer used. A *short branch* is merged back to the trunk once and never again used.

CVS permits a branch to be activated again at any time; it has no way of saying that a branch is no longer valid. Ending a branch is done by telling all developers that it will never again be used for active development.

Long branch, merging to branch

An ongoing branch for which the trunk merges repeatedly to the branch is useful for situations in which the trunk should not be affected by changes in the branch, but the branch needs changes from the trunk. Mirror web sites may use this method. See Figure 4-13 for an illustration of how this method works.

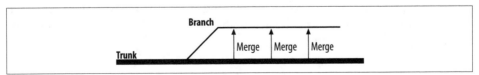

Figure 4-13. A trunk merging repeatedly to a long branch

Long branch, merging to trunk

An ongoing branch that merges repeatedly to the trunk is useful in situations in which the branch should not be affected by ongoing trunk development, but the trunk needs changes made in the branch. Any situation in which a branch is being tested and prepared for publication can use this branch style. Projects that are in testing can use this method, putting the content that is being tested on the branch and merging corrections back to the trunk. See Figure 4-14.

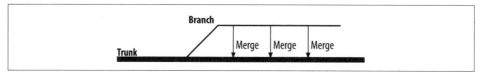

Figure 4-14. Long branch, merging to the trunk

Long branch, merging both trunk and branch

A long branch that merges in both directions ensures that changes from the branch are integrated to the trunk and that changes in the trunk are integrated into the branch. If the developers working on the branch are doing ongoing development of unstable code, the branch can be merged back to the trunk when each stage is completed, and the branch can be synchronized with changes from the trunk whenever the branch developers are prepared to merge those changes. This method can be useful when mature code is being rewritten one section at a time, while new features are being added on the trunk. See Figure 4-15.

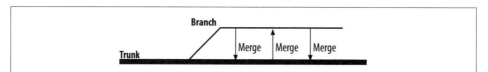

Figure 4-15. Long branch, merging both ways

Short branches

A short branch can be a standalone branch used for a simple change. If you want to add a single feature, write experimental code, or prepare for a release, a short, single-purpose branch may be ideal.

You can also use a series of short branches to simulate a long branch merged to and from the trunk. By using a series of short branches, you avoid having to merge branch changes to the trunk and then trunk changes to the branch. Instead, you merge changes from a branch to the trunk, and then start a new branch from the trunk. This method may be useful when both the trunk and the branch have significant changes. See Figure 4-16.

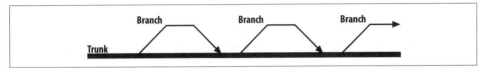

Figure 4-16. Short branches

Nested branches

CVS permits you to create branches off of branches. You then treat the root branch as a trunk and manage the subbranch using any of the branch styles discussed in the preceding sections. Nested branches are most useful when using CVS for configuration management. Minimize the nesting complexity to reduce confusion.

If you are writing a new set of features on a branch and need to give a feature to a tester while you continue to work on the branch, you can create a test branch off your feature branch. Figure 4-17 shows a set of nested branches off a trunk.

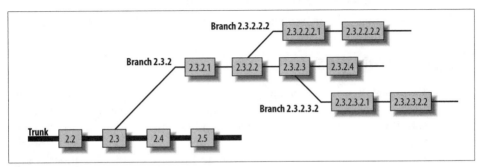

Figure 4-17. Nested branches

Branch Policies

Consistent policies can help ensure that branching assists your project. Without consistent rules, you may end up with a mess of branches that are difficult to keep track of.

Having and using consistent policies can also keep merging as simple as possible. Minimizing the amount of merging requires communication between the developers working on the branch and those working on the trunk.

Develop policies that work for your projects and your team. My coworkers and I have found the following policies useful:

- Have an overall design for the project.
- Ensure that each branch has a definite purpose and minimize the number of currently active branches.
- Minimize the complexity of your branching scheme. CVS permits nested branches, but there are few situations where multiple layers of nesting help a project.

- Use a consistent branch-naming scheme that expresses the purpose of each branch.

- Be aware of semantic differences between a branch and the trunk; good design and good communication can reduce these differences.

  An example of semantic difference is when a developer has changed the number (or worse, the order) of parameters in a function and other developers call the function with the old parameters.

- Avoid binary files where possible to allow CVS to merge files automatically.

- Merge back frequently; the fewer changes there are to the trunk, the easier they are to merge.

- Tag the branch at every merge point, so you can avoid merging the same changes twice.

- Tag the trunk at every branch point and just before and after every merge, in case you need to retrieve the trunk state at that time.

- Use consistent tag-naming schemes for the tags associated with the branches.

Merging Strategies

Chapter 3 contains a section on merging and resolving conflicts ("Updating the Sandbox Files from the Repository"). Conflicts are rare when the developers are working solely on the trunk and frequently committing to the same line of development. However, once a development team starts using branches, there is the potential for lines of development to be kept separate from each other for months at a time. This vastly increases the possibility for conflict, so I am expanding on the process of merging and resolving conflicts. Please read the section in Chapter 3 first, however, as this discussion is based upon knowledge of the information provided there.

The process for a merge is as follows:

1. If you're trying to merge a branch to a trunk, a branch to another branch, a trunk to a branch, or any other such combination, go to step 2. In all other cases, try to *commit*. If the commit succeeds, the process is finished. Otherwise, continue.

2. Run *update* to blend the files. Watch to see whether any files have conflicts. If none do, the process is finished. Otherwise, continue.

3. For each file that has a conflict, edit the file (text mode) or use the merge tool in your graphic client. Note the conflicting lines.

4. If the conflicting lines can peacefully coexist in the file, edit out the conflict markers and any duplicate lines. Go on to step 7.

5. If you need to consult with a coworker to decide what to do about the conflicting lines, use *log* or *annotate* to determine who wrote them. Consult with your coworkers and decide how to correct the conflict.

6. Edit the files to correct the conflict, remove conflict markers and remove any duplicate lines.

7. Check for any additional conflict markers in the current file. If there are no additional markers, commit the file. Otherwise, go back to step 3.

8. Use *status* to remind yourself which files still have conflicts. If there are any, choose one and go back to step 3. Otherwise, you are finished.

When Merging Is Easy

The easiest merges are the ones CVS can do by itself, with no human intervention. Those occur when a *cvs update* produces an M or P result against a file, and doesn't require any work from you. Those merges don't need any particular explanation, so this section is about the second-easiest merges.

Merging is easy when you can simply include both sets of changes. Let's look at a case where the two changes are a comment on an existing function and the creation of a new function. In cases like this, where the changes don't affect each other, you can remove the conflict markers and any duplicate lines and recommit the file.

Both Bob and Lisa check out revision 1.3. The relevant section of revision 1.3 looks like this:

```
              TotalTime+=temp-time;
              Add(event,temp-time);
              }
       time=temp;
       }
   Record[total++]=time;
   }
```

Bob adds a comment at the end of the function. He commits, and his version now becomes revision 1.4. His section now looks like this:

```
              TotalTime+=temp-time;
              Add(event,temp-time);
              }
       time=temp;
       }
   Record[total++]=time;
   }

   /* Have we considered the null event? */
```

Lisa starts a new function on the same line. Her code looks like this:

```
              TotalTime+=temp-time;
              Add(event,temp-time);
```

```
            }
    time=temp;
            }
Record[total++]=time;
}

long GetEvent( )
{
```

She tries to commit, but gets the conflict warning.

```
bash$ cvs commit
cvs commit: Examining .
cvs server: Up-to-date check failed for `timed-events.c'
cvs [server aborted]: correct above errors first!
cvs commit: saving log message in /tmp/cvsgmS8tS
```

So she runs *update* and crosses her fingers that she just gets an M or a P (merge or patch). But no, she gets a C, for conflict.

```
bash$ cvs update
cvs server: Updating .
RCS file: /home/cvs/src/timed-events.c,v
retrieving revision 1.3
retrieving revision 1.4
Merging differences between 1.3 and 1.4 into timed-events.c
rcsmerge: warning: conflicts during merge
cvs server: conflicts found in timed-events.c
C timed-events.c
```

She opens the file, and sees this:

```
                TotalTime+=temp-time;
                Add(event,temp-time);
                }
        time=temp;
            }
<<<<<<< timed-events.c
 Record[total++]=time;
   }

/* Have we considered the null event? */
=======
   Record[total++]=time;
   }

long GetEvent( )
{
>>>>>>> 1.4
```

Oh well. It's not a major issue. She edits the file, removing the conflict markers, and commits. The new revision 1.5 is this:

```
                TotalTime+=temp-time;
                Add(event,temp-time);
```

```
            }
        time=temp;
        }
    Record[total++]=time;
    }

    /* Have we considered the null event? */

    long GetEvent( )
    {
```

When Merging Is Difficult

Having had it so easy, Bob and Lisa have become overconfident. They're not talking to each other enough, and they are both working on the same function. This often leads to problems. They check out revision 1.8, which looks like this:

```
long GetEvent( )
{
    /* FIXME: Currently returns true regardless of events */
    return TRUE;
}
```

Lisa commits first, and revision 1.9 has a change to the parameters of the function.

```
long GetEvent(int* currentkey)
{
    /* FIXME: Currently returns true regardless of events */
    return TRUE;
}
```

Bob also changes the parameters (obviously, they both intend to change the content of the function as well):

```
long GetEvent(char* name)
{
    /* FIXME: Currently returns true regardless of events */
    return TRUE;
}
```

Bob tries to commit and has the same problem Lisa did. He tries the update, just as she did, and gets a conflict marker. He opens the file and sees this:

```
<<<<<<< timed-event.c
long GetEvent(int* currentkey)
=======
long GetEvent(char* name)
>>>>>>> 1.9
{
    /* FIXME: Currently returns true regardless of events */
    return TRUE;
}
```

He's not entirely sure who the other person editing the file is. He thinks it's Lisa, but just to be certain, he uses *cvs annotate* on the file.

```
Annotations for timed-event.c
***************
    .
    .
    .
1.9        (lisa    13-Apr-2006): long GetEvent(int* currentkey)
1.5        (lisa    11-Apr-2006): {
1.5        (lisa    11-Apr-2006):          /* FIXME: Currently returns true regardless
of events */
    .
    .
    .
```

It is Lisa. He goes to her desk with the issue, and the pair of them discuss it. They agree on which parameters the function needs, and Bob then edits the file and commits. The function signature in revision 1.10 looks like this, and all is right in the world (until the next merge!):

```
long GetEvent(int* currentkey, char* name)
```

## CHAPTER 5

Multiple Users

This chapter explains how CVS can be used for source or content control—how to manage a group of developers working together on a project without having them overwrite each other's work, causing loss of data. It also describes commands that show what each person has done to a file.

The problem of source control occurs when you don't have any management software. If you have a central location for data and two people are using the same storage, such as the same file, the second person to save that file will overwrite the first person's changes. Source control software can prevent this, either by capturing both sets of changes and merging them together, or by preventing two people from having the same file checked out at the same time.

CVS is designed to allow developers to work simultaneously on a file. Several people can work on the same file, each in their own sandbox, and CVS tries to merge their changes to the data in the central repository. If the changes can't be merged easily, the developer who commits the second set of changes is asked to resolve the conflict. This pattern is explained in Chapter 3.

An alternative to simultaneous development is exclusive development, where one developer at a time has the editing rights for a file. Some development teams prefer to use exclusive development, which is effective for files that can't be merged. CVS supports the exclusive development of files with a choice of two methods:

- The first method permits, but does not enforce, exclusive development. This method uses the *cvs watch*, *cvs edit*, and *cvs unedit* command set.
- The second method uses the *cvs admin* command to emulate file locking with reserved checkouts and relies on the *rcslock* script in the *contrib* directory of the CVS source code. This method requires that the user have privileges to modify the repository, or the assistance of the repository administrator.

Whether you use exclusive or simultaneous development, source control works only if your project members use it. It is also essential that they communicate the basic design and structure of the project with each other. No source control system can take the place of a shared vision of the project.

Once you are working in a team, you need to be able to see the changes made by other team members. Studying the history of changes can help keep the team working toward the same goals, or it can help determine where the team's goals have diverged. CVS provides a range of commands for viewing changes.

The *diff* and *rdiff* commands display the changes made between specific revisions of a file and also allow you to make patches that can be installed with the GNU *patch* program. The *annotate* command displays the most recent change to each line of a file, along with the revision number of the revision in which the line was changed and the username of the user who made the change. The *log* command displays the log messages and status information for files.

Using Simultaneous Development

Simultaneous development allows multiple developers to work on the same file at the same time. If you and your coworker are working on different sections of a file, you can both edit the file and then have a program (such as CVS) merge the two versions of the file. Simultaneous development is also useful when you have developers distributed across many time zones, as it eliminates the need to check with other team members before editing a file.

CVS supports simultaneous development without requiring any configuration changes or setup. Simultaneous development is most helpful when you are using text or other line-based files, because CVS merges are based on the changes in lines. CVS is less adept at merging binary files.

When multiple developers use the same repository directory, each should check out her own sandbox, develop in that sandbox, commit to the repository frequently, and update frequently. CVS merges most changes automatically, and if you update and commit frequently, there should be few cases where a human has to merge conflicting changes.

Watching a File

CVS provides a set of commands to notify users when a file is being edited or committed. You can use these commands to monitor what each member of your team is doing and reduce the necessity of merging files when *cvs update* is run. Together, the *cvs watch*, *cvs edit*, and *cvs unedit* commands make up the *watch* method of exclusive development, which is a lightly enforced method of exclusive development.

The watch method requires the repository administrator to set up the notify and *users* files in the *CVSROOT* directory of the CVS repository; it requires the developers to check whether a file is being edited before they attempt to edit it.

Use *cvs watch* like this:

1. Check out your sandbox, including the files you want to watch.

2. Issue the *cvs watch on* command to mark files for watching. (This does not set you as the watcher for the files; it just informs CVS that the files can be watched.) Once a file has been marked for watching, it remains marked unless it is cleared with *cvs watch off*.

 You need to run *cvs watch on* for a file only once, unless someone clears the setting. Usually, your project leader decides which files can be watched and marks those files for watching.

3. Issue the *cvs watch add* command to set yourself as a watcher of the files you want to watch.

4. Issue *cvs edit* to inform CVS and other users that you intend to edit a specific file. Other users watching the file will be notified that you are editing it.

5. Edit the file in any editor.

6. Commit your changes with *cvs commit*. This command saves the changes to the repository and releases the file for others to edit. CVS notifies other users watching the file that you have committed it.

7. If you don't want to commit your changes, but instead want to revert to the state of the file before you edited it, run *cvs unedit* to release it for others to edit. CVS notifies anyone watching the file that you are no longer editing it.

The watch method is voluntary; there is nothing preventing another user from making changes to a file you are editing. However, the *cvs edit* command automatically designates you as a temporary watcher on a file until you release the file. So, if another developer runs *cvs edit* on the file, you are notified and can contact them to coordinate your changes.

The *cvs edit* and *cvs unedit* commands work in conjunction with CVS's watch feature to enable you to keep track of activity in your project's files. The *watch*ing and *edit*ing features can also be used independently of each other. The next few sections show how to use the *watch* method to coordinate development and monitor activity in your project files.

Figure 5-1 shows the Cervisia menu for the watch-related commands. Figure 5-2 shows a TkCVS display with the *server.cc* file claimed by user jenn.

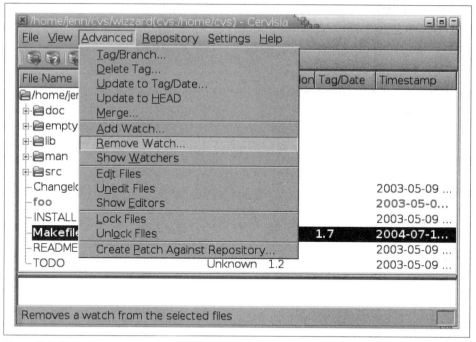

Figure 5-1. Cervisia watch menu

Configuring Watches

Before using the *watch* commands, you need to designate files as watchable and configure how you want CVS to notify watchers. You can designate which files are watchable with the *cvs watch on* command, which marks a file as watchable but does not make you a watcher.

CVS notifies a file's watchers when the file is committed, marked for editing, or released from editing. When the conditions exist for CVS to notify a watching user, CVS runs the commands in the repository's *CVSROOT/notify* file. This file usually contains a single line that causes the watcher to be emailed with the notification. (It may be commented out at installation). Such a line is shown in Example 5-1.

 The default *notify* file assumes that the repository server is configured to send email with the command *mail*. If your server is not, you can use a different form of notification that is configured (such as some form of instant messaging), or set it up for mail.

I like the explanation of mail servers in *Running Linux*, by Matt Welsh et al. (O'Reilly). It is Linux-focused, but the explanation of email is valid for all systems, and their preferred mail transport agent (Postfix) will work on Unix, Linux, and Mac OS X.

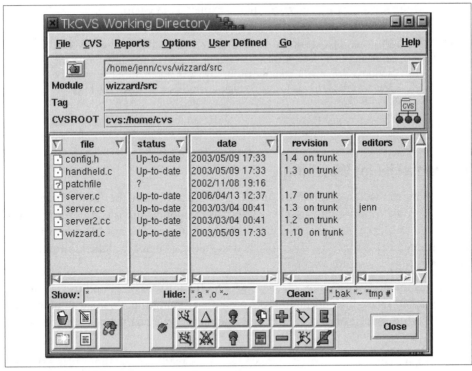

Figure 5-2. TkCVS showing a current editor

Example 5-1. The file CVSROOT/notify

```
ALL mail %s -s "CVS Notification"
```

The *notify* file in Example 5-1 sends an email to the user's CVS username at the computer that the repository is on. If there are users whose mailboxes (or other notification method) are not on the same computer or use different usernames, create a *users* file in the repository's *CVSROOT* directory. The format of this file is a separate line for each user, consisting of the CVS username and the email address to send notifications to, in the following format:[*]

```
username:email_address
```

Example 5-2 shows an example of a *users* file.

Example 5-2. CVSROOT/users

```
jenn:jenn@helit.example.com
doppel:doppel@teppic.example.com
```

---

[*] The CVS username is usually the system username, but it may be a special username if you are connecting with pserver (see "The pserver Access Method" in Chapter 8).

The full syntax for the *notify* and *users* files is explained in Chapter 6.

When working with the files in the *CVSROOT* directory, such as *notify* and *users*, check them out into a sandbox and edit them in the sandbox. When you commit them, CVS will automatically install the clear-text file it needs for its configurations. (See "CVSROOT Files" in Chapter 6.)

The command to create a *CVSROOT* sandbox is *cvs -d repository_ path checkout CVSROOT*.

Marking a File for Watching

Before using the watch commands on a file, you need to set the file for watching. Files that are set for watching are checked out as read-only, and the intent is that you run *cvs edit* to set the file's permissions to allow editing, and to notify other watchers that you intend to edit it. If a directory is designated as being watched, all new files in that directory are set for watching.

Use the command *cvs watch on filename* to set a file for watching, and use *cvs watch off filename* to revert it to normal mode. Note that setting the file for watching does not add you to the list of people watching the file; it only enables the watch system for that file.

The watch system is honor-based. You can set a file read-write without using the *cvs edit* command and then edit it without ever notifying other users. (They get a message when you commit the file, however.) CVS also won't stop another user from using *cvs watch off* to turn off the watch you set. If you need a more restrictive system, consider using the *rcslock* system described in "Reserving Files," later in this chapter.

Setting Your Watch

Watching a file sets CVS to notify you when someone signals their intent to edit the file, when someone commits that file, or when someone signals that they have stopped editing the file. CVS does not notify you of your own changes to the file. Use the command *cvs watch add filename* to add yourself to the list of people watching a file. *cvs watch add* takes the *-a* command option, which restricts the actions CVS should notify you of. The *-a* option has the parameters *edit*, *unedit*, *commit*, *none*, or *all*. The default case is *all*.

To stop watching a file, use *cvs watch remove filename*. *cvs watch remove* also takes the *-a* option with the same parameters as *cvs watch add*. Both commands use *-R* to operate recursively down a directory tree and *-l* to operate locally.

You can use *cvs watch add* or *cvs watch remove* without having the file set for watching—in other words, without executing *cvs watch on* first—but CVS can inform you of an edit only if the other developer uses *cvs edit*. If the file is not set for watching, the other developer is not reminded to use *cvs edit*.

Unfortunately, the *cvs watch* commands do not provide helpful feedback when they are called; they do provide error messages if appropriate. Example 5-3 shows the use of the *cvs watch* commands.

Example 5-3. Using cvs watch

```
bash-2.05a$ cvs watch on Makefile
bash-2.05a$ cvs watch add -a edit Makefile
bash-2.05a$ cvs watch remove Makefile
bash-2.05a$ cvs watch off Makefile
bash-2.05a$
```

Example 5-4 shows the mail CVS sends as a result of a *cvs edit* command.

Example 5-4. Mail from CVS

```
From:      doppel@example.com
To:        jenn@helit.example.com
Subject:   CVS Notification
Date:      17 Apr 2006 22:13:45 +1000
wizzard Makefile
---
Triggered edit watch on /var/lib/cvs/wizzard
By Poppel
```

The syntax of the *cvs watch* command is:

```
cvs [cvs-options] watch {on|off|add|remove} [command-options] [filenames]
```

The *cvs watch* command can take filenames, directory names, or modules as parameters and use the sandbox directory as a parameter if no other parameter is given. If no -a option is given to *cvs watch add* or *cvs watch remove*, -a all is the default.

Example 5-5 demonstrates using *cvs watch* locally to set a specific watch for a directory, but not subdirectories. It also uses the *watchers* command to show some of the results of the watch.

Example 5-5. Using cvs watch options

```
bash-2.05a$ cvs watch add -l -a commit .
bash-2.05a$ cvs watchers .
Changelog   jenn     unedit   commit
INSTALL     jenn     unedit   commit
Makefile    jenn     edit     unedit   commit
README               jenn     unedit   commit
TODO                 jenn     unedit   commit
doc/design/AcceptanceTest.doc        jenn     unedit
doc/design/Analysis.rtf              jenn     unedit
.
.
```

Example 5-5. Using cvs watch options (continued)

```
.
src/config.h       doppel   edit        unedit   commit
   jenn     edit    unedit
.
.
.
```

The *cvs watch* command doesn't work if either the server or the client is running CVS version 1.6 or earlier.

Editing a File

Signal your intent to edit a file with the *cvs edit filename* command. This sets the file's permissions to read-write, signals CVS to notify all watchers who are interested in edits, and temporarily adds you as one of the file's watchers. If you do not wish to watch the file, you can use *-a none*.

Before you run *cvs edit* on a file, check your notification (usually email) to determine whether someone else has claimed it.

Once you have signaled your intent to edit a file, use your usual editor to make your changes. When you are finished, use *cvs commit* to save changes or *cvs unedit* to revert them.

The syntax of *cvs edit* is:

```
cvs [cvs-options] edit [command-options] [filenames]
```

The syntax of *cvs unedit* is:

```
cvs [cvs-options] unedit [command-options] [filenames]
```

Both commands can take filenames, directory names, or modules as parameters and use the sandbox directory as a parameter if no other parameter is given. Both commands use *-R* to operate recursively down a directory tree and *-l* to operate locally. The *edit* command also supports *-a* with the same parameters as *cvs watch*. If no *-a* option is given to *cvs edit*, *-a all* is set by default.

The *cvs edit* command does not restrict anyone else from editing the file you're working on; it only signals to them that you're editing it. It doesn't warn you if someone else is already editing the file.

Aborting an edit

When you commit a file with *cvs commit*, CVS clears the file's edit mark. If you want to clear the edit on a file but don't want to commit your changes, you can use the *cvs unedit filename* command, use *cvs release* on the directory the file is in, or delete the file and use *cvs checkout* or *cvs update* to recreate it.

The *cvs unedit* command sets the target file's permissions to read-only, notifies CVS to signal users watching for unedits, clears you from watching the file if you had a temporary, *cvs edit*-based watch, and reverts the file to the repository revision on which it was based.

 If you call *cvs unedit* on a file that is not currently set for watching, CVS can revert the file only if CVS can contact the server.

Deleting the file and issuing *cvs checkout* or *cvs update* notifies watchers, clears you from watching the file, returns the file to the latest repository revision, and sets the file's permissions to read only if it is still a watched file.

Issuing *cvs release* or deleting the file and then issuing *cvs checkout* or *cvs update* sends a notification to users watching for an *unedit* and clears you from a temporary watch. Using *cvs release* also sets the directory to no longer be a sandbox directory.

Committing an edit

Use *cvs commit* to save your changes to the repository. This command also clears your edit signal, sets any watched files' permissions to read only, signals users watching for commits, and clears you from watching the file if you were temporarily watching it (i.e., if you used *cvs edit* and didn't use the *-a none* option).

 If both the client and the server are CVS 1.12.10 or later, you can use *edit* and *commit* with the *-c* option. Used with *commit*, *-c* causes the commit to fail if the user is not the current listed editor of the file, and to succeed if the user is the listed editor. Used with *edit*, *-c* causes the edit to fail if anyone else is registered as the editor, but to succeed if the file is currently unclaimed.

If you want to use the *-c* options, it is useful to put them in the *.cvsrc* of all developers. The *.cvsrc* file is explained in Chapter 3.

CVS 1.12.10 also added the *-f* option to *edit*, which forces the edit through regardless of other editors. It overrides *-c*, and is useful when *-c* is in the user's *.cvsrc* but the user has reason to edit a file even though someone else has claimed exclusive development.

Listing Watchers and Editors

Before editing a watched file, you should use the *cvs editors* command to see whether anyone else has issued *cvs edit* to indicate they are editing the file. You might also want to know who is watching the file you're about to edit.

The *cvs watchers filename* command lists the people currently watching the file, showing their username as stored in the *notify* or *users* files in the repository's *CVSROOT* directory.

The *cvs editors filename* command lists the people currently editing the file, their email addresses, the time they began working with the file, and the host and path of the directory containing the file.

See Example 5-6 for an example of the *cvs watchers* and *cvs editors* commands.

Example 5-6. Using cvs watchers and cvs editors

```
bash-2.05a$ cvs watchers
Changelog   doppel    edit     unedit      commit
INSTALL     doppel    edit     unedit      commit
Makefile    doppel    edit     unedit      commit
      jenn  edit      unedit   commit
bash-2.05a$ cvs editors Makefile
Makefile      jenn     Tue Apr 17 12:13:44 2006 GMT      helit /home/jenn/cvs/wizzard
```

The syntax of *cvs watchers* is:

```
cvs [cvs-options] watchers [command-options] [filenames]
```

The syntax of *cvs editors* is:

```
cvs [cvs-options] editors [command-options] [filenames]
```

Both commands can take filenames, directory names, or modules as parameters and use the sandbox directory as a parameter if no other parameter is given. Both accept the *-l* (local) and *-R* (recursive) command options.

Reserving Files

CVS has a method of exclusive development that is based on reserving the ability to commit files, so that only a single user can commit a reserved file. This feature is useful when you want to enforce exclusive development, especially when you have files that cannot be merged and users who are not comfortable with the honor system that *cvs watch* relies on.

This method requires the *rcslock* script (distributed in the *contrib* subdirectory of the CVS source code), file locking set to strict (the CVS default), the assistance of the repository administrator, and the active support of the developers. The *rcslock* script is provided as is; currently, it is an unsupported part of the CVS distribution.

File locking is set to strict by default in CVS, so there should be no need to set it that way manually. You can confirm the lock status of a file with the command *cvs log -h filename*.

Do not use the *cvs admin -U* command on any files in your project. This sets file locking to nonstrict and can cause problems. File locks can be set strict again with *cvs admin -L*.

Installing and Configuring rcslock

The *rcslock* script is distributed with the CVS source code. Chapter 2 includes the URL for the CVS source code, and most Linux or Unix packaging systems include an option to install the source from the package. The file in the package may be an *rcslock.pl* or an *rcslock.in* file, or even just *rcslock*. In recent versions of CVS, the CVS build script attempts to generate a version called *rcslock*, with a Perl invocation as the first line.

You may also find an *rcslock* that corresponds to your installed version of CVS lurking somewhere on your filesystem. For example, on Mac OS X, you can find it in */usr/share/cvs/contrib/rcslock*. On Ubuntu, it's the (compressed) file */usr/share/doc/cvs/contrib/rcslock.gz*.

Install the *rcslock* script by copying it from the *contrib* directory to a sensible location and ensuring that your CVS users have permission to execute it. I recommend using */usr/local/lib/cvs* as the location for this script, because */usr/local/lib* is a standard location for components of locally installed software such as CVS. Edit the *commitinfo* file in the repository's *CVSROOT* directory and add a line to invoke the script:

```
ALL /usr/local/lib/cvs/rcslock [options]
```

When working with *commitinfo* or other files in the *CVSROOT* directory, check them out into a sandbox to edit them, as explained in "Configuring Watches" earlier in this chapter.

If you are using a copy of *rcslock* that has the *.pl* extension, include the full filename, with extension, in the *commitinfo* file. The *ALL* keyword may be replaced by a regular expression that covers the directories or files for which you wish to reserve checkouts. The regular expression patterns used in CVS are explained in Chapter 11. Example 5-7 shows a *commitinfo* file that includes *rcslock* configured for the *wizzard* project. The characters after *wizzard* prevent CVS from matching names like *wizzard-libs* and *wizzardly*, yet still match *wizzard/src* or *wizard/docs*.

Example 5-7. Configuring commitinfo to include rcslock

```
^wizzard\(/\|$\)  /usr/local/lib/cvs/rcslock
```

The path in the *rcslock* file should be the path you installed the script to. The available options for the script are *-v* and *-d*, for verbose and debugging modes, respectively. The *rcslock* script runs quietly if no options are given.

 If your copy of *rcslock* has an *.in* extension, it needs to be processed before it's ready for use. Run *./configure* from the top directory of your CVS source tree, which will create a *Makefile* in the *contrib* directory of the CVS source tree. Change directory into the *contrib* directory and run *make*. This will create your final *rcslock* file.

Reserving a File

When using *rcslock*, reserve a file before you start editing it. Reserving the file ensures that no one else can commit it until you commit it or release it.

To reserve a file, lock it with the command *cvs admin -l filename*. The *cvs admin -l* command is a CVS frontend to the RCS file-locking command (RCS, or Revision Control System, is a tool that CVS uses to store files, and that the *rcslock* script exploits to do its job). The *rcslock* script runs when CVS commits a file, and uses the RCS file lock to prevent anyone else from committing to the file before you do. CVS prevents you from locking a file that is already locked on the same branch or trunk. CVS and *rcslock* automatically release the lock when you run *cvs commit* on the file.

 Three programs work to make the *rcslock* system work: RCS, CVS, and the *rcslock* script.

Example 5-8 shows an attempt to lock a file that has already been reserved.

Example 5-8. Failing to lock a reserved file

```
bash-2.05a$ cvs admin -l Makefile
RCS file: /var/lib/cvs/wizzard/Makefile,v
cvs [server aborted]: Revision 1.6 is already locked by doppel
```

Example 5-9 shows locking a file using *cvs admin*.

Example 5-9. Locking with cvs admin

```
doppel@teppic$ cvs admin -l Makefile
RCS file: /var/lib/cvs/wizzard/Makefile,v
1.3 locked
done
```

Committing a File

When *rcslock* is active, you cannot commit a file if someone else has a lock on that file. Example 5-10 shows the error message CVS displays when you attempt to commit a file reserved by another user.

Example 5-10. Failing to commit a reserved file

```
jenn@helit$ cvs commit Makefile
cvs [server aborted]: Revision 1.3 is already locked by doppel
cvs commit: saving log message in /tmp/cvsuFw5r5
```

Example 5-11 shows a successful commit of a file reserved with *rcslock*. Committing a file also unlocks it so that another person can reserve it.

Example 5-11. Committing a reserved file

```
jenn@helit$ cvs commit Makefile
Checking in Makefile;320C written
/var/lib/cvs/wizzard/Makefile,v  <--  Makefile
new revision: 1.4; previous revision: 1.3
done
```

Releasing a File

If you wish to abort the changes to a file, unlock it so that someone else can reserve it. To unlock a file without committing changes, run the command *cvs admin -u filename*. This command is the CVS frontend to the RCS file-unlocking command. Example 5-12 shows unlocking a file with *cvs admin*.

Example 5-12. Unlocking with cvs admin

```
doppel@teppic$ cvs admin -u Makefile
RCS file: /var/lib/cvs/wizzard/Makefile,v
1.3 unlocked
done
```

Combining rcslock with watch

I recommend using the *rcslock* file-reserving technique in combination with *cvs watch*. Use *cvs watch* to allow your project team to communicate which person is editing which file, and use *rcslock* to enforce exclusivity.

If you are using the command-line client, you can create a shell script that calls both *cvs edit* and *cvs admin -l*, to cut down on typing. You may also want a script for *cvs unedit* and *cvs admin -u*. Example 5-13 shows a *bash* script that executes both *cvs edit* and *cvs admin -l* on every file it acts on. Call this script with `scriptname filenames`. This script works only for files without whitespace in the filename.

Example 5-13. Script for cvs edit and cvs admin -l

```
#! /bin/sh
cvs edit $*
cvs admin -l $*
```

Comparing File Revisions

As your project develops, you sometimes need to compare a current revision with an old one, or compare two older revisions with each other. This usually happens when several developers are working on the same file and you need to know which changes were made to a file since you last worked on it.

The *cvs diff* command compares two revisions of a file and displays the differences. It uses a version of the GNU *diff* program internal to CVS; this code is also used when revisions are merged during *cvs update*.

The *diff* command and the similar *rdiff* command are also useful for creating patches to be installed by the GNU *patch* program.

cvs diff has the following syntax:

```
cvs [cvs-options] diff [command_options] [filenames]
```

You can call *cvs diff* with filenames, directories, or module names. If you don't give a filename, the current working directory is the default.

Usually, you call *cvs diff* with at least one *-r tag* or *-D date* command option. If you invoke it with a single *-r* or *-D* parameter, CVS compares the current copy in the working directory with the version in the repository. For example, if you check out revision 1.6 of *Makefile*, edit the file, then run *cvs diff -r 1.6 Makefile*, *diff* displays the changes you made to *Makefile* since you checked it out.

If you invoke *cvs diff* with two *-r* or *-D* options, CVS compares the two revisions against each other. The command *cvs diff -r 1.5 -r 1.7 Makefile* displays the changes between revisions 1.5 and 1.7.

Example 5-14 shows a *diff* command that compares revisions 1.2 and 1.3 of the *Makefile* file, using the *-c* option to display a few lines of context around each change. The output starts with a header listing the filename, the repository copy of the file (listed as *RCS file*), the revisions to be retrieved, the *diff* options, and the number of times the revisions were committed.

diff then shows the sections that were changed. The *diff* in Example 5-14 shows the changes that occur when keywords are expanded, so the contents of the lines should help you understand the *diff*.

Example 5-14. Using cvs diff

```
bash-2.05a$ cvs diff -c -r 1.2 -r 1.3 Makefile
Index: Makefile
===============================
RCS file: /var/lib/cvs/wizzard/Makefile,v
retrieving revision 1.2
retrieving revision 1.3
diff -c -r1.2 -r1.3
*** Makefile      1 Apr 2006 06:57:23 -0000      1.2
--- Makefile     12 Apr 2006 12:57:40 -0000      1.3
***************
*** 2,10 ****
  # Makefile for the Wizzard project
  # First created by J Vesperman, 1 Apr 2006
  #
! # Current revision $Revision$
  # On branch $Name$ (not expanded if this is the trunk)
! # Latest change by $Author$ on $Date$
  #

  # Initial declarations
--- 2,10 ----
  # Makefile for the Wizzard project
  # First created by J Vesperman, 1 Apr 2002
  #
! # Current revision $Revision$
  # On branch $Name$ (not expanded if this is the trunk)
! # Latest change by $Author$ on $Date$
  #

  # Initial declarations
***************
*** 34,39 ****
--- 33,41 ----
  #
  # Log record for Makefile changes:
  # $Log$
  # Revision 1.3  2006/03/07 21:52:50  madd
  # madd SC edits
  #
  # Revision 1.2  2006/02/27 21:47:43  madd
  # madd R2 conversion edits
  #
  # Revision 1.1  2006/02/26 22:22:10  madd
  # Initial revision
  #
+ # Revision 1.3  2005/09/12 12:57:40  jenn
+ # Trying again with the wrappers..
+ #
  # Revision 1.2  2005/09/01 06:57:23  jenn
  # Initial code in the Makefile.
  #
```

The first change occurs in the headers to the *Makefile*, when the revision number and date are changed. These changes overwrite lines in the old revision, so the changed lines are denoted with an exclamation point (!) in the left column. The revision listed first in the parameter list is shown first, followed by the second revision.

The second change to the file is the new log message. This is shown only once, with plus marks (+) in the left column to show that the line was added.

Graphic clients tend to produce side-by-side *diff* displays, with color coding for the differences. Figure 5-3 shows the Cervisia *diff* display.

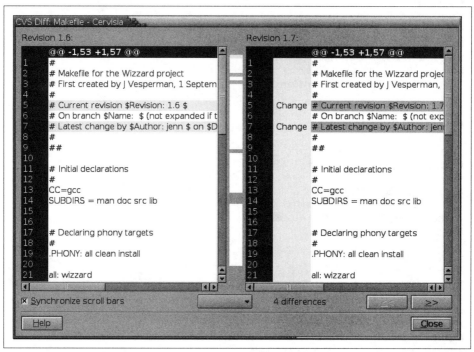

Figure 5-3. Graphic diff display

Chapter 10 provides the full list of symbols and meanings for *cvs diff*.

 In CVS 1.11.1 and later, you can also use *cvs diff* to generate files for the Unix and Linux program *patch*. The *patch* program is designed to update a text file from one version to another, automatically.

The *cvs rdiff* command is a variant of *cvs diff* that can be used to create a patch file that can be installed using the standard GNU *patch* command. *cvs rdiff* is useful for publishing updates of programs. It does not require a sandbox but does require file, directory, or module name parameters. If *cvs rdiff* is used outside a sandbox, the repository path must be given with the *-d* CVS option or the *CVSROOT* environment variable. If *cvs rdiff* is used in a sandbox that connects to a repository other than the one you want to work from, the repository path must be given with the *-d* CVS option.

cvs rdiff has the following syntax:

```
cvs [cvs-options] rdiff [command_options]   filenames
```

The *filenames* parameter can be one or more directories, filenames, or module names. Output from *cvs rdiff* is directed to *stdout*. If you intend to use the output as a patch file, you can redirect it to a file using the > shell operator. Example 5-15 shows how to make a patch for *handheld.c* that upgrades the file from revision 1.1 to the most current revision.

Example 5-15. Making a patch file

```
bash-2.05a$ cvs rdiff -r 1.1 -r HEAD wizzard/src/handheld.c  > patchfile
bash-2.05a$
```

cvs diff and *cvs rdiff* take two types of options. The first are standard options that determine which revisions of which files are checked and which keyword mode is used. The second set of options determines the output format and affects how CVS compares the files. Chapter 10 provides the full list of options to *cvs diff* and *cvs rdiff*.

One of the most useful *cvs diff* (and *cvs rdiff*) options is *-y*, also available as *--side-by-side*. This option displays the differences between the files by showing the relevant lines beside each other. Open your terminal window as wide as possible when using this option. Example 5-16 shows a side-by-side *diff* between the current revision of a file in the sandbox and the most recent revision in the repository.

Example 5-16. Displaying diff side-by-side

```
bash-2.05a$ cvs diff -y server.c
Index: server.c
===============================
RCS file: /var/lib/cvs/wizzard/src/server.c,v
retrieving revision 1.1
diff --side-by-side -r1.1 server.c
/*                              /*
 * server.c                      * server.c
 * Apr 13 2006                   * Apr 13 2006
 * Developer: Jenn Vesperman     * Developer: Jenn Vesperman
 *                               *
 * server code file              * server code file
 */                              */
                               >
                               > #include <iostream.h>
                               >
                               > int main (  ) {
                               >   cout << "Hello World\n";
                               >   return (0);
                               > }
```

Displaying Recent Changes

The *cvs annotate* command displays the most recent change for each line of a file in the repository. This command is very helpful when you need to know which change broke the compilation or who rewrote a key paragraph in the documentation incorrectly. This command works off the repository copy, not the sandbox copy, so it does not show any changes in the sandbox that were not committed.

For each line, *cvs annotate* shows the revision number for the last change, the user, the date, and the contents of the line. This is a quick way of discovering who made which change. Example 5-17 shows some of the annotations for the *wizzard.h* file.

Example 5-17. Using cvs annotate

```
bash-2.05a$ cvs annotate src/wizzard.h
Annotations for src/wizzard.h
***************
1.6      (doppel  15-Apr-06): #include "config.h"    /* using autoconf */
1.6      (doppel  15-Apr-06): #include "options.h"   /* manual options that can't
1.1      (jenn    11-Apr-06):
1.2      (jenn    13-Apr-06): #define TRUE 1
1.2      (jenn    13-Apr-06): #define FALSE 0
```

cvs annotate has the following syntax:

```
cvs [cvs-options] annotate [command-options] [filenames]
```

If you don't provide a filename, *cvs annotate* attempts to run *annotate* on all the files in the current sandbox. The filenames can be directories or modules.

> *annotate* doesn't work correctly on binary files. CVS tries to display them as text files, which can trigger the bell character and mess with your terminal window.

Use the *-F* option to run *cvs annotate* on binary files. You can select which revision to display with *-D date* and *-r revision* (or *tag*), and you can use the *-f* option to force CVS to use the most recent revision on the trunk if no revision matches the specified date, revision, or tag. *cvs annotate* uses the usual *-l* and *-R* options to control local and recursive operation, respectively.

Graphic clients also use pretty colors for *annotate*. Figure 5-4 shows the annotate display in TkCVS.

Displaying File History

The *cvs log* command displays information about files, directories, or modules. You pass a parameter to specify which file, directory, or module you are interested in. If you don't specify anything, *cvs log* displays log information about all files in the current

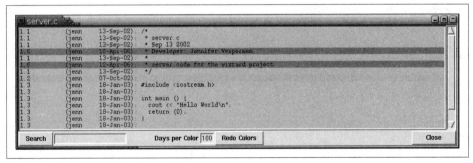

Figure 5-4. Graphic display of annotate

sandbox directory. The user-provided part of this log information is entered when you run *cvs commit* or when you set the *-m* command option to *cvs add*.

cvs log is often used to help decide which of two revisions to use to create a patch file, to determine a branch point, or to provide a quick guide to what the other developers are doing in a multiuser environment. Informative log messages are very important for all of these uses.

The options to *cvs log* reduce the amount of information it shows. By default, it displays everything it can. For each file, it displays a header; then, for each revision of the file, it displays the revision number, date, author, state, log message, and number of lines added and deleted in that revision.

Example 5-18 shows a simple use of *cvs log*. Note that the keyword-substitution mode is the default mode, generating both keyword and value, and that the log message in revision 1.1 mentions both files that were added at the time.

Example 5-18. Using cvs log

```
bash-2.05a$ cvs log main.c
RCS file: /var/lib/cvs/wizzard/src/main.c,v
Working file: main.c
head: 1.9
branch:
locks: strict
access list:
symbolic names:
        beta_0-1_branch: 1.9.0.2
        beta_0-1_branch_root: 1.9
        pre_beta_0-1: 1.8
keyword substitution: kv
total revisions: 9;      selected revisions: 9
description:
----------------------------
revision 1.9
date: 2005/09/12 08:14:19;  author: jenn;  state: Exp;  lines: +0 -0
Final test of re-addition methods.
    .
    .
    .
```

Example 5-18. Using cvs log (continued)

```
----------------------------
revision 1.1
date: 2005/09/11 13:33:13;  author: jenn;  state: Exp;
Added main.c: parses parameters and calls functions in other files.
Added wizzard.h: defines compile-time global variables.
==============================
```

The header for each file includes the path to the repository copy of the file, the name of the sandbox (or *working*) file, the revision number of the head revision, the current branch, if any, the lock status, the access list, tag (or *symbolic*) names and revision numbers, any keyword-substitution modes, the number of total revisions for the file, the number of revisions the *log* command is to display, and any description of the file stored in CVS.

The access list and the description are historical and exist because the files are stored in an RCS-based format. CVS relies on strict locking, so the lock status should always be strict. CVS files are created with strict locking; locking can only be set non-strict through the *cvs admin* command or through editing the file directly.

cvs log has the following syntax:

```
cvs [cvs-options] log [command-options] [filenames]
```

If no file, directory, or module names are given, *cvs log* assumes the current sandbox directory as the parameter. The options to *cvs log* differ from the standard options for most other commands.

Most of the options to *cvs log* restrict the revisions for which information is displayed. *cvs log* normally displays only those revisions that match all the options you specify, so as you add options, you tend to reduce the set of revisions for which *cvs log* displays information. For example, if both *-b* and *-r* options are selected, *cvs log* displays only the revisions that match both *-b* and *-r* parameters. If other options are also selected, *cvs log* displays the revisions that match *-b* and *-r* and also fit the other options.

The *-b* option limits the *cvs log* output to the default branch, usually the latest branch off the trunk. *-rrevision-range* restricts the output to the revisions given in the revision range. Chapter 10 provides the syntax to use in specifying the revision range.

The *-w usernames* option limits *cvs log* output to revisions checked in by users in a comma-separated list of usernames. The list of usernames should not include spaces, and there should be no space between the *-w* and the list.

The *-h* and *-t* options limit the amount of information *cvs log* displays with each file. *-h* limits it to the header, and *-t* limits it to the header and the description. Using the *-S* option tells *cvs log* not to display the header of files where at least one revision will be displayed.

Graphic clients can produce extremely helpful and useful displays with the data from CVS log. TkCVS provides a diagram of the tree structure of a file, as shown in Figure 5-5.

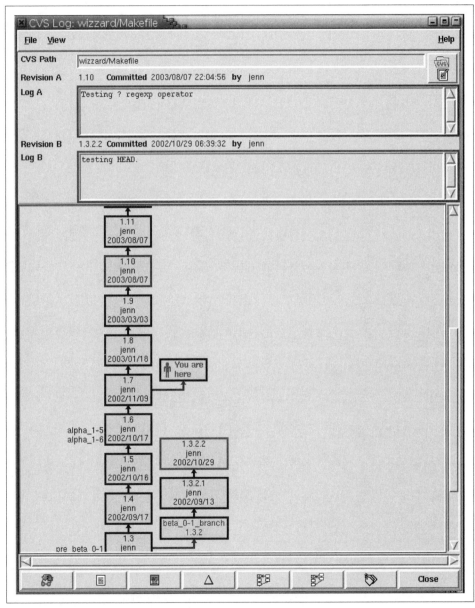

Figure 5-5. Graphic display of log

Chapter 10 provides the full list of options for *cvs log*.

## PART III

CVS Administration

This part of the book is for project managers and repository administrators. The chapters can be read in any order, but later chapters assume familiarity with commands explained in earlier chapters. Part III includes the following chapters:

Chapter 6, *Repository Management*
> This chapter discusses repository management and the modules in the repository. It covers creating a repository and estimating disk space, the structure of the CVS repository, configuration and permissions, repository security, and hand-editing a repository.

Chapter 7, *Project Management*
> This chapter covers the tools used by project administrators. Topics include importing and exporting projects, using the *cvs admin* and *cvs history* commands, and using the *info* configuration files to interact with bug-tracking systems or to enforce log-message formats.

Chapter 8, *Remote Repositories*
> Most projects involve a repository on a different machine from the client. This chapter discusses the security considerations and methods of remote access and how to set up each method.

Chapter 9, *Troubleshooting*
> Every tool has its caveats and gotchas. This chapter provides examples of things that can go wrong when using CVS and how to fix them.

## CHAPTER 6

Repository Management

Topics covered in this chapter include repository creation, configuration, security, backup, and recovery. It also covers the structure of the repository and the sandbox, the file locking that CVS uses internally, how to edit the repository manually, and the CVS administrative files and environment variables. This chapter is about the repository and the projects stored in it. If you want a quick guide to creating an initial repository, see the instructions in Chapter 2.

In this chapter, I assume that the reader is skilled with Unix and/or Linux operating systems. *Running Linux*, by Matthias Kalle Dalheimer and Matt Welsh (O'Reilly), is an excellent introduction to Linux systems. *Learning the Unix Operating System*, by Jerry Peek et al. (O'Reilly), provides information on Unix.

Repository administrators using CVSNT can still use the information in this chapter: I have tried to identify places where I use Unix/Linux-specific terminology, and to provide a generic term as well. There are differences between the CVSNT and the CVS server, so the instructions given here will vary from those for CVSNT.

 CVS on Mac OS X behaves just like it does on Unix and Linux, so Mac users will be able to open a Terminal window and follow the instructions in this chapter.

CVS uses the term *CVSROOT* in two different ways. As the environment variable, it refers to the root directory (topmost folder) of the repository. However, inside the repository is a directory called *CVSROOT*. To avoid confusion, this chapter never refers to the root directory of the repository as *CVSROOT*, and, except when mentioning the environment variable, this chapter uses the term *CVSROOT* solely to refer to the *CVSROOT* subdirectory of the repository root directory.

If your repository is in */var/lib/cvs*, then */var/lib/cvs* is the repository root directory and */var/lib/cvs/CVSROOT* is the repository's *CVSROOT* directory.

Creating a Repository

The repository root directory and the administrative files should be owned by a user made specifically for CVS; typically, the user is named *cvs*. This system reduces the damage a malicious or careless user can do to the repository, as long as she doesn't have *root* (superuser) access.

To create a repository, create the directory that you want to use as the repository root directory on the computer that will act as the CVS server and ensure that the repository root directory is owned by the user who will ultimately own the repository. A recommended repository root directory is */var/lib/cvsroot*.

Execute the command `cvs -d repository_root_directory init,` where `repository_root_directory` is the name of your directory: this command sets up that directory as a CVS repository. The root directory given must be an absolute path, not a relative path. Example 2-5 (in Chapter 2) shows repository creation.

The *cvs init* command sets up the directory as a CVS repository by creating the *CVSROOT* subdirectory and the initial files for *CVSROOT*, with their default configurations.

A repository may hold many projects, so to determine how much space you need to allow for your repository, you need to calculate the space for each project. The repository itself will have a small amount of overhead: I allow 500 K for a small repository, and a megabyte or two for most commercial repositories.

For any project, ensure enough room on the partition for three times the expected final size of the project. If you intend to store binary files, multiply their expected size by at least five. Monitor the repository's partition; your users may have a use pattern that requires more or less space than this.

For most projects, the amount of RAM on the repository server is not an issue. CVS is usually modest in its memory requirements, and a server with 256 MB of RAM can handle most repositories. The two major areas of memory use are large *checkout*s and large *diff*s.

For each *checkout* request from a client, CVS spawns two processes. The smaller process uses a negligible amount of memory, but the larger consumes at least 2 MB and can grow to just over the size of the files in the directory being checked out. Fortunately, the larger process can use swap space rather than physical memory. Allow enough memory for several of these processes to run simultaneously, and base your calculations on the project directory that occupies the most disk space.

The *diff* process can also use swap space and runs at each commit. For efficient processing, allow enough swap space or physical memory to store ten times the size of the largest file you expect to commit. If memory is a problem, allow five times the size of the largest file. The *diff* process is fairly fast, so there is rarely need to allow for simultaneous processes.

The repository is user data, and it should be on a partition that is backed up and that won't shut down the machine if it is filled. I recommend */var/lib/*, as it is the most appropriate in the Filesystem Hierarchy Standard.

Ensure that the repository is on a machine accessible to everyone who needs to use the repository. The repository can be local to a user, or it can be accessed remotely across a network. Remote access methods are explained in Chapter 8.

Deleting a Repository

A CVS repository that is no longer needed can be removed as you would remove a normal directory tree. All the information CVS stores about the repository and the projects in it are stored within the repository tree, most of it in the *CVSROOT* subdirectory of that repository.

If you have edited the scripting files in the *CVSROOT* directory, they may refer to scripts stored elsewhere. Check the scripting files; if the referenced scripts are no longer needed, they can also be removed.

Once you have backed up any projects you may need to refer to later, remove the repository with *rm -rf repository_root_directory*.

Securing Your Projects

The security of your projects relies on the security of your CVS repository, the repository's computer and its environment, all the computers that contain sandboxes, your access method, your backup storage, and your developers' working environments. The security of access methods is covered in Chapter 8. General computer security is outside the scope of this book, but you should consider it when securing your repository.

Both sandbox and repository security is based on the filesystem security for the operating system that the repository is running under. The specific instructions in this section are based on traditional Unix and Linux filesystem permissions, but the principles can also be used to secure a repository running under systems with more extensive security options, such as Access Control Lists (ACLs).

CVS 1.12.2 introduced experimental support for PAM (Pluggable Authentication Modules). PAM allows system administrators to configure their choice of authentication and other security measures, rather than accepting the range of measures implemented in the application. I discuss this further in Chapter 8.

CVS's PAM support is under active development. The information in this book is correct for CVS 1.12.13, but you can expect changes if your version is later than that.

I strongly encourage you to provide feedback about PAM and CVS. The appropriate forums for this feedback are the mailing lists *info-cvs@nongnu.org* and *bug-cvs@nongnu.org*.

Sandboxes

Sandbox security relies on the security features installed in the filesystem that the sandbox is stored on. CVS expects to find separate user and group ownership, and separate read, write, and execute permissions for files. Fortunately, these features are available in all the systems for which CVS clients are available. Sandboxes are checked out of the repository with the username of the user who creates them (with *cvs checkout*). If the client's computer has a group that matches the group ownership of files in the repository, files in the sandbox are stored with that group ownership.

Read and write permissions in a sandbox depend on the settings for new files in the sandbox computer's operating system, on whether the user has the *CVSREAD* environment variable set, and on whether the files are being watched with the *cvs watch* commands. The *CVSREAD* environment variable is described in "Client Environment Variables," later in this chapter.

If a file is imported or added as executable, it is set as executable in the repository and the executable setting is preserved in the sandboxes.

If your project must be kept secure, ensure that the computers that the sandboxes are on are kept secure. Keep an eye on the location of any printouts your developers make, and any copies they may make outside their sandboxes. Remember that you need to track the data, not just the CVS files.

Repository Root Directory

Secure the repository root directory so that only the CVS owner and users who are allowed to create new projects have write access to this directory. Users who will be using existing repository projects, even though they may be creating and writing to project files, should have read access to this directory.

Securing the repository root directory usually involves creating a group for the users with the right to import projects, setting the repository root directory read-write-execute for the repository's owner and that group, and setting it read-execute for all others. It's fairly typical for write access to the repository root to be limited to the system administrator and her assistants, or to the CVS repository administrator if that person is different from the system administrator.

You may also want to set the Set Group ID (SGID) bit on the repository root directory to ensure that all projects are imported with a reasonably secure group. You'll see how to do this in the upcoming section "Project Directories."

In many cases, people who can create projects can also be trusted with the *CVSROOT* subdirectory, so you can set that directory read-write for those same users. Be aware, however, that these people will have access to scripts that will run arbitrary commands when CVS users check in files. See the following section for more information on the *CVSROOT* directory.

Example 6-1 shows a small repository and the permissions and groups set for it. The user *cvs* is the owner of the repository, and the group *cvs* is the group for people who can create new projects. The user *doppel* created the *wowow* project for the people in the group *sauce*, and the user *jenn* created the *wizzard* project for those in the group *wizzard*.

Example 6-1. Repository permissions

```
/var/lib/cvs$ ls -la
drwxrwsr-x   39 cvs      cvs       4096 Sep 17 22:52 .
drwxrwsr-x   41 root     staff     4096 Sep 17 23:07 ..
drwxrwsr-x    4 cvs      cvs       4096 Sep 17 23:30 CVSROOT
drwxrwsr-x    4 doppel   sauce     4096 Aug 17 12:08 wowow
drwxrwsr-x    4 jenn     wizzard   4096 Sep 24 20:14 wizzard
```

CVSROOT Directory

The permissions on the *CVSROOT* directory in the repository should be considered carefully. A user who can modify the files in this directory may be able to cause CVS to run arbitrary commands on the repository computer. These files are the *scripting files* explained in Chapter 7; they're run as the user who commits a file to CVS, and they can run any command or script. Only trusted users should have write access to this directory or most of the files in this directory.

All users who will have access to CVS should have read access to all the files in the *CVSROOT* directory.

Two files should be writable (as well as readable) to all users who will be running CVS commands: the *history* file and the *val-tags* file. If the *history* file exists, most CVS commands attempt to append to it, and fail if they can't. Many commands attempt to modify *val-tags*. Neither of these files trigger scripts or arbitrary commands; both are purely informational.

Project Directories

CVS allows you to have any number of projects in the same repository, and each project can be secured separately. Create a group for each project, and add the users who should be changing project files to that group.

It's good practice to give each project its own group, even if two projects have the same development team when the projects are created. Over the lifetime of the projects, their teams may diverge.

> If you want to split off a directory from an old project into a new project, perhaps because what seemed like a small issue has become a large one, you can do so. See "Moving Files and Directories" later in this chapter.

Group ownership of project files and directories controls project security. Ensure that each project is group-owned by a group with appropriate membership, and set the group permissions for the project files to the project's group. Also set the SGID bit, as described earlier in "Repository Root Directory."

You have only directory-level control over the security of project files. CVS sets the permissions of files stored in the repository and overwrites any read or write permissions you set when it next changes the files. When a file is changed, CVS writes a temporary version of the file, then copies the temporary file over the original file. The resulting file is owned by the person who last changed it. The group of users who change the files in a project repository must have read, write, and execute access to the project directories. Because files are overwritten when changed (during the commit process), a user changing a file needs write permission to the directory the file is in, but not to the file itself.

Users reading project files must have read and execute access to the project directories and write access to the location of the project's locks—usually the project's directories. The *LockDir* option in the *config* file in the repository's *CVSROOT* directory can change the location of the lock files if you want to avoid giving out write permission to the repository's project directories.

> Read-only, anonymous access to a CVS repository can be done in two ways:
>
> - The recommended way is to use your operating system's security mechanisms. Create an account with no password and ensure that it can run only CVS. Give that account read access to the projects you want it to access, and give the account both read and write access to the directory tree listed in *LockDir*.
> - The other way is explained in Chapter 8. It uses the *pserver* access method with no password and relies on a permissions system internal to CVS.

To ensure that group ownership is set correctly, have your project directories automatically create the correct group permissions for new files. To do this, set each directory's SGID bit: this tells the operating system to set the group ID for new files or directories to the group ID of the directory they are created in. Use the command *chmod g+s directory* to set the SGID bit. The directories in Example 6-1 have their SGID bits set.

If a file is executable when it is imported or added, CVS sets it to executable in the repository. The executable bit in the repository copy of the file is preserved when the file is checked out to the sandbox. If a file should be executable but isn't, or shouldn't be but is, change the setting in the repository with *chmod*.

When you change the settings on a file in the repository, the file permissions of existing files in existing sandboxes are unaffected. To correct the sandbox permissions, delete the file from the sandbox and then retrieve a new copy with *cvs update*.

Committing a file with sandbox permissions that differ from the repository permissions does not affect the permissions in the repository version. Repository files acquire sandbox file permissions only during an *add*.

General Information on Security

If you need to set project file permissions differently from your usual file permissions, you can use the *CVSUMASK* environment variable, which specifies a *umask* setting for CVS to use. The CVS process on the repository server reads the calling user's *CVSUMASK* and, if this variable is present, uses the *umask* to set the permissions of any files or directories the CVS process creates. The format of *CVSUMASK* is the same as the Unix and Linux shell setting *umask*.

A *umask* is a "user file creation mode mask." It's an octal number that is used to set the file permissions of newly created files. The file permissions are determined by doing a bitwise exclusive *OR* operation between the *umask* and the octal number 777. The result is the octal form of the file permission.

For more information, see either of the Unix/Linux books recommended at the start of this chapter, or any book with a good section on Unix or Linux file security.

CVS normally uses the project's repository directories for lock files. Consider designating an alternate directory by using the *LockDir* setting in the *config* file in the repository's *CVSROOT* directory. This setting allows you to restrict users from writing to the project directories. If you use *LockDir*, remember to modify any scripts that you are using to freeze the repository (see "Freezing a Repository," later in this chapter). Also, when you need to remove a lock manually, be sure to look in the *LockDir* directory. Changing the lock directory is rarely needed, but you should be aware that it is possible.

If you want to use *setuid*, *setgid*, or similar ownership-changing systems, be aware that CVS is not designed to prevent a determined user from escaping from CVS and gaining access to the shell.

Repository Structure

A CVS repository is composed of the project directories, and the special *CVSROOT* administrative directory. All the general CVS administrative files and configuration files are kept in *CVSROOT*. Most of the project-specific CVS administrative files are kept in *CVSROOT* as well, but there are exceptions, which are detailed next.

The project directories contain the project's files and subdirectories. The project's files are stored in RCS format and have a *,v* file suffix.

Any project directory or subdirectory may contain *Attic* or *CVS* directories. An *Attic* subdirectory stores any file from the directory it's part of that doesn't exist on the trunk (the main development line for the file). A *CVS* subdirectory stores metadata for the files in its directory.

The server also stores files in a temporary directory set by either the *TMPDIR* environment variable or the *-T* command-line option. These files are under a directory called *cvs-serverPID*, where *PID* is the process ID of the server. If the server is shut down and unable to clean up after itself, the files may be left in place. They can be removed safely if there is no CVS process running with the relevant process ID.

Attic Subdirectory

The *Attic* subdirectory stores files that have been removed from the trunk (the main line of development), or that were never added to the trunk. If a file exists on only one or more branches, it is kept in the *Attic*. Each *Attic* subdirectory contains files that are related to the directory the *Attic* is in.

CVS manages the *Attic* itself—you need to be conscious of it only on the rare occasions when you are editing the repository directly.

CVS Subdirectory

The repository contains CVS subdirectories, which contain the file *fileattr*, which lists the file attributes of the files in the parent directory. The file attributes are settings for the *cvs watch* commands. In later versions of CVS, the *fileattr* file may be used for other attributes or the *CVS* subdirectory may be used for other files.

The format for *fileattr* is one line per attribute, each line containing information as follows:

```
entry-type filename (tab) attribute-name = attribute-value
    [;attribute-name = attribute-value...]
```

Attribute names starting with an underscore (_) are reserved for CVS. Future versions of CVS may allow user-defined attributes, but they're not currently permitted.

The *F* entry type specifies that a line contains attributes for a file. The *D* entry type with no filename specifies that the line contains default attributes for all files in the directory that includes the *CVS* subdirectory.

These are the supported attributes:

_watched
> Indicates that the file is being watched and should be checked out read only.

_watchers
> Lists the users watching the file. The value is in the form:
>
>   watcher > type [, watcher > type...]
>
> *watcher* is a username; *type* is *edit*, *unedit*, *commit*, or some combination of those keywords, separated by plus symbols (+). The *tedit*, *tunedit*, and *tcommit* types refer to the temporary watches created by the *cvs edit* command.

_editors
> Lists the users editing the file. The value is in the form:
>
>   editor > value [, editor > value...]
>
> *editor* is a username and *value* is *time+hostname+pathname*, where *time* indicates when the *cvs edit* command was run and *hostname* and *pathname* specify the sandbox from which the command was run.

Example 6-2 shows a *fileattr* file.

Example 6-2. CVS/fileattr

```
Fconfig.h   _watchers=doppel>edit+unedit+commit;_watched=
Fhandheld.c _watchers=doppel>edit+unedit+commit;_watched=
Fmain.c     _watchers=doppel>edit+unedit+commit,jenn>
edit+unedit+commit+tedit+tunedit+tcommit;_watched=;_editors=jenn>Fri Sep 27 19:15:18 2002
GMT+helit+/home/jenn/cvs/wizzard/src
Fserver.c   _watchers=doppel>edit+unedit+commit;_watched=
D           _watchers=doppel>edit+unedit+commit
```

Locks

CVS uses read and write locks to prevent processes from simultaneously writing to or reading from the same repository files. These locks are signaled by the presence of a file or directory with a specific name pattern in project directories. Most CVS users never need to know about these locks; the only time end users will notice the locks is when two people try to commit to the same directory simultaneously, or when a CVS process crashes and leaves a spurious lock file. However, information on CVS's locks is useful to repository administrators who may want to lock a repository when backing the repository up, or may want to write software to interact with the repository.

The instructions for clearing a lock caused by a CVS process that crashed are in the "Editing a Repository" section, later in this chapter.

CVS locks the repository one directory at a time, each lock locking a directory, its *Attic* and *CVS* subdirectories, and all files in that directory. A lock does not lock subdirectories, so to lock an entire directory tree, each subdirectory must be locked individually.

 Because CVS locks the repository one directory at a time, it is possible to check out a sandbox that constitutes part of another user's committed sandbox. This happens when user A's process locks the *foo* subdirectory and commits to it while user B's process locks the *bar* subdirectory and updates from it, then user A commits to the *bar* subdirectory while user B updates from *foo*, which now contains A's changes. In actual practice, this scenario rarely causes problems.

These are the file and directory names that indicate CVS locks:

#cvs.lock
> The presence of this directory in any repository directory indicates that a process holds the master lock in the current directory.

#cvs.rfl or *#cvs.rfl.**
> The presence of a file with this name or name pattern in a repository directory indicates that a process holds a read lock in the current directory.

#cvs.wfl or *#cvs.wfl.**
> The presence of a file with this name or name pattern in a repository directory indicates that a process holds a write lock in the current directory.

Holding a master lock prohibits programs (such as the freeze script shown later) that honor such locks from creating new locks in the locked directory. Any program that honors the locks will not read from or write to a file unless it has locked the directory the file is in. Master locks are directories, because in most operating systems, directory creation is done as a single operation and can't be interrupted by another process.

A read lock is a nonexclusive lock, which permits others to read files while the directory is locked but not to write to them. You create a master lock before you create a read lock, to ensure that no one else locks the directory while you are trying to lock it. You can release the master lock once you have your read lock, to allow others to read the files as well.

To obtain a read lock:

1. Create the *#cvs.lock* directory in the directory that you wish to lock. In most operating systems, directory creation is an atomic process. Check the response code for the directory-creation command; if it fails because the directory already exists, try again later.

2. Once you have the master lock, create *#cvs.rfl* or *#cvs.rfl.extension* in the *#cvs.lock* directory. *extension* is any data you wish to add and is often a process ID. Remove the *#cvs.lock* directory to release the master lock.

3. When you are finished reading in the *#cvs.lock* directory, you must remove the *#cvs.rfl* file to release the read lock.

A write lock is an exclusive lock, which prohibits others from reading or writing the files while you hold the lock. CVS prohibits reading or writing by having processes that use a write lock also hold the master lock until after they release the write lock. The write-lock file exists primarily to provide the process ID, so that you can identify which process is holding the lock if you need to clear it.

To obtain a write lock:

1. Obtain the master lock in the same way that you obtain a read lock.

2. Check for the presence of a read lock by looking for a *#cvs.rfl* or *#cvs.rfl.** file. If there is a read lock, release the master lock, wait, and try again.

3. Once you have a master lock on a directory with no read lock, create a write lock by creating a *#cvs.wfl* or *#cvs.wfl.extension* file in the target directory, where the *extension* may be a process ID or other identifier. Retain the master lock.

4. When you are finished writing to the repository, release the write lock first. Then release the master lock.

If you are trying to lock multiple directories simultaneously and you encounter an existing lock, you should release all the locks you have obtained before waiting and trying again. This approach helps avoid deadlocks.

A deadlock occurs when two processes attempt to lock multiple directories and each is holding one directory locked while attempting to lock a directory that the other is holding. Such a deadlock prevents either process from continuing.

CVSROOT Files

The *CVSROOT* directory contains administrative files that contain information about the projects stored in CVS. The *CVSROOT* directory can be checked out to a sandbox, edited, and committed in the same way as any other directories or files managed by CVS.

As part of the process of committing an administrative file, CVS exports a clear-text copy into the *CVSROOT* directory. The *CVSROOT* directory contains both RCS-format repository copies of administrative files and clear-text copies of the latest revision of the files. The RCS-format files are named `filename,v`. While CVS is creating the clear-text copies, it prints the message *cvs commit: Rebuilding administrative file database*.

Some of the files in *CVSROOT* allow you to run user-created scripts during the execution of CVS commands. Therefore, it's important to restrict the number of people authorized to commit or edit files in the *CVSROOT* directory.

It's good practice to have a specific user be the owner of the *CVSROOT* directory and the repository root directory, and for this user to also be the initial owner of the *CVSROOT* files. This practice restricts the amount of damage that can be done to these files by a malicious or careless user, unless she happens to have *root* permissions.

Create a group to have the group ownership of the *CVSROOT* directory and files, and include only trusted people in that group. If this group should be permitted to create new projects, and consists of all the people who can, it can also own the repository root directory. The *CVSROOT* directory and most of the files should be writable only by the repository's owner and the group, but they must be readable by all users who will be running CVS commands. The directory's SGID bit should be set, to ensure that new files are created with the same group ownership as the directory.

Two files in the *CVSROOT* directory should be writable by all the users who will be using the CVS commands: the *history* and *val-tags* files. These files may have a different group ownership than the rest of the files in this directory.

Example 6-3 shows a CVSROOT directory and its permissions. The initial owner of the files is *cvsown*, the group with write permissions to the directory is *cvsgrp*. The *cvsusrs* group consists of those authorized to use CVS, but not to modify the repository administrative files.

We have this directory locked down fairly tightly—the only writable files are *history* and *val-tags*, and those are only writable by the members of *cvsusrs*. The other files (except for *passwd*) can be read by anyone, and checked out by anyone, but only those in *cvsgrp* can commit to them. (Note that write access to the directory is sufficient to permit committing.) We could improve security by further restricting read access to the files.

Files with a *,v* extension are the RCS format repository copies; the ones without are the clear-text versions that CVS reads. The *passwd* file is normally edited in place rather than checked out, and in this case has never been used.

Example 6-3. CVSROOT permissions

```
/home/cvs/CVSROOT$ ls -la
drwxrwsr-x    4 cvsown    cvsgrp  4096 2006-08-08 04:13 .
drwxrwsr-x   63 cvsown    cvsgrp  4096 2006-08-05 09:02 ..
-r--r--r--    1 cvsown    cvsgrp   495 2006-05-13 22:02 checkoutlist
-r--r--r--    1 cvsown    cvsgrp   695 2006-05-13 22:02 checkoutlist,v
-r--r--r--    1 cvsown    cvsgrp    35 2003-08-07 22:36 commitinfo
-r--r--r--    1 cvsown    cvsgrp  1308 2006-05-13 22:02 commitinfo,v
-r--r--r--    1 cvsown    cvsgrp    15 2002-10-16 23:49 config
-r--r--r--    1 cvsown    cvsgrp  1902 2006-05-13 22:02 config,v
-r--r--r--    1 cvsown    cvsgrp   602 2006-05-13 22:02 cvswrappers
-r--r--r--    1 cvsown    cvsgrp   802 2006-05-13 22:02 cvswrappers,v
-rw-rw-r--    1 cvsown    cvsusrs 34507 2006-08-08 05:25 history
-r--r--r--    1 cvsown    cvsgrp   403 2001-09-26 01:00 loginfo
-r--r--r--    1 cvsown    cvsgrp  2139 2001-09-26 01:00 loginfo,v
-r--r--r--    1 cvsown    cvsgrp   587 2003-01-26 06:46 modules
-r--r--r--    1 cvsown    cvsgrp  1351 2006-05-13 22:02 modules,v
-r--r--r--    1 cvsown    cvsgrp   752 2006-05-13 22:02 notify
-r--r--r--    1 cvsown    cvsgrp   952 2006-05-13 22:02 notify,v
-r--r-----    1 cvsown    cvsgrp     0 2002-10-17 00:08 passwd
-r--r--r--    1 cvsown    cvsgrp   649 2006-05-13 22:02 rcsinfo
-r--r--r--    1 cvsown    cvsgrp   849 2006-05-13 22:02 rcsinfo,v
-r--r--r--    1 cvsown    cvsgrp  2096 2006-05-13 22:02 taginfo
-r--r--r--    1 cvsown    cvsgrp  2296 2006-05-13 22:02 taginfo,v
-rw-rw-r--    1 cvsown    cvsusrs   114 2002-09-13 07:30 val-tags
-r--r--r--    1 cvsown    cvsgrp  1357 2006-05-13 22:02 verifymsg
-r--r--r--    1 cvsown    cvsgrp  1557 2006-05-13 22:02 verifymsg,v
```

It is possible to commit an administrative file that has settings that prevent CVS from committing anything else. If this happens, you can edit the clear-text repository copy of the file directly to enable CVS to commit again. To ensure that your version-controlled copy matches with the hand-edited copy, overwrite your sandbox copy with the corrected, hand-edited copy and commit the sandbox again.

Configuration Files

The files described in the next few subsections allow you to modify CVS's behavior. Three of these files are explained in more detail in chapters about the tasks the files are associated with, but the *config* file is fully explained here.

config

The *config* file contains CVS configuration options. Lines that start with a # are comments. Other lines are in the form *keyword=value*, one pair per line. Whitespace is significant, including carriage returns, tabs, and extra spaces.

These are the most useful of the configuration options:

ImportNewFilesToVendorBranchOnly
> This option is a repository-wide version of the *-X* command option to *cvs import*: during an import, new files are added only to the vendor branch, and not to the trunk. Chapter 7 explains vendor branches.

KeywordExpand=value
> This option controls which keywords may be expanded. It affects all files in all projects in the repository it's configured in. The value is in the format *i|e[keyword list]*, where *keyword list* is a comma-separated list of keywords. The keywords may be any of the standard CVS keywords, or any local keyword as defined in the *LocalKeyword* configuration option (see the following entry).

> If the first character is *i*, the keywords in the list will be the only keywords which CVS expands. If the first character is *e*, the keywords in the list will not be expanded. A typical entry might be *KeywordExpand=Author, Id, Locker*, which would limit expansion to the Author, ID, and Locker keywords.

LocalKeyword=value=keyword.
> This option creates a keyword that is local to the current repository, which is an alias for one of the existing keywords. For example, you could use *LocalKeyword=Filename=RCSfile*, which would mean you could use *$Filename$* instead of *$RCSfile$* as the keyword that generates the name of the current file. (Or *Path=Source* to get the full path from the repository root.)

LockDir=directory
> This option is available only in CVS versions 1.10.2 and later. If this setting is enabled, CVS puts lock files in the nominated *directory* rather than in the repository. This option allows you to set the repository directories to read only for people who should not be committing changes.

> You need to create *directory*, but CVS creates all of the necessary subdirectories itself.

> Do not use *LockDir* if any of your users are running CVS 1.9 or earlier and accessing a local repository, as users will then be putting locks in two different places and not honoring each other's locks. CVS 1.10 doesn't use *LockDir*; it displays an error and does not work. Versions prior to 1.10 ignore *LockDir* silently.

LogHistory=value
> The text in *value* controls which actions are logged to the *history* file in the repository's *CVSROOT* directory. The valid values are any combination of the following letters:

> A   Log when a file is added to the repository.

> C   Log when a file would have been updated in a sandbox, but needed to be merged and there were conflicts in the merge.

E   Log when a file or files are exported.

F   Log when a file or files are released.

G   Log when a file is updated in a sandbox with a successful merge.

M   Log when a file is modified (a sandbox revision is added to the repository).

O   Log when a file or files are checked out.

P   Log when a file is patched.

R   Log when a file is removed from the repository.

T   Log when a file or files are tagged or rtagged.

U   Log when a file is updated in a sandbox with no merge required.

W   Log when a file is deleted from a sandbox during an update because it is no longer active in the repository.

RereadLogAfterVerify=value

This option is useful only if the *verifymsg* file in the repository's *CVSROOT* directory is in use. It applies to CVS versions 1.11.2 and later.

The log message saved during *cvs commit* might be changed if the *verifymsg* file is in use. This option controls whether the message is reread after the program listed in *verifymsg* file is run.

These are the available options:

always or *yes*

Reread the log message after the *verifymsg* file has been processed. This is the default case.

never or *no*

Do not reread the log message after the *verifymsg* file has been processed.

stat

Check whether the log message has been changed, using the filesystem's *stat( )* command. If the log message has changed, reread it. This option can take up to an extra second per directory to process.

SystemAuth=value

This option is useful only if the client connects to CVS in *pserver* mode. It applies to CVS versions 1.9.14 and later.

If *value* is *yes*, the server authenticates the connecting user with the *passwd* file in the repository's *CVSROOT* directory. If the user fails to authenticate there, the server authenticates the user against the main user database for the operating system.

If *value* is *no*, the server authenticates the user only against the *passwd* file.

The default value is *yes*. Consider setting the value to *no* if you run *pserver*, as the *pserver* access mode transmits passwords with minimal security. See Chapter 8 for more information.

TopLevelAdmin=value

> If *value* is *yes*, a *CVS* subdirectory is created in the current working directory when you check out a sandbox.
>
> If *value* is *no*, the *CVS* subdirectories are created only in the actual sandbox directory tree. The default is *no*.
>
> The *yes* setting is useful if you run CVS commands in the working directory above your sandboxes. The *CVS* subdirectory contains a *Root* file, so you don't need to specify the *-d repository* option to CVS commands. If you use other *CVS* subdirectory files (such as *Template*), they will also be stored in the *CVS* subdirectory.
>
> If your repository is for public use, you should probably keep this option set to *no*. Your end users may want to have sandboxes from various different repositories in the same directory, and a CVS subdirectory in that directory may cause unexpected effects (such as *CVS/Root* overriding the *CVSROOT* environment variable).
>
> *TopLevelAdmin* is valid in CVS 1.9.29 and later.

UserAdminOptions=value

> This option is available in CVS 1.12.1 and later. If *value* exists, then any user can run *cvs admin* options listed in *value*. The contents of *value* must be a string of letters with no separators or spaces, and the letters must be the command options (without parameters) for *cvs admin*.
>
> If the *cvsadmin* group exists on the server machine, then only members of the *cvsadmin* group are allowed to run commands not listed in *value*.

Example 6-4 shows a configuration file (with all comments removed).

Example 6-4. CVSROOT/config

```
SystemAuth=no
LockDir=/var/lock/cvs
LogHistory=TMAR
RereadLogAfterVerify=stat
```

cvswrappers

The *cvswrappers* file contains a line-separated list of wrappers that control the merge method or keyword-substitution mode of files, based on a filename pattern. Wrappers are explained in Chapter 3.

There are two additional functions for wrappers. These are not available in CVS 1.11.5, so check the documentation for your version before relying on them. They are:

-f path_to_filter

> Process the file through the specified filter program every time the file leaves the repository.

-t path_to_filter

> Process the file through the specified filter program every time the file enters the repository.

modules

The *modules* file contains information about projects in the repository and can group arbitrary files or directories into a single module. Information in this file must be created by the repository or project administrator; CVS does not update this file when a new project is imported.

Once a module is defined, the project files and directories it defines can be checked out into a sandbox using either the module name or the name of the repository directory it represents. A module can represent a directory and all its files and subdirectories, a file, or any collection of such files or directories. Directories can also be excluded from a module explicitly.

Module definitions are useful for splitting a project into several virtual projects, especially when you need to have several projects that share common files. You can also use module definitions to merge projects into a single virtual project.

If you intend to use modules for project organization, be aware that modules are not versioned. If you change the structure of the project, you may not be able to retrieve old releases with the module names in effect at the time those releases were current.

For example, if you create an *animal* project with *elephant* and *turtle* subprojects, then later change the name of *turtle* to *tortoise*, there is no way to record that versions of the project prior to the change use *turtle* and versions after the change use *tortoise*.

The *modules* file can also specify programs to run when files in the module are committed, exported, updated, checked out, or tagged with *rtag*. These programs can be used to integrate CVS with bug trackers or other project-management or program-development tools. The developers of CVS recommend that you use the scripting files rather than the options in the *modules* file.

Use the files described in "Scripting Files," later in this chapter, to define programs to run during the operation of certain commands.

Chapter 7 explains the *modules* file in detail.

notify

The *notify* file contains the commands to run when conditions exist for *cvs watch* to notify a user of a change to a watched file. Chapter 5 explains uses for the *notify* file and provides an example of its use (see Example 5-1).

The syntax of the *notify* file is a series of lines, each line appearing as follows:

```
filename-pattern command
```

The filename pattern can be *ALL* or it can be any CVS standard pattern, as used in *cvsignore* and *cvswrappers* and explained in Chapter 11. The command can be any *sh* shell command, but it must contain a *%s*, which is replaced by the name of the user to notify. The rest of the notification information is provided to the command through standard input—*stdin*, in Unix or Linux.

CVS does not notify you of your own changes to a file.

Scripting Files

The files described in this section control scripts that run at specific times when the repository is modified. They can be used to interface CVS to bug-management or change-tracking systems, integrated development environments, or other tools; to enforce compliance with a project policy; or to trigger processes such as automated export programs to keep an up-to-date copy of the project files on a file server.

If you allow a Perl script to be run from these scripting files, ensure that *taint-checking* is enabled. You do this with the -*T* option in the #! line of the script, e.g., *#!/usr/local/bin/perl -T*. (In Perl 4, use *taintperl* instead: *#!/usr/local/bin/taintperl*.)

Read *perldoc perlsec* for more information on Perl security.

These files usually are configured on a per-project basis, so Chapter 7 explains them in detail. This chapter provides only a basic summary. The syntax of the files changed in CVS 1.12.6, and new files were added in 1.12.10.

In the old format, the syntax is a series of lines, each containing information in the following pattern:

```
name_pattern action
```

The *name_pattern* specifies which files the action is run for and may include the project's root directory. The action is used to specify programs, and the programs defined in these files are passed the results or parameters of CVS commands, either as parameters or via standard input.

The new format is explained in Chapter 7.

commitinfo

The *commitinfo* file indicates programs to run while a commit is being processed, before the file is written to the repository. Typical uses include determining whether a file meets your project's coding standards or whether a system configuration file has the correct syntax. If any of the programs exit with a nonzero exit status, the commit will not proceed.

editinfo

The *editinfo* file is obsolete and has been replaced effectively by *verifymsg* and *rcsinfo*. It has been removed as of CVS 1.12.2.

In CVS versions that use *editinfo*, the file enforces the use of a specific editor when entering log messages. If CVS is called from a remote client or if the *-m* or *-F* command options are used with *cvs commit*, the *editinfo* file is not used. If the editor exits with a nonzero exit status, the commit will not proceed.

loginfo

The *loginfo* file defines programs to run when a file has been committed successfully. The *loginfo* file is intended as a way to record log messages to specific places, such as a *ChangeLog* generation program, but is often used to trigger automated export programs.

postadmin

The *postadmin* file was added in CVS 1.12.10. It specifies scripts to be run immediately after any *cvs admin* command which changes one or more project files.

postproxy

The *postproxy* file was added in CVS 1.12.10. It specifies scripts to be run immediately after a secondary server has connected to a primary server, before the secondary server permits the client to use the connection.

Of all the scripting files, this and *preproxy* are most likely to be of interest to a repository administrator. See Chapter 7 for detailed information on this file.

posttag

The *posttag* file was added in CVS 1.12.10. It specifies scripts to be run immediately after any *cvs tag* or *rtag* command that changes one or more project files.

postwatch

The *postwatch* file was added in CVS 1.12.10. It specifies scripts to be run immediately after any *cvs edit*, *unedit*, or *watch* command that changes the CVS watch administration file (*fileattr*).

preproxy

The *preproxy* file was added in CVS 1.12.10. It specifies scripts to be run before a secondary server has connected to a primary server, after the client has requested the connection.

Of all the scripting files, this and *postproxy* are most likely to be of interest to a repository administrator. See Chapter 7 for detailed information on this file.

rcsinfo

The *rcsinfo* file does not actually trigger any scripts, but it uses the same syntax as the scripting files. It specifies forms to be displayed as the template for commit log messages.

taginfo

The *taginfo* file specifies programs to run before a file is tagged. Typical uses include determining whether tag names meet your project's standards, and logging tags. If any of the programs exit with a nonzero exit status, the tag will not proceed.

verifymsg

The *verifymsg* file specifies programs to run after a log message for a commit has been entered but before the commit takes place. The programs are passed the log message and can modify it or parse it to ensure that all essential fields have been filled in. The *verifymsg* file usually is used in tandem with the *rcsinfo* file to manage log messages, and sometimes to interact with bug-tracking programs. If any of the programs exit with a nonzero error status, the commit is aborted.

Informational Files

The files in this section contain information that CVS refers to when processing commands. You can set the information for most of these files, but *history* and *val-tags* should be written to only by CVS.

checkoutlist

The *checkoutlist* file contains a list of user-defined files stored in the *CVSROOT* directory and exported into that directory when they're committed, in the same way that the standard administrative files are. This can be a useful way to store user-defined scripts for the other administrative files.

The file format is simply a list of the names of the files, one file per line. Paths are not needed; all files must belong in the *CVSROOT* directory. Example 6-5 shows a *checkoutlist* file.

Example 6-5. CVSROOT/checkoutlist

```
passwd
wiz_bugzilla
```

cvsignore

The *cvsignore* file contains a list of filenames or filename patterns indicating files that CVS should not attempt to store in the repository. These files are also ignored when CVS displays informational messages, such as during *update*, *commit*, or *status* commands. The syntax for this file is a space-separated or line-ending-separated list of filenames or name patterns. Example 6-6 shows a *cvsignore* file.

Example 6-6. CVSROOT/cvsignore

```
*~ ignoreme ChangeLog
test.prog testing* a?out
```

In any of the lists of filenames to be ignored, the special filename *!* causes CVS to clear the ignore list. While creating its ignore list, if CVS encounters a *!* in a list of patterns to be ignored, it clears the list it has created to that point and starts a new ignore list with the next filename pattern it encounters.

> The *!* makes sense when you understand how CVS builds up its complete ignore list. I describe that process shortly.

The special filename *** causes CVS to ignore everything. *cvsignore* uses the standard CVS pattern matching explained in Chapter 11.

The *cvsignore* file is space-separated, so it is difficult to ignore filenames that include spaces. You can attempt to work around this problem using the pattern-match syntax *foo?bar*, but that not only matches the file *foo bar*, it also matches *fooxbar* and *foombar*. Unfortunately, there is no perfect solution for ignoring filenames that contain spaces.

CVS includes a default list of filenames and filename patterns that are either CVS special files or common files that users don't want to store, such as C object code files. The default list is coded into the CVS source code:

```
. .. core RCSLOG tags TAGS RCS SCCS .make.state
.nse_depinfo #* .#* cvslog.* ,* CVS CVS.adm .del-* *.a *.olb *.o *.obj
*.so *.Z *~ *.old *.elc *.ln *.bak *.BAK *.orig *.rej *.exe _$* *$
```

There are many places where you can specify files for CVS to ignore. Not only can you have a *cvsignore* file in your repository's *CVSROOT* directory, but all CVS users can also have their own *.cvsignore* (note the dot) files in their home directories or in subdirectories in a sandbox. Files to ignore can also be specified via environment variables and command-line options. CVS generates the list of files to ignore in the following sequence:

1. Create the ignore list with the default filenames and filename patterns.

2. Add the entries from *cvsignore* in the repository's *CVSROOT* directory.

3. Add the entries from *.cvsignore* in the user's home directory. (The *.cvsignore* file is explained later in this chapter.)

4. Add the entries from the user's *CVSIGNORE* environment variable.

5. Add the entries from the *-I* command option.

6. Add the entries from the *.cvsignore* file in the current sandbox directory. These entries apply only to the directory they are in, not to any subdirectories. Each sandbox directory or subdirectory, excluding the administrative *CVS* directories, can have a *.cvsignore* file. (The sandbox *.cvsignore* file is explained later in this chapter.)

The CVS command-line option *-I !* causes CVS to process every file, except any files that are specified in *.cvsignore* in the sandbox (or, if importing, the import directory). That's because *-I !* resets the ignore list at step 5 in the previous list. This behavior is extremely useful when you're using *cvs import* on a directory that contains only files that you want to store, as it ensures that every file in the directory is added to the CVS repository even if it would otherwise be ignored. Later versions of CVS may alter the processing sequence so that *-I !* will clear sandbox *.cvsignore* lists too.

history

The *history* file contains the information displayed by the *cvs history* command. It must be writable by all CVS users, and it is created by *cvs init* to be owner- and group-writable. This file should not be edited manually; all changes should occur through CVS.

If you wish to turn history logging off, rename the *history* file.

passwd

The *passwd* file contains the usernames and passwords used for the *pserver* remote-access method. Chapter 8 explains this file.

This file usually is edited in place, not checked out like the other administrative files. If you wish to check it out, add it to the *commitinfo* file, but be aware of the security risks explained in Chapter 8.

readers

The *readers* file contains the usernames of people who have read-only access to the repository via the *pserver* remote-access method. (Also see the *writers* administrative file.) Chapter 8 explains this file.

users

The *users* file provides a list of email addresses for users whose mailboxes are not on the same machine as the CVS repository. This list is used by the command given in the *notify* file, and the email address provided for the relevant username becomes the input represented by the *%s* string.

The format of this file is a separate line for each user, each line consisting of the username and the email address to send notifications to:

    user:email

Chapter 5 explains the use of this file and provides an example.

val-tags

The *val-tags* file contains a list of valid tag names, acting as an internal cache for CVS. It must be writable by all CVS users, and it is created by *cvs init* to be owner- and group-writable. This file should not be edited manually; all changes should occur through CVS.

writers

This file contains the usernames of people who have read-write access to the repository via the *pserver* remote-access method. If this file exists, any username not in this file is given read-only access. A username listed in both *writers* and *readers* is given read-only access. Chapter 8 explains the *readers* and *writers* files.

Variable Expansion

The administrative files in *CVSROOT* can use several types of variables, including internal, user-defined, environment, and shell variables.

The syntax to use when referencing CVS internal variables is *${VARIABLE}*. If the character immediately following the variable is neither alphanumeric nor an underscore (_), you can use the alternative syntax *$VARIABLE*. These are the internal variables:

CVSROOT
> The path to the repository root directory (not to the *CVSROOT* directory within the repository). This variable contains the path only; it does not contain any access method or host information.

CVSEDITOR or *EDITOR* or *VISUAL*
> The editor CVS calls for *commit* or *import* commands. This variable is calculated after the *-e* CVS option or the client's environment variables have been read.

RCSBIN
> The path to the *rcs* program. This variable applies only to CVS 1.9.18 or earlier.

USER
> The username (on the server machine, if in client/server mode) of the user running CVS.
>
> In the *pserver* access method, *USER* represents the third field of the appropriate line in the *passwd* file in the repository's *CVSROOT* directory; or, if there is no username there, *USER* is the name in the leftmost field.

CVS recognizes two shell variables within the CVS administrative files:

~/ The home directory of the user calling the CVS process

~username

    The home directory of the user identified as *username*

CVS sets three environment variables in the environments of scripts run via the CVS administrative files:

CVS_USER

    This variable is meaningful only with the *pserver* access method. It refers to the CVS-specific username provided in the leftmost field of the appropriate line in the *passwd* file in the repository's *CVSROOT* directory. If this username does not exist, the variable expands to an empty string.

LOGNAME or *USER*

    The username of the user calling the CVS process. In the *pserver* access method, this is the third field of the line in the *passwd* file; or, if there is no username there, *LOGNAME* or *USER* is the same as the *CVS_USER*.

CVS permits user-defined variables that can be passed to administrative files from the client, allowing CVS users to pass information to the scripts and commands set up by project leads and repository administrators. In an administrative file, read such a variable with the syntax *${=VARIABLE}*. In the command line, use the *-s variable=value* CVS option to pass the variable to CVS.

Example 6-7 shows how to call CVS while providing and defining the user variable *${=TESTDIR}*. Use the variable *${=TESTDIR}* in one of the administrative files under *CVSROOT*.

Example 6-7. User-defined variables

```
cvs -s TESTDIR=/home/jenn/tests commit
```

I suggest using the contents of *${=TESTDIR}* to point to either a location for test files, or a source of test data. In an administrative file (possibly the *loginfo* file described in Chapter 7), I suggest calling a test script with the *${=TESTDIR}* variable as a parameter to the script. The *loginfo* file is read after the commit has been processed, so use that script to run an automated test suite over a program, using the contents of the directory provided with *${=TESTDIR}* as the data for that test suite. If you have two teams working on the same project but with different test data or standards, you can use user-defined variables to allow each team to provide their own information source.

All strings that contain the $ symbol, other than the variables, are reserved for CVS internal use. There is no way to escape the $ symbol.

Server Environment Variables

CVS reads some of the calling user's environment variables whenever you run a command for which the variable may affect the results. These variables, shown in the following list, are read and used by the process that runs on the repository's server. Note that these variables must be in the calling user's environment on the repository server, so different users may cause different behaviors.

CVS_SERVER_SLEEP

Delays the start of the client/server process by *CVS_SERVER_SLEEP* seconds to allow a debugger to be attached to it. Use this variable only when debugging the server in client/server mode.

In local-access mode, CVS uses both client and server environment variables.

CVSUMASK

Sets the default permissions of files in the repository. See "Securing Your Projects" earlier in this chapter.

PATH

Locates any programs whose paths are not coded into the CVS program. It is also used for the programs called in the scripting files. The *PATH* variable is less important to CVS than it was when the *rcs*, *diff*, and *patch* programs CVS now uses were not included with CVS.

TMPDIR

Sets the temporary directory CVS stores data in. It defaults to */tmp*. CVS creates temporary files with *mkstemp* (BSD 4.3) if possible. It determines what is available at compile time, and if it can't find *mkstemp* it tries *tempnam* (SVID 3), *mktemp* (BSD 4.3), or *tmpnam* (POSIX), in that order. If it uses *tmpnam*, it cannot use the *TMPDIR* environment variable, and files will be created in */tmp*.

Currently, some parts of CVS use */tmp*, regardless of the contents of *TMPDIR*. This is a bug and should be fixed in a later version.

Backing Up a Repository

A CVS repository can be backed up using the same backup tools and schedule that you use for ordinary text and binary files. You must be able to restore the repository with the same permissions and structure it had when it was backed up. You must restore the *CVSROOT* directory and its contents before the project directories are useful, but you can restore project root directories and their contents independently of each other.

If a file in a repository is being written to while a backup is in progress, it is possible that the file could be backed up in a state that might make it difficult for CVS to read it accurately when it is restored. For this reason, you should prevent processes from writing to the repository during a backup.

Freezing a Repository

"Freezing a repository" is CVS-speak for the act of preventing users from changing the repository. The most common reason to freeze a repository is to ensure that a backup operation copies all the repository files in a consistent state.

The simplest way to freeze a repository is to block clients from accessing the CVS server. There are many ways to do this, such as shutting down the CVS server program, disallowing logins to the server system, blocking the server with a firewall rule, setting the server to single-user mode, or pulling out the network cable. Rather than blocking access to the server completely, you can use CVS's locks to read-lock the repository.

To keep the server running and allow clients to continue to read the repository files while a backup or other critical work takes place, use a script that creates lock files like CVS's internal locks. CVS honors these locks as if they were its own. Lock the directories you want to back up, make your backup, and then unlock the directories. See "Locks," later in this chapter, for a full explanation of CVS locks.

Ideally, you should write your backup script to leave out the lock files when it's backing up CVS; if you don't, you'll need to remove those locks as part of the restoration. Example 6-8 shows a script that locks an entire repository. It attempts to lock the repository and backs off if it can't lock the whole repository. The backing off is necessary to prevent deadlocks. Example 6-9 shows a script that unlocks a repository. If it can't lock the repository within nine attempts, the script backs off, reports an error, and exits. This prevents it from trying endlessly when there's a stale lock from a crashed CVS program. (See "Clearing Locks," later in this chapter, for how to fix stale locks.)

 Because the *for* loop in *bash* breaks on spaces, this script will not work if there are spaces in the filenames. A variant of this script, done in a language such as Perl, Python, or Ruby, would work.

Example 6-8. Script to lock a CVS repository

```
#!/bin/sh
# Freeze - Lock a whole repository for backup.

KEYMAGIC=$$
TMPFILE=/tmp/freeze.$KEYMAGIC
bail_out ( ) {
        # Exit abruptly. Return a failure code and display
```

Example 6-8. Script to lock a CVS repository (continued)

```
        # an error message.
        echo "$1"
        rm -f $TMPFILE
        exit 1
}

freeze_directory ( ) {
        echo "FREEZE: $1"
        # Obtain the master lock
        mkdir "$1/#cvs.lock"
        if [ $? != 0  ]
                then
                # Could not get master lock
                return 1
                fi
        # Create the read lock
        touch "$1/#cvs.rfl.$KEYMAGIC"
        # Record it in case of trouble
        echo $1 >> $TMPFILE
        rmdir "$1/#cvs.lock"
        return 0
}

thaw_repository ( ) {
        # If we encounter anyone else playing with the
        # CVS locks during this, then there's a small risk
        # of deadlock. In that event, we should undo everything
        # we've done to the repository, wait and try again.
        # This function removes all the locks we've produced during
        # the run so far.
        for dir in `cat $TMPFILE`
                do
                echo "** THAW ** $dir"
                mkdir "$dir/#cvs.lock"
                if [ $? ]
                        then
                        # Remove read lock
                        rm -f "$dir/#cvs.rfl.$KEYMAGIC"
                        # Remove masterlock
                        rmdir "$dir/#cvs.lock"
                        fi
                done
        return 0
}

freeze_repository ( ) {
        for dirname in `find $CVSROOT/$REPOSITORY -type d ! -iname CVS ! \
        -iname Attic ! -iname "#cvs.lock"`
                do
                freeze_directory $dirname
                if [ $? != 0 ]
                        then
```

Example 6-8. Script to lock a CVS repository (continued)

```
                        # We couldn't get the master lock.
                        # Someone else must be working on the
                        # repository
                        thaw_repository
                        return 1
                        fi
                done
        return 0
}

if [ "$CVSROOT" =  = "" ]
        then
        echo "No CVSROOT specified in the environment"
        bail_out "Aborting"
        fi

if [ "$KEYROOT" =  = "" ]
        then
        KEYROOT="$CVSROOT"
        fi

if [ "$1" =  = "" ]
        then
        echo "No Repository specified."
        echo "Usage: $0 repository"
        bail_out "Aborting"
else
        REPOSITORY="$1"
        fi

# Double-check the validity of supplied paths
KEYFILE=$KEYROOT/.$REPOSITORY
test -d $CVSROOT || bail_out "Can't access $CVSROOT - is it a directory?"
touch $KEYFILE || bail_out "Can't access $KEYFILE - aborting"

TRIES=0
while   ! freeze_repository
        do
        let TRIES=$TRIES+1
        echo "Could not freeze. Repository in use. (Attempt $TRIES)"
        if [ $TRIES -gt 9 ]
                then
                bail_out "Giving up"
                fi
        echo " Sleeping 1 second."
        sleep 1
        rm -f $TMPFILE
        echo "Trying again.."
        done
echo "** Repository $REPOSITORY frozen"
echo "$KEYMAGIC" >> $KEYROOT/.$REPOSITORY
```

Example 6-8. Script to lock a CVS repository (continued)

```
rm -f $TMPFILE
exit 0
```

Example 6-9. Script to unlock a CVS repository

```
#!/bin/sh
# Unfreeze - Unlock a whole repository.

bail_out ( ) {
        # Exit abruptly. Return a failure code and display
        # an error message.
        echo "$*"
        rm -f $TMPFILE
        exit 1
}

unfreeze_directory ( ) {
        echo "UNFREEZE: $1"
        mkdir "$1/#cvs.lock"
        if [ $? != 0  ]
                then
                # Could not get master lock
                return 1
                fi
        test -f "$1/#cvs.rfl.$KEYMAGIC" || echo "THAW: Expected to find a lock file: \
                $1/#cvs.rfl.$KEYMAGIC"
        # Proceed anyway.
        rm -f "$1/#cvs.rfl.$KEYMAGIC"
        rmdir "$1/#cvs.lock"
        return 0
}

unfreeze_repository ( ) {
        TMPFILE=/tmp/freeze.$KEYMAGIC
        for dirname in `find $CVSROOT/$REPOSITORY -type d ! -iname CVS ! \
        -iname Attic ! -iname "#cvs.lock"`
                do
                unfreeze_directory $dirname
                if [ $? != 0 ]
                        then
                        return 1
                        fi
                done
        return 0
}

if [  "$CVSROOT" =  = "" ]
        then
        echo "No CVSROOT specified in the environment"
        bail_out "Aborting"
        fi
```

Example 6-9. Script to unlock a CVS repository (continued)

```
if [ "$KEYROOT" = = "" ]
        then
        KEYROOT="$CVSROOT"
        fi

if [ "$1" = = "" ]
        then
        echo "No Repository specified."
        echo "Usage: $0 repository"
        bail_out "Aborting"
else
        REPOSITORY="$1"
        fi

# Double-check the validity of supplied paths
KEYFILE=$KEYROOT/.$REPOSITORY
test -d $CVSROOT || bail_out "Can't access $CVSROOT - is it a directory?"
test -f $KEYFILE || bail_out "No $KEYFILE appears to exist. Repository does \
not appear to be frozen"
TRIES=0

# Walk through each of the keys that the repository has been frozen with
# and unlock each one in turn. A single run of unfreeze thaws multiple
# runs of freeze.
for KEYMAGIC in `cat $KEYFILE`
        do
        unfreeze_repository
        if [ "$?" = "1" ]
                then
                echo "** Unable to obtain master locks for all directories."
                let TRIES=$TRIES+1
                if [ "$TRIES" = "10" ]
                        then
                        bail_out "Too many attempts. Giving up."
                        fi
                sleep 1
                echo "** Trying again."
        else
                echo "** Repository $REPOSITORY thawed from freeze $KEYMAGIC"
                fi

        done
echo "** Unfreeze complete"
echo "** Repository $REPOSITORY thawed"
rm -f $KEYFILE
exit 0
```

If you need to freeze the repository entirely, preventing anyone from either reading or writing, modify the scripts in Examples 6-8 and 6-9 to create and remove write locks. For example, you need to do this when attempting to restore a backup of the whole repository.

Restoring a Backup

A CVS repository can be restored using the same tools that you use to restore ordinary text and binary files. You must restore the *CVSROOT* directory and its contents to be able to use the project files reliably. You need not restore every project in the repository, but when you restore a project, you should restore all its files and directories.

 If the repository was locked for backup, and the locks were not removed in the backup script, remove them before the repository can be used again.

When you restore a repository, you must ensure that no one can write to it. You can do this by freezing the repository as described earlier in "Freezing a Repository," but if you use locks, you must use write locks rather than the read locks described in that section, because the repository will be in an inconsistent state while the files are being restored; you don't want anyone to read from or write to the repository during the restore process.

After you have restored a CVS repository from a backup, it is safest to assume that any sandbox files are based on revisions that do not exist in the backup of the repository. This means that individual developers are likely to have changes in their sandboxes that need to be committed (or recommitted) to the repository in order to bring it up to date.

Here is the simplest way to restore changes that have been preserved in sandboxes:

1. Check out a new sandbox from the restored repository.
2. Try to use commands such as *cvs diff*, *cvs status*, and *cvs update* on a sandbox from before the repository was restored, to determine which files have been changed and what the changes are. If this does not work, try using the Unix *diff* program to determine the differences between an old and the new sandbox.
3. Copy the old sandbox files you want to commit or recommit into the new sandbox.
4. Commit the changes as if they were ordinary changes.
5. Make sure the log message indicates what happened.

Distributed Repositories

Many CVS systems use only a single, central repository, but not all. Many open source projects that rely on CVS use mirrored repositories to distribute the latest source, and many of those have a version of the repository available on the World Wide Web. Recently, write-proxying has been enabled for mirror repositories: this process allows the user to connect to the mirror as if the mirror were the central repository.

Mirroring a Repository

Many project teams have public, read-only CVS repositories. If you want to do likewise, you can copy the repository, reserve the original repository for your project work, and use the copy (or mirror) repository as a public repository.

The copy can be on the same computer as the original or on a different computer or even a different network. Having two or more copies of a repository allows you to put one copy on a trusted network for your developers and another on a more public part of your network for the general public.

 You can't commit to a repository mirror, but CVS permits you to make a mirror repository into a write-proxy for a primary repository. See the following section on write proxies.

Mirror a repository by copying the repository files. To avoid getting part of one release and part of another due to the copy overlapping with a commit, freeze the repository with read locks before mirroring and unfreeze it afterward.

The Unix and Linux *rsync* program is a useful tool to use when mirroring. It allows you to recursively transfer only the changed files between any two directories and recovers properly if it's interrupted. It also has an optional CVS-exclusion mode, called with the *--cvs-exclude* option, which ignores the same files CVS ignores by default. By default, *rsync* uses SSH, but if your system is configured differently, you can use the *-e ssh* option to *rsync* to transfer using the SSH protocol. An *rsync* command or script can be triggered at either the central repository or the mirror.

There is also a repository mirroring tool called CVSup. It's designed specifically for use with CVS, and parses the CVS data files to do the mirroring as efficiently as possible. It is triggered by the mirror, and is most often updated on a daily basis, triggered by an automation application such as *cron*.

To keep a secondary repository up to date with all changes from the primary repository, trigger an *rsync* script in all four of the *loginfo*, *postadmin*, *posttag*, and *postwatch* scripting files. You can't as easily keep a CVSup'd mirror constantly up to date, because the CVSup system is designed to be triggered from the mirror rather than from the central repository.

Example 6-10 shows a typical *rsync* line for the scripting files. Add this line to all four of the *loginfo*, *postadmin*, *posttag*, and *postwatch* files to generate an *rsync* attempt with the mirror repository in the directory */usr/local/cvs* on the machine *mirror1*. Configure *rsync* and SSH so that they don't need a password—see your SSH documentation for details. Note that *rsync* has many useful options other than the ones I've included, which are to preserve permissions, group, and owner, and to use compression.

Because we're trying to mirror the repository, I've chosen not to use *--cvs-exclude* and thus kept the CVS administrative files. The *%p* is an internal CVS variable (valid in recent versions only) and is explained in the section "Running Scripts" in Chapter 7.

Example 6-10. Mirroring with rsync

```
ALL rsync -pgoz -e ssh ./ mirror1:/usr/local/cvs/%p &
```

Write Proxies

In CVS version 1.12.10, the developers added the ability for CVS mirrors to act as write proxies for the central repository. The mirror (or secondary repository, in the proxy system) handles all read requests itself, but passes write requests to the central (primary) repository.

> The write proxy system does not modify the secondary repository, nor does it do anything to keep the secondary repository up to date. Use the techniques explained in "Mirroring a Repository," earlier in this chapter, to update your secondary repositories.

To configure a write proxy system, edit the *CVSROOT/config* files in your secondary repositories. The *PrimaryServer* configuration option must specify the repository path of the primary repository: be aware that at present, you must use the *:ext:* or *:fork:* connection methods. There is no mandatory configuration on the primary repository for write proxying itself, but almost all administrators will choose to configure a mirroring system of some sort.

> CVS clients older than CVS 1.12.9 do not recognize write proxying. In the new clients, the secondary server requests that the client redirect the write request to the primary server. To support older clients, the secondary server will act as a transparent proxy to the primary server. Unfortunately, this requires additional configuration.
>
> The good news is that if all your clients are newer than 1.12.9, the extra configuration is unnecessary.
>
> To support pre–CVS 1.12.9 clients, your primary and secondary servers must be compatible. Ideally, use the same version of CVS for both; otherwise, you will need to ensure that the same write requests are used both by primary and secondary server.
>
> Also (still supporting older clients), you should ensure that all secondary servers are invoked with the parameter *--allow-root=secondary repository root*. You will probably need to do this by installing an alias or a script on your server's machine.

Web-Viewable Repositories

An alternative way to distribute a repository—for read-only access—is across the Web. The current favorite tool for doing this is ViewVC (formerly ViewCVS), which generates HTML navigation for CVS and Subversion repositories, and is available at *http://www.viewvc.org*. A similar tool is CVSWeb, which has gone through several incarnations and is currently being maintained as FreeBSD-CVSWeb.

Web distribution is very popular in open source projects, or in other projects where a variety of people using a variety of platforms will want read-only access to the documents stored in CVS.

The INSTALL document included in the ViewVC source distribution is very clear and easy to read, and the installation is automated. Configuration is done by editing the file *viewvc.conf*, which itself contains clear and concise examples.

Editing a Repository

There are times when you need to restructure a project or fix things up when something has gone wrong in the repository. In an ideal world, restructures or repairs would all be done using the CVS commands explained in Chapter 3 or the *cvs admin* command explained in Chapter 7. Sometimes, however, those commands can't do what you're trying to achieve, and you need to modify the repository directly.

The main problem with editing the repository directly is that you may lose historic data. Removing files or directories affects retrieval of older releases of a project and may affect build scripts. Moving or renaming files or directories can affect older releases, build scripts, and instructions within your files.

 Always freeze a repository with write locks before hand-editing it.

Always consider backing up and freezing the directories you're hand-editing. If you're just removing a stale lock, this isn't necessary. But you should back up and freeze directories if you're moving, removing, editing, or renaming content files. Try to get your users to *commit* and *release* their sandboxes before you hand-edit the repository. They can *checkout* new sandboxes afterwards.

If a user does not release an old sandbox and tries to act on a filename that the sandbox has records of, but the repository does not have the file, the user will receive strange errors. Correct these errors by releasing the user's sandbox copy of the file in question and then checking out the file again using the new filename.

If you are using the scripting files in the *CVSROOT* directory, you may need to edit them when a directory is moved or removed.

Moving Files and Directories

CVS does not have a built-in command for moving or renaming a file or directory. This doesn't mean that you can't move or rename files and directories; it just means that doing so requires ingenuity.

 To rename a file or directory, move it from the old name to the new name. To create a new project from parts of an older project, move the files into a directory in the repository root directory, or move a whole subdirectory into the repository root.

As shown in Chapter 3, the simplest way to move a file involves using *cvs remove* and *cvs add* on the sandbox copy of the file. This method is simple, retains the history of the file, and allows mistakes to be corrected easily. The revision numbering for the file starts over at 1.1, but if you find that bothersome, you can change the revision numbering with *cvs commit -r revision filename*. If this method for moving or renaming a file doesn't suit your needs, you can edit the repository.

There are two ways to move a file by editing the repository and two ways to move a directory. Directories can't be moved easily with CVS commands, as they can't be deleted without editing the repository. Chapter 3 explains how to get the effect of moving a directory without losing historic information.

Prerequisites to moving a file

To move a file by editing the repository directly, you need to move all the file's data. Most of this data is stored in the file itself, but if the file is being watched or is flagged for editing with *cvs edit*, there may be data about it in the *fileattr* file in the CVS subdirectory of the directory your file is stored in.

If there is data in *fileattr* about the file you want to move, the record for that file needs to be cleared before you move or remove the file. It is best to clear this record with CVS commands—by having users use *cvs release* or *cvs unedit*, and *cvs watch remove*—and then use *cvs watch off* on the file. If you can't clear information for a file out of *fileattr* with CVS commands, edit *fileattr* directly and copy the lines with that file's filenames to the *fileattr* file in the new location. If you're renaming the file but keeping it in the same directory, replace the old name with the new name.

Moving a file: Method 1

The first method for moving a file is to move the file:

1. Have users *cvs release* their sandboxes.
2. Freeze the repository directory that contains the file and the directory it will be moved to, to prevent people from reading or writing to them.

---

3. Remove any information about the file from the *CVS/fileattr* file in the same directory. Save this information, if there is any, for step 6.

4. Move the file with Unix's *mv* command (e.g., *mv old,v new,v*).

5. Change any build scripts or other files that refer to the old name.

6. Restore *fileattr* data in the new location.

7. Unfreeze the repository and allow users to check out sandboxes.

This method for moving a file doesn't affect the file's revision numbering, and it allows the old directory to be removed if all the files are taken out of it in this way.

However, this method damages the historic record for the file being moved. When old revisions of the file or old releases of the project are checked out, the file is retrieved with its new name. There will also be no record of when the name was changed and why.

Moving a file: Method 2

This method involves copying the file, then using CVS commands to move the old copy to the *Attic* as a dead revision, and finally removing tags from the new copy. Removing the tags ensures that retrieving old revisions by tag works as expected—retrieving the old filename, not the new one.

1. Freeze at least part of the repository (for writing) in a way that allows you to access it as a client, possibly from a sandbox on the same machine as the repository. You need to freeze only the directory that contains the file you want to move and the directory to which it is moving. Because you need to use a sandbox, it may be easier to limit access to the server—effectively freezing the whole repository—than to use write locks on the affected directories.

2. Make sure you have an active sandbox that contains the file you want to move.

3. In the repository, copy the file using the Unix *cp* command (e.g., *cp oldfile,v newfile,v*). You can now remove the lock on the old directory.

4. Copy the relevant line of the *fileattr* file from the file's old location to its new location.

5. In the sandbox, remove the old file with *cvs remove oldfile*. Commit this change with a message that you've moved the file to the new filename.

6. In the sandbox, retrieve the new file with *cvs update newfile*.

7. Remove any nonbranch tags from the new file with *cvs tag -d tagname newfile*. Use *cvs status -v newfile* to get the tagnames. This works because CVS stores tags inside the repository copy of project files.

8. Merge the file to other active branches, if necessary.

9. Change any build scripts or other files that refer to the old name.

10. Unfreeze the repository and allow users to resume work.

This method has the following advantages:

- Checking out old revisions by tag works perfectly.
- The log of changes is intact.
- Revision numbers are intact.

This method has a few problems. The move is recorded only in the commit message in the old file, and retrieving old revisions by date retrieves old revisions with the new filename as well as the old one.

Another issue with this method involves branch tags. Removing the branch tags prevents old branch revisions from appearing under the new name, which is desirable but also means that the new file is not on the branch.

You can remove the old branch tags from the new file to prevent old revisions from being retrieved incorrectly, then add the new file to the branch with *cvs add* to put the file back onto the branch. But because of the way CVS stores branched files, this approach may corrupt the file if some of the information in the new file can't be retrieved properly. I recommend that you do not do this, as the data can be difficult to recover if you change your mind.

 If you need to move a branched file, I recommend you use method 1 to move it, or omit the step of removing the tags if you use method 2. And if you do remove branch tags, make a backup first.

Examples 6-11 and 6-12 show how to move a file with this method. Example 6-11 shows the command to copy the file in the repository, and Example 6-12 shows the commands used in the sandbox.

Example 6-11. Moving files with method 2, repository view

```
/var/lib/cvs/wizzard/src$ cp main.c,v wizzard.c,v
/var/lib/cvs/wizzard/src$
```

Example 6-12. Moving files with method 2, sandbox view

```
bash-2.05a$ cvs remove -f main.c
cvs server: scheduling `main.c' for removal
cvs server: use 'cvs commit' to remove this file permanently
bash-2.05a$ cvs update wizzard.c
U wizzard.c
bash-2.05a$ cvs status -v wizzard.c
===============================
File: wizzard.c          Status: Up-to-date

    Working revision:    1.8
    Repository revision: 1.8     /var/lib/cvs/wizzard/src/wizzard.c,v
    Sticky Tag:          (none)
    Sticky Date:         (none)
    Sticky Options:      (none)
```

Example 6-12. Moving files with method 2, sandbox view (continued)

```
   Existing Tags:
   pre_beta_0-1          (revision: 1.8)

bash-2.05a$ cvs tag -d pre_beta_0-1 wizzard.c
D wizzard.c
bash-2.05a$ cvs commit -m "Moved main.c to wizzard.c"
cvs commit: Examining .
Removing main.c; 9L, 316C written
/var/lib/cvs/wizzard/src/main.c,v  <--  main.c
new revision: delete; previous revision: 1.8
done
bash-2.05a$ cvs commit -f -m "Moved main.c to wizzard.c" wizzard.c
Checking in wizzard.c;
/var/lib/cvs/wizzard/src/wizzard.c,v  <--  wizzard.c
new revision: 1.9; previous revision: 1.9
done
```

Moving a directory: Method 1

Moving a directory within the repository damages the historic record for the project. When old releases of the project are checked out, the directory and the files it contains are retrieved with the new name. There is no record of when the name was changed and why. To move a directory:

1. Have users run *cvs release* on their sandboxes.

2. Freeze the repository directory to be moved, any subdirectories, and the parent directory, to prevent people from reading from or writing to them.

3. Edit any of the scripting files in the *CVSROOT* directory of the repository that refer to the directory you are moving. The most likely of these files is *modules*. CVS does not edit the scripting files itself, so you need to check only files that you or others with write access to the *CVSROOT* directory have changed.

4. Move the directory with *mv old new.*

5. Correct any build scripts or other files that refer to the old name.

6. Unfreeze the repository and allow users to check out new sandboxes.

Moving a directory: Method 2

This alternative method of moving a directory preserves the old structure of the project, which can allow older build scripts to continue to work on old versions of the project. This method leaves the old directory in place, available for new files to be added to that directory. You may not always want this result.

1. Follow steps 1 through 3 from method 1.

2. Move the directory with *cp old new.*

3. Correct any build scripts or other files that refer to the old name.

4. Unfreeze the repository enough to allow you to create a single sandbox with permissions to the old directory.

5. From that sandbox, remove all the files in the old directory with *cvs remove*.

6. Unfreeze the repository and allow users to check out new sandboxes.

Deleting Files and Directories

Before deleting any files or directories manually, have your users run *cvs commit* and *cvs release* on their sandboxes. They will get odd errors if they try to commit or work with files and directories that no longer exist in the repository.

Deleting a file

When you delete a file with the *cvs remove* command, CVS sets its state to *dead* (see "Editing a Project's RCS Files," later in this chapter). If the revision you deleted was the head revision of the trunk, CVS stores the file in an *Attic* subdirectory of its original directory.

To remove a file from the repository entirely:

1. Have users run *cvs release* on their sandboxes.

2. Freeze the affected repository directory, to prevent people from reading from or writing to it.

3. Check whether the file is recorded in the *CVS/fileattr* file and remove the reference if it is. (See "Moving Files and Directories," earlier in this chapter.)

4. Remove the file with the Unix *rm* command.

5. Unfreeze the repository and allow users to check out new sandboxes.

Deleting a directory

CVS does not provide any way to delete a directory with CVS commands, because removing a directory necessitates removing its *Attic* subdirectory. Even if the directory is empty of active files, if it has ever contained files, it will have an *Attic* subdirectory, which needs to exist to allow old revisions of files or old releases of the project to be retrieved.

If you will not need to retrieve any files stored in a directory's *Attic* subdirectory, you can delete the directory in the repository with the following method:

1. Have users run *cvs release* on their sandboxes.

2. Freeze the repository directory that contains the directory to be removed, to prevent people from reading from or writing to it.

3. Move any project files as shown earlier in "Moving Files and Directories." Use the *cp* method (method 2) if you want to retain old revisions; use either method if you don't.

4. Delete any lock files, the *Attic* subdirectory, and the *CVS* subdirectory with *rm* or *rmdir*.

5. Delete the directory with *rm* or *rmdir*.

6. Unfreeze the repository and allow users to check out new sandboxes.

Deleting a Project

A project can be deleted by deleting its directory, as described in the previous section. However, a project directory is more likely to have entries in the scripting files in the *CVSROOT* directory. The most critical scripting file to check is *modules*, as this file defines module names that can be used as parameters to most CVS commands.

Ensure that all users have committed and released their project sandboxes before you delete the project. If they attempt to work on a project that has been removed, they will get interesting error messages.

Editing a Project's RCS Files

The project files in the repository are stored in Revision Control System (RCS) format and are easily recognized by the *,v* at the end of the filename. *Applying RCS and SCCS*, by Don Bolinger and Tan Bronson (O'Reilly), explains RCS in detail. The RCS format is also explained in the CVS source-code document *RCSFILES* (in the *doc* directory) and in the Unix and Linux manual page *man 5 rcsfile*.

 In CVS 1.12.12, a *commitid* field was added to the RCS files. This identifies which *commit* or *import* the file was last changed in, and is unique to the particular commit or import session. It is the same in all files committed or imported during the session.

If you think you need to edit the repository copy of a project file in order to solve a problem, always try to use the *cvs admin* commands to fix the problem first. These commands include most of the functions RCS provides for managing an RCS-format file. The *cvs admin* commands are explained in Chapter 7.

CVS edits an RCS file by editing a copy of the file, then replacing the existing RCS file with the edited copy. Lock the repository directory; then follow this same procedure if you are editing a file manually. You can edit an RCS file with any plain-text editor.

Example 6-13 shows the header of an RCS file.

Example 6-13. RCS file header

```
head   1.2;
access;
symbols
```

Example 6-13. RCS file header (continued)

```
  beta_0-1_branch:1.1.0.2
  beta_0-1_branch_root:1.1
  pre_beta_0-1:1.1;
locks; strict;
comment @ * @;
```

The header contains metadata about the file, including the head (most recent) revision of the trunk, the revisions and names for each tag, the RCS lock status (always *strict* for CVS files), and a comment field bounded with @ symbols.

After the header, the RCS file contains revision metadata for each revision in the file. This metadata includes the revision number, date, author, state, any branches that use that revision as their base node, and the *next* revision. The *next* revision is the revision that is one revision older than the current revision on the same branch (or trunk) of the file. After all the revision metadata, the RCS file has a space to store a file description. The file description is bounded by @ symbols.

Example 6-14 shows RCS revision metadata. Note that the branch revision 1.1.2.1 is in the dead state, which means that the revision has been removed with *cvs remove*. The description of this file is empty, but the @ symbols that would bound a description are present on the line under *desc*.

Example 6-14. RCS revision metadata

```
1.2
date  2006.04.13.07.26.27;  author jenn;  state Exp;
branches;
next  1.1;

1.1
date  2006.04.12.08.56.41;  author jenn;  state Exp;
branches
   1.1.2.1;
next  ;

1.1.2.1
date  2006.04.13.07.42.06;  author jenn;  state dead;
branches;
next  ;

desc
@@
```

The rest of the RCS file contains the file content—the actual text of the file and the log messages. The head revision contains the bulk of the file content. Every other trunk revision contains only the differences between that revision and the revision that is one revision newer than it. These differences are stored in the same format used by the *diff* and *patch* programs.

Trunk revisions are stored in reverse order. To retrieve any trunk revision, CVS starts with the contents of the head revision and recursively applies the patches stored with each revision to those contents. CVS then works backward chronologically until it reaches the desired revision. The *next* field in the revision metadata tells CVS which revision's patches should be applied in the next recursion.

Branch revisions are slightly different. If your desired revision is on a branch, CVS starts with the most current revision of the trunk and works backward to the branch point, then works forward through branch revisions.

Revision 1.1 in Example 6-15 contains the code d12 3, which means delete 3 lines starting at line 12.

Each revision starts with the revision number, then the log message (preceded by *log* and bounded by at symbols (@)), then the revision text or *diff* (bounded by at symbols). If an @ is required inside a section, it is escaped with another @. An email address looks like this: *jenn@@nosuch.com*.

Example 6-15. RCS file body

```
1.2
log
@Minor tweaks to the config file.
@
text
@/*
 * Wizzard.h
 * Apr 12 2006
 * Developer: Jenn Vesperman (jenn@@nosuch.com)
 *
 * Headers, macros and constants file for the Wizzard project.
 *
 */

#include "config.h"    /* using autoconf */
#include "options.h"   /* manual options that can't be done in autoconf */

#define TRUE 1
#define FALSE 0
@

1.1
log
@Moving src/wizzard.h to src/config.h
@
text
@d12 3
@
```

Clearing Locks

When a CVS client process is waiting on a lock in a repository, the client displays messages such as those shown in Example 6-16.

Example 6-16. Waiting for a lock

```
cvs server: [23:30:43] waiting for jenn's lock in /var/lib/cvs/wizzard/src
cvs server: [23:31:13] waiting for jenn's lock in /var/lib/cvs/wizzard/src
cvs server: [23:31:43] waiting for jenn's lock in /var/lib/cvs/wizzard/src
```

The process waits 30 seconds between tries. If the process is still waiting for a commit after an unusually long time, you may need to check whether the other user's CVS process has crashed and (if so) remove the lock manually. In CVS 1.11.3 and later, CVS provides the time in UTC. In earlier versions, the time is given in the server's time zone.

The simplest way to determine whether a process has crashed is to check with the user running the client program. If he's uploading large files over a slow link, wait a little longer.

If you can't get in touch with the user directly, you can check the status of the user's process on the repository server by using whatever commands are appropriate on your system (for example, *ps -ef* or *ps -auwx* on many Unix systems). CVS puts the process ID in the name of the lock file. Check whether that process is still alive and functioning, and see if it is a CVS process. If the process has died or if some other program has taken the process ID, you can remove the lock safely by removing the lock file.

To remove a lock manually, check for a lock file or files in the directory given in the error message. There may be a lock file and a master directory belonging to the user's process. The lock file or files will be the *#cvs.lock* directory or files whose names start with *#cvs.rfl* or *#cvs.wfl*. Remove these files to remove the lock.

In Example 6-17, I determine that the process 20233 on the server named *nest* belongs to a crashed CVS client, so *#cvs.wfl.nest.20233* is redundant. The master lock *#cvs.lock* is owned by the same user and also belongs to the crashed client. Example 6-17 shows how to remove the lock files.

Example 6-17. Clearing a lock, server view

```
jenn@nest:/var/lib/cvs/wizzard/src$ ls
#cvs.lock  #cvs.wfl.nest.20233  main.c,v  wizzard.h,v
jenn@nest:/var/lib/cvs/wizzard/src$ ps -p 20233
  PID TT STAT     TIME COMMAND
jenn@nest:/var/lib/cvs/wizzard/src$ rm *cvs.wfl.nest.20233
jenn@nest:/var/lib/cvs/wizzard/src$ rmdir *cvs.lock
```

Example 6-18 shows the CVS output to the client that was waiting for the lock, once the lock files are cleared.

Example 6-18. Clearing a lock, client view

```
cvs server: [23:33:13] obtained lock in /var/lib/cvs/wizzard/src
RCS file: /var/lib/cvs/wizzard/src/main.c,v
done
.
.
.
done
bash-2.05a$
```

Sandbox Structure

A CVS sandbox is composed of a sandbox root directory, the project files and directories, and a special *CVS* subdirectory in the root directory and in every project directory. The sandbox root directory usually has the same name as the module it was created for, or it takes the name of the project root directory in the repository.

Project files in a sandbox are in editable form, just as if they were exported from the repository for release. The *CVS* subdirectory in each project directory stores metadata for the files in the project directory it is part of. This metadata is contained in a number of files (and one directory). Each of the sandbox directories may also contain a *.cvsignore* file.

CVS Subdirectories

Each project directory in a sandbox contains a subdirectory named *CVS*. This *CVS* subdirectory contains the files that store the administrative data for the files in the project directory. The following list describes the files and directories you will most likely find in a *CVS* directory. Files that are rarely encountered or are temporary are not included in this list. The full list of files is available in Chapter 11.

Base
> Stores the pre-editing revision of any files that are being edited with *cvs edit*. This is a directory, not a file.

Baserev
> Contains the revision information for every file in the *Base* directory, in the format *name/revision/*. Later versions of CVS may add to this format.

> If you need to edit any of these files manually, back the file up before you start.

Checkin.prog
> Used if the *modules* file in *CVSROOT* has an *-i* option for the module in this sandbox. *Checkin.prog* stores the program used when the module is committed. This file is obsolete in CVS 1.11.5 and later.

Entries

Contains a line for each file and directory in the relevant sandbox directory. Lines for files have the format:

```
/name/revision/timestamp[+conflict]/options/tagdate
```

Lines for directories have the format:

```
D/name////
```

There may be text between or after the empty slashes in the directory form, but in the current version of CVS (1.11.5), this text is ignored. The space is reserved for future expansion.

Entries.Log

Used to record planned changes to the *Entries* file, one change per line. Lines to be added to the *Entries* file start with *A*; lines to be removed start with *R*. There must be a space after the *A* or *R*, followed by the line to be added or removed from *Entries* in the same format as in that file.

Programs that read *Entries* should also check for *Entries.Log*. If this file exists, the programs should read *Entries*, apply the changes from *Entries.Log*, then rewrite *Entries* and remove *Entries.Log*.

Entries.Static

If this file exists, CVS did not receive a complete set of files from the repository and this sandbox directory is static; CVS will not create new files in the parent directory. This file can be cleared by using *update -d* to download a full set of files and subdirectories for the parent directory.

Notify

Contains any *cvs watch* notifications that have not yet been sent to the server.

Repository

Usually contains the path from the repository root to the repository directory that the relevant sandbox directory is a reflection of. This file may contain the full path, including the path to the root of the sandbox's repository.

If the current sandbox directory does not have a related repository directory, this file contains *CVSROOT/Emptydir*.

Root

Contains the path to the root of the sandbox's repository.

Tag

Used to store a sticky tag or date that applies to the whole parent directory, if one exists. This sticky tag or date is usually used to add the relevant tag or date to new files in the directory, especially when using branch tags.

If the first character in the *Tag* file is *T*, the *Tag* file designates that the parent directory has a sticky branch tag. *N* is a nonbranch tag, and *D* is a date.

Template

In client/server mode, this file stores the login template specified in the *rcsinfo* file in the repository's *CVSROOT* directory.

Update.prog

Used if the *modules* file in *CVSROOT* has a *-u* option for this sandbox's module. The file stores the program used when the module is updated. This file is obsolete in 1.11.5 and later.

Dot Files in Sandbox Directories

The *.cvsignore* file can be used in any sandbox subdirectory or sandbox root directory. It contains a list of files that CVS should not process from the directory. This file uses the same format as *cvsignore* in the repository's *CVSROOT* directory, but its list applies only to files in the directory it is contained in.

Dot Files in User Home Directories

CVS reads several files and one directory in the calling user's home directory. These files and the directory are described in the following list. All but the *.rhosts* file are read and used by the process that runs on the client computer. *.rhosts* is used with *rsh* and resides in the user's server-side home directory. Note that these files and the directory must be in the calling user's directory, so different users may cause different behavior.

.cvsrc

Contains a list of CVS commands and the options the user wants as default options for those commands. See Chapter 3 for more details on command options.

.cvsignore

Contains a list of files CVS should not process. This file uses the same format as *cvsignore* in the repository's *CVSROOT* directory.

.cvswrappers

Contains a list of wrappers that affect how a file is stored, based on the filename. See Chapter 3 for more details.

.cvspass

Used in *pserver* remote-access mode. This file contains the user's password, stored in a simple form of encoding. Be aware that the file is human-readable and the password is easy to decode.

.rhosts

Used when connecting with *rsh*. This file should be in the user's home directory on the server machine, and it should contain the client's computer hostname and the username on the client machine. See Chapter 8 for more details.

.ssh

Used when connecting with SSH. This directory should be in the user's home directory on both client and server machines. See your SSH documentation for details.

Client Environment Variables

CVS reads the calling user's environment variables, described in the following list. The variables in the list are read and used by the process that runs on the client computer. Note that these variables must be in the calling user's environment, so different users may experience different behavior.

CVS_CLIENT_LOG

Used for debugging CVS in client/server mode. This variable should be set to a *filename*. If it is set, everything sent to the server is stored in the *filename.in* file and everything received by the client is stored in *filename.out*.

CVS_CLIENT_PORT

Used to set the port the client uses to connect to the CVS server in *kserver*, *gserver*, and *pserver* modes. By default, clients use port 2401 (*gserver* or *pserver*) or port 1999 (*kserver*) to connect to the server.

CVSIGNORE

A list of filename patterns—separated by whitespace—that should be ignored. See *.cvsignore* in the previous section.

> In local-access mode, CVS uses both client and server environment variables.

CVSEDITOR or *EDITOR* or *VISUAL*

Used to set the editor CVS calls when it opens an editor for log messages. On Unix and Linux systems, this defaults to *vi* if these variables are unset. Using *CVSEDITOR* to customize CVS is preferred, as the other variables may be used by other programs as well. *CVSEDITOR* is searched first, then *EDITOR*, and *VISUAL* last. If the *-e editor* CVS option is used, it overrides the environment variables.

CVS_PASSFILE

Used to change the file CVS uses to store and retrieve the password in *pserver* remote-access mode. The file defaults to *.cvspass* in the user's home directory.

CVSREAD

If this variable is set to 1, CVS tries to check sandboxes out in read-only mode. (CVS actually checks whether this variable is nonnull, so it works regardless of the setting. This behavior may change in the future.)

CVSROOT

May contain the full pathname of a CVS repository, as described in Chapter 3. When working in a sandbox, this variable is not needed. If working outside a sandbox, either this variable must be present or the *-d repository_path* command-line option must be used.

CVS_RSH

Used to set the program CVS calls to connect to a remote repository when using *ext* mode. The program defaults to *rsh*.

CVS_SERVER

If connecting to a CVS server using *rsh*, this variable is used to determine which program to start on the server side. In *ext* and *server* modes, the program defaults to *cvs*. In *fork* mode, this variable defaults to the full path of the executing CVS client program.

CVSWRAPPERS

May contain one *wrapper*, as explained in Chapter 3.

HOME or *HOMEPATH* or *HOMEDRIVE*

Used to determine the location of the user's home directory, to enable CVS to locate its dot files. On Unix, Linux, and related systems, only *HOME* is used. On Windows systems, *HOMEDRIVE* and *HOMEPATH* are used together. Some Windows operating systems (NT and later) set these variables automatically. If yours doesn't, *HOMEDRIVE* should be set in the format *C:*, and *HOMEPATH* should be set in the format *\home\jenn*.

RCSBIN

This environment variable became obsolete in CVS 1.9.20. It was used for the path to the external *rcs* program before *rcs* was added to the CVS distribution.

Exit Status

You may at some point want to write a script that includes one or more CVS commands, such as a script to automatically export files from a repository to a web server, or a script to automatically update a test directory and attempt to build a program. If you do, you will need to know whether a given CVS command succeeded.

CVS commands set an exit status when they complete processing. A successful command always returns the *success* status. A failing command prints an error message and returns the *failure* status.

The *cvs diff* command behaves differently from the other commands. It returns success if it finds no differences and failure if it finds differences or encounters an error. This behavior may change in later versions of CVS.

Testing the exit status depends on the operating system. In Unix and Linux, the *sh* shell variable *$?* is *0* if CVS returns success, and nonzero if it returns a failure. Example 6-19 shows a script to test a CVS return value, and Example 6-20 shows a Windows version of the same script.

Example 6-19. Testing return values in bash

```
cvs commit -m "Automated commit"
if [ $? -eq 0 ]; then
        echo "Commit successful."
else
        echo "Commit failed with return code $?"
fi
```

Example 6-20. Testing return values in Windows

```
@echo off
cvs commit -m "Automated commit"
if %ERRORLEVEL% GEQ 1 goto ERR
goto OKAY
:ERR
  echo "Commit failed with return code %ERRORLEVEL%"
  goto END
:OKAY
  echo "Commit successful."
:END
```

## CHAPTER 7

Project Management

The team leader responsible for a project needs to know more about the project's tools than most other developers, or to have a team member who knows about the tools. This chapter is for the team leader and the CVS specialist on the team. It concentrates on the files and directories that make up a project and how they are stored and managed in CVS, rather than on managing the development process itself.

The topics covered include initial creation of a project's CVS files, configuring a project as a module, exporting a project, integrating CVS with build systems and bug trackers, and configuring scripts to run when certain CVS commands are used.

This chapter also covers a special type of branch called a *vendor branch*, and concludes with a discussion of strategies and practices for using CVS that you may find helpful.

Creating a Project

A *project* is any group of files and directories that exist beneath one project root directory. Every project must include at least one directory, because CVS needs to be able to create a subdirectory to store metadata about the project.

Most often, a project represents one program, one set of related configuration files, or one web site. Sometimes, a project is a collection of related items. For instance, I store all my articles for *http://www.oreillynet.com* in one project, with each topic grouped under a subdirectory. Sometimes a project is a subsection of something larger.

If you want to create a project right now with default settings and minimal reading, read "Importing Projects" in Chapter 2. That section walks you through the process of importing a project.

Preparing a Project

To create a project in CVS, you need a copy of the files and directories you want to import, or an idea of which files and directories you want to make. If you are planning to import an existing project, be sure to make a backup of it before you proceed.

If you have an existing set of files and directories, check whether you have files that can be generated from other files, such as compiled code. Files that can be generated easily do not usually need to be stored in CVS and can be removed from the copy of the project. It is good practice to store the commands that generate these files in CVS as part of the project, usually as a build script or as part of the installation document.

If you have a set of files stored in another version control system and want to save their revision history, see "Importing from Other Version Control Systems" later in this chapter. If you don't need to retain their revision history, export the files from the other system using a command that gives you a clean copy of the project with no administrative files, and use that copy to import from.

If you don't have any existing files, you can import a single directory with the project name. If you are more comfortable with a structure to work from, create an initial directory structure for your project and import that.

If you cannot easily fit the task you are trying to accomplish into a single project, you can use the *modules* feature of CVS to give each development team a smaller section to work from, or you can create several projects and use a module to combine projects into a larger unit when needed. Modules are explained in "The modules File" and "Project Structure and Sandboxes," both later in this chapter.

Be aware that CVS restricts the filename *CVS* for its own purposes. You should also avoid using *Attic*, *.cvsignore*, and any filename in the format *.#filename.revision*.

Once you have at least one directory ready to add to the repository, you need to decide how to add it. There are two methods, which are explained in the following section "Importing a Project" and in "Alternatives to Importing," later in this chapter.

Importing a Project

The *cvs import* command is used for both creating a new project and updating the vendor branch. Vendor branches are explained in "Vendor Branches," later in this chapter.

To create a new project, make your initial directory structure and place in it the initial files for your project, or set out your existing code that is ready for importing, as described in the preceding section, "Preparing a Project." Run the *cvs import* command from within the root directory of that structure. CVS takes the files and directories from the initial directory structure and copies them into the repository. The syntax for *cvs import* is:

cvs [*cvs-options*] import [*command-options*] *project_name vendor_tag release_tag*

cvs import requires a log message and calls an editor if it is not invoked with the *-m* option. You'll then be able to type a message into the editor to record the purpose of the import. See Chapter 2 for more information about the log message.

Check out a sandbox to test whether the *import* command has worked. If the files are in the sandbox correctly, you can remove or store the original files or directories as you see fit; CVS no longer needs them. *cvs import* doesn't change the files it imported from, and it doesn't convert them into a sandbox.

Example 7-1 shows how to import a project and create an initial project sandbox. The vertical ellipsis indicates where CVS calls the editor so you can enter a log message. Note that I change directories before checking out the test sandbox.

Example 7-1. Importing with cvs import

```
bash-2.05a$ cd wizzard
bash-2.05a$ cvs -d cvs_server:/var/lib/cvs import wizzard wizzard ver_1-0
.
.
.
"/tmp/cvsfaQoRz" 5L, 287C written
N wizzard/Makefile
N wizzard/README
N wizzard/TODO
No conflicts created by this import
bash-2.05a$ cd ~/cvs
bash-2.05a$ cvs -d cvs_server:/var/lib/cvs checkout wizzard
cvs server: Updating wizzard
```

cvs import saves the data from the files to both the project trunk and to the special branch known as the vendor branch. Unless specified otherwise with *-b*, the vendor branch is given the ID 1.1.1. The *vendor tag* parameter is used for the branch tag, and the *release tag* tags the branch at the current (just-imported) revision. These tags can consist of only alphanumeric characters, hyphens, and underscores.

If you need to import binary files or other files that are not plain text, see the information on binary files in Chapter 3 before adding them to the repository.

The *cvs import* command honors *cvsignore* and *cvswrappers* files and recognizes the standard *-k*, *-I*, and *-W* options (also used by *cvs checkout* and *cvs update*) explained in Chapters 3 and 10. The *-d* option causes CVS to record the time of import based on a file's last modification time, rather than the current time.

Like *cvs update*, *cvs import* reports on the status of files it adds to the repository. These are the output codes for *cvs import*:

C *file*

> The file already exists in the repository and has been modified locally. A conflict must be resolved.
>
> This code is usually seen when a project is reimported (see the next section, "Vendor Branches").

I *file*

> The file has matched a *cvsignore* pattern and has been ignored.

L *file*

> The file is a symbolic link and has been ignored.

N *file*

> The file is new and has been added to the repository.

U *file*

> The file already exists in the repository and has not been locally modified. A new revision has been created.
>
> This code is usually seen when a project is reimported (see "Vendor Branches," next).

Vendor Branches

A vendor branch is a special type of branch that CVS creates automatically when you *import* a project. If your project is based on code external to the project itself, such as in-house patches to a vendor's code base, the vendor branch provides a way to merge updates from the external source with your own code.

If you intend to use vendor branches, create your project with *cvs import*, using the vendor's code as the initial directory for the project. Make your changes on the main trunk and run the project normally; the vendor branch is used only when the vendor releases a new set of code.

When the vendor provides a new release, use the *cvs import* command to add the new code to the same CVS project with the same vendor tag and a new release tag. In effect, this is a special *cvs commit* to the vendor branch.

Example 7-2 shows a vendor-branch import to the *wizzard* project. Note the new release tag. The project name and vendor tag remain the same as in Example 7-1.

Example 7-2. Importing a vendor branch

```
bash-2.05a$ cvs -d cvs_server:/var/lib/cvs import wizzard wizzard ver_2-0
C wizzard/TODOf" 5L, 270C written
```

Example 7-2. Importing a vendor branch (continued)

```
C wizzard/README
C wizzard/Makefile
C wizzard/INSTALL
.
.
.
C wizzard/doc/design/Specification.rtf
C wizzard/doc/design/Requirements.doc
C wizzard/doc/design/Design.rtf
C wizzard/doc/design/Analysis.rtf
C wizzard/doc/design/AcceptanceTest.doc

17 conflicts created by this import.
Use the following command to help the merge:

    cvs -d cvs_server:/var/lib/cvs checkout -j<prev_rel_tag> -jver_2-0 wizzard
```

If a file is changed on the vendor branch and the local file has not changed, CVS sets the trunk revision of the file to the new vendor-branch revision.

If both the vendor-branch copy and the local copy of a file have changes, CVS reports this as a conflict with the message "*N* conflicts created by this import," where *N* is the number of conflicts. CVS also provides a suggested variant of *cvs checkout* to help you resolve all the conflicts, using two *-j* command options to merge the vendor branch with the trunk.

> Beginning with CVS 1.12.10, if you want to import new files only to the vendor branch and not to the trunk, you can use the *-X* command option to *cvs import*.
>
> If the client version number is less than 1.12.10 but the server's is greater, you can have the repository administrator use the configuration option instead.

CVS 1.11.5 tries to provide the exact *cvs checkout* command you can use to find the differences between the previous release and the current release of the vendor branch and merge those differences to the trunk. If your version doesn't do this, try the following command:

```
    cvs checkout -j previous_release_tag -j current_release_tag projectname
```

You may also need to include the *-d repository_path* CVS option if you run this command from outside the sandbox, where CVS can't find the repository path in the sandbox administrative files.

"Merging Branches" of Chapter 4 explains how the *-j* option works and how to resolve any conflicts that arise from this type of merge. Tag the vendor branch once these conflicts have been resolved, and use that tag as the *previous_release_tag* when you next merge changes from a vendor branch.

If the vendor branch contains binary files or files with keywords, use the keyword (*-k*) and wrappers (*-W*) command options to *cvs import*. Keywords and wrappers are discussed in Chapter 3.

If you have more than one external source for a project, you can use the *-b* command option to run *cvs import* on an arbitrary branch number. This creates an additional vendor branch with the specified branch number. Create a separate vendor branch for each separate code source for your project, to help you keep track of which changes came from which vendor.

When selecting a branch to use as a new vendor branch for a new code source, determine that there is no preexisting branch with the number you choose. When updating an existing vendor branch (other than the default branch), use the *-b* option with the numeric ID of the branch, to specify the target branch for the current import.

 Be careful when using *-b*, as CVS doesn't check whether the branch number corresponds to the vendor tag given in the *import* command. You can accidentally overwrite one vendor branch with another branch's files.

Alternatives to Importing

If your project does not contain files provided outside the project, it is unlikely you will need to use vendor branches. If this is the case, you can bypass *cvs import*. To do so, create a new project by adding a new subdirectory to the repository root directory, either by editing the repository directly or by checking out the repository root directory and then using *cvs add* in that sandbox.

If you do not need the vendor-branch capability of *cvs import*, the choice between *cvs import* and the combination of *cvs checkout* and *cvs add* is a matter of personal taste. However, I recommend that you use either of those methods—using CVS commands to create a new project—rather than editing the repository directly.

Creating a project with cvs add

To create a project with CVS commands other than *cvs import*, you need to check out a sandbox that contains only the repository root directory, create the new project root directory, and add that directory with *cvs add*.

To check out the repository root directory, use a period (.) as the project name. Use the *-d name* command option to specify a directory name in which to check out the sandbox. To avoid including subdirectories, use the *-l* command option to *cvs checkout*.

Example 7-3 shows how to create a project and an initial project sandbox by checking out the repository root directory and using *cvs add*.

Example 7-3. Importing without cvs import

```
bash-2.05a$ cvs -d cvs_server:/var/lib/cvs checkout -l -d cvsroot .
cvs server: Updating cvsroot
bash-2.05a$ cd cvsroot
bash-2.05a$ mkdir wizzard
bash-2.05a$ cvs add wizzard
Directory /var/lib/cvs/wizzard added to the repository
bash-2.05a$ cd ~/cvs
bash-2.05a$ cvs -d cvs_server:/var/lib/cvs checkout wizzard
cvs server: Updating wizzard
```

These are the steps for this method:

1. Check out the entire top-level directory of the repository, renaming the sandbox root directory with a name such as *cvsroot*, as shown in Example 7-3.

2. Change the directory into *cvsroot* and create the new project root directory. In Example 7-3, the project directory is *wizzard*.

3. If you have existing files or directories to import, copy them into your newly created directory.

4. Use *cvs add* to add the new files and directories to the repository. If you add files as well as directories, you also need to run *cvs commit*. Example 7-3 shows directory addition only.

   As explained in Chapter 3, the *cvs add* command adds directories immediately, but files are added to the repository only after the next *cvs commit*.

5. Change directories to a working directory and check out the new project to test whether the import worked successfully, as shown in Example 7-3.

6. Use *cvs release* to remove the repository root sandbox you checked out in step 1. Remove any temporary files you created when preparing to import the project.

Creating a project by editing the repository

The second way to create a new project and bypass *cvs import* is to edit the repository directly. Editing the repository always involves the risk of making a minor typing error and affecting other projects (or your own), so I suggest you back up the repository before editing it.

To create a new project by editing the repository:

1. Log in to the repository computer with any user that has write access to the repository root directory.

2. Change the directory into the repository root directory.

3. Use *mkdir project_root_name* to create the project root directory.

The rest of this process is optional and is needed only if you have existing files to add to the project:

4. Log in to a workstation computer.

5. Use *cvs -d repository_path checkout project_root_name* to check out a sandbox.

6. Copy any existing project files and directories into the new sandbox.

7. Use *cvs add* to add the new files and directories to the repository. If you add files as well as directories, you also need to use *cvs commit*.

Importing from Other Version Control Systems

You might want to import a project, including the project's history, from a different version control system into CVS.

If the other version control system can export files into RCS format, use the following steps to install the RCS files into CVS:

1. Ensure that the latest revision in each RCS file isn't locked, the access list is empty, and the file-locking type is set to *strict*, using the tools available in your version control system if possible.

   If your version control system doesn't have tools to do these things and you have RCS installed, use *rcs -elL filename* to set locking and access appropriately.

 If RCS isn't available, you can proceed to steps 2 and 3 anyhow, but once the files are in the repository, use *cvs admin* commands to set locking and access.

2. Create the project's directory structure in CVS using *cvs import* or one of the alternative methods described earlier.

3. Copy the RCS files directly into the appropriate directories in the repository.

If the other version control system can't make *RCS* files, write a script to check out each revision of each file from the other system and commit it into CVS, or create an RCS file with the RCS *ci* command and use *ci* to add each revision of the original file to the RCS file. If you create RCS files, you can install them to CVS as described earlier.

The *contrib* directory in the CVS source contains scripts that convert SCCS and PVCS files to files that CVS can use. These scripts can be used as templates for scripts to convert files from other version control systems. Appendix B contains more information about the *sccs2rcs* and *pvcs2rcs* scripts.

Distributing Files

All project leads need to distribute completed work at various stages of a project. When working with some projects, such as content management of web sites, you need to distribute files frequently with small changes. With others, such as large programming projects, you need to distribute files less often and with larger changes.

checkout and update

One way to distribute files is to use the *cvs checkout* command to produce a set of files for distribution. Another way is to use the *cvs update* command on an existing set of files.

The *checkout* and *update* commands are designed to produce a sandbox suitable for editing the files being checked out or updated. The commands create administrative files in the sandbox that most project leads don't want in a public distribution, so you may need to remove the administrative files in the *CVS* subdirectory from each of the checked-out directories.

There is a benefit to using *checkout* and *update* to distribute files. When you use either command on an existing sandbox, CVS sends only the differences between the revisions currently in the sandbox and the revisions requested from the repository. This approach uses less bandwidth than the *export* command, which retrieves entire files.

Exporting Files

Although *cvs checkout* creates a sandbox suitable for editing copies of a project's files, *cvs export* creates a release of the project's files that is suitable for publication. This command uses most of the same internal code as *cvs checkout*, but *cvs export* does not create any *CVS* subdirectories or CVS administrative files.

cvs export requires that you use a date or tag command option. The *-D now* or *-r HEAD* options export the latest revisions of all files in a project.

If you don't have any binary files in your project, you can export with *-kv* to set the keyword-substitution mode to values only, so that the string *$keyword: value$* shows in each exported file as *value*. This can be an advantage when you are publishing a completed release of your project. For example, the string *$Revision$* displays as *5.7* and the string *$Author$* displays as *jenn*. Keywords are commonly used in "About this program" displays.

The syntax for *cvs export* is:

```
cvs [cvs-options] export [command-options] project_name
```

cvs export uses a subset of the options available with *cvs checkout*. It accepts the *-D date*, *-r revision*, and *-r tag* options to specify the revision to be exported. You can also use the *-f* option, which instructs CVS to use the *HEAD* revision if the specified revision is not available.

The *-l* and *-R* options specify local or recursive operation, and the *-k mode* option is used to set the keyword-expansion mode. Use the *-n* option to prevent CVS from running an export program specified in the *modules* scripting file.

The *-d directory* option provides a directory name for CVS to export the files to. Otherwise, CVS exports the files and subdirectories to a directory named for the module, or for the project root directory.

If you use *-d* and are exporting only one file from a subdirectory, CVS removes intermediate directories. For example, *cvs export -d shortpath /long/path/to/file* will produce a directory *shortpath* containing *file*. Use *-N* with *-d* to prevent CVS from removing intermediate directories.

Example 7-4 shows an export of the *wizzard* project.

Example 7-4. Using cvs export

```
bash-2.05a$ cvs -d cvs_server:/var/lib/cvs export -D now wizzard
cvs export: Updating wizzard
U wizzard/Changelog
U wizzard/INSTALL
U wizzard/Makefile
U wizzard/README
U wizzard/TODO
cvs export: Updating wizzard/doc
cvs export: Updating wizzard/doc/design
U wizzard/doc/design/AcceptanceTest.doc
U wizzard/doc/design/Analysis.rtf
U wizzard/doc/design/Requirements.doc
U wizzard/doc/design/Specification.rtf
cvs export: Updating wizzard/doc/plan
U wizzard/doc/plan/Schedule.rtf
cvs export: Updating wizzard/lib
cvs export: Updating wizzard/man
cvs export: Updating wizzard/src
U wizzard/src/config.h
U wizzard/src/handheld.c
U wizzard/src/server.c
U wizzard/src/wizzard.c
```

If you are using CVS to manage a web server, FTP site, or other publication system, you may want to ensure that the latest revisions of the project files are in your publication directory. You can do this by automatically exporting the files on a regular basis using *cvs export*, *cvs checkout*, or *cvs update*.

cvs export attempts to write the full revision of each file, and it will not export a file if an existing file of the same name is in the directory it is trying to write to. If you want to overwrite an existing copy of the project or if you want to transmit only changes, *cvs checkout* or *cvs update* may be more useful. See the "checkout and update" section earlier in this chapter for more details.

You may need to set up permissions, create symbolic links, or move files after they have been exported. A build tool such as *make* can be useful for this.

Example 7-5 shows a simple script that exports a project, tests whether the export worked, and then runs an installation script using the *make* utility. The script in the example could be called from *cron* or any other Unix or Linux scheduler.

Example 7-5. Export cron script

```
cd /ftp/internal
/bin/rm -r wizzard
/usr/bin/cvs export -D now wizzard
if [ $? -eq 0 ]; then
      cd wizzard
      /usr/bin/make install
else
      /bin/cat "Export failed with return code $?" | /usr/bin/mail wizmanager -s \
        "Wizzard export failed"
fi
```

You can also run a script similar to the one in Example 7-5 to export your project whenever a file has been changed, using the *loginfo* administrative file or the *-i* option in the *modules* file. These files are explained in the following section.

Running Scripts

In the repository's *CVSROOT* directory, there are several *scripting files* that allow you to run scripts while a project is being committed, tagged, updated, or modified in other ways. The scripts called from scripting files are often used to interact with other programs or to enforce standards.

 The *CVSROOT* directory and its files were described in Chapter 6. This section explains the scripting files in more detail.

Example 7-6 shows a *commitinfo* scripting file that runs a layout-testing program called *indent-tester* on the *wizzard* project files. CVS calls scripts in *commitinfo* before files are committed.

Example 7-6. Sample commitinfo file

```
^wizzard/src\(/\|$\) /var/lib/cvs/CVSROOT/indent-tester -gnu %r/%p %s
```

To make Example 7-6 work with CVS versions prior to 1.12.6, remove the *%r/%p %s*.

When a project file is committed, CVS searches the *commitinfo* file for rules that match the project file's path; if CVS finds a rule, it runs the script given in that rule. The rule in Example 7-6 matches all files in the *src* directory (and its subdirectories) of the *wizzard* project and tells CVS to run the *indent-tester* script on those files, also providing the parameters the script expects. (Later in this chapter, Example 7-8 shows the *indent-tester* script that can be used to enforce indentation standards for a project.)

CVS processes the scripting files separately for each directory that is affected by a command, and it calls the script in the scripting file once for each directory it matches. If you run *cvs commit wizzard*, CVS checks *commitinfo* for patterns that match *wizzard* and runs the script once for the files in the *wizzard* directory, then does the same for each subdirectory, checking for patterns that match *wizzard/doc* and processing its files, followed by *wizzard/lib* and *wizzard/src*.

Working with Scripting Files

The scripting files are all stored in your repository's *CVSROOT* directory. The purpose of each file is described in the section of this chapter named for that file. Most of these files use a common syntax.

Some files don't use the common syntax. In such cases, the syntax is described in the same section as the file.

The common syntax is rule-based, one line per rule, and each rule consists of a pattern to be matched and an action to be taken. When CVS reads a scripting file, it tries to match the pattern to project files. If the pattern matches the file that CVS is currently processing, CVS runs the action. The action is usually a pathname to a script and parameters for that script. The common syntax is described in the next section.

To edit any of the scripting files, check out the file with the following command:

```
cvs -d repository_path checkout CVSROOT/filename
```

Edit the file with any text editor, then commit the file with *cvs commit*. CVS stores these files in the repository's *CVSROOT* directory in both plain-text and RCS formats and updates both types of file every time a file is committed. When you check them out, you'll only see the plain-text format in the *CVSROOT* sandbox directory.

You can also store the scripts you call from these files in your repository's *CVSROOT* directory or a subdirectory of *CVSROOT*. Add such scripts to the *checkoutlist* file in *CVSROOT*, so that they are automatically exported to the *CVSROOT* directory when they're committed. The *checkoutlist* file is described in Chapter 6.

 It is tempting to store scripts called by the scripting files in the project or module they are called for. Resist this temptation, because CVS then tries to call such a script when the script is itself being committed. Also be aware that if you store scripts in a project or module, they'll be stored on the repository machine in RCS format only; scripts can't be run from that format.

Do not attempt to interact with the user from scripts called from the scripting files. Some remote-access methods do not support such interaction at all, and other methods can be affected by having unexpected data go through their socket. Users other than the one involved in the interaction may also be left waiting on the first user until the interaction is complete.

If any script contains a CVS command, be aware that the command that calls the script will not finish until the script does. You may find that some directories have been locked by the original command, which can't finish and release them until the script is finished, but the script can't finish because the second command can't run until those same locks are released. This situation can be prevented by having your script call any CVS commands in the background or by calling the script in the background (which probably necessitates having the script report any errors by email to the repository or project administrator).

Scripts called from all files except the *modules* file are run on the computer that hosts the repository. Two of the *modules* scripts run on the sandbox computer; the others run on the repository computer.

If you do not provide a full path for a script, CVS searches the user's *PATH* environment variable. To prevent the wrong script from being called, I recommend using the full path in all scripting files.

Your repository administrator may limit your access to the scripting files for security reasons. Work with the repository administrator; you are asking for permission to run arbitrary scripts, so try to address her concerns.

Common Syntax

Most of the scripting files in *CVSROOT*—including *commitinfo*, *loginfo*, *editinfo*, *rcsinfo*, and *verifymsg*—share a common syntax. The *modules* file does not use the common syntax, as described in the next section.

If your version of CVS is older than 1.12.6, see the "Common Syntax: Pre-1.12.6" sidebar for information on the syntax you should use.

The developers of CVS have been very busy with the scripting files: if you are running a version of CVS newer than 1.12.13 (the current version while I'm writing this), check the documentation to see if they've added new and useful features.

In versions later than 1.12.6, whether you use the new or old syntax for the scripting files is controlled by the configuration option *UseNewInfoFmtStrings*. The valid options are yes (to use the new syntax) and no (to use the syntax prior to 1.12.6). These options are set in the *config* file, normally stored in the *CVSROOT* directory.

There is a very temporary feature in current versions of CVS: if there is no format string in a line in a scripting file, CVS will append as arguments the information it appended before 1.12.6. Please *do not* rely on this feature continuing.

The file syntax is as follows:

```
name-pattern action format_string
```

The *name-pattern* is a regular expression that must match a relative path within the repository, or one of the special words *DEFAULT* and *ALL*. It is separated from the *action* by one or more spaces or tabs. Regular expressions are explained in Chapter 11.

The *action* is a command-line template, or the filename (and path) of a script plus any parameters required for that script. Good practice is to use the full pathname of the script, with the *$CVSROOT* variable standing in for the repository path. You may embed one or more format strings in the template or among the script's parameters; you may also use the variables listed later in this chapter, in the section *CVSROOT Variables*.

The character # at the start of a line signals a comment. Blank lines are ignored. There is no way to break a long line in current versions of CVS.

CVS processes the file by matching the current repository directory to the regular expression. It looks for the first matching line, and runs the action provided on that line, and also runs the actions on any line with a name-pattern of *ALL*. Note that *DEFAULT* as a name-pattern is deemed to match everything, so ensure that it is the last name-pattern other than *ALL*.

Even though you can call several actions with separate *ALL* lines, the actions are not guaranteed to run in sequence. If you have inter-dependent actions, use a script called by a single *ALL* line, rather than a set of *ALL* lines.

The format strings are processed by CVS before being passed to the action's script or command. Before processing, the format string consists of a %, followed by a single variable optionally enclosed in braces ({ }), or by a set of variables enclosed in braces. Some of the variables represent individual values, and other represent list values. A set of variables enclosed in braces must all represent list values.

Each value represented by a format string variable is passed to its script as a single argument, irrespective of white space within the value. A list on its own is passed as a single argument for each element of the list.

A set of list values are also passed as a single argument for each element of each list, but are collated. For instance, *%{sVv}* in the *taginfo* file will produce a list of arguments in the format *file1 oldversion1 newversion1 file2 oldversion2 newversion2 file3 oldversion3 newversion3*.

The format string variables which are valid in all files represent single values, and are:

%   A literal percent sign (i.e., %% will become %).

c   The name of the command which triggered the execution of the script. In a script run because of a *cvs commit*, for instance, the format string will be replaced with commit.

n   The null string.

p   The name of the directory in the repository that's currently being processed.

r   The path of the repository root directory.

R   Relevant in repositories which are involved in proxy setups. This is the referrer, or the repository which the client contacted and which referred the operation to this server.

The modules File

The *modules* file is used to define CVS modules. A *project* is defined by the project root directory and contains all files and subdirectories; a *module* can be an arbitrary set of directories and files. Once a module is defined, the files and directories it describes can be checked out into a sandbox by either the module name or the name of the repository directory (or directories) it represents. The *modules* file can also specify scripts to run when CVS acts on a file within a module.

Each module definition needs to be on a line of its own. When adding directories to module definitions, use relative paths from the repository root directory.

Example 7-7 shows a *modules* file. The lines in the file are explained in the following sections on module definition.

Example 7-7. CVSROOT/modules

```
# wizzard project. Project lead: jenn. Module type: regular.
wiz -s development wizzard

# singer project. Project lead: doppel. Module type: alias.
singer -a music/descant !chorus/tenor !chorus/bass chorus

# wizsinger project. Project lead: doppel. Module type: regular
wizsinger -i /var/lib/cvs/CVSROOT/export &wiz &singer
```

Example 7-7. CVSROOT/modules (continued)

```
#wizmake project: retrieves just the Makefile from wizzard.
wizmake wizzard Makefile

# wizhandheld project: retrieves just the handheld.c file.
wiztest wizzard/src handheld.c
```

Updating Old Scripting Files

If you're using scripts designed for the old format, you will want to either use the old format for the scripting files, or add format strings to the scripting files that duplicate the old format.

I recommend adding the format strings. Eventually, the developers will remove the *UseNewInfoFmtStrings* configuration option—probably not for years, but it'll be easier in the long run to just edit the files now.

To add the strings, edit the scripting file and add the following to each line of the file:

- In *commitinfo*: %r/%p %s
- In *taginfo*: %t %o %p %{sv}
- In *verifymsg*: %l

To see this update, look at Example 7-6. In the first edition of this book, the line was:

```
^wizzard/src\(/\|$\) /var/lib/cvs/CVSROOT/indent-tester -gnu
```

In this edition, the line is:

```
^wizzard/src\(/\|$\) /var/lib/cvs/CVSROOT/indent-tester -gnu %r/%p %s
```

The *loginfo* file always had a format string, so it's more difficult to update. Ideally, you should rewrite your scripts to use the new syntax: most importantly, to treat each item generated by the format string as a separate argument.

If that's not feasible, there's a temporary fix available. In each format string, put a 1 immediately after the percent sign. For example, if you had the string *%{Vv}*, you should now have *%1{Vv}*. Also, replace the implicit directory path that *loginfo* used to pass with an explicit one—the string for that is *%p*.

Be aware that CVS will provide deprecation warnings if you use the temporary fix— you can ignore them for now, but eventually the developers intend to remove support for the old syntax entirely.

Alias modules

An *alias module* can group files and directories into a single module, regardless of where they are stored in the repository tree. The syntax for an alias module definition is:

```
module-name -a path [path...]
```

The *path* may be an existing module, a pathname to a file, or a directory path, and there may be any number of paths. If the path leads to a directory, the directory and all subdirectories and files are included in the module.

If you wish to exclude a subdirectory in an alias module, use an exclamation mark (!) in front of the directory name.

Alias modules cannot have options, nor can you specify scripts to run for them. If you need to use options or scripts, you can define an alias module as part of a regular module, or you can simply use a regular module instead.

Alias modules are easier to use than are regular modules (described in the next section). You define alias modules with a space-separated list of all the items you want in the module; regular modules have a more complicated syntax. You can also add multiple directories, files, and modules in an alias module; a regular module allows only one directory.

The *singer* project in Example 7-7 defines an alias module that includes all files and directories in the *chorus* directory, except those under the subdirectories *tenor* and *bass*. This project also includes the *descant* file from the *music* directory.

When you use an alias module's name in a CVS command which acts on the repository, CVS treats the module name as if the list of items in the *path* were used instead. When you use an alias module in the *checkout* command, CVS creates a separate sandbox for each item in the *path*.

Regular modules

A *regular module* defines options for a project. It can also define subsets of a project or group modules together. If you have a particularly complex project, you may need to define your project with a combination of alias and regular modules.

Using alias modules in a complex definition allows you to add multiple directories with one alias, and the regular module allows you to define options to use when calling that module.

The syntax to define a regular module is:

```
module-name [options] [directory [filename|subdir...]] [&module...]
```

The directory should be a path relative to the repository root directory. If filenames or subdirectory names are included, they should refer to files or subdirectories in the directory. The module definition then applies only to those files or subdirectories. Note that you need a space between the directory and the files within the directory, and you can define only one directory within a regular module.

You can include an existing module in a regular module by prefixing the existing module name with an ampersand (&) and listing it in the regular module definition. The existing module can be an alias or a regular module. If it is not defined in the *modules* file, it must be a directory path relative to the repository's root directory. This rule is illustrated in the *wizsinger* module definition in Example 7-7, which includes two existing modules. The sequence of the module definitions doesn't matter; you can include a module in an earlier line than the module's own definition.

Module options and scripts

Most of the options for a regular module define scripts to run immediately after a CVS command on the files in the module. Here is the full list of options:

-d directory_name
> Use *directory_name* rather than the module name as the name of the sandbox root directory.

-e script
> Run the specified script whenever the module is exported. This script is given the module name as an argument.

-i script

> Run the specified script whenever the module is committed. This script is given the full pathname of the relevant repository directory as an argument.
>
> This option was removed in CVS 1.11.6 for security reasons.

-o script

> Run the specified script whenever the module is checked out. This script is given the module name as an argument.

-s status

> Provide a *status* for the module. This has no meaning internal to CVS, but when the command *cvs checkout -s* runs, the display output is sorted in ascending order by *status*. You can use the *status* string for anything; examples include the name of the person responsible for the module or whether the module is in active development.
>
> CVS allocates an 11-character space for the status string when it is displayed, but the string is not truncated if it is longer than 11 characters.

-t script

> Run the specified script whenever *rtag* is used on the module. This script does not run when *tag* is used. The *taginfo* file is a better way to run a script when files are tagged. This script is given two arguments: the module name and the name of the tag.

-u script

> Run the specified script whenever the module is updated. This script is given the full pathname of the affected repository directory as an argument.
>
> This option was removed in CVS 1.11.6 for security reasons.

The scripts designated in the *modules* file run after their respective processes have been completed.

If the repository is not on the same computer as the client, CVS stores the scripts for the *-i* and *-u* options in the *Checkin.prog* and *Update.prog* files in the *CVS* subdirectories in the sandbox. These scripts will run on the client computer (and are no longer available, as of 1.11.6). All other scripts called from the modules file run on the repository server computer.

> The behavior of *Checkin.prog* and *Update.prog* changed in CVS 1.11.6 for security reasons.

The sandbox copies of the *Checkin.prog* and *Update.prog* files are not changed when the *modules* file or the repository computer's copies of the scripts are changed. If you change a module definition or the *commit* or *update* scripts for your project, your users must release and recreate their sandboxes.

The commitinfo File

The *commitinfo* file is processed before a file is committed and is usually used to enforce project standards for file format or content. It runs very early in the commit, during the tests to determine which files have changed.

commitinfo uses the syntax described in "Common Syntax" earlier in this chapter, with one rule per line and each rule consisting of the following elements:

```
name_pattern action format_string
```

If a *name_pattern* matches the name and path of the directory or module parameter to *cvs commit*, CVS calls the *action* and appends as parameters the result of the expanded *format_string*. In addition to the usual format string variables, it allows *s*, a list variable containing the names of the files to be committed. The *name_pattern* may contain *DEFAULT*, but not *ALL*.

> In versions prior to 1.12.6, CVS appends as parameters the full path of the repository and the filenames of all files to be committed, and does not have a format string.

If you run *cvs commit* from a sandbox directory without specifying a project, CVS tries to match the repository path that corresponds to your current sandbox directory with a rule in *commitinfo*. If you run *cvs commit* with a file or directory parameter, CVS tries to match the repository path that corresponds to that parameter.

CVS makes a set of normal-format files from the data it receives from the CVS client and stores them in a temporary directory to allow the action to read a normal file rather than an RCS file. If CVS is running in client/server mode, the script or command in the action runs on the repository computer in a directory that is a copy of the sandbox directory being committed. If this script returns a nonzero value, the commit does not proceed. The script cannot change the file that is being checked; so although you can use a layout-testing program such as the one shown in the following example, you cannot successfully use one that modifies the layout.

Example 7-8 shows an indentation tester that can be used with the *commitinfo* file in Example 7-6. Note that this tester assumes that all files it is called for can be tested validly with *indent*.

Example 7-8. Indentation tester

```
INDENTOPTS=$1
shift
while test "$1" != ""
  do
  FILENAME=$1
  TMPFILE="$TMP/id.$$"
  cat $FILENAME | indent $INDENTOPTS > $TMPFILE
  diff $FILENAME $TMPFILE 2>/dev/null >/dev/null
```

Example 7-8. Indentation tester (continued)

```
  if [ $? -ne 0 ]; then
    return 1
  shift
  done
return 0
```

The loginfo File

The *loginfo* file is processed after files have been committed to the repository. During a *commit*, the file is processed once per directory, after each directory's changes have been successfully stored. During an *import*, the file is processed once, after the import is complete. During a directory *add*, it's processed after the directory has been created. *loginfo* uses the syntax described in "Common Syntax" earlier in this chapter, with one rule per line and each rule consisting of the following elements:

```
    name_pattern action format_string
```

If a *name_pattern* matches the name and path of the directory parameter to *cvs commit*, CVS calls the *action* and passes it the log message from the *commit* on the standard input. CVS also passes the repository path being committed to, followed by an expanded format string. The *action* can consist of a script, a shell command, or a group of shell commands that will run as one command. The script or command in the action runs on the repository computer.

The *name_pattern* supports both *DEFAULT* and *ALL*. In addition to the standard format string variables, *loginfo* supports:

s   This list variable expands to the names of the current files being processed.

T   This list variable expands to the tag name of the destination, or the empty string if there is no relevant tag name.

V   This list variable expands to the files' revision number prior to the commit.

v   This list variable expands to the files' revision number after the commit.

 If you run the *cvs* command that triggered the *loginfo* script from a sandbox directory, CVS tries to match the repository path that corresponds to your current sandbox directory with a rule in *loginfo*. If you run the command with a file or directory parameter, CVS tries to match the repository path that corresponds to that parameter.

The *loginfo* file is usually used to control where (aside from the repository) the log information from *cvs commit* is sent. It can also be used to trigger actions, such as notifying all developers of changes, maintaining a file that logs a record of changes, or exporting the changed files to a file server.

Example 7-9 shows a *loginfo* file that emails the log message for every change to the user *cvsadmin*. This file also runs the *changelog* script that is stored in *CVSROOT* for every file that is committed to the *wizzard* project. The line for the *teppic* project demonstrates a way to call an export script in the background.

Example 7-9. A loginfo file

```
^wizzard\(/\|$\) /var/lib/cvs/CVSROOT/changelog %{sv}
^teppic\(/\|$\) /var/lib/cvs/CVSROOT/export &
ALL mail -s "CVS commit" cvsadmin
```

Old loginfo Format Strings

The format string is stored in the *loginfo* file and controls the information that CVS passes to the script or command. The string consists of a , followed by a space, a single variable, or a set of variables enclosed in braces ({ }). These are the variables:

s

Expands to the name of the current file being processed.

V

Expands to the file's revision number prior to the commit.

v

Expands to the file's revision number after the commit.

When CVS processes the format string, the output is in the form:

"*variable_expansion* [*variable_expansion*...]"

The output includes a variable expansion for each file that was committed. The variable expansion is a comma-separated set of strings, such that %{sV} could be expanded to a string such as *main.c,1.3*. Dollar signs ($), backticks (`` ` ``), backslashes (\), and quotation marks (") in the repository path or filename are escaped with backslashes.

The postadmin File

The *postadmin* file defines programs to run after any *cvs admin* command that modifies a file is run. These programs run on the repository computer. This file is available only in versions 1.12.10 and later.

This file uses the standard scripting file syntax, and supports both *DEFAULT* and *ALL*.

The postproxy File

The *postproxy* file defines programs to run after a secondary server has completed a connection to a primary server, and before the secondary server releases the connection to the client. These programs run on the secondary server, and are called once per directory. It is recommended that the *postproxy* file include a command to update the secondary server's copy of the repository. This file is available only in versions 1.12.10 and later.

This file uses the standard scripting file syntax, and supports both *DEFAULT* and *ALL*. It has the additional format variable *P*, the repository path of the primary server.

The posttag File

The *posttag* file defines programs to run after any *cvs tag* or *rtag* command that modifies a file is run. These programs run on the repository computer. This file is available only in versions 1.12.10 and later.

This file uses the standard scripting file syntax, and supports both *DEFAULT* and *ALL*. It permits the same format string attributes as the *taginfo* file: see the later section "The taginfo File" for more information.

The postwatch File

The *postwatch* file defines programs to run after any *cvs watch*, *edit*, or *unedit* command that modifies the repository's watch administrative file, *fileattr*. See Chapter 6 (specifically the information on *fileattr*) for more information on which commands are affected. These programs run on the repository computer. This file is available only in versions 1.12.10 and later.

This file uses the standard scripting file syntax, and supports both *DEFAULT* and *ALL*.

Note that *edit* and *unedit* do not always contact the server, and sometimes cache their notification to be run later.

The preproxy File

The *preproxy* file defines programs to run before a secondary server connects to a primary server, and after the client has contacted the secondary server. These programs run on the secondary server, and are called once, from the top directory specified by the client's request. This file is available only in versions 1.12.10 and later.

This file uses the standard scripting file syntax, and supports both *DEFAULT* and *ALL*. It has the additional format variable *P*, the repository path of the primary server.

The rcsinfo File

The *rcsinfo* file is processed before a file is committed. It uses the syntax described in "Common Syntax" earlier in this chapter. The action in each rule of an *rcsinfo* file should not be a path to a script; it should be a path to a template file that will be displayed when CVS asks the user for a log message during a *cvs commit* operation.

If you run *cvs commit* from a sandbox directory, CVS tries to match the repository path that corresponds to your current sandbox directory with a rule in *rcsinfo*. If you run *cvs commit* with a file, directory, or module parameter, CVS tries to match the repository path that corresponds to that parameter. The *DEFAULT* and *ALL* rules described in "Common Syntax" are honored. There is no need for a format string.

If CVS finds a match, it displays the contents of the template file when it opens an editor to receive a log message. If there is a matching rule and an *ALL* rule in *rcsinfo*, CVS displays the contents of the file each rule refers to (that is, it displays the contents of two files). Subject to any editing you do when you commit, the contents of the template file (or files) are stored as part of the log message.

 If you use *-m message* or *-f file* as options to *cvs commit*, the *rcsinfo* file is ignored.

If CVS is running in client/server mode, it stores a copy of the template file in the *Template* file in the *CVS* subdirectory of the sandbox when the sandbox is checked out. In CVS versions prior to 1.12.1, this file is not updated with other sandbox files, so if the *rcsinfo* file or the templates it refers to are changed, your users should release and recreate their sandboxes. (In 1.12.1, the behavior was changed, and template files are updated with other sandbox files.)

The taginfo File

The *taginfo* file is processed before a file is tagged using either the *tag* or the *rtag* commands. *taginfo* uses the syntax described in "Common Syntax," earlier in this chapter, with one rule per line and each rule consisting of the following elements:

    name_pattern action format_string

If a *name_pattern* matches the name and path of the directory or module parameter to *cvs tag* or *cvs rtag*, CVS calls the script or command in the *action* and appends as parameters the result of the expanded *format_string*. It supports both *DEFAULT* and *ALL*. In addition to the usual format string variables, it allows:

b   Tag type. This is a single element variable, and evaluates to *T* for a branch, *N* for a nonbranch, or *?* for unknown.

o   Operation. This is a single element variable, and evaluates to *add*, *del*, or *mov* for additions, deletions, or moving of a tag.

s   This is a list variable, and evaluates to the current file name(s).

T   This is a list variable, and evaluates to the tag name of the destination, or the empty string if there is no such tag name.

t   This is a single element variable, and evaluates to the new tag name.

V   This is a list variable, and evaluates to the old version number (as for a move or delete operation).

v   This is a list variable, and evaluates to the new version number (as for an add or move operation).

 In versions prior to 1.12.6, CVS does not use a format string, and instead appends a parameter string. The parameter string has the following format:

```
tagname operation repository_path file_revision_pair [file
revision_pair...]
```

The *file_revision_pair* is a space-separated pair of filename and revision number, and there is a pair for each file to be tagged.

The operations CVS provides are *add*, *mov*, and *del*. The *mov* operation is provided when *tag* or *rtag* is called with the tag-moving option *-F*, and *del* is provided when *tag* or *rtag* are called with the tag-deletion option *-d*. The *add* operation is provided when a new tag is added.

If CVS is running in client/server mode, the script given in the *action* runs on the repository computer. If the script exits with a nonzero exit status, the *tag* or *rtag* operation does not proceed. The script cannot modify the tag.

The *taginfo* file is often used to enforce tag name standards in a project. Example 7-10 shows the first part of a parser subroutine that returns 1 if a tag name doesn't fit the project's standards and 0 if it does.

Example 7-10. Parsing tag names

```
$TAGNAME=$ARGV[0];
$OPERATION=$ARGV[1];
$REP_PATH=$ARGV[2];
%FILE_REV=splice(@ARGV,3);

@tagfields=split('-',$TAGNAME)
if (!is_in(('prealpha','alpha','beta','stable'),$tagfields[1])) {
    return 1;
}
.
.
.
return 0;
```

The verifymsg File

The *verifymsg* file is processed before a file is committed and after you enter the *cvs commit* log message, either in the editor that CVS opens or by using the *-m message* or *-F file* options to *cvs commit*.

---

verifymsg uses the syntax described in "Common Syntax" of this chapter, with one rule per line and each rule consisting of the following elements:

```
name_pattern action format_string
```

If a *name_pattern* matches the name and path of the directory or module parameter to *cvs commit*, CVS calls the *action* and appends as parameters the result of the expanded *format_string*. It supports *DEFAULT* but not *ALL*. In addition to the usual format string variables, it allows:

l   The full path to a temporary file containing the log message.

s   A list variable containing the file names.

V   A list variable containing the version numbers prior to the commit. In versions prior to 1.12.6, CVS passes the script specified in *action* the path to a temporary file containing the *cvs commit* log message, and a copy of the log message on standard input (*stdin*).

If the repository is not on the same computer as the client, the script given in the *action* runs on the repository computer. If the script returns a nonzero value, the commit does not proceed.

The *verifymsg* file is usually used to enforce project standards for *commit* log messages, and the script often either checks or modifies the log message you enter when you commit files.

The script can modify the log message, and the *RereadLogAfterVerify* option in the *config* file in the repository's *CVSROOT* directory determines whether the original or the modified log message is used. (If the log message is reread, CVS reads it from the temporary file.) See Chapter 6 for information on the *config* file.

Interfacing with External Programs

CVS is rarely used alone. There are a number of project-management tools available, each used to perform a different set of tasks. The scripting files can be used to connect CVS to other project-management tools, such as bug trackers and build scripts.

Interfacing with Bug Trackers

Interfacing with a bug tracker is easiest if the tracker accepts input from standard input or via an email form. Use the *rcsinfo* file to have the *cvs commit* editor screen include the template your bug tracker requires, and use the *verifymsg* file to ensure that all fields are filled in appropriately. Then have a script in *verifymsg* or *loginfo* mail the log data to your bug tracker.

Examples 7-11 and 7-12 show how to integrate with the Bugzilla bug-tracking tool, available at *http://bugzilla.mozilla.org*. These examples assume that the Bugzilla email gateway has been enabled. The *@resolution* field in the message template allows you to change a project's status and is supported directly by Bugzilla.

Use the *verifymsg* script in Example 7-11 to separate out the bug ID so it can be used in the mail subject (which must have the format [Bug XXXX]). The rest of the log message can be sent as the mail body. The script uses the *read* command to get the bug ID from the first line of the log message, checks that the first line it reads uses the format it expects, and then mails the bug ID and the rest of the *stdin* input to the user *bugzilla* on the same computer. The script returns 1 if the format was wrong and 0 if it succeeds in mailing everything to Bugzilla.

Example 7-11. Interfacing with Bugzilla, verifymsg

```
#! /bin/bash
read prompt bugid
if [ $prompt != '@bugid' ]; then
    return 1
else
    mail -s "[Bug $bugid]" bugzilla
fi
return 0
```

Example 7-12 shows an *rcsinfo* template file that contains the *@bugid* string that Example 7-11 expects and the *@resolution* and *@message* strings that Bugzilla supports. Enter the bug ID, resolution status, and a log message to the right of each of these prompts.

Example 7-12. Interfacing with Bugzilla, message template

```
@bugid
@resolution
@message
```

A more complete *verifymsg* script than the one shown in Example 7-11 would include a facility to strip comments out of the template file, and the template file would have comments explaining what to write beside each prompt. (CVS strips lines that start with the string CVS:, so you can use that mechanism instead of your own comment-stripping code.)

Example 7-13 shows the lines in the *verifymsg* and *rcsinfo* files that would call these scripts for the *wizzard* project, if the scripts were called *bugzilla-mail* (Example 7-11) and *bugzilla-template* (Example 7-12).

Example 7-13. Interfacing with Bugzilla, scripting files

```
# In verifymsg, call the script bugzilla-mail
^wizzard\(/\|$\) /var/lib/cvsroot/CVSROOT/scripts/bugzilla-mail

# In rcsinfo, call bugzilla-template
^wizzard\(/\|$\) /var/lib/cvsroot/CVSROOT/scripts/bugzilla-template
```

Interfacing with Build Scripts

A build for publication should be slightly different from a build for development. During development, your developers want to start with a recent sandbox, build from that sandbox, make their changes, and then test only those changes. However, a build for testing or publication should be taken from a known set of revisions, frequently the most up-to-date revisions.

Fortunately, both building for incremental testing and building for a major release can be done using the same build script. If the script is included in the project files and designed to be able to be run from a sandbox, the developers can run their test builds from their sandboxes and the project lead can run testing or publication builds from an exported copy of the project files. Note that it's good practice to tag the project's files just before a testing or publication build, so that the exact revisions can be easily retrieved later.

If your developers are sharing a central set of files and have only a partial set of the project's files in their sandboxes, you can have the build script set up symbolic links to the shared files from their sandboxes or call files from a central location.

If your developers are changing copies of a set of files but will eventually want to distribute your project's files across several unrelated directories, it is best to develop the project to build under a single root directory, then distribute the files across multiple directories as part of the installation script.

Example 7-14 is a script for the *wizzard* project that tags the head revisions of all files, then builds and installs the project (assuming that the *Makefile* is properly configured). To create a build of this script for development, produce a smaller script that contains only the *make* and *make install* commands and run that smaller script from a developer's sandbox. To create a build of the project for testing or publication, run the full script given in Example 7-14 from any directory.

Example 7-14. Building for testing or publication

```
/usr/bin/cvs -d cvs:/var/lib/cvs rtag -r HEAD $1 wizzard
if [ $? -eq 0 ]; then
    cd /tmp
    /usr/bin/cvs -d cvs:/var/lib/cvs export -r $1 wizzard
    if [ $? -eq 0 ]; then
        cd wizzard
        /usr/bin/make
        /usr/bin/make install
    else
        echo "Export failed."
    fi
else
    echo "Tag failed."
fi
```

Enforcing Standards

The different scripting files can be used in the following ways to enforce project standards:

commitinfo
> Can be used to run a program through a layout checker, run a system configuration file through a syntax checker, or run a documentation file through a spelling and grammar checker. If the checker returns a nonzero exit status, the file is not committed and the commit fails for all files in that commit.

verifymsg
> Can be used to ensure that log messages meet the project's standards and contain the correct fields. This file can also be used to generate fields and include them in the log message.

taginfo
> Can be used to enforce a standard format for tag names.

Making Patchfiles

A *patchfile* is a special file that can be used by the *patch* utility to update a set of files from one revision to another. You don't need to use a patchfile to change files stored under CVS—but you may have exported and distributed your project and want to update the exported sets with only the changes.

To make a patch, use *cvs diff* or *cvs rdiff*, and redirect the output to a file. In most shells the command would be *cvs diff -r old -r new filenames > patchfile*. You can replace *filenames* with any project, file, module, or directory names that are compatible with *cvs diff* or *rdiff*. The parameters *old* and *new* are the old and new revision numbers or tags, and *patchfile* is the name of the file you want to create. The > symbol tells the shell to redirect the output into the file.

> CVS *diff* is the GNU *diff* tool, with additional features specifically to make it work well with CVS. Because of this, you can get further information about CVS *diff* from resources about GNU *diff*, such as the official GNU *diffutils* manual, found at *http://www.gnu.org/software/diffutils/diffutils.html*.

If your installation script rearranges the exported files so that they're in different places from where they are in a sandbox, use the GNU *diff* utility rather than the CVS *diff* utility. Export and install the old version in one directory, then export and install the new version in another. Run *diff -Nuar old new > patchfile*, where *old* and *new* are the names of the two top-level directories of the two installations. The result of the *diff* is your *patchfile*; test it by typing *patch -p1 old patchfile*, This command should update the older revision so it matches the newer revision.

I recommend the *diffutils* manual for information on using GNU *diff*, including ideas on creating top-quality *patchfiles*.

Tools

Project administrators should be aware of the CVS commands described in Chapters 3 and 5. You may also want to read Chapters 4 and 6.

In addition to the commands described in those chapters, there are two commands that are particularly useful to project administrators: *cvs admin* and *cvs history*. *cvs admin* allows you to use RCS-like commands on files stored in the repository. *cvs history* provides a record of the actions performed on a project's files and is similar to *cvs log* or *cvs annotate*.

The cvs admin Command

The *cvs admin* command is used to edit the RCS files directly in the repository. It is more accurately thought of as a set of commands than a single command, as it provides many of the commands that RCS would make available, though not all of these commands are usable or have an effect that matters to CVS. These commands are present mostly for historic reasons and backward compatibility with early versions of CVS.

If there is a system group called *cvsadmin* on the repository server, only users in that group can use the *cvs admin* command. If this group does not exist, any user can use the *cvs admin* commands on any repository files they have permission to change. Consider using the *cvsadmin* system group, as some of the *cvs admin* commands can prevent CVS from using the affected file or files.

 There is a new option in the *config* file of CVS 1.12.1 and later. The *UserAdminCommands* option allows the system administrator to set *cvs admin* options that users who are not in the *cvsadmin* group can run.

The syntax for *cvs admin* is as follows:

```
cvs [cvs-options] admin command-options [filename...]
```

 I strongly recommend always stating the filenames that you wish *cvs admin* to act on, as some of the *cvs admin* commands can be difficult or impossible to recover from if you accidentally apply them to the wrong file. If you do not specify a filename, *cvs admin* operates on all files in the current sandbox directory and moves recursively down its subdirectories.

Each of the RCS commands that *cvs admin* provides is represented by a command option to *cvs admin*. RCS commands that are obsolete or meaningless when used with CVS are not listed in this chapter. For many of the commands, there can be no space between an option and its argument. See Chapter 10 for the full list of *cvs admin* command options.

The most commonly used *cvs admin* option is the *-k* option, which sets the default keyword-substitution mode for a file. This option is explained in the "Binary Files and Wrappers" of Chapter 3. If you forget to set the *-kb* keyword-substitution mode of a binary file when you add it to the repository, you can use *cvs admin -kb filename* to correct the mistake.

If you use the *rcslock* script to reserve development of files, as described in Chapter 5, you use *cvs admin -l filename* and *cvs admin -u filename* to lock and unlock the file you are reserving.

The *-o* option is used in one of the methods of moving files, as described in Chapter 6. This option allows you to remove old revisions of a file, effectively collapsing the changes from those revisions into a single revision. It cannot be reversed once it is done, so be very careful and test it on a copy of the repository (not just a copy of the sandbox!) first. The full syntax of the *-o* option is provided in Chapter 10.

The *-m* option allows you to replace a log message. The *-s* option is used to set the state of a file. The state is shown in *cvs log* output and in the results of the *Log* keyword. The *-t* option is used to set a description of the file, which is also shown in *cvs log* output.

> The *-U* option to *cvs admin* sets file locking to nonstrict, which prevents CVS from working with a file effectively. The *-L* option repairs this problem by setting the file locking to strict. The *-U* and *-L* options should not be used, but if someone accidentally uses *-U* while trying to use *-u*, you now know you can use *-L* to repair the damage.

The cvs history Command

The *cvs history* command reports on the history of actions performed on the files in a repository. This command is a variation of the *cvs log* command explained in Chapter 5. The *cvs log* command displays only commit actions; *cvs history* can display most types of actions.

The history file

cvs history uses the *history* file in a repository's *CVSROOT* directory as a database and displays only events that have occurred while the file is present and writable. The *cvs init* command creates the *history* file by default. Note that CVS will not report an error if the *history* file is removed.

The *history* file must be writable by all users. Because it never causes a script to be executed, this is not a security issue. The actions that are logged to the history file are controlled by the *LogHistory* setting in the *config* file in the repository's *CVSROOT* directory.

cvs history output

The format of the output of the *cvs history* command varies, depending on the options chosen. The basic format of each line of the *history* output is:

```
type date timezone user {revision|path|branch} {module|directory|tag|filename}
[module|project-root-directory] access_type
```

The *type* is a single letter, representing one of the types given in the list at the end of this section. The *timezone* is +0000 (i.e., UTC) if not specified otherwise. The *access_type* is *remote* or *local*; if it is *local*, it shows the directory the sandbox was in when the command recorded in the *history* file was run.

Example 7-15 shows an example of most of the output types for *cvs history*. Whitespace has been removed to prevent the output from wrapping.

Example 7-15. cvs history command output

```
bash-2.05a$ cvs history -e -zUTC
O 2006-08-22 05:42 UTC jenn wizzard =wizzard= <remote>/*
O 2006-10-03 08:38 UTC jenn wizzard =wizmake= /tmp/*
O 2006-10-03 08:38 UTC jenn wizzard/src =wiztest= /tmp/*
M 2006-08-22 08:00 UTC jenn 1.8 1-introduction.sxw cvsbook = = <remote>
A 2006-08-29 12:17 UTC jenn 1.1 Z-copiesto cvsbook = = <remote>
W 2006-09-12 04:36 UTC jenn wizzard.h wizzard/src = = <remote>/src
C 2006-09-12 05:32 UTC jenn 1.2 main.c wizzard/src = = <remote>
G 2006-09-12 05:32 UTC jenn 1.4 wizzard.h wizzard/src = = <remote>
R 2006-09-12 06:07 UTC jenn 1.3 main.c wizzard/src = = <remote>
T 2006-09-13 04:04 UTC jenn wizzard [pre_alpha_0-2:HEAD]
T 2006-09-13 04:04 UTC jenn wizzard [pre_alpha_0-2:2006.09.13.04.04.22]
T 2006-09-13 07:12 UTC jenn wizzard [beta_0-1_branch:beta_0-1_branch_root]
E 2006-10-01 07:00 UTC jenn [2006.10.01] wizzard =wizzard= <remote>/*
F 2006-10-02 17:48 UTC jenn =wizzard= <remote>/*
```

Using the cvs history command

The syntax for the *cvs history* command is:

```
cvs [cvs-options] history [command-options] [filenames...]
```

The options to *cvs history* modify how much of the history is shown for which users and modules. The *-T*, *-c*, and *-o* options display the records for tags, commits, and checkouts, respectively. The *-e* option displays all record types. The *-z timezone* option converts times and displays them in the specified time zone.

CVS does not allow you to combine the -T, -c, -o, -x, and -e options. If you wish to display multiple action types, use the -x option with a *type* letter.

The types shown in the *history* output are designated by letters, which can also be used with the -x option to specify the types of events you wish to display. Multiple types can be specified. These are the types:

A   Report on records of files added to the repository (a committed add).

C   Report on records showing files that would have been updated in a sandbox, but that needed to be merged and for which there were conflicts in the merge (compare with G and U).

E   Report on records of files being exported.

F   Report on records of files being released.

G   Report on records of a file being updated in a sandbox with a successful merge (compare with C and U).

M   Report on records of a file being modified (a successful commit of a sandbox revision).

O   Report on records of files being checked out.

R   Report on records of files being removed from the active part of the repository (a committed remove).

T   Report on records of files being rtagged.

U   Report on records of a file being updated in a sandbox with no merge required (compare with C and G).

W   Report on records of a file being deleted from a sandbox during an update because it is no longer active in the repository.

The full list of command options for *cvs history* is provided in Chapter 10.

Strategies and Practices

CVS is a tool that can help you manage a project, but you need to decide how to use CVS with your project to make it work effectively for you and your team. The following sections present some ideas to help you integrate CVS into your working practices.

Tag and Branch Strategies

Decide whether and how you will use tags and branches, and then decide on the format to use for tag and branch names. Branching philosophies, styles, and policies are explained in the "Branching Strategies" section of Chapter 4.

I strongly recommend keeping almost-complete work separate from experimental work. In programming projects, I recommend keeping bug fixes separated from the main body of development by putting either bug corrections or development on a branch.

If you use branches, designate an owner for each branch. The owner should be responsible for seeing that the branch is used for its specified purpose, for maintaining a record of the changes made to that branch, and for managing merges to or from that branch.

I strongly recommend tagging at strategic points in development, at the root of each branch, and at each merge point. See "Tagging Strategies" in Chapter 4 for more suggestions on tagging.

Automation Strategies

Automation can be helpful in ensuring that a project moves smoothly to completion. Generally, automation translates into consistency. When using CVS on a project, you may find the following automation strategies to be helpful:

- Use the scripting files in *CVSROOT* to enforce project standards and assist project communication.
- Automate builds to encourage projects to be tested frequently. This practice also ensures that the entire build process is recorded and performed correctly every time.
- Integrate CVS to your change-tracking program in order to minimize the effort developers have to put in to do both version control and change tracking.
- Keep computer clocks synchronized with each other to ensure that CVS can read accurate last-modified times.

Project Structure and Sandboxes

Good project structure remains good structure, regardless of the use of version control. You know how to structure your project, whether it's a small web site or a complicated client-server application: you're the expert on your particular project and how to lay it out.

As long as your project can be developed and tested under a single top-level directory (and without symbolic links), you need not modify it at all for use under CVS. If it can't, consider developing it under a top-level directory, and using a build system such as *make* to distribute the files for testing. If your project is particularly large, consider breaking it into subprojects or using modules so that each developer needs to check out only her part of the project.

In small projects, each sandbox can contain the entire source tree. In larger projects, use symbolic links or other tools to allow the developers to share a central set of standard files. In such projects, each developer's sandbox should contain only the files that developer needs to work on, and the build script in each developer's sandbox should include commands to create the necessary symbolic links to the central files. This practice allows developers to compile and test their own code without having to compile files they haven't changed.

Consider having a central build sandbox that is automatically updated and built on a regular schedule. This sandbox can be used to test the integration of the whole project. If developers fail to commit all their necessary files, the central build usually fails, because the update is unable to retrieve the uncommitted files. This makes it obvious when someone has forgotten to commit a crucial file.

Each task should have its own sandbox; each developer, tester, and editor should work from his own sandbox, and anyone who is working on multiple branches should work from a different sandbox for each branch. If there is a central build, it should be in its own sandbox. If there is a file server, it should be a separate sandbox.

Use *cvs release* to remove sandboxes. This helps prevent modified or new files from being forgotten. If the *history* file is in use, this command records the removal of a sandbox.

Structure Examples

A company is producing a small client-server application. Neither the client nor the server share actual code, and different development teams are handling each side of the project. The project lead has three major choices for how to structure the project:

- She can store it all as one project, with the code intermingled. If she creates and maintains modules (see "The modules File," earlier in this chapter), the developers can each check out their relevant section of the project. This choice requires that the module be maintained, but is the best option for permitting shared files later in the project. If she chooses not to use modules, developers will need to check out the whole project.

- She can store it under one project name, but have subdirectories for client and server side. This allows the developers to check out *projectname/client* or *projectname/server* sandboxes and requires no module maintenance, but if a later file turns out to be useful as a shared file, it's difficult to determine where to keep it.

- She can have three subdirectories—*client*, *server*, and *shared*. Developers would then check out both their relevant subdirectory and the shared subdirectory.

Another company is producing a web site, where most of the project structure will be placed under a single directory, but there is also a set of CGI files that need to be in a *cgi-bin* directory, elsewhere on the server.

The project lead decides to make the top directory of the project an administrative directory, with a build script. Under that, she'll place the web site pages in the repository in the same layout she intends to use in production. Also under the top directory is the *cgi-bin* directory. The build script contains *rsync* commands to recursively copy the two subdirectories to their test (or installation) locations on the test (or production) server.

Client and Server Version Mismatch

The CVS 1.12 line of development provides many new and useful tools to repository administrators and project managers. It's extremely tempting to run 1.12 and use the new features—believe me, I know! Unfortunately, many of us don't control the software our users use. Here's a partial list of problems you can encounter if you're running a 1.12 server, but your users are running a recent 1.11 client.

commitid
> This will not be displayed in the log and status output of 1.11 series clients.

cvs log time
> Log outputs the local time if both server and client are newer than 1.12.9.

import -X
> The *-X* option to import doesn't exist in 1.11, but you can set the server to default to this behavior using the *ImportNewFilesToVendorBranchOnly* option in the *config* file.

write proxy
> The earlier clients don't support the proxy code, so some extra configuration is required if you're using write proxies. See "Distributed Repositories" in Chapter 6.

The following features are available only in 1.12 series clients (and later):

* Connection method options for repository paths
* The *cvs ls* command
* The *revision:date* format for command options other than *-j*

Practices for Development

Decide whether to use the simultaneous development model or one of the watching files or reserving files models of exclusive development. These models are explained in Chapter 5, which also explains how to use each model in CVS.

Consider using watches, notification emails sent via scripting files, or other tools to keep developers informed of what is happening during a project's development.

Develop strategies for updating and committing sandboxes. Sandboxes and the repository need to be kept synchronized to minimize conflicts and to ensure that a project is fully backed up. Deciding how frequently your users update and commit is a matter of judging the risk of breaking the build with incomplete work versus the benefits of storing data, even when it won't compile. The risk of breaking the build can be minimized with the careful use of branches.

The most common work pattern for development projects is *update-edit-test-commit*. In this pattern, your developers update a sandbox first thing in the morning, work on their files, test their files, and commit at the end of the day. Some groups commit at lunchtime and update again after lunch, working on a shorter cycle.

The greatest risk with frequent commits occurs in environments where one person can break something for everyone, such as a programming environment. If a person's code doesn't compile and this broken code is propagated to the entire team, no one can compile until that code is either removed or fixed. For this reason, many programming teams have a rule against committing before your code compiles.

The rule about not committing until your code compiles works well in some situations, but if a person is doing long-term experimental code, the code might not be in the repository for days. If the sandboxes aren't backed up, that's several days of work at risk. In such cases, I recommend letting the person work on an experimental branch and commit to the branch.

Some teams prefer to restrict updates rather than restrict commits. These teams update stable code into their sandbox and work from that stable code base until they have completed a feature. Then they update from a new stable code base. The risk in this case is that the changes one person has made to the code will conflict with changes from a team member in a way that CVS cannot merge, and someone will have to merge those changes by hand. The benefit is that team members are working against a known code base. This system can be duplicated by using a branch to build the feature on, then merging the branch and the new feature to the trunk. Using the branch also provides a way to commit the partially completed feature without affecting other people's sandboxes, which helps protect against mistakes.

## CHAPTER 8

Remote Repositories

Most projects involve a *remote repository* (one that's on a different machine than the clients). This chapter discusses remote repositories, access methods, how to set up each access method, and security considerations for each type of access.

This chapter also discusses the two access methods for local repositories: *local* and *fork*. The *fork* method presents a way to access a local repository as if it were a remote repository.

CVS can operate equally well as a single program that handles both the sandbox and the repository or as a pair of programs—a client managing the sandbox and a server managing the repository.

CVS can run as a single program if both sandbox and repository are on the same computer, or if the repository is on a file server and the computer that the sandbox is on perceives the shared directories as local.

If you have a personal repository for private work, you may choose to keep the repository on the same computer as your sandbox. If you are sharing a server with several other people, you may have a shared repository on the same server as your sandboxes. In such situations, be particularly careful to back up the repository. When the repository and the sandbox are on different computers, each acts as a partial backup of the other. When they are on the same computer, that inherent backup is not available.

Specifying Repository Paths

Whenever CVS runs a command from a client, it needs to know where to find the CVS repository. The address of the repository is called the *repository path*. CVS looks for repository paths in the sandbox, the *CVSROOT* environment variable, and the *-d repository_path* command option.

If you run a CVS command from within a sandbox, CVS uses the repository path that is stored in the sandbox. When a sandbox is not available—such as when you're creating a sandbox or issuing a command from outside a sandbox—you must specify which repository you are attempting to access. You also need to specify the repository path if you are in a sandbox but wish to access a different repository than the one the sandbox uses.

You can specify a repository path from the command line with the *-d repository_path* option, or you can specify it with the *CVSROOT* environment variable. CVS uses the path given with the *-d* option in preference to the path in the sandbox, and it uses either the sandbox or the *-d* path in preference to the path in the environment variable.

 The *rtag*, *rlog*, *rdiff*, *rannotate*, and *export* commands can run without a sandbox. If these commands are run outside a sandbox, they need either the *-d* option or the *CVSROOT* environment variable.

The format for a repository path is:

    [:method[;option=arg...]:][[[user][:password]@]hostname[:[port]]]/path

The *method* can be one of the following:

local
> For the local machine

ext
> For externally defined *rsh* or *rsh*-like connection methods (such as SSH)

fork
> For connecting to a local machine as if it were a remote machine (useful if you are trying to diagnose problems)

server
> For the internal *rsh* server; available only on some operating systems (including Windows)

gserver
> For connections through the GSS-API (currently Kerberos 5.0)

kserver
> For connections through Kerberos 4 and earlier

pserver
> For the *pserver* (built-in password server) connection method

Everything except the path itself can be left out of a repository path definition.

If the method is left out, and the host is not included or is the local host, CVS uses the *local* access method. If the method is left out but the host is included, CVS uses either the *server* or the *ext* methods, depending on whether an internal *rsh* server is available. If *user* is left out, CVS uses the username in the current environment. If *password* is left out and is required, CVS asks for it. If the *port* is left out and the method requires a port, CVS uses the default port for that method. (The default port for each access method is given in the following sections on each method.) If the *host* is left out, *localhost* is assumed.

If you put a colon immediately after the username, CVS attempts to connect with an empty password.

If an element of the repository path is included but not needed for the current method, CVS displays a message stating which element is not necessary.

Method Options

In version 1.12.7, CVS added two options to the connection methods: the *proxy* and *proxyport* methods that permit a client to connect to a server via an HTTP proxy. In 1.12.11, three other options were added (*CVS_RSH*, *CVS_SERVER*, and *Redirect*).

Options are included in the method section of a repository path. The repository path without options is usually something similar to the following:

```
:ext:cvs_server:/var/local/cvs
```

The repository path with an option would look like this:

```
:ext;CVS_RSH=/bin/ssh:cvs_server:/var/local/cvs
```

It's possible to use multiple options in the same repository path. To do this, chain them with semicolons:

```
:ext;CVS_RSH=/bin/ssh;CVS_SERVER=/bin/cvs;Redirect=false:cvs_server:/var/local/cvs
```

 The binaries for *cvs* and *ssh* are more likely to be found under */usr* or */opt* than */bin*. I thought that using */usr/local/bin/cvs* or */opt/cvs-1.12.13/bin/cvs* made the examples awkward. Those are, however, more likely places to find the commands.

The methods are:

CVS_RSH=path
> This method allows you to declare your *rsh* replacement command on the command line, instead of as an environment variable. It overrides the *CVS_RSH* environment variable. Most of the time, this will be *ssh*. See "The ext and server Access Methods," later in this chapter, for an explanation of the *rsh* replacement.
>
> This option is valid only with the *ext* method, and was added in 1.12.11.

CVS_SERVER=path
> This method allows you to declare the server program you wish to use on the command line, instead of as an environment variable. It overrides the *CVS_SERVER* environment variable. In most cases, neither this nor the *CVS_SERVER* variable is necessary, but it's useful if you are testing a server that has been compiled with a different configuration from the default server, or are testing an upgrade of the CVS software.
>
> This option is valid only with the *ext* and *fork* methods, and was added in 1.12.11.

proxy=hostname

proxyport=port

CVS can connect through an HTTP proxy. The proxy must be using the HTTP protocol, and must be a tunnel that leads to a CVS server. *hostname* is the name of the proxy, and *port* is the number of the port to connect to.

These options are valid only with the *gserver* and *pserver* methods, and were added in 1.12.7.

Redirect=boolean

This method determines whether the server you connect to may redirect your request to another server. At present, it is useful only when connecting to a secondary server that may act as a write proxy for a primary server. The *boolean* value may be *on* or *true* to permit redirection; or *off* or *false* to prohibit redirection. The default is to permit redirection.

This option is valid only with the *ext* method, and was added in 1.12.11.

The local Access Method

If your repository is on the same computer as your sandbox (or the sandbox you want to make) or on a shared filesystem that is accessed as if it were a local partition, you can use the *local* method to access the repository.

For the *local* access method, the repository path format is:

```
[:local:]/path
```

When running a command that requires an explicit path declaration, put the repository path in your *CVSROOT* environment variable or use the path as the argument to the *-d repository_path* option. You will most likely need this path declaration when creating a sandbox, but it is also necessary for *cvs export* and *cvs rtag*.

 If you just enter the directory path with no hostname or method declaration, CVS uses the *local* access method.

With local access, CVS does not run in client/server mode. One program manages both the sandbox and the repository. The program runs under the username that it was called with, and it has the access permissions of that user. Any programs that CVS calls (such as programs called from a scripting file) run with the same username and access permissions.

If *local* access mode is being used on a single-user computer, security normally is not an issue. On shared filesystems or servers, your repository security problems are the same as the usual security issues for file sharing. Use the security services of your operating system to secure a shared repository that is accessed with the *local* method.

Example 8-1 shows how to check out a sandbox using the *local* access method.

Example 8-1. Using the local access method

```
jenn@helit:/tmp$ cvs -d :local:/var/lib/cvs checkout wizzard
cvs checkout: Updating wizzard
U wizzard/Changelog
U wizzard/INSTALL
U wizzard/Makefile
```

The ext and server Access Methods

In my experience, *ext* is the most commonly used access method, and it is usually used with SSH. *ext* stands for external, which refers to an external (to CVS) *rsh* or remote shell program. This method uses a remote shell program to connect the sandbox client computer to the repository server computer. The *server* method is almost the same as the *ext* method. The only difference is that *server* uses a remote shell program that is included with CVS.

To use a program other than *rsh* with the *ext* connection method, the *CVS_RSH* environment variable on the client should be set to the name of the program and the directory containing the program should be in the user's *PATH* on the client computer. Alternatively, you can set the *CVS_RSH* environment variable to the absolute path to the program without modifying the *PATH* variable. You may also use the *CVS_RSH* method option, described in "Method Options" earlier in this chapter.

ext accepts any command-line-based program that can be called with the following syntax:

```
program [-b] [-l username] host commands
```

The program must run the commands in a remote shell and pipe standard input (*stdin*) and standard output (*stdout*) without filtering the content. The *-b* is necessary only if the program is running on OS/2 and is used to force *rsh* to run in binary mode, without end-of-file conversion. The *-l username* is used (by CVS) only if there is a username included in the repository path.

For the *ext* access method, the repository path format is:

```
[:ext:][user@]hostname[:]/path
```

The user needs a username on both the client computer and the server computer. If these names are the same, the *user@* part of the repository path isn't needed. In versions of CVS prior to 1.11.1, the colon between *hostname* and *path* was required.

The user's *PATH* environment variable on the server must include the directory that contains the *cvs* executable, the user's *CVS_SERVER* environment variable on the client must contain the path to the *cvs* executable on the server, or the *CVS_SERVER* method option must be set to the path to the *cvs* executable on the server. If you're using *PATH*, this variable must be set in a configuration file, such as *.cshrc* or *.bashrc*, that is read by nonlogin shells.

The *rsh* (or *rsh*-like) program starts the *cvs* executable on the server computer, using the username and permissions of the user the *rsh* program has connected as. Any programs CVS calls (such as programs called from a scripting file) run with this username and access privileges.

As a trouble-prevention measure, before trying to use your *rsh* or *rsh*-like program with CVS, attempt to log in to the server with it, using the *program [-b] [-l username] host commands* command format, as shown in Example 8-2.

Example 8-2. Testing SSH for ext

```
bash-2.05a$ ssh -l jenn helit ls
jenn@helit's password:
Mail
MyMozilla
MyPilot
...
```

 Neither the *rsh* nor the *server* methods use encryption, and both transmit a clear-text username and password to a valid user account on the repository server. For this reason, I strongly recommend that you use SSH or some other secured connection whenever you connect across an untrusted network. You should consider using a secured connection even on a trusted network. If there is any external connection to your network (even through a firewall), I recommend encrypting the connection.

Example 8-3 shows how to check out a sandbox using the *ext* access method.

Example 8-3. Using the ext access method

```
bash-2.05a$ cvs -d :ext:jenn@cvs_server:/var/lib/cvs checkout wizzard
cvs server: Updating wizzard
U wizzard/Changelog
U wizzard/INSTALL
U wizzard/Makefile
```

rsh

rsh is the default program used with the *ext* method. If no other program is specified in the *CVS_RSH* environment variable, CVS calls *rsh*. If *rsh* is not in the user's *PATH* on the client or is not available on the server, CVS cannot connect.

On the server, the user's *.rhosts* file in the user's home directory must have a line in the format *client_name username*, where *client_name* is the name of the client computer and *username* is the user's name on the client computer.

The *rsh* program provided with Windows NT (and later) modifies end-of-line characters and is unsuitable for use with CVS. In the HP-UX operating system, use the *remsh* program rather than *rsh*, as *rsh* is a different program entirely. Use the *CVS_RSH* environment variable to define the replacement programs for both operating systems.

The server Access Method

The *server* access method uses a version of *rsh* internal to CVS. The *.rhosts* file on the server must be set, as described in the preceding section on "rsh".

To determine whether the *server* access method is available, you can attempt to check out a sandbox with the method, as shown in Example 8-4.

Example 8-4. Testing for server mode

```
bash-2.05a$ cvs -d :server:cvs_server:/var/lib/cvs checkout wizzard
cvs [checkout aborted]: the :server: access method is not supported by this port of CVS
```

The *server* method is not available in all operating systems. Both client and server must be able to run the internal *rsh* program.

SSH

Secure Shell (SSH) is an *rsh* replacement that encrypts the data stream. You can authenticate your SSH connection with a pair of keys (private and public) or with a password.

There are two SSH protocols: SSH1 and SSH2. The server must be running an SSH daemon that understands the protocol the client is using. SSH clients also come with a key-generation program that generates the private and public keys that will be used to encrypt the data stream.

To use SSH with CVS:

1. Install an SSH client on the sandbox computer and a daemon on the repository server, as given in the instructions for your SSH programs (Linux and Mac OS X normally include *openssh* as part of the core installation). Ensure that the path to the SSH program is in the *PATH* environment variable on the client computer.

2. Ensure that the server speaks the same protocol as the client. If the documentation for either program doesn't specify whether it uses SSH1 or SSH2, it probably uses the older SSH1 protocol.

3. Ensure that the user has a username and password for the server as well as the client.

4. (This step is optional.) Generate an SSH key for the client, using the key-generation program. Under *openssh*, this is *ssh-keygen*. Once you've run this command, you'll

have two files in your *~/.ssh* directory: *id_rsa* and *id_rsa.pub*. *id_rsa* is your private key: keep it secret, keep it safe. You'll need to copy the contents (it's one very long line) of *id_rsa.pub* (your public key) into the *~/.ssh/authorized_keys* file on the server. Once you've done this, you'll be prompted for your public key's passphrase instead of your password on the server. You can avoid having to type your password over and over by running these commands:

```
$ eval `ssh-agent`
$ ssh-add
```

When you run the second command, you'll be prompted for your passphrase. You should be able to execute SSH operations, including CVS commands, without being prompted again for your passphrase as long as your shell is open. The instructions differ for different versions of SSH.

5. Test whether the connection works by attempting to log in to the server with the username from step 3, as shown in Example 8-5.

6. Put the name of your SSH program (or its path) into the *CVS_RSH* environment variable on the client computer.

7. Run CVS using *ext* as the method in the repository path, as shown in Example 8-3.

Example 8-5 shows a test connection to a server with an SSH client program, as described in step 5.

Example 8-5. Connecting with SSH

```
bash-2.05a$ ssh -l jenn helit
Linux helit 2.4.19-686-smp #1 SMP Thu Aug 8 22:06:13 EST 2006 i686 unknown unknown GNU/
Linux
.
.
.
Last login: Tue Jul 15 17:43:40 2006 from 10.0.2.2
jenn@helit:~$
```

I recommend *http://www.openssh.org* and the FAQ file at *http://www.openssh.org/faq.html* as sources of information on SSH. This site also provides free SSH client and server programs.

Other Connection Programs

The *ext* method can run with any other program that calls a remote program in the way that *rsh* and *ssh* do. The program must not modify data in transit, and it must be called using the format:

```
program [-b] [-l username] host commands
```

If you wish to use Kerberos with CVS, you can use the Kerberos version of *rsh* to connect using the *ext* method. If you wish to use Kerberos more directly, use the *kserver* or *gserver* access methods.

If you need to call *rsh* or *ssh* with an option, write a shell script like the one in Example 8-6 and put the path to that shell script in your *CVS_RSH* variable. CVS invokes the shell script, which in turn invokes *rsh* or *ssh* with the options you desire.

Example 8-6. Invoking ssh with command-line options

```
#! /bin/bash
exec ssh -F ~/.sshconf "$@"
```

The fork Access Method

The *fork* access method acts like *ext* without the external connection. You can use it only when the repository and the sandbox are on the same computer. *fork* makes CVS run in client/server mode and is most useful for debugging—to isolate whether a fault is in CVS's remote protocols or in the networking—but it is also used as a substitute for the *local* method.

The *fork* method uses the *CVS_SERVER* environment variable, as described in "The ext and server Access Methods," earlier in this chapter.

The repository path format for *fork* is:

```
[:fork:]/path
```

With the *fork* access method, both client and server programs run under the username that the client was called with and have the filesystem access of that user. Any programs that CVS calls (such as programs called from a scripting file) run with the same username and access.

Security normally is not an issue with the *fork* access method if the method is used on a single-user computer. However, be aware of the security issues of shared filesystems or shared servers; use the security services of your operating system to secure a shared repository that is accessed with the *fork* method.

Example 8-7 shows how to check out a sandbox using the *fork* access method.

Example 8-7. Using the fork access method

```
jenn@helit:/tmp$ cvs -d :fork:/var/lib/cvs checkout wizzard
cvs server: Updating wizzard
U wizzard/Changelog
U wizzard/INSTALL
U wizzard/Makefile
```

The gserver Access Method

The *gserver* access method uses the GSS-API (Generic Security Service Application Programming Interface) to support authentication and encryption of the CVS connection. The GSS-API in itself does not authenticate or encrypt the connection; these processes are performed by an authentication or encryption system configured to work with the GSS-API. The most common system used with the GSS-API is Kerberos 5.

The GSS-API is explained in RFC 2743, available at *http://www.ietf.org/rfc/rfc2743.txt*. RFC 1964 explains how the GSS-API interacts with Kerberos 5. To use Kerberos 5 with CVS, use the GSS-API and the *gserver* access method. Kerberos 4 is used with the *kserver* access mode, explained in the next section.

The repository path format for the GSS-API is:

```
:gserver:[user@]hostname[:[port]]/path
```

The default port for *gserver* is 2401. If *user* is not specified, the client sends the username of the calling user on the client computer.

The CVS client and server must both be compiled to run the GSS-API. If you intend to encrypt the data stream, you also need to have encryption enabled at compile time. You can test whether your CVS program has the GSS-API compiled by attempting to check out a sandbox. Example 8-8 shows the result when CVS does not support the GSS-API.

Example 8-8. Testing for gserver mode

```
bash-2.05a$ cvs -d :gserver:cvs_server:/var/lib/cvs checkout wizzard
cvs checkout: CVSROOT is set for a GSS-API access method but your
cvs checkout: CVS executable doesn't support it.
cvs [checkout aborted]: Bad CVSROOT: `:gserver:cvs_server:/var/lib/cvs'.
```

You can test for encryption support by checking the options list, as shown in Example 8-9.

Example 8-9. Checking for encryption

```
bash-2.05a$ cvs --help-options
CVS global options (specified before the command name) are:
    .
    .
    .
    -x              Encrypt all net traffic.
    .
    .
    .
(Specify the --help option for a list of other help options)
```

To recompile CVS to support the GSS-API, see the following instructions. A more detailed discussion on installing from source is provided in Chapter 2, but the examples in that discussion do not include the GSS-API.

You need to use the *--with-gssapi[=directory]* option to configure CVS to use the GSS-API. If you want encryption, use *--enable-encrypt* as well.

> Check the *INSTALL* file from the CVS source distribution for the exact syntax of configuration options in your version of CVS.
>
> On some operating systems, the GSS-API is installed automatically. If that's the case with your system, you may need to use *--without-gssapi* if you don't also have Kerberos 5 available.

To compile CVS with GSS-API support:

1. Ensure that your computer has an installation of both the GSS-API and Kerberos 5, with the header files.
2. *cd* to the CVS source directory.
3. Run *make distclean* to remove any cached configuration information or other remnants of previous compilations.
4. Run *./configure* with the arguments you need. To configure CVS for the GSS-API, you need *--with-gssapi[=header files]*. To enable encryption, use *--enable-encrypt*. The *header files* argument to *--with-gssapi* should be the path of the *GSS_API* directory that contains libraries and include files (or a directory above that directory).
5. Run *make*.
6. Change user to *root* or another privileged user.
7. Run *make install*.

> Check the output of *configure* carefully to ensure that it was able to locate the GSS-API include files. The output from *configure* is saved in *config.log*.

Using the GSS-API, CVS can authenticate and encrypt the data stream, but it does not do these things by default. Use the *-a* CVS option to authenticate the data stream, and use the *-x* CVS option to encrypt it. You may want to include these options in your *.cvsrc* file. For example, to both authenticate and encrypt the data stream, place the following in *.cvsrc*:

```
cvs -ax
```

To support the *gserver* access method, CVS needs to run a server on the computer that hosts the repository. CVS uses most of the same code to support the *gserver* and *pserver* methods. To configure the repository to run the CVS server, edit *inetd.conf* and add *cvs pserver* (not *gserver*). See "Using inetd with gserver, kserver, and pserver" later in this chapter for more information on this configuration.

Install and configure Kerberos 5, per the instructions for your Kerberos system. The principal name for CVS is *cvs/HOSTNAME*, where *HOSTNAME* is the canonical name of the host.

 CVS 1.11.2 has a bug in its GSS-API code. It fails to connect and produces the following error message whenever it attempts to connect to a GSS-API server: *cvs [import aborted]: gserver currently only enabled for socket connections*.

Later versions do not have this problem, and there is a patch for 1.11.2 in the archives of the *info-cvs* mailing list.

The extent to which the GSS-API is secure depends on the particular system you choose and whether you choose to authenticate or encrypt the message stream. It's useful because of that flexibility: you can determine precisely which level of security you want. At present, the only system available to work with the GSS-API and CVS is Kerberos 5, which provides a high level of authentication security across an untrusted network, if the hosts connecting through it are secure.

Once the GSS-API and Kerberos 5 are installed and configured and CVS is recompiled, you can get a Kerberos ticket for your user on the client and then run CVS commands normally. Example 8-10 shows how to check out a sandbox using the *gserver* access method.

Example 8-10. Using the gserver access method

```
bash$ cvs -d :gserver:helit:/var/lib/cvs checkout wizzard
cvs server: Updating wizzard
U wizzard/Changelog
U wizzard/INSTALL
U wizzard/Makefile
```

The kserver Access Method

The *kserver* method is used to connect using Kerberos 4. If you do not have an existing Kerberos 4 installation on your CVS repository server, I recommend you use Kerberos 5, described in the preceding section. Kerberos 4 has known weaknesses that Kerberos 5 resolves. This section assumes that you have an existing Kerberos 4 installation and the documentation to configure and use it.

Kerberos 4 is a reasonably secure authentication system, but it has known flaws. Kerberos 5 fixes some of them; most critically, it prevents a replay attack. In Kerberos 4, there is a five-minute window in which an attacker can sniff an authentication request, modify and resend it, and get an authentication ticket. Kerberos 5 allows only one ticket to be produced per request.

The repository path format for Kerberos is:

```
:kserver:[user@]hostname[:[port]]/path
```

The default port for *kserver* is 1999. If *user* is not specified, the client sends the username of the calling user on the client computer.

The CVS client and server must both be compiled to run Kerberos 4. If you intend to encrypt the data stream, you also need to have encryption enabled at compile time. You can test whether your CVS program has compiled *kserver* support by checking the command list, as shown in Example 8-11.

Example 8-11. Testing for kserver mode

```
bash-2.05a$ cvs --help-commands
CVS commands are:
.
.
.
        kserver     Kerberos server mode
.
.
.
(Specify the --help option for a list of other help options)
```

You can test for encryption support by checking the options list, as shown earlier in Example 8-9.

To use CVS with *kserver*, install and configure Kerberos 4 as described in your Kerberos manual. You need to have the header files for Kerberos 4 available for CVS to link to. The *principal name* for CVS is *cvs*.

To recompile CVS to support Kerberos 4, follow the instructions in Chapter 2 on installing from source. Use the *--with-krb4[=header-files]* option to *configure* to get Kerberos authentication support. Use the Kerberos directory as the argument to *--with-krb4*. (You need the Kerberos directory you intend to compile against, usually one with *include* and *lib* subdirectories.) If you also desire encryption, use *--enable-encrypt* as well.

Check the *INSTALL* file for the exact syntax of *configure* options in your version of CVS.

CVS needs to run a server on the repository computer to support the *kserver* access method. Edit *inetd.conf* and add a line for *cvs kserver*. See "Using inetd with gserver, kserver, and pserver" later in this chapter for details on how to edit *inetd.conf*.

Using Kerberos 4, CVS can encrypt the data stream, but it does not do this by default. Use the *-x* option to encrypt the data stream. You may want to include this option in your *.cvsrc* file. For example:

```
cvs -x
```

To run CVS, get a Kerberos ticket for the user on your client; then call CVS the usual way with the *kserver* method. Example 8-12 shows how to check out a sandbox using the *kserver* access method.

Example 8-12. Using the kserver access method

```
bash$ cvs -d :kserver:helit:/var/lib/cvs checkout wizzard
cvs server: Updating wizzard
U wizzard/Changelog
U wizzard/INSTALL
U wizzard/Makefile
```

The pserver Access Method

The *pserver* method allows users to connect to the repository with a username and password that are stored on the repository server. The main advantage of *pserver* is that it permits anonymous, passwordless, read-only access. The main disadvantages of *pserver* mode are that it uses a trivial encoding scheme for passwords and the data stream is not encrypted. *pserver* mode is included in CVS automatically, but it requires a password file that needs to be configured.

To use *pserver*, you need a username on the repository computer, to enable CVS to run programs on that computer. You may share this username (your *system username*) with other users and have a separate *CVS username* to identify you to CVS as an individual. You also need to log in before running other commands.

To support the *pserver* access method, CVS needs to run a server on the computer that hosts the repository. To configure the repository to run the CVS server, edit *inetd.conf* and add *cvs pserver*. See "Using inetd with gserver, kserver, and pserver" later in this chapter for more information on *inetd* configuration.

The repository path format for *pserver* is:

```
:pserver:[[user][:password]@][hostname:[port]]/path
```

The default port for *pserver* is 2401. If the user is not specified, the client sends the username of the calling user on the client computer.

You need to configure the *passwd* file and possibly the *readers* and *writers* files before you can use *pserver*. These files are explained in "The passwd File" and "The readers and writers Files" later in this chapter. You also need to use the *login* command, explained in "login and logout."

> You can bypass the *passwd* file by using the *SystemAuth* configuration option in the *config* file (explained in Chapter 6).
>
> If you bypass the *passwd* file using *SystemAuth*, CVS uses the shell account passwords for your users with the minimal security it uses for *pserver* passwords. Be sure that you take the security risks into account if you choose to do this.

Once CVS is configured for *pserver*, you can check out a sandbox or use other CVS commands normally, using the *pserver* repository path when necessary. Example 8-13 shows how to check out a sandbox using the *pserver* access method.

Example 8-13. Using the pserver access method

```
bash-2.05a$ cvs -d :pserver:jenn@cvs_server:/var/lib/cvs login
Logging in to :pserver:jenn@cvs:2401/var/lib/cvs
CVS password:
bash-2.05a$ cvs -d :pserver:jenn@cvs_server:/var/lib/cvs checkout wizzard
cvs server: Updating wizzard
U wizzard/Changelog
U wizzard/INSTALL
.
.
.
```

The passwd File

The *passwd* file in the repository's *CVSROOT* directory stores passwords and user-names for the *pserver* access method. The format is as follows:

    CVS_username:password:system_username

The *CVS_username* is the name the user sends to CVS. The *system_username* is the name the CVS programs run under. If these names are the same, the *system_username* does not need to be given, because it defaults to the *CVS_username*. The *CVS_username* is shown in the *author* field of *cvs log* output.

> In CVS 1.11.11 and later, you cannot configure the *pserver* password file with a superuser as the system username.

The *system_username* must exist on the repository server. The *CVS_username* doesn't need to exist on the server unless it's the same as the *system_username*. If the *system_username* does not exist on the server, the commands fail, even if the user authenticates as far as CVS is concerned.

If the *password* field is empty, the user automatically authenticates, even with no password.

Example 8-14 shows a *passwd* file.

Example 8-14. A passwd file

```
anonymous:
jenn:ENCRYPTEDPASSWORD
doppel:ENCRYPTEDPASSWORD
chris:ENCRYPTEDPASSWORD:cvsusers
peter:ENCRYPTEDPASSWORD:cvsusers
asmith:ENCRYPTEDPASSWORD:anne
```

The passwords are encrypted with the standard Unix *crypt( )* function and need to be encrypted elsewhere and pasted in; there currently is no code that edits this file. You can use the Unix *mkpasswd* utility to create a suitable encrypted string from a plaintext password.

> Another way to generate passwords is to use the Perl command *perl -e 'print crypt "password", "salt";'*. Replace *salt* with any two characters to randomize the results.

A single system username can be shared by multiple users with different CVS usernames. This can be used to allow several people to work on a project and record the changes across multiple users. (Of course, this could also be done with group permissions.) If appropriate for your security needs, you can restrict the system usernames so that they can only run CVS.

The *passwd* file should be edited in place; it should not be checked out to sandboxes.

> You can grant anonymous, read-only access to CVS using *pserver*. Set up the *passwd* file in the *CVSROOT* directory with the user *anonymous* (or any other username) with no password or system name, and add the user *anonymous* to the *readers* file.
>
> A better way to grant anonymous, read-only access is to use the operating system's built-in security. This method is explained in Chapter 6.
>
> The *readers* file is described in the next section.

The readers and writers Files

The *readers* and *writers* files in the repository's *CVSROOT* directory control whether someone using the *pserver* access method has permission to write to the repository. These files affect only users using the *pserver* access method; repository access using the other access methods is controlled by the filesystem permissions.

The *readers* and *writers* files use the CVS username, not the system username, to determine whether a user has access.

Users gain access to the repository according to the following rules:

- If a user is listed in the *readers* file, she has read-only access to the repository.
- If the *writers* file exists and a user is not listed in the *writers* file, she has read-only access to the repository.
- If a user is listed in the *writers* file but not in the *readers* file, she has read-write access to the repository.
- If a user is listed in both *readers* and *writers*, CVS takes the conservative choice and she has read-only access to the repository.

Both files are one name per line. You must have a newline character after the last username. An example *readers* or *writers* file is shown in Example 8-15.

Example 8-15. readers or writers file

```
jenn
doppel
asmith
peter
```

login and logout

The *passwd* file controls whether the CVS server requires a password for any given user. If the server requires a password, *pserver* requires you to use the *cvs login* and *cvs logout* commands. Run the *cvs login* command before any other CVS command, setting the repository path, if necessary, with one of the usual methods. Example 8-16 shows how to log in with *pserver* mode.

Example 8-16. Logging in with pserver

```
bash-2.05a$ cvs -d :pserver:jenn@cvs.example.net:/var/lib/cvs login
Logging in to :pserver:jenn@cvs:2401/var/lib/cvs
CVS password:
```

You can also supply the password during the command, as shown in Example 8-17.

Example 8-17. Giving a password at login

```
bash-2.05a$ cvs -d :pserver:jenn:password:@cvs.example.net:/var/lib/cvs login
Logging in to :pserver:jenn@cvs:2401/var/lib/cvs
```

Once you have successfully logged in, CVS records the password and other data in the *.cvspass* file in your home directory on your client computer. This filename can be changed by putting the path to the new file in the *CVS_PASSFILE* environment variable in the client before you run *login*. CVS stores the data indefinitely in the format */1 user@host:port/path Aencoded_password*, one repository to a line. (Yes, there is a literal A before the password; that's an internal version identification system.)

You can remove this line from the file by using *cvs logout* with the same *CVSROOT*, in which case you would need to log in again the next time you wish to use *pserver* access to connect to that repository.

The password is encoded using a simple encoding scheme and can be decoded easily by a malicious user. It is encoded against inadvertent, nonmalicious reading, but it is not secure.

Security

CVS searches the *passwd* file in the *CVSROOT* directory for usernames and passwords for *pserver* access. Because of the trivial encoding, passwords used for *pserver* access should not be the same as the passwords used for access to the main filesystem of the repository server. The *passwd* file should not be included in the *checkoutlist* list in the *checkoutlist* file. It should always be edited in place, because multiple copies of the passwords in various sandboxes is a security risk.

CVS can also fall back to system-level user authentication. If a user is not found in the *passwd* file, CVS (by default) authenticates the user with the system's normal authentication method. To prevent users from connecting to CVS with systemwide passwords, this fallback system should usually be disabled; it should definitely be disabled if the data might be transmitted across an untrusted network. Disable it by editing the *config* file in the *CVSROOT* directory and setting the *SystemAuth* value to *no*.

If users with *pserver* access can edit the *CVSROOT* scripting files, an attacker who decrypts a *pserver* access password can force CVS to run arbitrary scripts. Fortunately, scripts run with the access level of the system user as determined when CVS reads the *passwd* file; the access level is not determined by the daemon that runs CVS.

Be aware that once an intruder has write access to the CVS repository, he may be able to gain additional access to the system. If your communications travel over an untrusted network, don't use *pserver* for access where users can change data. *pserver* can be useful for read-only, anonymous access, but I recommend you use something else for other kinds of access. If you need to use *pserver*, an SSH tunnel may be a reasonable compromise.

Using inetd with gserver, kserver, and pserver

gserver, *kserver*, and *pserver* access modes require a server to run on the repository computer. For these modes, the server is started with *inetd* or *xinetd* . *inetd* is configured in the "Other services" section of */etc/inetd.conf*, as shown in Examples 8-18 and 8-19. Note that the configuration must be all on one line. After you edit *inetd.conf*, you should send it a HUP signal, as in *killall -HUP inetd*.

Example 8-18. Inetd for gserver and pserver

```
#:OTHER: Other services
2401 stream tcp nowait root /usr/bin/cvs cvs -f --allow-root=/var/lib/cvs pserver
```

Example 8-19. Inetd for kserver

```
#:OTHER: Other services
1999 stream tcp nowait root /usr/bin/cvs cvs -f --allow-root=/var/lib/cvsroot kserver
```

The *gserver* access method connects to a *pserver* CVS server. The code that runs the server end of *pserver* checks whether it has been connected to with the *pserver* or *gserver* access method and runs the appropriate server code.

The parameter to the *--allow-root* option is the path to the repository root directory. If there will be several different repository root directories, add more *--allow-root* options. If *inetd* complains about the line length or command length, have *inetd* call a script which runs CVS with the appropriate options.

You can use the *-T* option or the *TMPDIR* environment variable to set a specific temporary directory. If no directory is listed, */tmp* is used.

> It can be useful to run the server as a special user, possibly named *cvs*, to limit the amount of damage that can be done if one of the arbitrary scripts (or CVS itself) is insecure. If you do this, ensure that the repository root directory and the *CVSROOT* files start out being owned by the *cvs* user, and make sure that the *cvs* user is in all the groups that can use the repository. You also need to ensure that all users run as user *cvs*, perhaps by having that as the system username in *pserver* access mode.
>
> If CVS has *root* privileges, it runs the scripts called from the scripting files as the user who calls CVS, not the user named in *inetd*, so this is not a special concern.

If your version of *inetd* doesn't allow you to specify port numbers in *inetd.conf*, add lines to */etc/services*, as shown in Example 8-20. Then use those service names instead of the port numbers in *inetd.conf*.

Example 8-20. Port services

```
cvspserver 2401/tcp
cvs 1999/tcp    cvskserver
```

CVS looks for the *cvs* service if it is running *kserver* access mode, and it looks for *cvspserver* if it is running in *gserver* or *pserver* mode. If you installed CVS from a package, CVS may have been modified to use *cvskserver*. Once *inetd.conf* is set up, you'll need to restart *inetd* with the HUP signal, as described earlier.

If you use *xinetd* instead of *inetd*, create */etc/xinetd.d/cvspserver* or */etc/xinetd.d/cvskserver* and enter code similar to the code shown in Example 8-21, rather than editing */etc/inetd.conf*.

Example 8-21. xinetd

```
service cvspserver
{
    port = 2401
    socket_type = stream
    protocol = tcp
    wait = no
    user = root
    passenv = PATH
    server = /usr/bin/cvs
    server_args = -f --allow-root=/var/lib/cvs pserver
}
```

When you have edited the *xinetd* configuration, restart it by logging in as the superuser and running *service xinetd restart* or */etc/init.d/xinetd restart*.

The *-f*, *-T*, and *--allow-root* options to the CVS server are the same as they are for *inetd*. To use the code in Example 8-21 for the *kserver* access method, change the filename and port and use *kserver* instead of *pserver* in the *server-args* line. If *cvspserver* or *cvskserver* are defined in */etc/services*, the line that defines the port is not needed.

Client Ports

If you're using *pserver* or *gserver*, the client defaults to use port 2401. If your repository server is listening on a different port, specify the port in the repository path or set the *CVS_CLIENT_PORT* environment variable on the client computer. You can also compile the client with the *CVS_AUTH_PORT* macro set to the new port.

If you're using *kserver*, the client defaults to use port 1999. If your repository server is listening on a different port, you can use the repository path or the *CVS_CLIENT_PORT* environment variable. The *CVS_PORT* macro sets the default port for *kserver* mode during compilation.

PAM

PAM (Pluggable Authentication Modules) provides an interface that programs can use to connect to whatever authentication methods are desired. Authentication can be as trivial as the user typing "hello world", as complex as biometrics, or as prosaic as passwords. I think PAM is a great boon for system administrators, and I'm excited to see it in CVS.

PAM works by having the system administrator define which *modules* she wants run for each application. The application calls PAM, PAM checks its configuration files, and then PAM calls the relevant modules. If the module requires additional data (such as a password), the module requests it from PAM, and PAM requests it from the application, then hands it to the module. The module runs, and reports its results to PAM.

PAM combines the results of all the modules it's configured to run for the application, and then returns a single combined *success* or *failure* to the application, depending on a strict set of criteria. The criteria are also configured by the system administrator.

At the moment, PAM support in CVS is experimental, and is limited to the fallback option in the pserver connection method. To get PAM support for CVS, configure your CVS executable with *--enable-pam*, having *SystemAuth* set to *yes* in your *CVSROOT/ config* file, and leave *CVSROOT/passwd* empty.

 My article "Introduction to PAM" explains how to configure PAM on your system, and it is available at *http://www.linuxdevcenter.com/pub/ a/linux/2001/09/27/pamintro.html*.

The default PAM configuration file for CVS is */etc/pam.d/cvs*. If your version of PAM uses a single */etc/pam.conf* file instead of a separate file for each application, the application name is *cvs*. The PAM application name (or configuration file name) can be configured at compilation time with *-with-hardcoded-pam-service-name=name*. Use *./configure* to set the PAM compilation options. Make sure you read the *INSTALL* file in the CVS source code, and the installation instructions in Chapter 2.

Each PAM configuration file contains a series of lines. Those lines have the format `module-type control-flag module-path arguments`. The module type defines the aspect of authentication that the line controls. The module path and arguments control what is done for that line. The control flag specifies how PAM should react to the results of the module defined in the module path.

CVS uses the *auth*, *account*, and *session* module types, but not *passwd*. This means that the system administrator will be responsible for defining and updating the authentication token for each user. The module types are:

account
> Nonauthentication account management, such as limiting the maximum number of users or restricting root access

auth
> User authentication, group assignment, and other authentication- and permission-related tasks

session
> Anything the user needs to have done to connect, such as mounting drives or logging connections

passwd
> Updating the authentication token

PAM can call any number of modules for each module type, but calls only one module type at a time: it will call all *auth* modules when CVS is identifying the user, or all *session* modules when CVS is starting a connection. The control-flag for each module controls how PAM calculates success or failure for that module, and for the *stack* of all modules of the type. If you're accustomed to using PAM, there's a complicated syntax for the control flags that gives you truly fine-grained control. If not, use these four flags:

optional
> Not critical to the success or failure of the stack. If at least one nonoptional module succeeds or fails, the result of this module is ignored when calculating the success or failure of the stack.

required
> The module must succeed for the stack of this module type to succeed. If this module fails, all other modules in the stack are executed but the stack is considered to fail.

requisite
> The module must succeed for the stack of this module type to succeed. No later module of its type is executed; failure is reported immediately. The return value is that of the first module in the stack to fail.

sufficient
> Success of this module is sufficient for the stack of this module type to succeed. If no previous *required* module has failed, no other modules of this module type are invoked. (This overrides the *required* execution of all other modules.) Failure of this module does not inherently prevent the stack from succeeding.

A basic PAM configuration might be:

```
account    required     /usr/lib/security/pam_unix.so
auth       requisite    /usr/lib/security/pam_nologin.so
auth       required     /usr/lib/security/pam_unix.so
session    required     /usr/lib/security/pam_unix.so
```

PAM has hundreds of modules available, including modules to authenticate users via LDAP or Kerberos, cryptography cards and buttons, or classic Unix authentication. Every time I look, there are even more interesting and useful modules. I use the Linux-PAM web site at *http://www.kernel.org/pub/linux/libs/pam/*, but you can also find out about PAM news at *http://www.openwall.com/pam/* or *http://www.sun.com/ software/solaris/pam/*.

 The PAM method has all the security problems of the *pserver* method. The password (or other security token) is still stored and transmitted with trivial encoding, and there is no easy method within CVS of updating the passwords.

If you use the PAM system, or have comments about it, please consider mailing them at the CVS mailing lists: *info-cvs@nongnu.org* or *bug-cvs@nongnu.org*. The developers are actively requesting feedback.

CHAPTER 9

Troubleshooting

It would be nice if CVS were perfect, but it isn't. There are times when CVS doesn't work as expected, but with the techniques and information in this chapter, you should be able to fix the most common problems.

General Troubleshooting Techniques

Most of the CVS error messages are helpful but concise. They usually tell you what is wrong and may contain key words or phrases that lead you toward a resolution to the problem. Few of the error messages actually provide a resolution, however, because usually there are several possible causes of any given problem.

If your problem seems to be confined to a single sandbox, the simplest solution is usually to check out a new sandbox. To save changed files, copy them to the new sandbox before erasing the old sandbox. (If the new sandbox has newer revisions of some files, don't copy over them.)

To fix problems in a single sandbox directory, check the sandbox administrative files in the *CVS* subdirectory. If a command has been aborted, the administrative files may have been partially changed. Chapter 6 explains the sandbox administrative files.

Many repository problems are caused by permissions errors. If a user (system user-name) can't read the repository and the problem doesn't seem to be a networking issue, check the repository permissions. The username of the user must be a member of a group with access to the files that they're trying to read. Thankfully, permissions problems are easy to fix. Chapter 6 covers permissions in detail.

Finding Help

CVS is an open source software program that was created by a group of program-mers, rather than by a specific company.* Because there is no company that created

---

* Open source software is explained at *http://www.opensource.org*.

CVS—which means that there is no company that gains revenue from selling it—there is no official source of commercial support. Companies in many parts of the world provide high-quality commercial support for open source products. CVS is a widely used version control system, so most of these companies have staff who are familiar with CVS.

See the CVS wiki at *http://ximbiot.com/cvs/wiki/* and *http://ximbiot.com/cvs/wiki/index.php?title=Commercial_Support* for a list of some of the commercial companies that provide CVS support.

Mail and newsgroups

There are also sources of help on the Internet, such as mailing lists and newsgroups. These are meeting places for people who are familiar with CVS, and for those who need help with it.

The official mailing list is monitored by several CVS developers. Subscribe to the list at *http://mail.gnu.org/mailman/listinfo/info-cvs*.

The *fa.info-cvs* and *gnu.cvs.help* newsgroups were established specifically for CVS. *comp.software.config-mgmt* is a general newsgroup for software-configuration management, defined in the *comp.software.config-mgmt* FAQ as:

> The management of software development projects with respect to issues such as multiple developers working on the same code at the same time, targeting multiple platforms, supporting multiple versions, and controlling the status of code.

The Web

When searching the Web for CVS information, you can avoid references to CVS pharmacies or curriculum vitae by using a search string such as *CVS -pharmacy -resume* or *CVS +version*.

When you have an error message you don't understand, you can often find an explanation by pasting the text of the error message into a web search engine. Example 9-1 shows an attempt to retrieve a revision that does not yet exist (at the time, the highest revision of *Makefile* was 1.7).

Example 9-1. Web searching

```
bash-2.05a$ cvs update -r 3.2 Makefile
cvs server: Makefile is no longer in the repository
```

To search for information on this error, use the search string "is no longer in the repository". This is the longest string that does not contain the name of a file. In many search engines, a quoted string is searched as the phrase, not as the individual words. The results from searching for a string like this often include a series of help requests and answers archived from a technical mailing list.

Another useful search is the name of the command (such as "cvs commit") for which you received the error. Results for this search may lead to a tutorial, mailing-list archives, or other useful information.

Reporting Bugs

If you believe that you've uncovered a bug in the CVS software, you can report that bug to the CVS development team. They can then verify, prioritize, and perhaps fix the bug in a future release of the CVS software.

The first step of reporting a bug is to decide whether the behavior you are experiencing is a bug or whether it is intentional. To do this, read the official documentation for CVS: *Version Management with CVS*, by Per Cederqvist et al. This document is provided with Linux and Unix distributions and is available at the official CVS web site at *http://cvs.nongnu.org*. On Linux or Unix, you can display it with the *info cvs* command. If CVS does not work as described in the official documentation you get from *info cvs*, there is a bug in either CVS or the documentation.

Report bugs to the location listed in the *BUGS* section of *info cvs*. In the current version (and for the foreseeable future), this location is the *bug-cvs@gnu.org* mailing list. You can subscribe to this mailing list at *http://mail.gnu.org/mailman/listinfo/bug-cvs*.

When reporting a bug, include the command you used, what you expected the command to do, and what the command actually did. It is also helpful to list the page in *info cvs* that describes the behavior you expected and to indicate the version of CVS you are using. Be prepared to answer questions about your computer's configuration and your CVS installation.

You can also use the *cvsbug* program, distributed with CVS, to report a bug to CVS. *cvsbug* opens an editor, provides a template for you to fill out, and automatically includes some information about your configuration. Once you close the editor, it sends the problem report to the CVS development team.

Making Your Own Changes to CVS

If you want to add new features to CVS or know how to correct a problem, you may want to make your own changes to CVS and run a modified version at your site.

The functions for most CVS commands are in the *src* subdirectory of the CVS source code, in files named after the command names. For example, the *add* command is implemented by the *add.c* file. Not all commands follow this pattern. The *export* command is in the *checkout.c* file, as it uses most of the same code, and both *export* and *checkout* use functions in *update.c*.

If you wish to submit your changes for inclusion in future versions of CVS, read the *HACKING* and *DEVEL-CVS* files in the CVS source code directory. The *HACKING* file also contains useful advice on CVS coding standards.

Connectivity Problems

If you are having difficulty connecting to a repository, first confirm that the repository path is declared correctly. The most common mistake when checking out a new sandbox is to forget to specify the repository path at all. Another common mistake is to forget to specify the connection method if you are using a method other than *local* or *ext*.

If you want to examine the data sent to or received from the server, set the *CVS_CLIENT_LOG* environment variable to a filename. It must be set on the client computer, and the traffic is logged in files in the current working directory named for that filename, with the suffixes *.in* and *.out*. For instance, if you set *CVS_CLIENT_LOG* to *cvslog*, the traffic is logged to *cvslog.in* and *cvslog.out*. (Traffic to the server is logged to *cvslog.in*, and traffic from the server is logged to *cvslog.out*.)

The *gserver*, *kserver*, and *pserver* connection methods rely on a server that is started with *inetd*. *inetd* sets a limit on the number of connections per unit of time and delays further connections. If you expect heavy use of CVS, you may need to configure *inetd* to accept more connections per minute. Not doing so may cause "connection refused" error messages.

If you're having trouble with the *write proxy* system, the most likely cause is the client being an older client and the server not being configured correctly to support it. See Chapter 6 for the configuration information.

Root and Repository File Problems

If you are in an active sandbox and are receiving an error like the one shown in Example 9-2, the *Root* or *Repository* file in the *CVS* subdirectory of the current sandbox directory has become unreadable. Chapter 6 includes an explanation of these files and what they should contain, but the simplest way to correct a problem in a sandbox is to remove and recreate the sandbox. If there are changes in the sandbox files, be sure to preserve them before removing the sandbox.

Example 9-2. Repository undeclared

```
cvs update: No CVSROOT specified!  Please use the `-d' option
cvs [update aborted]: or set the CVSROOT environment variable.
```

Certain changes in a repository or a repository's host environment can cause the *Root* and *Repository* files in a sandbox to be out of date. Examples of these changes include a change to the repository computer's hostname, a change to the user's username, and a change in the preferred connection method. The traditional way to manage these changes is to commit and release the sandbox beforehand and create a new sandbox afterward.

If you do not want to create a new sandbox, you can edit the appropriate files in the sandbox. Example 9-3 is a small script that relies on *bash* and *perl* to change the hostname in a sandbox *Root* file automatically. In the example, *helit* is the old hostname, and *lat* the new.

Example 9-3. Changing the Root files automatically

```
find ~/cvs/wizzard -name Root | xargs perl -p -i'.bak' -e "s/helit/lat/;"
```

Misconfigured Access Methods

Some of the access methods require configuration. The *pserver*, *kserver*, and *gserver* methods require configuration at the repository, and the *ext*, *kserver*, and *gserver* methods require configuration at the sandbox. Example 9-4 shows the error that occurs when the *pserver* method is used but the user does not exist in the repository's user database. Example 9-5 shows the error that occurs when *kserver* is used but the client is not compiled to support it.

Example 9-4. Pserver misconfiguration

```
bash-2.05a$ cvs -d :pserver:cvs_server:/var/lib/cvs checkout wizzard
no such user jenn in CVSROOT/passwd
```

Example 9-5. Kserver misconfiguration

```
bash-2.05a$ cvs -d :kserver:cvs_server:/var/lib/cvs checkout wizzard
cvs checkout: CVSROOT is set for a kerberos access method but your
cvs checkout: CVS executable doesn't support it.
cvs [checkout aborted]: Bad CVSROOT: `:kserver:cvs_server:/var/lib/cvs'.
```

In addition to checking the configuration of the access method, check whether the username you're trying to use exists on the server and has access to the repository project files you are trying to reach.

If you are using the *pserver* access method, also check that the *passwd* file in the repository's *CVSROOT* directory is mapping your CVS username onto an existing system username with the appropriate permission. If you are using Kerberos 4 or the GSS-API with Kerberos 5, ensure that you have a Kerberos username and a current ticket and that the CVS server has its ticket. System times are also critical with Kerberos.

Isolating Connectivity Problems

Isolating a problem is a common and useful troubleshooting tactic. If you are having trouble accessing a repository, there may be a problem with the protocol you are using to connect with, the configuration of either CVS or the protocol, or, more rarely, the CVS code. To fix your problem, you need to figure out where it is.

There is a common set of client and server code used by all CVS remote-access methods. The *fork* connection method can be used to determine that this common CVS code is functioning correctly. To determine whether Kerberos, the GSS-API, *rsh*, or your *rsh* replacement are working, you can use a simple service with the same protocol as the method you are having trouble with.

To test whether a connection problem is caused in CVS itself, try using the *fork* access method to create a sandbox on the same computer as the repository. If this fails, check your repository path and check that the project name you are using is valid. If both are correct, there is a problem in the CVS client and server code that should probably be reported as a bug. Example 9-6 shows what should happen when you test the server with *fork*.

Example 9-6. Testing the server with fork

```
jenn@helit:/tmp$ cvs -d :fork:/var/lib/cvs checkout wizzard
cvs server: Updating wizzard
U wizzard/Changelog
U wizzard/INSTALL
U wizzard/Makefile
U wizzard/README
U wizzard/TODO
cvs server: Updating wizzard/doc
cvs server: Updating wizzard/doc/design
.
.
.
```

If the *fork* test shows that your repository path and project name are valid and that the common CVS server is functioning correctly, you can isolate the problem further by testing the access method with a simple program that uses the same protocol. You must do this with the protocol client you are attempting to use with CVS, and you must use the same hostname. Kerberos 4 or 5 can be tested with the Kerberos *rsh* replacements, and *ext* or *server* can be tested with *rsh*. If *ext* is used with a replacement for *rsh*, that replacement should be used in the test. You can test *pserver* with *telnet*.

Example 9-7 shows a successful attempt to connect to a host named *helit* using the SSH protocol. SSH clients are commonly used as *rsh* replacements.

Example 9-7. Testing ext

```
bash-2.05a$ ssh helit
Linux helit 2.4.19-686-smp #1 SMP Thu Apr 8 22:06:13 EST 2006 i686 unknown unknown GNU/
Linux
.
.
.
Last login: Mon Mar 11 04:24:55 2006 from 10.0.2.2
jenn@helit:~$
```

rsh-Replacement Problems

If you are using the *ext* connection method, you can choose from many programs to manage your connection; however, such a choice can cause problems.

The replacement must not convert line endings, as CVS expects to do that itself. If your replacement converts line endings, CVS is unable to determine where the end of each line is, so the merge methodology fails.

It's highly unlikely that you'll find an *rsh* replacement that isn't *8 bit clean*, but if you're using binary files or compression and you get strange file corruption problems, you just might have found one. *8 bit clean* refers to how the program handles character sets: *7 bit* programs kept the eighth bit of the byte for use as a parity or flag bit.

The replacement must accept the following syntax:

```
program [-b] [-l username] host commands
```

The *-b* is optional if you are not using OS/2, but the rest of the syntax is required.

The repository server must be running a server process that can accept the protocol the replacement is using and that can run the commands sent by the *rsh*-replacement program. To test most of these requirements, you can run a command that uses the full syntax, as shown in Example 9-8.

Example 9-8. Testing ssh for suitability

```
bash-2.05a$ ssh -l jenn cvs_server ls /tmp
iio
makemain
wizzard
```

If you need to pass a command or call an option to your *rsh* replacement, you can do so by creating a small script and calling that script instead of the replacement program. Example 9-9 shows one such script.

Example 9-9. ssh script

```
#!/bin/bash
exec ssh -i /home/jenn/.RSAkey "$@"
```

Filename Problems

CVS reserves some filenames for its own uses, and other filenames are included in the default ignore list.

If you have a file that CVS appears to be ignoring, check the default ignore list and any *cvsignore* files in your repository, home directory, or sandbox. The default list is provided in "cvsignore" of Chapter 6. If the *-I!* option to a CVS command causes CVS to recognize the file, then you can be sure the file is in a *cvsignore* list. You can temporarily force CVS to recognize an ignored file by stating it explicitly as a command parameter.

CVS uses *CVS* and *Attic* directories in the repository. CVS prevents you from using the filename *CVS* but permits you to create files or directories called *Attic*. If you use an *Attic* directory and look in the repository, the *Attic* directory has files that don't exist on the trunk from the directory above it, as well as those you are currently using in your sandbox version of the *Attic*. You should avoid using *Attic* as a file or directory name.

CVS may ignore a filename with a # or .# prefix, as CVS reserves some files with the prefix .# for its own use. In the sandbox, CVS uses the .# prefix for copies of files it has overwritten during a merge. In the repository, lock files start with #.

Another cause of filename problems is a conflict between the filesystem on a client computer and the filesystem on a repository. For example, filename case is significant in Linux and Unix filesystems, but not in Windows filesystems, and the significance of filename case varies in Macintoshes—depending on which filesystem they're using, and on a configuration option. If two filenames vary only in case and you are checking them out to a filesystem that ignores case, the second file to be checked out may overwrite the first. This action can also cause problems when you attempt to change the case of a file in Windows. Another possible case-related problem is that if you are disconnected from the network, on an operating system that doesn't consider case relevant, then you *cvsremove FiLe* and try to *cvs add file*, CVS may search the pending requests, see that *FiLe* existed, and perceive *cvs add* as an unremove.

Line-Ending Problems

If CVS is reporting lines as longer or shorter than they should be, there may be a problem with the line-ending conversion from one filesystem to another.

If you are using the *ext* access method with an *rsh* replacement, your replacement may be trying to convert line endings. CVS relies on being able to do the conversion itself.

If this is not the problem and the file in question is a text file, you might have binary keyword-expansion mode set for the file. Use the command *cvs status filename* to show the keyword-expansion mode, and use *cvs admin -kkv filename* to fix the file in the repository by setting its keyword-expansion mode to the default for text files. If a binary file is corrupted, it might be set as a text file. The command *cvs admin -kb filename* sets the binary file's keyword-expansion mode correctly, but it might not repair the damage to the local file. To retrieve the original version of the file, use *cvs update -r 1.1 -p > filename*.

Permission Problems

For all access methods except *pserver*, CVS relies exclusively on the filesystem to manage permissions. Each user must have a username on the repository server, and must have write access to every directory that contains files they will need to commit.

You can control permissions only at a directory level. If a user will need to commit to any file in a directory, she needs read and write access to the whole directory.

 Once, I was working on a project where I had to connect to the repository server through an intermediate proxy server. We kept getting permission errors and eventually tracked it to the intermediary. We all had membership in the *col* group on the client and repository servers, but not on the intermediary. As files passed through the intermediate server, their group membership information was lost, so they were saved in the repository with no group ownership. We corrected this by setting the repository directories' SGID flags on the repository server.

The *history* and *val-tags* files in the repository's *CVSROOT* directory must be writable to all CVS users. The *history* file can be removed if none of your users use the *cvs history* command.

pserver Problems

The *pserver* connection method uses a more complicated permission system than the one other connection methods use. The *passwd* file in the repository's *CVSROOT* directory can cause a user to have two effective usernames: one that affects only CVS and another that affects the filesystem. If a user has permission within one but not the other, he may be unable to access his project files. For instance, if his CVS username is in the *writers* file in the *CVSROOT* directory, CVS attempts to allow him to write to his project files. If, however, his system username is not allowed to write to the project directories, the operating system denies access and CVS is unable to write to the files.

The *readers* and *writers* files in the repository's *CVSROOT* directory set read-only or read-write permission based the on CVS username. These files must have a newline character after each username, including the last.

Lock Files

CVS removes its lock files when a CVS process completes properly, but processes that are killed can sometimes leave lock files in place. Chapter 6 explains the process of removing lock files and provides an example of the messages CVS displays when a lock file is present.

If you have to wait for valid lock files frequently, you may need to reduce the length of time a lock file is active in the repository. Locks are based on the directory that is being locked, so if you have frequently accessed project directories with many files or large files, you may benefit from splitting them into smaller directories.

If you are waiting for lock files frequently, you can also check whether your system is being overloaded. You may have network trouble, or large checkouts or commits may be overloading your system memory or swap space. Check the load average on the repository server, and find out what the CPU is doing. If you have insufficient memory, your server will be spending a lot of time swapping. You might also experience delays due to slow hard drive access times.

Time Issues

The most common cause of CVS timing problems is a mismatch in the time settings of the server and the client. Ideally, both server and client should maintain their base time clock in UTC and convert to local time for display. Having one (or both) maintaining their base time clock in local time is acceptable, provided that the machine is configured to know that it's maintaining local time.

Trouble comes if one or both is maintaining local time but thinks that it's maintaining UTC, or if the two machines disagree on what time it is. Fortunately, NTP (network time protocol) can ensure the machines keep the same time, and modern operating systems make time configuration easy.

## PART IV

Reference

This part of the book is designed to be used as a reference. Part IV includes the following chapters:

Chapter 10, *Command Reference*
> This chapter is a reference of CVS commands, providing the syntax and options for each command.

Chapter 11, *Miscellaneous Topics Reference*
> This chapter covers CVS administrative files, environment variables that affect CVS, date formats, pattern matching, and the repository access methods, in reference form.

Command Reference

This chapter is a comprehensive reference of all CVS commands, with a brief summary of what each does. It is intended to be useful as a quick reference, not a tutorial.

If you have never used CVS before, read Chapter 2 or Chapter 3 before reading this reference. Those chapters explain the basic concepts of CVS and how to use it effectively.

CVS Command-Line Options

CVS supports a number of command-line options that you can use to control various aspects of CVS behavior. Command-specific options are described in "CVS Commands," later in this chapter. This section focuses on options that you pass to the *cvs* executable itself, not to any specific CVS command.

The syntax of any CVS command is as follows:

```
cvs [cvs-options] [command] [command-options-and-arguments]
```

The specific *cvs-options* modify the behavior of the main CVS code, rather than the code for a specific command. The following options are valid:

-*a*   Authenticate all network traffic. Without this option, the initial connection for the command is authenticated, but later traffic along the same data stream is assumed to be from the same source.

     This option is available only with GSS-API connections. (If you use *ssh* as your *rsh* replacement in the *ext* connection mode, *ssh* authenticates the data stream, and you don't need extra authentication.)

     Support (in the client) for this option is generated when CVS is compiled. You can test whether your installation supports -*a* by checking whether it is listed in *cvs --help-options*. The command-line client can be compiled to support it by using the *--enable-client* option to the *configure* script.

     The server always supports -*a*. See also -*x*.

--allow-root=directory

Used as part of the *inetd* command string for *server*, *kserver*, and *pserver* connection methods. The *directory* is the repository root directory that the server allows connections to. Using *--allow-root* more than once in a command allows users to connect to any of the specified repositories.

 This option is only relevant when configuring the CVS server, so if you're not a server administrator, you can safely ignore it. (If you are a server administrator, see Chapter 8 for more information.)

-b directory

Exists for backward compatibility with old versions of CVS (before 1.9.18) and does nothing in current versions. It used to specify the *directory* for the RCS executables.

-d repository_path

Use *repository_path* as the path to the repository root directory. This option overrides both the *CVSROOT* environment variable and the contents of the *Root* file in the sandbox's *CVS* subdirectory. It also overrides the contents of the *.cvsrc* file.

The syntax for the repository path is:

    [:method[;option=arg...]:][[[user][:password]@]hostname[:[port]]]/path

Chapter 8 contains a full explanation of each element of the repository path. Chapters 2 and 3 contain simpler explanations of repository paths.

-e editor

Use the specified *editor* when CVS calls an editor for log information during the *commit* or *import* process. This option overrides the *EDITOR*, *CVSEDITOR*, and *VISUAL* environment variables and the contents of the *.cvsrc* file.

Prevent CVS from reading the *~/.cvsrc* file and from using the options in it.

--help or *-H*

If called as *cvs -H* or *cvs --help*, CVS displays a general CVS help message.

If called as *cvs -H command* or *cvs --help command*, CVS displays the available options and help information for the specified command. (Contrast with *--help-commands*.)

--help-commands

List the available CVS commands with brief descriptions of their purposes.

--help-options

List the available *cvs-options* with brief descriptions of their purposes.

--help-synonyms

List the valid synonyms (short names) for the CVS commands.

Dropped into an Unfamiliar Editor?

Unix and Linux systems traditionally use editors that don't have menus or "what you see is what you get" interfaces. If you don't set an editor, and use command-line CVS rather than a graphical client, CVS will probably open an old-style (but very good) editor, usually *emacs*, *vi*, or a more recent variation on *vi* called *vim*.

If you find yourself in an unknown editor with no visible help or menus, try this command sequence: try pressing Ctrl-H then t. If this brings up a tutorial, you're in *emacs*. If it doesn't, try pressing Escape, then type :h, then press Return. If this sequence brings up a help screen, you're in *vi*.

To exit *vi* (without saving changes), type :q!. To exit *emacs* without saving, press Ctrl-X Ctrl-C.

I have noticed that some modern distributions use an editor (such as *pico* or *nano*) with menus along the top or bottom, instead of *vi*, as their default editor. I think this is a good change: those of us who prefer *vi* or *emacs* can set it as our defaults; those who don't aren't left trapped in an editor with obscure commands. For more information on these editors, see *Learning the vi Editor*, by Linda Lamb and Arnold Robbins (O'Reilly), and *Learning GNU Emacs*, by Debra Cameron et al. (O'Reilly).

-l   Do not log the current command to the *history* file in the repository's *CVSROOT* directory. The command will not show in subsequent *cvs history* output. This option is removed in CVS 1.11.7.

-n   Execute only commands that do not change the repository or sandbox. Using this option with *cvs update* can provide a status report on the current sandbox.

The displayed screen messages may be different if you run a command with and without the -n option. If you use this option, you won't get output that would normally be part of the process of modifying the repository copies of files.

-q   Run in *quiet mode*. This option causes CVS to display only some of the usual informational messages.

-Q   Run in *very quiet mode*. This option causes CVS to display only the most critical information.

-r   Set files that are checked out to the sandbox as read only. This option affects only newly checked-out files.

Normally, files are checked out as read-write, but if a file is being watched with *cvs watch*, read-only is the default. This option overrides settings in the *.cvsrc* file, and has the same effect as the *CVSREAD* environment variable. See also -w.

-R   Enables CVS to work (in a limited fashion) with read-only repositories, such as a repository on a CD-ROM. (This option is present in CVS 1.12.1 and later.)

-s variable=value

> Set a user variable for use with one of the scripting files in *CVSROOT*. The user variables are explained in Chapters 6, 7, and 11.

-t   Display messages that trace the execution of the command. This option can be used with *-n* to determine precisely what a command does without actually changing a file (within the limits of the *-n* command).

-T directory

> Use the named *directory* to store temporary files. This option overrides the *TMPDIR* environment variable, and if run on the server, also overrides the setting in the *CVSROOT/config* file in the repository. This option has a local effect: if given in the client, it affects the client but not the server. If given in the server, it affects the server but not the client.

--version or *-v*

> Display CVS version and copyright information.

-w   Set files checked out to the sandbox as readable and writable. This option only sets the permissions of newly checked-out files and overrides the *CVSREAD* environment variable. This option overrides settings in the *.cvsrc* file. See also *-r*.

-x   Encrypt all data that travels across the network between the client and the server. This option is currently available in GSS-API or Kerberos mode only. (If you use *ssh* as your *rsh* replacement in the *ext* connection mode, *ssh* encrypts the data stream by default.)

> This option is available only if the client is compiled to support it. You can check by seeing if it is listed in *cvs --help-options*. You can compile the command-line client to support it by using the *--enable-client* and *--enable-encryption* options to the *configure* script.

> The server always supports *-x*. See also *-a*.

-z #

> Compress all network traffic by using the specified *gzip* compression level (the *#* symbol here represents a *gzip* level number). The compression levels range from *0* (no compression) to *9* (maximum compression). This option overrides settings in the *.cvsrc* file.

CVS Commands

Most of your interaction with CVS is through the various CVS commands. Even if you use a graphical client, most of the functions the client uses call the CVS commands.

Most commands have a shortened nickname that you can type instead of the longer command name. These are called *command synonyms* in CVS jargon.

add

cvs [*cvs-options*] add [-k *mode*] [-m *message*] *files*

Adds a file or directory to the repository. This command can also be used to undo an uncommitted file deletion or to restore a deleted file. A file that is added with this command is not uploaded to the repository until the next *cvs commit*. A directory is added immediately (unless you are using a client with an "offline" mode, and are offline).

Command options

-k mode

> Add a file or files with the designated keyword-expansion mode. This option also sets the default keyword mode for the file. If you forget to set the default keyword mode when you *cvs add* a file, you can do so later with *cvs admin*, unless the repository administrator has limited the users of *cvs admin*.
>
> The keyword-expansion modes are listed in "Keywords and Keyword Modes" of Chapter 11 and are explained in "Keywords" in Chapter 3.

-m message

> Use the specified *message* as the description of the newly added file. The description is shown in *cvs log* output.

Description

Files and directories added with this command must already exist, and must be within a sandbox. They are added to the directory in the repository that corresponds to the one in the sandbox.

If you are using branches, be aware that the file or directory is added only to the branch or trunk that the sandbox directory is part of. To add it to other branches as well, you will need to merge it; see Chapter 4 for more information.

Note that you must explicitly state which files are added, though you can use wildcards like * to specify a group of files.

In Example 1, I add a single file. Example 2 shows the use of wildcards. Example 3 shows a correction of an unwanted file removal.

Example 1

```
jenn@soldier:~/wizzard/doc/design$ cvs add Design.rtf
cvs server: scheduling file `Design.rtf' for addition
cvs server: use 'cvs commit' to add this file permanently
```

Example 2

```
jenn@soldier:~/wizzard/lib$ cvs add *.h
cvs add: scheduling file `acconfig.h' for addition
cvs add: scheduling file `getdate.h' for addition
cvs add: scheduling file `gettext.h' for addition
cvs add: scheduling file `utils.h' for addition
cvs add: use `cvs commit' to add these files permanently
```

Example 3

```
jenn@soldier:~/wizzard/src$ cvs add handheld.c
cvs add: `handheld.c', version 1.3, resurrected
U handheld.c
```

---

admin
Synonyms: *adm, rcs*

cvs [*cvs-options*] admin [-iILqU] [-*ausernames*] [-A*filename*] [-b[*revision*]] [-c*string*]
[-e[*usernames*]] [-k*mode*] [-l[*revision*]] [-m*revision:message*] [-n*tagname*[:[*revision*]]]
[-N*tagname*[:[*revision*]]] [-o*range*] [-s*state*[:*revision*]] [-t[*filename*]] [-t-*string*] [-u
[*revision*]] [-VN] [-x*suffix*] [*files...*]

Use a variety of special administrative commands (RCS commands) on the repository copy
of project files. Many of these commands have no effect on CVS, and exist mostly as
historic artifacts—though the more guru-like of the repository administrators may find
uses for them.

Command options

-*ausernames*

> (No effect in CVS.) Append the comma-separated list of *usernames* to the RCS access
> list in the repository (RCS-format) copy of a file.
>
> See also -*A* and -*e*.

-A*filename*

> (No effect in CVS.) Append the RCS access list in *filename* to the access list of the files
> being operated on.
>
> See also -*a* and -*e*.

-b[*revision*]

> (Use with great caution!) Set the default branch of a file to the named branch revision;
> or, if no revision is named, set the default branch to the highest branch revision on the
> trunk. This option should be used very rarely in CVS; it is better to check out a
> sandbox as a branch sandbox with the -*r* option to *checkout* or *update*.
>
> You can use this option to revert a file or project to the vendor's version, if you are
> using vendor branches, which are explained in Chapter 7.

-c*string*

> Set the RCS comment leader of a file to the specified *string*. This option is significant
> if the configuration option *UseArchiveCommentLeader* is set to *true*.

-e[*usernames*]

> (No effect in CVS.) Remove the comma-separated list of *usernames* from the RCS
> access list in the repository (RCS-format) copy of a file. If no list of *usernames* is
> provided, remove all names.
>
> See also -*a* and -*A*.

-i   (Not used in CVS.) Create and initialize an RCS file. This option is not used in CVS
      (use *cvs add* instead), and it is not available in CVS 1.9.14 and later.

-I   Run interactively. This option does not work in client/server-mode CVS and may be
      removed from later versions of CVS.

-kmode

Set the default keyword-expansion mode for a file.

The keyword-expansion modes are listed in the "Keywords and Keyword Modes" section of Chapter 11 and explained in "Keywords" in Chapter 3.

-l[revision]

Lock the specified *revision* of a file so that another user cannot commit to it. If *revision* is omitted, CVS locks the latest revision on the current sandbox's branch or the trunk. To work with CVS, the lock requires a script such as the *rcslock* script in the *contrib* directory of the source. Chapter 5 explains how to use this option.

See also *-u*.

-L   Set RCS locking for a file to *strict*, which means that the owner of the file must lock the file before committing. (This locking is done by the CVS code and need not be done manually.)

File locking must be set to strict for CVS to work properly.

See also *-U*.

-mrevision:message

Replace the log message of the designated *revision* of a file with the specified *message*.

-ntagname[:[revision]]

(Use with caution!) Tag the designated *revision* or branch of a file with the *tagname*. If there is no *revision* and no colon, delete the tag; if there is a colon but no *revision*, tag the latest revision on the default branch, usually the trunk. If the *tagname* is already present in the file (and the operation isn't *delete*), this option prints an error and exits.

Generally, it is better to use *cvs tag* and *cvs rtag* to manipulate tags.

See also *-N*.

-Ntagname[:[revision]]

(Use with caution!) Tag the designated *revision* or branch of a file with the *tagname*. If there is no *revision* and no colon, delete the tag; if there is a colon but no revision, tag the latest revision on the default branch—usually the trunk. If the *tagname* is already present in the file (and the operation isn't *delete*), this option moves the tag to the new revision.

Generally, it is better to use *cvs tag* and *cvs rtag* to manipulate tags.

See also *-n*.

-orange

(Use with extreme caution!) Delete the revisions specified in the *range*. The revisions given in the range can be revision numbers or tags, but be wary of using tags if multiple tags in a file denote the same revision.

 There is no way to undo a *cvs admin -orange* command.

If using tags rather than revision numbers, be very careful with this—you could delete a file revision you had not intended to. (If the tags *alpha*, *beta*, and *gamma* refer to the same revision number in a file, and you delete *alpha:beta*, you have also lost *gamma*.) You cannot use tags with the :: versions of this command.

CVS does not cope well if you delete a revision and someone then tries to commit changes made against that revision. If this happens, you will almost certainly need to restore from backup.

The *range* can be any of the following:

revision1:revision2
> Delete revisions between *revision1* and *revision2*, including *revision1* and *revision2*.

revision1::revision2
> Delete revisions between *revision1* and *revision2*, excluding *revision1* and *revision2*.

revision:
> Delete *revision* and all newer revisions on the same branch (or the trunk).

revision::
> Delete all revisions newer than *revision* on the same branch (or the trunk).

:revision
> Delete *revision* and all older revisions on the same branch (or the trunk). This range does not delete the base revision of the branch or revision 1.1.

::revision
> Delete all revisions older then *revision* on the same branch (or the trunk). This range does not delete the base revision of the branch or revision 1.1.

revision
> Delete *revision*.

-q   Run quietly, without printing diagnostics (redundant with *cvs -q admin*).

-sstate[:revision]
> Set the *state* of the designated *revision* of a file, or set the last revision on the trunk or the current branch if no *revision* is listed. The *state* should be a string and is shown in the output of *cvs log* and by the *Log* and *State* keywords. The *dead* state is reserved for CVS internal use.

-t[filename]
> Write the contents of the file specified by *filename* to the description of each file listed in the command. The description is shown in *cvs log* output. This option deletes any existing description. If the *filename* is omitted, CVS seeks input from standard input (*stdin*), ending with a period (.) on a line by itself.

> See also *-t-string*.

-t-string
> Write the contents of the *string* to the description of each file listed in the command. The description is an RCS field, shown in *cvs log* output. This option deletes any existing description.

> See also *-t[filename]*.

-u[revision]
> Unlock the specified *revision* of a file so that another user can commit from that revision. If the *revision* is omitted, this option unlocks the latest revision on the current sandbox's branch or the trunk. This option requires a script such as the *rcslock* script in the *contrib* directory of the source. Chapter 5 explains how to use this option.

> See also *-l*.

-U (Can prevent CVS from working!) Set RCS locking for a file to nonstrict, which means that the owner of the file does not need to lock the file before committing. (This locking is done by the CVS code and need not be done manually.)

File locking must be set to strict for CVS to work properly. This option should never be used on CVS-stored files.

See also *-L*.

-VN
(Not used in CVS.) Write an RCS file compatible with RCS version *N*. This option is not used in CVS anymore, and it is not available in CVS 1.9.20 and later.

-xsuffix
(Not used in CVS.) Specify the *suffix* for the RCS file. All CVS files use *,v*, so this is an unused command.

Description

The *cvs admin* command is a frontend for a range of useful (though sometimes useless to CVS) RCS-based commands. Project files are stored in the repository in RCS format, so it is useful to have a way to use some of the RCS commands on the files directly. This command and the useful options are explained in Chapter 7.

Note that if the *cvsadmin* group exists on the server, only members of that group can use *cvs admin*. A limited set of commands can be made available to general users with the *UserAdminOptions* setting in the *config* file in *CVSROOT*.

The *-c*, *-k*, *-s*, and *-t* options are useful to general users, as are *-l* and *-u* if you're using *rcslock* (see Chapter 5). I would recommend setting an empty *cvsadmin* group (to prevent anyone using most of these commands), and setting *UserAdminOptions* to permit the three (or five) useful options.

The *-m* option permits users to modify old log messages, and is either useful or dangerous depending on how strictly you want to maintain the history of project changes. (I can envision potential mischief with it.) Think carefully about whether or not you want to add it to *UserAdminOptions*.

In Example 1, I tell CVS to treat a Word document as binary. In Example 2, I am setting the RCS comment leader of all the *.h* files in the current directory.

Example 1

```
jenn@soldier/wizzard/doc/design$ cvs admin -kb AcceptanceTest.doc
RCS file: /var/lib/cvs/wizzard/doc/design/AcceptanceTest.doc,v
done
```

Example 2

```
jenn@soldier:~/wizzard/lib$ cvs admin -c"Log: " *.h
RCS file: /var/lib/cvs/wizzard/lib/acconfig.h,v
done
RCS file: /var/lib/cvs/wizzard/lib/getdate.h,v
done
RCS file: /var/lib/cvs/wizzard/lib/gettext.h,v
done
RCS file: /var/lib/cvs/wizzard/lib/utils.h,v
done
```

annotate

cvs [*cvs-options*] annotate [-fFlR] [-D *date*] [-r *revision*] [*files...*]

Displays a file or files with annotations about the last change of each line. The annotations give the editor, and the revision number of the latest revision. If no files are used in the argument, the files in the current sandbox are shown.

See also *rannotate*.

Command options

-D date
  Run *annotate* on the latest revision of a file that is as old as or older than the date or time specified by *date*.

-f Use the latest (*HEAD*) revision of a file that is on the current branch or trunk if no revision matches a specified date or revision number. This option applies only if *-r* or *-D* is used.

-F Show annotations for binary files. (Note that binary files may have extremely long lines.)

-l Run *annotate* on the files in the local directory only. (Do not recurse into subdirectories.)

-r revision[:date]
  Run *annotate* on the specified *revision* or tag of a file. If this option refers to a branch, run the command on the latest (*HEAD*) revision of the branch.

  The *date* can be used only if the revision designates a branch, and specifies the latest revision on that date (the *:date* option is available as of 1.12.12).

-R Run *annotate* on the files in the local directory and all subdirectories and recurse down the subdirectories. This option is the default.

Example 1

```
jenn@soldier:~/wizzard$$ cvs annotate Makefile

Annotations for Makefile
***************
1.2  (jenn    01-Sep-06): #
1.2  (jenn    01-Sep-06): # Makefile for the Wizzard project
(jenn    01-Sep-06): # Created by J Vesperman, 1 September 2002
```

Example 2

```
jenn@soldier:~/zebedee/src$ cvs annotate utils.cc

Annotations for utils.cc
***************
1.4        (dancer    14-Apr-06): #ifdef HAVE_CONFIG_H
1.4        (dancer    14-Apr-06): #include <config.h>
1.4        (dancer    14-Apr-06): #endif
1.1        (jenn    13-Apr-06): #include "utils.h"
1.1        (jenn    13-Apr-06):
1.9        (dancer    19-Apr-06): #include <string>
```

```
1.10          (jenn  17-Oct-06): extern std::string config_prefix;
1.10          (jenn  17-Oct-06): const std::string fixpath(const std::string &
oldpath)
```

checkout   Synonyms: *co, get*

cvs [*cvs-options*] checkout [-AcflnNpPrs] [-d *directory-name*] [-D *date*] [-j *revision*[:
date]] [-j *revision2*[:*date2*]] [-k *mode*] [-r *revision*] projects...

Creates a new sandbox in the current working directory, or updates an existing sandbox. (The *update* command is preferred for updating a sandbox, because it doesn't have the additional code for creating a new sandbox.)

See also *export* and *update*.

Command options

- -A   Clear sticky tags, dates, and keyword-expansion modes from a project and replace the current files with the head of the trunk. See "Stickiness" in Chapter 4.

- -c   Display the contents of the *modules* file in the repository's *CVSROOT* directory. This option lists the modules in the current repository and the options applicable to those modules.

     See also -s.

   checkout -c lists only those projects that have entries in the *modules* file.

-d *directory-name*
     Check a sandbox out into a directory called *directory-name* instead of using the repository directory name or the name designated in the *modules* file in the repository's *CVSROOT* directory. This is particularly useful when creating a second sandbox for a project.

     CVS usually creates the same directory structure that the repository uses. However, if the *checkout* parameter contains only one file or directory and the -d option is used, CVS does not create any intervening directories, thus shortening the directory path to the single file or directory. Use -N to prevent CVS from shortening the path.

     For example, if the repository contains a project *my*, with a file at *my/very/long/path/to/beachfront.txt*, and you use *checkout -d beach my/very/long/path/to/beachfront.txt*, CVS will produce a sandbox *beach* containing only *beachfront.txt*.

     If you use *checkout -N -d beach my/very/long/path/to/beachfront.txt*, CVS will produce a sandbox *beach* containing the entire directory chain *very/long/path/to*, with *beachfront.txt* in the directory *to*.

-D *date*
     Check out the latest revision of each file in a project that is as old as or older than the date or time specified by *date*. This option implies the -P option and produces a sticky date on the new sandbox.

-f   Use the latest (*HEAD*) revision on the current branch or trunk if no revision matches the date or revision number. This applies only if *-r* or *-D* is used.

-j revision[:date]

Determine the common ancestor of the revision the files in the sandbox are based on and the specified *revision*, then determine the changes between that common ancestor and the revision specified, and merge those changes to the sandbox.

If two *-j* options are used, determine the changes between the first *-j* revision and the second *-j* revision and merge those changes to the sandbox.

The *date* can be used only if the revision designates a branch. *date* specifies the latest revision on that date.

-k mode

Check out a sandbox with the designated keyword-expansion mode. This option also sets a sticky keyword mode for the sandbox, so that later commands operate with the same keyword-expansion mode unless a *-k* option overrides that mode. Prior to CVS 1.12.2, the *-k* option overrides the default mode for each file. After that version of CVS, *-kb* will not be overridden.

The keyword-expansion modes are listed in "Keywords and Keyword Modes" of Chapter 11 and are explained in "Keywords" in Chapter 3.

-l   Run *checkout* on the local directory only. (Do not check out subdirectories.)

See also -R.

-n   Do not run any program listed in the *modules* file for this directory.

-N   Do not shorten the path. CVS usually creates the same directory structure that the repository uses. However, if the *checkout* contains only one file and the *-d* option is used, CVS does not create any intervening directories unless *-N* is also specified.

-p   Check out the listed files to the standard output (usually the screen), rather than to a sandbox.

-P   Do not include empty directories in the sandbox.

-r revision[:date]

Run *checkout* on the specified *revision* or tag. If this option refers to a branch, run the command on the latest (*HEAD*) revision of the branch. This option implies the *-P* option and produces a sticky tag on the new sandbox.

The *date* can be used only if the revision designates a branch, and specifies the latest revision on that date (the *:date* option is available as of 1.12.12).

-R   Run *checkout* on the local directory and all subdirectories and recurse down the subdirectories. This option is the default.

See also -l.

-s   Display the contents of the *modules* file in the repository's *CVSROOT* directory. This option lists the modules in the current repository and their status.

See also -c.

Description

The *projects* argument to *checkout* may be one or more paths to directories within the repository, paths to files within the repository, or module names as specified in the *modules* file in the repository's *CVSROOT* directory. These paths must be separated by spaces, and are relative to the repository's root directory.

When creating a new sandbox, the repository path must be specified by using the *-d repository_path* CVS option or the *CVSROOT* environment variable. Repository paths are explained in more detail in Chapter 8.

If you are creating a new sandbox inside an existing sandbox, the *CVS/Root* file of the current directory in the existing sandbox can provide a repository path. In most cases, having a sandbox inside a sandbox is needlessly confusing.

Example 1 is a simple checkout of the *wizzard* project from the repository on *blackrock*. Example 2 is a checkout of the *beta_0-1-branch* of the *wizzard* project, into a sandbox named for the branch.

Example 1

```
jenn@soldier:~$ cvs -d :ext:blackrock:/var/lib/cvs checkout wizzard
cvs checkout: Updating wizzard
U wizzard/Changelog
U wizzard/INSTALL
U wizzard/Makefile
U wizzard/README
U wizzard/TODO
cvs checkout: Updating wizzard/doc
cvs checkout: Updating wizzard/doc/design
U wizzard/doc/design/AcceptanceTest.doc
U wizzard/doc/design/Analysis.rtf
U wizzard/doc/design/Design.rtf
U wizzard/doc/design/Requirements.doc
U wizzard/doc/design/Specification.rtf
cvs checkout: Updating wizzard/doc/plan
U wizzard/doc/plan/Schedule.rtf
```

Example 2

```
jenn@soldier:~$ cvs -d :ext:blackrock:/var/lib/cvs checkout \
> -rbeta_0-1_branch -dbeta_0-1_branch wizzard
cvs checkout: Updating beta_0-1_branch
U beta_0-1_branch/Changelog
U beta_0-1_branch/INSTALL
U beta_0-1_branch/Makefile
U beta_0-1_branch/README
U beta_0-1_branch/TODO
cvs checkout: Updating beta_0-1_branch/doc
cvs checkout: Updating beta_0-1_branch/doc/design
U beta_0-1_branch/doc/design/AcceptanceTest.doc
U beta_0-1_branch/doc/design/Analysis.rtf
U beta_0-1_branch/doc/design/Requirements.doc
U beta_0-1_branch/doc/design/Specification.rtf
cvs checkout: Updating beta_0-1_branch/doc/plan
U beta_0-1_branch/doc/plan/Schedule.rtf
```

commit

cvs [*cvs-options*] commit [-flnR] [-m *message* | -F *logfile*] [-r *revision*] [*files...*]

Commits changes in a sandbox to the repository.

Command options

-c This option is useful to encourage file watching (see Chapter 5). It blocks *commit* from working unless the files being committed have been properly flagged with *cvs edit*. If you are using file watching, have all your developers put the -c flag for *commit* and *edit* in their *.cvsrc*.

   (Requires both client and server to be CVS 1.12.10 or later.)

-f Force CVS to commit a file even if there have been no changes to the file. This option implies the -l option, but you can use both -f and -R to do a forced recursive commit.

   From CVS 1.12.10, -f causes -c to be ignored.

-F *logfile*
   Read a log message from the specified *logfile* rather than calling an editor.

-l Run *commit* on the files in the local directory only. (Do not recurse down subdirectories.)

   See also -R.

-m *message*
   Use the *message* when committing a file, rather than calling an editor.

-n Do not run any program listed in the *modules* file (in the repository's *CVSROOT* directory) for this directory.

-r *revision*
   Commit any changes to the specified *revision* number. The revision number must be higher than any current revision number for the file or files.

   If *revision* is a branch tag or a revision number on a branch, commit to the head of the branch.

-R Run *commit* on the files in the local directory and all subdirectories and recurse down the subdirectories. This option is the default.

   See also -l.

Description

The *cvs commit* command uploads changes in a sandbox to the repository. Until a *commit* is run, changes such as modified, new, or removed files are not reflected in the repository. If no files are listed as arguments, CVS uploads all changes in the current sandbox.

Unless you use either the -m or -F options, *commit* calls an editor to request a log message.

If there have been changes in the repository version of a file since it was last synchronized with the repository and the local version has also changed, you have a conflict and the file cannot be committed. You can try to commit the file again once you have updated it using *cvs update* or *cvs checkout*. The update will include an attempt to merge the file. See Chapter 3 for an explanation of file conflicts and how to resolve them.

Since CVS 1.12.12, a *commit id* is added to the file. This ID is unique for each commit, and is the same for all files committed at once.

Example 1 is a simple commit. In Example 2, I force CVS to commit the unchanged file *README* and to give it the revision number 1.6.

Example 1

```
jenn@soldier:~/wizzard$$ cvs commit
cvs commit: Examining .
cvs commit: Examining doc
cvs commit: Examining lib
.
.
.
RCS file: /var/lib/cvs/wizzard/doc/design/Design.rtf,v
done
Checking in doc/design/Design.rtf;
/var/lib/cvs/wizzard/doc/design/Design.rtf,v  <--  Design.rtf
initial revision: 1.1
done
```

Example 2

```
jenn@soldier:~/wizzard$ cvs commit -f -r 1.6 README
/var/lib/cvs/wizzard/README,v  <--  README
new revision: 1.6; previous revision: 1.2
```

---

diff
Synonyms: *di, dif*

`cvs` [*cvs-options*] `diff` [*format-options*] [`-lR`] [`-D` *date*] [`-D` *date2*] [`-f` *file*] [`-k` *mode*] [`-r` *revision*] [`-r` *revision2*] [*files...*]

Displays the differences between two revisions of a file or files. By default, *diff* checks the sandbox copy against the revision in the repository that the sandbox copy was last synchronized with. If the `files` argument is a directory, all files under that directory are compared and files in subdirectories are also compared recursively.

See also *rdiff*.

Standard options

Options described in this section determine which files and revisions are compared by *cvs diff*. These options are the same as the standard options for most CVS commands. The *-k* option may be used to slightly modify the data sent to *diff*.

-D date
> Display the differences between the current sandbox copy of a file and the latest revision on or before the date or time specified by *date*.
>
> If two *-D* options are used, display the differences between the latest revision before the first date and the latest revision before the second date. One or both *-D* options can be replaced with *-r*.

-k mode
> Run *diff* with the designated keyword-expansion mode. This option overrides the default mode and any sticky modes for each file. It's useful to use *-kk* with *diff* to avoid spurious differences being reported (such as expansion of the *$Revision$* keyword).

The keyword-expansion modes are listed in the "Keywords and Keyword Modes" section of Chapter 11.

-l   Run *diff* on the files in the local directory only. (Do not recurse down subdirectories.) See also *-R*.

-r revision[:date]

Display the differences between the current sandbox copy and the specified *revision*. The *date* can be used only if the revision designates a branch, and specifies the latest revision on that date.

If two *-r* options are used, display the differences between the first and second specified revisions. One or both *-r* options can be replaced with *-D*.

-R   Run *diff* on the files in the local directory and all subdirectories and recurse down the subdirectories. This option is the default.

See also *-l*.

Format options

These options determine how *cvs diff* displays any differences it finds. They represent the *format-options* portion of the syntax and operate in the same way as the options to the GNU *diff* program.

-number

Show *number* lines of context. This option is obsolete and should be replaced with either *-C number* or *-U number*. (If you do use it, this option must be combined with *-c* or *-u*.)

-a or *--text*

Compare files line by line, treating the files as text files.

-b or *--ignore-space-change*

Ignore trailing whitespace and consider all sequences of whitespace characters to be equivalent.

-B or *--ignore-blank-lines*

Ignore changes to blank lines, such as addition or deletion.

--binary

Read and write data in binary mode.

--brief

Report only whether the files are different, not how they are different.

-c or *-C number* or *--context[=number]*

Use context-output format, displaying *number* lines of context around each change. The default is two lines. If you are using *diff* to create a file to use with the *patch* program, you will need at least two lines of context.

-d or *--minimal*

Use an algorithm that is slower but tries to express the differences between the files in the fewest possible steps, sometimes creating a smaller list of changes to be made than the standard algorithm does.

-e or *--ed*

Produce the output in the form of a script that you can run with the *ed* text editor to convert the first revision to the second.

-f or *--forward-ed*

> Produce output that is similar to an *ed* script, but with the changes in the order in which they occur in the file. The resulting output is not a script; it is simply in a format similar to an *ed* script.

-F re or *--show-function-line=re*

> For each set of differences, show the most recent line that matches the regular expression *re*. See Chapter 11 for information on regular expressions.

-H or *--speed-large-files*

> Use heuristics that help make *diff* faster if it is reading large files with many scattered, small changes.

--horizon-lines=number

> If the files have a common header and footer, display the last *number* lines of the header and the first *number* lines of the footer.

-i or *--ignore-case*

> Do not report on changes of letter case. Consider upper- and lowercase letters as identical.

-I re or *--ignore-matching-lines=re*

> Do not report on changes that insert or delete lines that match the regular expression *re*.

--ifdef=NAME

> Produce a merged file as output, with C preprocessor *#ifdef=NAME* structures around the differences. This option is particularly useful if you can compare a version of a C (or related) program that has just had a feature added, to the version just before the feature was added (and nothing but the feature has changed). If you have coded it with this in mind, this allows you to toggle the feature at compile time, with a *#define*.

-L label or *--label label*

> Use *label* instead of the filename in the *diff* output headers.

--left-column

> (Side-by-side output only.) Where the lines are the same, display only the line in the left column.

-n or *--rcs*

> Produce a *diff* in RCS format rather than GNU format.

-N or *--new-file*

> If directories are being compared and a file is not found in one directory, treat the file as if it were there but empty.

-p or *--show-c-function*

> In the output, display the name of the C function each change is in. (Useful only if the files are written in C or related languages.)

-s or *--report-identical-files*

> Report files that are identical.

--suppress-common-lines

> In side-by-side format, do not display lines that are the same.

-t or *--expand-tabs*

> Display the output with spaces instead of tabs.

-T or *--initial-tab*
> Prepend a tab to the output to ensure that all subsequent tabs line up properly.

-u or *-U number --unified[=number]*
> Use unified-output format, displaying *number* lines of context around each change. The default is two lines.

-w or *--ignore-all-space*
> Ignore all differences in whitespace.

-W number or *--width=number*
> Produce side-by-side output that is no more than *number* columns wide.

-y or *--side-by-side*
> Use side-by-side output format.

Line and group format options

Line and group formats allow you to modify the way *diff* displays line changes. The group format options control the markers that surround the change, and the line format options control the marks on the changed lines themselves. Group format options are often used to create *if-then-else* structures for automated parsers to use.

The format options have a format string as a parameter and display the lines they affect according to the rule provided in the format string. The format string usually contains characters that are interpreted by your operating system's shell, so the string usually needs to be surrounded by your shell's quote character.

Following are the group format options, which affect the markers surrounding changed lines:

--old-group-format=format-string
> Display the text defined by the *format-string* for each group of lines from the first file that are different or missing in the second file.

--new-group-format=format-string
> Display the text defined by the *format-string* for each group of lines from the second file that are different or missing in the first file.

--changed-group-format=format-string
> Display the text defined by the *format-string* for each group of lines that are different between files—usually a concatenation of the old and new group format strings.

--unchanged-group-format=format-string
> Display the text defined by the *format-string* for each group of lines that are the same in both files.

Following are the line format options, which affect the lines themselves:

--old-line-format=format-string
> Display the text defined by the *format-string* for each line from the first file that is different or missing in the second file.

--new-line-format=format-string
> Display the text defined by the *format-string* for each line from the second file that is different or missing in the first file.

--unchanged-line-format=format-string
> Display the text defined by the *format-string* for each line that is the same in both files.

--line-format=format-string
> Display the text defined by the *format-string* for all lines.

The *format-string* for both group and line formats uses the percent character (%) as a special token, denoting a string to be evaluated by *cvs diff*. The string %% represents a single percent character. You also need to know your shell's escaping rules if you wish to include your shell's quote marks in the format string.

These are the special characters for a line *format-string*:

%l
> The contents of the line to be formatted, not including the newline character.

%L
> The contents of the line to be formatted, including the newline character. If a line does not contain a newline character, this character does not add it.

%[-][width][.[digits]][doxX]n
> A *printf*-style *format-string* that displays the line number of the current line. The hyphen (-) signals that the number should be left-justified. The *width* specifies the minimum field width, and the *digits* specifies the minimum number of digits. The other options are *d* (for decimal), *o* (for octal), and *x* or *X* (for lower- or uppercase hexadecimal).

%%
> The percent character.

%c'C'
> The character C, which cannot be a quote or a backslash.

%c'\O'
> The character represented by the octal string O.

These are the special characters for a group *format-string*:

%<
> The lines from the first file.

%>
> The lines from the second file.

%=
> Lines common to both files.

%[-][width][.[digits]][doxX]symbol
> A *printf*-style *format-string* that displays the number denoted by the *symbol*. The hyphen (-) signals that the number should be left-justified. The *width* specifies the minimum field width, and the *digits* specifies the minimum number of digits. The other options are *d* (for decimal), *o* (for octal), and *x* or *X* (for lower- or uppercase hexadecimal).

Lowercase *symbol*s denote the first file. Uppercase symbols denote the second file. The *symbol*s are:

E or e
> The line number of the line just before the group.

F or f
> The line number of the first line in the group.

L or l
> The line number of the last line in the group.

M or *m*

>The line number of the line just after the group.

N or *n*

>The number of lines in the group.

%(A=B?C:D)

>If *A* is equal to *B*, display *C*; otherwise, display *D*. *A* and *B* must be decimal constants or a single letter that is one of the symbols provided.

%%

>The percent character.

%c'C'

>The character *C*, which cannot be a quote or a backslash.

%c'\O'

>The character represented by the octal string *O*.

Example 1

This is a simple example to show how CVS displays the difference between the current and repository revisions of the *Makefile*:

```
jenn@soldier:~/wizzard$ cvs diff Makefile
jenn@blackrock's password:
Index: Makefile
===================================================================
RCS file: /var/lib/cvs/wizzard/Makefile,v
retrieving revision 1.17
diff -r1.17 Makefile
15d14
< testtesttesttes
30a30,32
> install:
>                        scp wizzard /usr/local/bin
>                        scp wizzard-doc /usr/local/man/wizzard
```

Example 2

This example is more complicated. It shows how to use *cvs diff* with group format strings. No revisions are specified, so CVS compares the repository and current sandbox revisions of the *cvs_admin.html* file. The *--old-group-format* option and the format string specified with it cause sets of lines from the older revision that are changed in the new revision to be surrounded by *#ifdef OLD* and *#else*. The *--new-group-format* option and its format string put *#endif* after sets of lines from the new revision. The quotes around the format strings prevent my shell from interpreting the strings.

```
jenn@soldier:~/oreilly/articles/cvs$ cvs diff \
> --old-group-format="#ifdef%c'\040'OLD%c'\012'%<%c'\012'#else%c'\012'" \
> --new-group-format="%>%c'\012'#endif%c'\012'" cvs_admin.html
Index: cvs_admin.html
===============================
RCS file: /var/lib/cvs/oreilly/articles/cvs/cvs_admin.html,v
retrieving revision 1.16
diff --old-group-format=#ifdef%c'\040'OLD%c'\012'%<%c'\012'#else%c'\012' --new-group-
```

```
format=%>%c'\012'#endif%c'\012' -r1.16 cvs_admin.html
<!DOCTYPE HTML PUBLIC "-//W3C//DTD HTML 4.01//EN"
    "http://www.w3.org/TR/html4/strict.dtd">
<html>
<head>
<title>CVS Administration</title>
</head>
<body>

    <h1>CVS Administration</h1>


<p>
#ifdef OLD
CVS - or Concurrent Versions System -  is a tool for saving the user's butt by
maintaining a history of changes. It allows the retrieval of older versions of files,
records who makes each change, and prevents simultaneous changes from overwriting
each other.
#else
CVS - or Concurrent Versions System - is a tool for protecting the user from their
own mistakes, by maintaining a history of changes. It allows you to fetch older
versions of files, records which person makes each change, and prevents simultaneous
changes from overwriting each other.

#endif
</p>
<p>
#ifdef OLD
CVS expects the files it maintains to be stored in modules - directories of related
files and subdirectories. A module can be as small as a single directory containing a
single file, or as large as you have disk space for.

#else
CVS expects the files it maintains to be stored in projects - directories of related
files and subdirectories. A project can be as small as a single directory containing
a single file, or as large as you have disk space for.

#endif
</p>
    .
    .
    .
```

edit

cvs [*cvs-options*] edit [-lR] [-a *action*...] [*files*...]

Marks a file as being edited by the current user.

See also *editors*, *unedit*, *watch*, and *watchers*.

Command options

-a action

> Notify the user when the specified *action* occurs to the file. This setting acts as a temporary watch (see *watch*) on the file and is removed when the file is no longer being edited. Each *-a* designates one of the possible actions. The *-a* option can be repeated to designate multiple actions.

> The *action* may be any of the following:

> *edit*

>> Notify the user if someone else has run *cvs edit* on the file.

> *unedit*

>> Notify the user when the file is no longer being edited by someone else. This notification is triggered by the user running *cvs unedit* or *cvs release* or by the file being deleted and recreated with *cvs update* or *cvs checkout*.

> *commit*

>> Notify the user when someone else commits changes to the file.

> *all*

>> Notify the user of all of the previous actions.

> *none*

>> Notify the user of none of the previous actions.

-c Causes *cvs edit* to fail if someone else is listed as editing the file. If the development team is using the *watch* system, *commit* and *edit* should both have the *-c* option in every user's *.cvsrc*.

> Available only if both client and server are running 1.12.10 or later.

-f Overrides the *-c* option, allowing *cvs edit* to work even if someone else is editing the file. Useful if *edit -c* is listed in the *.cvsrc* and the user is sure she's right to override the watch system.

> Only available if both client and server are running 1.12.10 or later.

-l Run *edit* on files in the local directory only. (Do not recurse down subdirectories.)

> See also *-R*.

-R Run *edit* on files in the local directory and all subdirectories and recurse down the subdirectories. This option is the default.

> See also *-l*.

Description

The *cvs edit* command is used as part of the *cvs watch* family of commands. If a file is being watched, it is checked out to the sandbox with read permissions but not write permissions. The *edit* command sets the sandbox file as writable, notifies any watchers that the file is being edited, and sets the user as a temporary watcher to be notified if certain actions are performed on the file by other users.

 CVS does not notify you of your own changes.

You can unedit (set read-only and clear the temporary watch) a file with *cvs unedit* or *cvs release*, or by removing the file and recreating it with *cvs update* or *cvs checkout*.

CVS uses any script in the *notify* file in the repository's *CVSROOT* directory to notify the user of changes.

See Chapter 5 for an explanation of the *watch* system.

Example

```
jenn@soldier:~/wizzard$$ cvs edit Makefile
jenn@soldier:~/wizzard$$
```

editors   Synonyms: none

cvs [*cvs-options*] editors [-lR] [*files...*]

Displays the list of people who have a current *edit* command for the file or files listed as parameters. If no files are listed, this command lists the editors for the files in the current directory and subdirectories.

See Chapter 5 for an explanation of the *watch* system.

See also *edit*, *unedit*, *watch*, and *watchers*.

Command options

-l   Run *editors* on files in the local directory only. (Do not recurse down subdirectories.)
     See also -R.

-R   Run *editors* on files in the local directory and all subdirectories and recurse down the subdirectories. This option is the default.
     See also -l.

Example

```
jenn@soldier:~/wizzard$$ cvs editors Makefile
Makefile jenn Sat Mar  4 04:42:35 2006 -0000 GMT helit /home/jenn/cvs/wizzard
```

export   Synonyms: *exp, ex*

cvs [*cvs-options*] export [-flnNR] [-r *revision*] [-d *directory-name*] [-D *date*] [-k *mode*] [-r *revision*] *project*

Create a directory containing all directories and files belonging to a specified release of a project, with no CVS administrative files. You must specify a revision or date.

See also *checkout* and *update*.

Command options

-d directory-name

> Export the project into a directory called *directory-name* instead of using the repository directory name or the name designated in the *modules* file in the repository's *CVSROOT* directory.

> CVS usually creates the same directory structure that the repository uses. However, if the export contains only one file and *-d* is used, CVS does not create any intervening directories, thus shortening the directory path to the single file or directory. Use *-N* to prevent CVS from shortening the path.

> For example, if the repository contains a project *my*, with a file at *my/very/long/path/to/beachfront.txt*, and you use *checkout -d beach my/very/long/path/to/beachfront.txt*, CVS will produce a sandbox *beach* containing only *beachfront.txt*.

> If you use *checkout -N -d beach my/very/long/path/to/beachfront.txt*, CVS will produce a sandbox *beach* containing the entire directory chain *very/long/path/to*, with *beachfront.txt* in the directory *to*.

-D date

> Export the latest revision of each file in a project that is older than the date or time specified by *date*. This option implies the *-P* option.

-f   Use the latest (*HEAD*) revision on the current branch or trunk of a project if no revision matches the date or revision number. This option applies only if *-r* or *-D* is used.

-k mode

> Export a release with the designated keyword-expansion mode. This option overrides the default mode for each file. Prior to CVS 1.12.2, the *-k* option overrides the default mode for each file. After that version of CVS, *-kb* will not be overridden.

> The keyword-expansion modes are listed in the "Keywords and Keyword Modes" section of Chapter 11.

-l   Run *export* on the files in the local directory only. (Do not recurse into subdirectories.) See also *-R*.

-n   Do not run any program listed in the relevant line of the *modules* file in the repository's *CVSROOT* directory.

-N   Do not shorten the path. CVS usually creates the same directory structure that the repository uses. However, if the export contains only one file and *-d* is used, CVS does not create any intervening directories unless *-N* is also specified.

-r revision[:date]

> Run *export* on the specified *revision* or tag of each file in a project. If this revision or tag refers to a branch, run the command on the latest (*HEAD*) revision of the branch. This option implies the *-P* option.

> The *date* can be used only if the revision designates a branch, and specifies the latest revision on that date (the *:date* option is available as of 1.12.12).

-R   Run *export* on the directory and all subdirectories and recurse down the subdirectories. This option is the default. See also *-l*.

Description

The *cvs export* command creates the directories and files that belong to a project as of a specific tagged release, revision number, or date. It acts like a *checkout* or *update* for that specific point, but it does not produce the CVS administrative files. *export* requires the *-r* or *-D* command options.

When exporting, the repository path must be specified by using the *-d repository_path* CVS option or the *CVSROOT* environment variable.

 You can imply the repository path by being in a sandbox, but exporting into a sandbox is not recommended.

The argument to *export* can be a directory name or path within the repository, a filename or path within the repository, or a module name as specified in the *modules* file in the repository's *CVSROOT* directory.

Example

```
jenn@soldier:/tmp$ cvs -d :ext:blackrock:/var/lib/cvs export -D now wizzard
cvs export: Updating wizzard
U wizzard/Changelog
U wizzard/INSTALL
U wizzard/Makefile
U wizzard/README
U wizzard/TODO
cvs export: Updating wizzard/doc
cvs export: Updating wizzard/doc/design
U wizzard/doc/design/AcceptanceTest.doc
U wizzard/doc/design/Analysis.rtf
U wizzard/doc/design/Design.rtf
U wizzard/doc/design/Requirements.doc
U wizzard/doc/design/Specification.rtf
cvs export: Updating wizzard/doc/plan
U wizzard/doc/plan/Schedule.rtf
```

history   Synonyms: *hi, his*

cvs [*cvs-options*] history [-aceloTw] [-b *string*] [-D *date*] [-f *file*] [-m *module*] [-n *module*] [-p *directory*] [-r *revision*] [-t *tag*] [-u *username*] [-x *flag...*] [-z *timezone*] [*files...*]

Displays the information stored in the *history* file in the repository's *CVSROOT* directory. The values of the *CVSROOT/config* file options *LogHistory*, *HistoryLogPath*, and *HistorySearchPath* affect what is stored in the history file, and where the file is.

To record changes, the file must be writable by all users who will run the commands that are to be logged. The users who run the history command must be permitted to read the history file.

The *-f*, *-l*, *-n*, and *-p* options for *cvs history* act differently than their normal uses in CVS.

Command options

-a Show history data for all users. By default, CVS shows only the data for the calling user.

-b string
Show data that is more recent than the newest record that contains the given *string* in the module name, filename, or repository path.

-c Report only commits—times when the repository was modified (equivalent to *-xAMR*).

-D date
Report data that is more recent than the given date or time. (See "Dates" in Chapter 11 for legal dates.)

-e Report on every record type. This option is equivalent to *-x* with every type specified.

-f file
Show data for the specified *file*. This option can be repeated to show data for multiple files.

-l Show only the most recent commit to the repository.

-m module or *-n module*
Show data for a particular *module*. Using *-m*, CVS checks the *modules* file in the repository's *CVSROOT* directory and then searches the *history* file for files and directories that belong to the *module*. Using *-n*, CVS searches only the *history* file for the specified *module* name.

-o Report on records of checkouts (equivalent to *-xO*). The default case is to report only on checkouts.

-p directory
Show records for a particular project *directory*. This option can be repeated to show records for several projects.

-r revision
Show data as of, or more recent than, the *revision* or tag. CVS searches the repository's project files to determine the timestamp of the *revision*.

-t tagname
Show data as of, or more recent than, the latest time a tag record with this *tagname* was stored in the *history* file by any user.

-T Report on records of tags (equivalent to *-xT*).

-u username
Report on records for the specified *username*. This option can be repeated to search for multiple users.

-w Report on records of actions that match the current working directory.

-x [ACEFGMORTUW]

Extract records that match the given flag or flags. Any number of flags can be used with the *-x* option. *cvs history* extracts all records in the *history* file that match this option and all other options. The flags may be any of the following:

A   Report on records of files added to the repository.

C   Report on records of files that would have been updated in a sandbox, but where the files needed to be merged and there were conflicts in the merge.

E   Report on records of files exported from the repository.

F   Report on records of files that were released.

G   Report on records of files updated in a sandbox with a successful merge.

M   Report on records of files that were modified (a sandbox revision added to the repository).

O   Report on records of files that were checked out.

P   Report on records of files that were patched in the sandbox.

R   Report on records of files that were removed from the repository.

T   Report on records of files that were rtagged.

U   Report on records of files updated in a sandbox file with no merge required.

W   Report on records of files deleted from a sandbox during an update because they were no longer active in the repository.

-z timezone

Produce output and convert times to the specified *timezone*. The best way to give a time zone is as an offset of UTC. Time is discussed in Chapter 11.

Example 1

```
bash-2.05a$ cvs history
O 2006-10-03 08:33 +0000 jenn wizzard/src =wizmain=    <remote>/*
O 2006-10-03 09:12 +0000 jenn wizzard     =wizmake=    <remote>/*
O 2006-10-03 09:12 +0000 jenn wizzard/src =wiztest=    <remote>/*
O 2006-10-25 08:58 +0000 jenn wizzard     =wizzard=    <remote>/*
```

Example 2

```
jenn@soldier:~/wizzard$ cvs history -e
O 2006-03-03 16:07 +0000 jenn wizzard     =wizzard=    <remote>/*
A 2006-03-03 16:17 +0000 jenn 1.1         acconfig.h   wizzard/lib == <remote>
A 2006-03-03 16:17 +0000 jenn 1.1         getdate.h    wizzard/lib == <remote>
A 2006-03-03 16:17 +0000 jenn 1.1         gettext.h    wizzard/lib == <remote>
A 2006-03-03 16:17 +0000 jenn 1.1         utils.h      wizzard/lib == <remote>
O 2006-03-03 16:27 +0000 jenn zebedee     =zebedee=    <remote>/*
O 2006-03-03 16:42 +0000 jenn [beta_0-1_branch] wizzard =beta_0-1_branch= <remote>/*
M 2006-03-03 17:02 +0000 jenn 1.1.6.1     README       wizzard     == <remote>
```

import

cvs [*cvs-options*] import [-b *branch*] [-d] [-I *ignore*] [-k *mode*] [-m *message*] [-W *wrapper*] *project-name vendor-tag release-tag*

Creates a new project in the repository or manages *vendor branches*.

Command options

-b *branch*

> Import to the specified vendor *branch*. If you have more than one external supplier for a project, you may need to use two or more distinct vendor branches to manage the project. If you are using multiple vendor branches, use the *-b* option to specify which branch you are importing to. *branch* must be the branch number, not a tag, and CVS does not check that the branch number given with the option and the symbolic tag provided as the *vendor-tag* argument to the command correspond to the same branch.
>
> I strongly recommend that you read "Vendor Branches" in Chapter 7 before using this option.

-d   When setting the timestamp on each imported file, use each file's last modification time rather than the current time.

-I *ignore*

> Ignore the named file when updating. *-I* can be used more than once. Use *-I !* to clear the list of ignored files. See "cvsignore" in Chapter 6.

-k *mode*

> Import the file or files with the designated keyword-expansion mode. This option also sets the default keyword mode for the file. If you forget to set the default keyword mode with *cvs import*, you can do it later with *cvs admin*.
>
> The keyword-expansion modes are listed in "Keywords and Keyword Modes" in Chapter 11.

-m *message*

> Use the *message* when committing a file. CVS does not call the editor the next time *cvs commit* runs.

-W *wrapper*

> Modify the import based on elements of each filename. Wrappers are explained in Chapter 3.

-X   Import any new files only to the vendor branch. (Default is to import them to the vendor branch and also add them to the trunk.) (CVS 1.12.10 and later.)

Description

To create a new project, lay out the project structure and any initial files. You can do this in a temporary directory, as CVS does not need the initial structure or files once the project has been imported. Change directories into the root directory of the new project, then run *cvs import*. You need to specify the repository path and provide a project name and two tags: a vendor tag and a release tag.

Test that you can *cvs checkout* the new project before removing the original files.

From 1.11.14, *import* will ignore files or directories named *CVS*.

The project name will become the project's root directory name. The tags are less critical; if you do not intend to use a vendor branch, a meaningless pair of tags such as *a1 b2* is sufficient. The tag names must conform to all the normal requirements for tags: they must start with a letter and can contain only alphanumeric characters, underscores (_), and hyphens (-). The *HEAD* and *BASE* tag names are reserved.

A vendor branch is a special branch that CVS provides to track third-party code that contributes to a project. If you use vendor branches, CVS uses the vendor tag as a branch tag for the vendor branch, and it uses the release tag to mark the current revisions of the vendor branch files.

Create a vendor branch by using *cvs import* to create the project. When you want to update to a new release from the vendor, run *cvs import* on the same project with the same vendor tag and a new release tag. See Chapter 7 for a full explanation of vendor branches.

In Example 2 below, the wrapper ensures that the **.doc* files are imported as binary files. Everything else is imported normally.

Example 1

```
bash-2.05a$ cvs -d cvs:/var/lib/cvs import wizzard wizproject ver_0-1
N wizzard/Changelong
N wizzard/INSTALL
N wizzard/Makefile
 .
 .
 .
"/tmp/cvsfaQoRz" 5L, 287C written
No conflicts created by this import
```

Example 2

```
jenn@soldier:/tmp/wizzard$ cvs -d :ext:blackrock:/var/lib/cvs import \
> -W"*.doc -k 'b'" wiztwo wizproject ver_2-0
N wiztwo/Changelog
N wiztwo/INSTALL
N wiztwo/Makefile
N wiztwo/README
N wiztwo/TODO
cvs import: Importing /var/lib/cvs/wiztwo/doc
cvs import: Importing /var/lib/cvs/wiztwo/doc/design
N wiztwo/doc/design/AcceptanceTest.doc
N wiztwo/doc/design/Analysis.rtf
N wiztwo/doc/design/Design.rtf
N wiztwo/doc/design/Requirements.doc
N wiztwo/doc/design/Specification.rtf
cvs import: Importing /var/lib/cvs/wiztwo/doc/plan
N wiztwo/doc/plan/Schedule.rtf
cvs import: Importing /var/lib/cvs/wiztwo/lib
```

```
N wiztwo/lib/acconfig.h
N wiztwo/lib/getdate.h
N wiztwo/lib/gettext.h
N wiztwo/lib/utils.h
cvs import: Importing /var/lib/cvs/wiztwo/src
N wiztwo/src/config.h
N wiztwo/src/handheld.c
N wiztwo/src/server.c
N wiztwo/src/server.cc
N wiztwo/src/server2.cc
N wiztwo/src/wizzard.c

No conflicts created by this import
```

init

cvs [*cvs-options*] init

Converts an existing directory into a CVS repository and creates and populates the *CVSROOT* directory that contains the administrative files for a CVS repository.

CVS creates the final directory in the path if it does not already exist. Previous directories in the path must exist. See Chapter 6 for more details.

Example

```
$ cvs -d /var/lib/cvsroot init
$
```

kserver

Synonyms: none

cvs [*cvs-options*] kserver

Runs the repository-server end of a Kerberos 4 connection. The *cvs kserver* command must be called from *inetd* or an equivalent server daemon. See Chapter 8 for more details.

See also *pserver*.

Example

```
#inetd.conf
#:OTHER: Other services
1999 stream tcp nowait root /usr/bin/cvs cvs -f --allow-root=/var/lib/cvsroot kserver
```

log

Synonym: *lo*

cvs [*cvs-options*] log [-bhlNRSt] [-d *dates*] [-r[*revisions*]] [-s *states*] [-w[*usernames*]] [*files...*]

Displays information about the files specified as parameters, or, if none are given, about the files in the current sandbox. The information this command provides is part of the metadata stored in the files in the repository, and the log messages created when files are imported or added, or changes are committed.

Dates and times are displayed in local time for the client, if the server is 1.12.9 or later and the client is 1.12.10 or later. Prior to that, they were given in UTC.

It's worth experimenting with option combinations, to learn which are useful and which aren't. For example, at first it seems that the options which specify revisions are useless in combination with options that prevent revision information from showing. However, if you add *-S* as well, you can get the header information from only the files which match the specified revisions.

With no options, *cvs log* displays all the information it has available. See also *rlog*.

Command options

-b   Display information only about the revisions on the default branch, normally the most recent branch on the trunk.

-d dates
Display information only on revisions checked in on or between the dates or times provided. Date and time formats are listed in Chapter 11. More than one date range can be given; ranges must be separated by semicolons. Date ranges can be specified according to the following list:

date1>date2 or *date2<date1*
Select all revisions between the two dates.

date1>=date2 or *date2<=date1*
Select all revisions on or between the two dates.

date> or *<date*
Select all revisions earlier than *date*.

date>= or *<=date*
Select all revisions on or earlier than *date*.

date< or *>date*
Select all revisions later than *date*.

date<= or *>=date*
Select all revisions on or later than *date*.

date
Select all revisions on *date*.

-h   Print only the header information for a file, not the description, the log messages, or revision information.

-l   Run *log* on the local directory only. (Do not recurse down subdirectories.)

-N   Do not list the tags (the symbolic names).

-r[revisions]
Provide information only on *revisions* in the ranges provided. More than one range can be given; ranges must be separated by commas. There must be no space between the *-r* and its argument. If no range is provided, the latest revision on the default branch, normally the trunk, is used.

Ranges can be specified according to the following list:

revision1:revision2 or *revision1::revision2*
> Select all revisions between *revision1* and *revision2*. The revisions must be on the same branch. With the double colon, CVS excludes *revision1*.

:revision or *::revision*
> Select revisions from the start of the branch or trunk the *revision* is on, up to and including the *revision*.

revision: or *revision::*
> Select revisions from *revision* to the end of the branch or trunk the *revision* is on. With the double colon, CVS excludes the *revision*.

branch
> Select all revisions on *branch*.

branch1:branch2 or *branch1::branch2*
> Select all revisions on both branches and any branches that split off from the two branches.

branch.
> Select the latest revision on *branch*.

-R   Display the name of the repository copy of a file only.

 Note that the usual CVS behavior with *-R* is to recurse down directories. *-R* works differently with *log* and *rlog*.

-s *states*
> Display only revisions with states that match one of the *states* in the comma-separated list.

-S   Do not display header information if there are no revisions to display.

-t   Print only the header information and description, not the log messages or revision information.

-w*[usernames]*
> Display only revisions committed by the specified list of users. Provide the list of users as a comma-separated list. If no usernames are listed, the revisions committed by the current user are displayed. There can be no space between *-w* and its argument.

Example

```
jenn@soldier:~/wizzard$ cvs log Changelog

RCS file: /var/lib/cvs/wizzard/Changelog,v
Working file: Changelog
head: 1.2
branch:
locks: strict
access list:
symbolic names:
        ver_2-0: 1.1.1.1
```

```
                wizzard: 1.1.1
                alpha_1-6: 1.1
                alpha_1-5: 1.1
                beta_0-1_branch: 1.1.0.2
                beta_0-1_branch_root: 1.1
                pre_beta_0-1: 1.1
        keyword substitution: kv
        total revisions: 3;      selected revisions: 3
        description:
        ----------------------------
        revision 1.2
        date: 2006-03-04 00:38:53 +1100;  author: jenn;  state: Exp;  lines: +0 -0;
        Testing keyword substitution modes.
        ----------------------------
        revision 1.1
        date: 2006-08-31 23:37:56 +1000;  author: jenn;  state: Exp;
        branches:  1.1.1;
        Creating a structure.
        ----------------------------
        revision 1.1.1.1
        date: 2006-01-06 23:39:45 +1100;  author: jenn;  state: Exp;  lines: +0 -0;
        Providing an example of vendor branches.
        =============================================================================
```

login

Synonyms: none

cvs [*cvs-options*] login

Logs in to a CVS *pserver* session. This command is needed only with the *pserver* connection mode. See Chapter 8 for more information.

See also *logout*.

Example

```
jenn@soldier:~/wizzard$ cvs -d \
> :pserver:jenn:password:@cvs.nosuch.net:/var/lib/cvs login
Logging in to :pserver:jenn@cvs:2401/var/lib/cvs
```

logout

Synonyms: none

cvs [*cvs-options*] logout

Logs out of a CVS *pserver* session. This command is needed only with the *pserver* connection mode. See Chapter 8 for more information.

See also *login*.

Example

```
jenn@soldier:~/wizzard$ cvs -d :pserver:jenn@cvs:/var/lib/cvs logout
Logging out of :pserver:jenn@cvs:2401/var/lib/cvs
```

ls

cvs [*cvs-options*] ls [-e | -l] [-RP] [-r *revisions*] [-D *dates*] [*files...*]

List the files and directories in the repository directory that corresponds to the current working directory (which must be in a sandbox). This is almost identical to what would be in the current sandbox directory after an update, but doesn't include files or directories which are local.

If you specify a filename or directory as a parameter to *cvs ls*, it will list the specified file or directory as it exists in the repository. These parameters should be given relative to the current working directory.

See also *rls*.

Command options

-d   List "dead" revisions, i.e., revisions which have been *cvs remove*d.

-D *date*
> List files as they were at the date or time specified by *date*.

-e   Display the output in the format used in the *CVS/Entries* file. (See Chapter 6 for information on this file.)

-l   List files in long form.

-P   Do not include empty directories in the output.

-r *revision[:date]*
> List files which belong to the specified *revision* or tag. If this option refers to a branch, run the command on the latest (*HEAD*) revision of the branch.
>
> The *date* can be used only if the revision designates a branch, and specifies the latest revision on that date (the *:date* option is available as of 1.12.12).

-R   List the local (or specified) directory and all subdirectories and recurse down the subdirectories. The default is to list only the local or specified directory.

Example 1

```
jenn@soldier: ~/wizzard$ cvs ls -l
---- 2006-03-04 00:38:53 +1100 1.2      Changelog
---- 2006-03-04 00:38:53 +1100 1.2      INSTALL
---- 2006-08-08 08:36:19 +1000 1.17     Makefile
---- 2006-03-04 04:05:15 +1100 1.6      README
---- 2006-03-04 00:38:53 +1100 1.2      TODO
d--- 2006-03-04 04:37:36 +1100          doc
d--- 2006-03-04 04:37:36 +1100          empty
d--- 2006-03-04 04:37:36 +1100          lib
d--- 2006-03-04 04:37:36 +1100          man
d--- 2006-03-04 04:37:36 +1100          src
```

Example 2

```
jenn@soldier:~/wizzard$ cvs ls -e
jenn@blackrock's password:
/Changelog/1.2/Mon Mar  3 13:38:53 2006//
/INSTALL/1.2/Mon Mar  3 13:38:53 2006//
```

```
/Makefile/1.17/Thu Aug  7 22:36:19 2006//
/README/1.6/Fri Mar  3 17:05:15 2006//
/TODO/1.2/Mon Mar  3 13:38:53 2006//
D/doc////
D/empty////
D/lib////
D/man////
D/src////
```

pserver

Synonyms: none

cvs [*cvs-options*] pserver [-c *path*]

Runs the repository-server end of a password server or Kerberos 5 (via the GSS-API) connection. This command must be called from *inetd* or an equivalent server daemon. See Chapter 8.

See also *kserver*.

-c path
> The path to the *config* file. By default, this is in the *CVSROOT* directory. (CVS 1.12.13 and later.)

Example

```
#inetd.conf
#:OTHER: Other services
2401 stream tcp nowait root /usr/bin/cvs cvs -f --allow-root=/var/lib/cvsroot pserver
```

rannotate

Synonyms: *ra, rann*

cvs [*cvs-options*] rannotate [-fFlR] [-D *date*] [-r *revision*] *files*...

Displays files with annotations about the last change of each line. The annotations give the editor and revision number of the latest revision. You can run *rannotate* without a sandbox, but you must have a repository specified if you do so. *rannotate* requires at least one filename, directory name, or module name from within the repository as an argument.

See also *annotate*.

Command options

-D date
> Run *rannotate* on the latest revision of a file that is as old as or older than the date or time specified by *date*.

-f
> Use the latest (*HEAD*) revision on the current branch or trunk if no revision matches the date or revision number. This applies only if *-r* or *-D* is used.

-F
> Show annotations for binary files. (Note that binary files may have extremely long lines.)

-l
> Run *rannotate* on files in the local directory only. (Do not recurse into subdirectories.)

-r revision[:date]

> Run *rannotate* on the specified revision or tag of a file. If the revision or tag refers to a branch, run the command on the latest (*HEAD*) revision of the branch.
>
> The *date* can be used only if the revision designates a branch, and specifies the latest revision on that date (the *:date* option is available as of 1.12.12).

-R   Run *rannotate* on files in the local directory and all subdirectories and recurse down the subdirectories. This option is the default.

Example

```
jenn@soldier:~$ cvs -d :ext:blackrock:/var/lib/cvs rannotate wizzard/Makefile

Annotations for wizzard/Makefile
***************
1.2        (jenn    01-Apr-06): #
1.2        (jenn    01-Apr-06): # Makefile for the Wizzard project
1.2        (jenn    01-Apr-06): # First created by J Vesperman, 1 April 2006
1.2        (jenn    01-Apr-06): #
1.17       (jenn    07-Apr-06): # Current revision $Revision$
1.3        (jenn    12-Apr-06): # On branch $Name$ (not expanded if this is the
trunk)
1.17       (jenn    12-Apr-06): # Latest change by $Author$ on $Date: 2006/Apr/12
22:25:48 $
1.2        (jenn    01-Apr-06): #
1.4        (jenn    12-Apr-06): ##
```

rdiff

Synonyms: *pa, patch*

cvs [*cvs-options*] rdiff [-flR] [-c|-u] [-s|-t] {-r *revision*|-D *date*} [-r *revision2* | -D *date2*] [-V *version*] *projects*...

Creates output that can be redirected into a file and used with the GNU (or equivalent) *patch* program. The output goes to the standard output (*stdout*). *rdiff* operates directly from the repository and does not need to be used from a sandbox. It does require a file-name, directory name, or module name as an argument, and you must specify one or two revisions or dates. If you specify one revision or date, *rdiff* calculates the differences between that date and the current (*HEAD*) revision. If two dates are specified, *rdiff* calculates the differences between the two.

See also *diff*.

 Most people use *rdiff* to make a file to use with *patch*. If you're using a *patch* file that was created over more than one directory, you may need to use the *-p* option to *patch*, so it can find all the appropriate directories.

Command options

-c   Use context output format, with three lines of context around each change. This is the default format.

-D date

> Display the differences between the current sandbox copy of a file and the latest revision as of the date or time specified by *date*. One or both *-D* options can be replaced with *-r*.

-f   Use the latest (*HEAD*) revision of a file on the current branch or trunk if no revision matches the date or revision number. This option applies only if *-r* or *-D* is used.

-k mode

> Run *diff* with the designated keyword-expansion *mode*. This option overrides the default mode and any sticky modes for each file. It's useful to use *-kk* with *diff*, to avoid spurious differences being reported (such as expansion of the *$Revision$* keyword).
>
> The keyword-expansion modes are listed in "Keywords and Keyword Modes" of Chapter 11.

-l   Run *rdiff* on files in the local directory only. (Do not recurse down subdirectories.)

> See also *-R*.

-r revision[:date]

> Display the differences between the current sandbox copy and the specified *revision*. The *date* can be used only if the revision designates a branch and specifies the latest revision on that date (the *:date* option is available as of 1.12.12).
>
> If two *-r* options are used, display the differences between the first and second specified revisions. One or both *-r* options can be replaced with *-D*.

-R   Run *rdiff* on files in the local directory and all subdirectories and recurse down the subdirectories. This option is the default.

> See also *-l*.

-s   Create a summary change report rather than a patch, showing which files have changed with one line per file.

-t   Produce a report on the two most recent revisions in a file. Do not use *-r* or *-D* with the *-t* option.

-u   Use *unidiff* format instead of *context* format.

-V version

> This option is now obsolete, but it used to allow you to expand keywords according to the rules of the specified RCS *version*.

Example

```
jenn@soldier:~/wizzard$ cvs rdiff -r 1.5 wizzard/Makefile
*** wizzard/Makefile:1.5      Thu Oct 17 08:50:14 2006
--- wizzard/Makefile    Fri Aug  8 08:36:19 2006
```

```
**************
*** 2,17 ****
  # Makefile for the Wizzard project
  # First created by J Vesperman, 1 September 2006
  #
! # Current revision $Revision$
  # On branch $Name$ (not expanded if this is the trunk)
! # Latest change by $Author$ on $Date$
  #
  ##

  # Initial declarations
  #
  CC=gcc
! SUBDIRS = man doc src lib ping


  # Declaring phony targets
--- 2,18 ----
  # Makefile for the Wizzard project
  # First created by J Vesperman, 1 September 2006
  #
! # Current revision $Revision$
  # On branch $Name$ (not expanded if this is the trunk)
! # Latest change by $Author$ on $Date$
  #
  ##

  # Initial declarations
  #
  CC=gcc
! SUBDIRS = man doc src lib
! oooofooofooofoo


  # Declaring phony targets
**************
*** 23,28 ****
--- 24,30 ----

  clean:
                  rm -f src/*.o
+                 rm -f lib/*.o
                  rm -f wizzard
                  echo "clean: make complete"

  .
  .
  .
```

release

cvs [*cvs-options*] release [-d] *directories*...

Makes a sandbox inactive. This command checks for uncommitted changes, removing any existing edit flags, and writes to the *CVSROOT/history* file that the sandbox has been released. You can use *release* on an entire sandbox or on one or more subdirectories.

Command option

-d   Delete the sandbox after it has been released.

 This command is recursive, and it deletes files and directories even if they have not been saved to the CVS repository. Use it carefully.

Example

```
jenn@soldier:/tmp$ cvs -d :ext:blackrock:/var/lib/cvs release -d wiztwo
You have [0] altered files in this repository.
Are you sure you want to release (and delete) directory `wiztwo': y
```

remove

cvs [*cvs-options*] remove [-flR] [*files*...]

The *remove* command removes a file or directory from the repository record for the current revision of the current branch or trunk. Committed data for the file remains in the repository, and old revisions can be retrieved with update or checkout as normal.

Remove can also be used to undo an uncommitted file addition.

Unless you use the *-f* option, you must have already removed the file from the sandbox.

 Any uncommitted changes are lost forever.

Command options

-f   Delete the files from the sandbox as well as removing them from the repository.
-l   Remove files in the local directory only. (Do not recurse down subdirectories.)
      See also -R.
-R   Remove files in the local directory and all subdirectories and recurse down the subdirectories. This option is the default.
      See also -l.

In Example 1, I remove a file which has been committed. In Example 2, I am undoing an unwanted addition that has not yet been committed.

Example 1

```
jenn@soldier:~/wizzard/src$ cvs remove -f handheld.c
cvs remove: scheduling `handheld.c' for removal
cvs remove: use `cvs commit' to remove this file permanently
```

Example 2

```
jenn@soldier:~/wizzard/src$ cvs remove -f handheld.h
cvs remove: removed `handheld.h'
```

rlog
Synonym: rl

cvs [*cvs-options*] rlog [-bhlNRSt] [-d *dates*] [-r[*revisions*]] [-s *states*] [-w[*usernames*]] *files*...

The *rlog* command is a remote version of the *log* command. *rlog* works without a sandbox and requires a file, directory, or module name from the repository.

See also *log*.

Command options

-b   Provide information only about the revisions or a file on the default branch, normally the highest branch on the trunk.

-d *dates*
      Provide information only on revisions of a file that were checked in on or between the dates or times provided. Date formats are listed in Chapter 11. More than one date range can be given; ranges must be separated by semicolons. Date ranges can be specified according to the following list:

date1>date2 or *date2<date1*
      Select all revisions between the two dates.

date1>=date2 or *date2<=date1*
      Select all revisions on or between the two dates.

date> or *<date*
      Select all revisions earlier than *date*.

date>= or *<=date>*
      Select all revisions on or earlier than *date*.

date< or *>date*
      Select all revisions later than *date*.

date<= or *>=date*
      Select all revisions on or later than *date*.

date
      Select all revisions on *date*.

-h   Print only the header information, not the description, log messages, or revision information.

-l   Run *rlog* on the local directory only. (Do not recurse into subdirectories.)

-N   Do not list the tags (the symbolic names).

-r[revisions]
Provide only information on *revisions* in the ranges provided. More than one revision range can be given; ranges must be separated by commas. There must be no space between the *-r* and its argument. If no range is provided, the latest revision on the default branch, normally the trunk, is used.

Ranges can be specified according to the following list:

revision1:revision2 or *revision1::revision2*
Select all revisions between *revision1* and *revision2*. The revisions must be on the same branch. With the double colon, *revision1* is excluded.

:revision or ::revision
Select revisions from the start of the branch or trunk the *revision* is on, up to and including the *revision*.

revision: or *revision::*
Select revisions from *revision* to the end of the branch or trunk it is on. With the double colon, the *revision* is excluded.

branch
Select all revisions on the *branch*.

branch1:branch2 or *branch1::branch2*
Select all revisions on both branches and any branches that split off between those two branches.

branch.
Select the latest revision on the *branch*.

-R   Display the name of the repository copy of the file only.

 Note that the usual CVS behavior with *-R* is to recurse down directories. *-R* works differently with *log* and *rlog*.

-s states
Display only revisions with states that match one of the *states* in the comma-separated list.

-S   Do not display header information of a file if there are no revisions to display.

-t   Print only the header information of a file and its description, not the log messages or revision information.

-w[usernames]
Display only revisions committed by the *usernames* in the comma-separated list. If there are no usernames listed, the revisions committed by the current user are displayed. There can be no space between *-w* and its argument.

Example

```
jenn@soldier:~$ cvs -d :ext:blackrock:/var/lib/cvs rlog wizzard/src
jenn@blackrock's password: ********
```

```
cvs rlog: Logging wizzard/src

RCS file: /var/lib/cvs/wizzard/src/config.h,v
head: 1.4
branch:
locks: strict
access list:
symbolic names:
        ver_2-0: 1.1.1.1
        wizzard: 1.1.1
        alpha_1-6: 1.3
        alpha_1-5: 1.3
        beta_0-1_branch: 1.1.0.2
        beta_0-1_branch_root: 1.1
        pre_beta_0-1: 1.1
keyword substitution: kv
total revisions: 7;     selected revisions: 7
description:
----------------------------
revision 1.4
date: 2006-03-04 00:41:46 +1100;  author: jenn;  state: Exp;  lines: +0 -0;
Yet more testing
----------------------------
revision 1.3
date: 2006-09-27 03:11:17 +1000;  author: jenn;  state: Exp;  lines: +5 -6;
Trying to find the cvs process
----------------------------
revision 1.2
date: 2006-09-13 17:26:27 +1000;  author: jenn;  state: Exp;  lines: +3 -0;
Minor tweaks to the config file.
----------------------------
revision 1.1
date: 2006-09-12 18:56:41 +1000;  author: jenn;  state: Exp;
branches:  1.1.1;  1.1.2;
Moving src/wizzard.h to src/config.h
```

---

rls   Synonyms: *rdir, rlist*

cvs [*cvs-options*] ls [-e | -l] [-RP] [-r *revisions*] [-D *dates*] [*files...*]

List the files and directories in the repository directory specified, or list the specified files. Files and directories must be given relative to the repository root directory. If no directory is specified, the repository root directory is listed.

See also *ls*.

-*d*   List "dead" revisions, i.e., revisions which have been *cvs remove*d.

-*D date*
        List files as they were at the date or time specified by *date*.

-*e*   Display the output in the format used in the *CVS/Entries* file. (See Chapter 6 for information on this file.)

-*l*   List files in "long" form.

-P   Do not include empty directories in the output.

-r revision[:date]
   List files which belong to the specified *revision* or tag. If this option refers to a branch, run the command on the latest (*HEAD*) revision of the branch.

   The *date* can be used only if the revision designates a branch, and specifies the latest revision on that date (the *:date* option is available as of 1.12.12).

-R   List the local (or specified) directory and all subdirectories and recurse down the subdirectories. The default is to list only the local or specified directory.

Example

```
jenn@soldier:~$ cvs -d :ext:blackrock:/var/lib/cvs rls
cvs rls: Listing module: `.'
CVSROOT
cvstraining
wiztwo
wizzard
wizzard-libs
zebedee
```

---

rtag
Synonyms: *rt, rfreeze*

cvs [*cvs-options*] rtag [-abBdfFlnR] {-D *date*|-r *revision*} *tagname files...*

Marks a revision of a single file with a meaningful name or marks a set of revisions of multiple files so that they can all be retrieved easily as a group.

See also *tag*.

Command options

-a   Clear a tag from files that have been removed from active development. Normally, removed files are not searched when tags are removed. This option works with the *-d* and *-F* options.

-b   Create a branch off the designated *revision*, using the designated *tagname* as the branch name. Chapter 4 explains branches and their uses.

-B   Allow *-F* and *-d* to act on branch tags.

 Back up the repository before you use this option, and be extremely careful. I strongly recommend reading Chapter 4 before using this option.

-d tagname
   Delete the specified tag. This removes the human-readable *tagname*. The revision that the *tagname* referred to remains in the file.

Do not delete branch tags unless you are absolutely certain you know what you're doing and have backed up your data: it can permanently corrupt the affected files.

-D date

Tag the latest revision of each file that is as old as or older than the date or time specified by *date*.

-f   Use the latest (*HEAD*) revision on the current branch or trunk if no revision matches the *date* or *revision* number.

-F tagname

Move the tag from the revision it currently refers to, to the revision specified in the *rtag* command.

Do not use this command on branch tags unless you are absolutely certain you know what you're doing and have backed up your data. Moving branch tags can permanently corrupt the affected files.

-l   Run *rtag* on files in the local directory only. (Do not recurse into subdirectories.) See also -R.

-n   Do not run any program listed in the appropriate line of the *modules* file of the repository's *CVSROOT* directory.

-r revision[:date]

Run *rtag* on the specified revision or tag. If *revision* refers to a branch, run the command on the latest (*HEAD*) revision of the branch.

The *date* can be used only if the revision designates a branch, and specifies the latest revision on that date (the *:date* option is available as of 1.12.12).

-R   Run *rtag* on files in the local directory and all subdirectories and recurse down the subdirectories. This option is the default.

See also -l.

Description

Use *rtag* to mark a revision of a single file with a meaningful name or to mark a set of revisions of multiple files so that they can all be retrieved easily as a group. Tagnames must begin with a letter and may contain only alphanumeric characters, underscores (_), and hyphens (-). There are two tags reserved for CVS: the *BASE* and *HEAD* tags.

The *tag* and *rtag* commands are also used to create branches. Branches and tags are explained in Chapter 4.

The *rtag* command does not need to run from a sandbox, but it does need to have a revision or date specified. It also requires a filename, directory name, or module name given as a parameter.

Example 1 adds the tag *bing* to the current (time *now*) revision of every file in the project *wizzard*. Example 2 removes that same tag.

Example 1

```
jenn@soldier:~$ cvs -d :ext:blackrock:/var/lib/cvs rtag -D now bing wizzard
cvs rtag: Tagging wizzard
cvs rtag: Tagging wizzard/doc
cvs rtag: Tagging wizzard/doc/design
cvs rtag: Tagging wizzard/doc/plan
cvs rtag: Tagging wizzard/empty
cvs rtag: Tagging wizzard/empty/design
cvs rtag: Tagging wizzard/empty/plan
cvs rtag: Tagging wizzard/lib
cvs rtag: Tagging wizzard/man
cvs rtag: Tagging wizzard/srcb
```

Example 2

```
jenn@soldier:~$ cvs -d :ext:blackrock:/var/lib/cvs rtag -d bing wizzard
cvs rtag: Untagging wizzard
cvs rtag: Untagging wizzard/doc
cvs rtag: Untagging wizzard/doc/design
cvs rtag: Untagging wizzard/doc/plan
cvs rtag: Untagging wizzard/empty
cvs rtag: Untagging wizzard/empty/design
cvs rtag: Untagging wizzard/empty/plan
cvs rtag: Untagging wizzard/lib
cvs rtag: Untagging wizzard/man
cvs rtag: Untagging wizzard/src
```

---

server   Synonyms: none

cvs [*cvs-options*] server [-c *path*]

The *server* command is used internally by CVS; the server is invoked by the CVS client when the client connects to the repository computer via the *ext* or *server* access methods.

See also *kserver* and *pserver*.

-c *path*
> The path to the *config* file. By default, this is in the *CVSROOT* directory. (CVS 1.12.13 and later.)

---

status   Synonyms: *st, stat*

cvs [*cvs-options*] status [-vlR] [*files...*]

Displays information about files, such as the current working or base revision, the current revision in the repository, and whether the files are currently synchronized with the repository. With the -v option, *status* also shows the files' tags.

Command options

-*l*   Run *status* on files in the local directory only. (Do not recurse down subdirectories.)
   See also -*R*.

-*R*   Run *status* on files in the local directory and all subdirectories and recurse down the subdirectories. This option is the default.
   See also -*l*.

-*v*   Include information about tags.

Example

```
jenn@soldier:~/wizzard$ cvs status Makefile
==============================
File: Makefile              Status: Locally Modified

    Working revision:    1.6
    Repository revision: 1.6      /var/lib/cvs/wizzard/Makefile,v
    Sticky Tag:          (none)
    Sticky Date:         (none)
    Sticky Options:      (none)
```

---

tag   Synonyms: *ta, freeze*

cvs [*cvs-options*] tag [-bcdfFlR] [-D *date*|-r *revision*] *tagname* [*files*...]

Marks a revision of a single file with a meaningful name or marks a set of revisions of multiple files so that they can all be retrieved easily as a group.

See also *rtag*.

Command options

-*b*   Create a branch off the specified *revision*, using the specified *tagname* as the branch name. Chapter 4 explains branches and their uses.

-*c*   Check whether the sandbox copies of the specified *files* have been modified since they were last synchronized with the repository. If they have been modified, do not tag them, and display an error. If they are unmodified, tag them with the specified *tagname*. This option is useful when tagging the current sandbox revisions.

-*d tagname*
   Delete the specified *tagname* from a file. (This option removes the human-readable tagname; the revision that the tagname used to refer to remains in the file.)

   Do not delete branch tags unless you are absolutely certain you know what you're doing it can permanently corrupt the affected files.

-*D date*
   Tag the latest revision of each specified file that is as old as or older than the date or time specified by *date*.

-f   Use the latest (*HEAD*) revision on the current branch or trunk if no revision matches the date, time, tag, or revision number. This applies only if *-r* or *-D* are used.

-F tagname
   Move the *tagname* from the revision it currently refers to, to the revision specified in the *tag* command.

 Do not use this command on branch tags unless you are absolutely certain what you're doing, and have backed up your data. Moving branch tags can permanently corrupt the affected files.

-l   Run *tag* on files in the local directory only. (Do not recurse down subdirectories.)
   See also *-R*.

-r revision[:date]
   Run *tag* on the specified revision or tag. If *revision* refers to a branch, run the command on the latest (*HEAD*) revision of the branch.

   The *date* can be used only if the revision designates a branch, and specifies the latest revision on that date (the *:date* option is available as of 1.12.12).

-R   Run *tag* on files in the local directory and all subdirectories and recurse down the subdirectories. This option is the default.
   See also *-l*.

Description

Use the *tag* command to mark a revision of a single file with a meaningful name or to mark a set of revisions of multiple files so that they can all be retrieved easily as a group. Tagnames must begin with a letter and may contain only alphanumeric characters, underscores (_), and hyphens (-). There are two tags reserved for CVS: the *BASE* and *HEAD* tags.

The *tag* and *rtag* commands are also used to create branches. Branches and tags are explained in Chapter 4.

If no revision number or date is given to the *tag* command, this command tags based on the most recent revision in the repository that was synchronized with the current sandbox directory (i.e., the most recently updated, checked-out, or committed revision). This revision can be seen as the *working revision* in the *cvs status* command.

Example 1

```
jenn@soldier:~/wizzard$ cvs tag alpha_1-5
cvs server: Tagging .
T Changelog
T INSTALL
T Makefile
T README
T TODO
.
.
.
```

Example 2

```
jenn@soldier:~/wizzard$ cvs tag -D now -F current
jenn@blackrock's password:
cvs tag: Tagging .
T Changelog
T INSTALL
T Makefile
T README
T TODO
  .
  .
  .
```

unedit

cvs [*cvs-options*] unedit [-lR] [*files...*]

Notifies watchers that a file is no longer being edited, clears the temporary watch, sets the file as read-only, and restores the file to the repository revision that the sandbox copy was based on.

See also *edit*, *editors*, *watch*, and *watchers*.

Command options

-l   Run *unedit* on files in the local directory only. (Do not recurse down subdirectories.)
      See also -R.

-R   Run *unedit* on files in the local directory and all subdirectories and recurse down the subdirectories. This option is the default.
      See also -l.

Description

The *cvs unedit* command is used as part of the *cvs watch* family of commands. If a file is being watched, CVS writes it (when it is checked out) to the sandbox with read permissions but not write permissions. The *edit* command sets the sandbox file as writable, notifies any watchers that the file is being edited, and sets the user as a temporary watcher to be notified if certain actions are performed on the file by other users.

The *unedit* command notifies watchers that the file is no longer being edited, clears the temporary watch, sets the file as read-only, and restores the file to the repository revision that the sandbox copy was based on.

The script in the *notify* file in the repository's *CVSROOT* directory is used to notify the user of changes.

See Chapter 5 for an explanation of the *watch* system.

Example

```
jenn@soldier:~/wizzard$ cvs unedit Makefile
jenn@soldier:~/wizzard$
```

update

cvs [*cvs-options*] update [-ACdflpPR] [-D *date*] [-I *ignore*] [-j *revision* [:*date*]] [-j *revision2* [:*date2*]] [-k *mode*] [-r *revision*] [-W *wrapper*] [*files...*]

Downloads changes from the repository to an existing sandbox.

See also *checkout* and *export*.

Command options

-A Clear sticky tags, dates, and keyword-expansion modes and replace the current files in a sandbox with the head of the trunk.

-C Replace any file that has been changed locally with the revision from the repository that the local file was based on. The modified local file is saved as *.#file.revision* in its local sandbox directory.

-d Create any directories that are in the repository but not in the sandbox. By default, *update* works only on the directories that are currently in the sandbox and ignores any new directories.

-D *date*
      Check out the latest revision of each file that is as old as or older than the date or time specified by *date*. This option produces a sticky date on the new sandbox. This also implies the -P option.

-f Use the latest (*HEAD*) revision on the current branch or trunk if no revision matches the date, time, tag, or revision number. This applies only if -*r* or -*D* are used.

-I *file_to_ignore*
      Ignore the named file when updating. -*I* can be used more than once. Use -*I !* to clear the list of ignored files. See "cvsignore" in Chapter 6.

-j *revision[:date]*
      Determine the older of the revision the files in the sandbox are based on and the specified *revision*, then determine the changes between that older revision and the *revision* specified, and merge those changes to the sandbox.

      If two -*j* options are used, determine the changes between the first -*j revision* and the second -*j revision* and merge those changes to the sandbox.

      The *date* can be used only if the *revision* designates a branch. If *date* is used, it specifies the latest revision on (not before) that date.

      From 1.12.12, you can use :*date* (with no revision) to specify a particular date on the trunk.

-k *mode*
      Update the files or sandbox with the designated keyword-expansion *mode*. This option also sets a sticky keyword mode for the files or the sandbox so that later commands operate with the same keyword-expansion mode unless a -*k* option overrides that mode. Prior to CVS 1.12.2, the -*k* option overrides the default mode for each file. After that version of CVS, -*kb* will not be overridden.

      The keyword-expansion modes are listed in "Keywords and Keyword Modes" in Chapter 11 and are explained in "Keywords" in Chapter 3.

-l Run *update* on files in the local directory only. (Do not recurse down subdirectories.)
      See also -*R*.

-p   Update the listed files, but write them to the standard output (*stdout*) rather than to the filesystem. Do not change the sandbox.

-P   Do not include empty directories in the sandbox.

-r revision[:date]
Run *update* on the specified revision or tag. If *revision* refers to a branch, run the command on the latest (*HEAD*) revision of the branch. This option produces a sticky tag on the new sandbox.

The *date* can be used only if the revision designates a branch, and specifies the latest revision on that date (the *:date* option is available as of 1.12.12).

-R   Run *update* on the local directory and all subdirectories and recurse down the subdirectories. This option is the default.

See also *-l*.

-W wrapper
Modify the *update* based on elements of each filename. Wrappers are explained in Chapter 3.

Description

The *cvs update* command brings changes from the repository to an existing sandbox. While doing this, *update* merges changes from the repository into changed files in the sandbox.

If *update* cannot merge repository changes with sandbox changes without losing data, it reports a conflict. Resolving conflicts is explained in Chapter 3.

If *update* is not given any filenames or directory names as parameters, it acts on the current sandbox.

Example 2 was run on a sandbox containing the current trunk, and is an example of merging the branch back to the trunk. Someone will have to edit *Makefile* and resolve the conflicts.

Example 1

```
jenn@soldier:~/wizzard$ cvs update
cvs server: Updating .
U wizzard/Changelog
U wizzard/INSTALL
U wizzard/Makefile
    .
    .
    .
```

Example 2

```
jenn@soldier:~/wizzard$ cvs update -j beta_0-1_branch_root -j beta_0-1_branch
jenn@blackrock's password: ********
cvs update: Updating .
RCS file: /var/lib/cvs/wizzard/Makefile,v
retrieving revision 1.3
retrieving revision 1.3.2.2
Merging differences between 1.3 and 1.3.2.2 into Makefile
rcsmerge: warning: conflicts during merge
```

```
cvs update: Updating doc
.
.
.
```

version

Synonyms: *ve, ver*

```
cvs [cvs-options] version
```

Displays the version information for the current installation of CVS.

Example

```
jenn@soldier:~/wizzard$ cvs version
Client: Concurrent Versions System (CVS) 1.12.12 (client/server)
Server: Concurrent Versions System (CVS) 1.12.12 (client/server)
```

watch

Synonyms: none

```
cvs [cvs-options] watch {on|off|add|remove} [-lR] [-a action] [files...]
```

Sets files to be watched or adds users to the file watch list. Users who are watching a file are notified via the script in the *notify* file in the repository's *CVSROOT* directory when other users perform specific actions. Chapter 5 explains uses of the *cvs watch* family of commands.

 CVS does not notify you of your own changes.

See also *edit*, *editors*, *unedit*, and *watchers*.

Command options

on and *off*

> The *on* and *off* subcommands control whether the file or files are marked as being watched. If a file is marked as being watched, CVS sets it as read-only when it is checked out of the repository. Without this read-only setting, your developers might forget to use *cvs edit* when editing a file.

> If the argument is a directory, all current files in the directory and all new files added to that directory in the future are set as being watched.

> The *on* and *off* subcommands set whether a file is watchable, but they do not set who is watching it.

add and *remove*

> Use the *add* and *remove* subcommands to set or remove files you want to watch. Use the -*a* option to specify which actions you want to be notified of.

> The *add* and *remove* subcommands set whether or not you are watching a file.

-a action

> Notify the user when the designated actions occur to the file. Each *-a* designates one possible action. The *-a* option can be repeated to designate multiple actions. The *-a* option is usable only with the *add* and *remove* subcommands.
>
> These are the possible actions:
>
> *edit*
>
>> Notify the user if someone else has run *cvs edit* on the file.
>
> *unedit*
>
>> Notify the user when the file is no longer being edited by someone else. Notification occurs when *cvs unedit* or *cvs release* runs or when the file is deleted and recreated with *cvs update* or *cvs checkout*.
>
> *commit*
>
>> Notify the user when someone else commits changes to the file.
>
> *all*
>
>> Notify the user in all of the previous cases.
>
> *none*
>
>> Notify the user in none of the previous cases.

-l   Run *watch* on files in the local directory only. (Do not recurse down subdirectories.)

> See also *-R*.

-R   Run *watch* on files in the local directory and all subdirectories and recurse down the subdirectories. This option is the default.

> See also *-l*.

Example

```
jenn@soldier:~/wizzard$ cvs watch on Makefile
jenn@soldier:~/wizzard$ cvs watch add Makefile
jenn@soldier:~/wizzard$
```

---

watchers

Synonyms: none

```
cvs [cvs-options] watchers [-lR] [files...]
```

Displays the list of users who are watching the files listed as parameters. If no files are listed, this command lists the watchers for the files in the current directory and its subdirectories.

See Chapter 5 for an explanation of the *watch* system.

See also *edit*, *editors*, *unedit*, and *watch*.

Command options

-*l*   Run *watchers* on files in the local directory only. (Do not recurse down subdirectories.) See also -*R*.

-*R*   Run *watchers* on files in the local directory and all subdirectories and recurse down the subdirectories. This option is the default.

    See also -*l*.

Example

```
jenn@soldier:~/wizzard$ cvs watchers Makefile
Makefile doppel edit unedit commit
        jenn edit unedit commit
```

CHAPTER 11
Miscellaneous Topics Reference

This chapter is a comprehensive reference of CVS topics other than commands. It is intended to be useful as a quick reference, not a tutorial.

If you have never used CVS before, I suggest you read Chapters 2 and 3 before reading this reference. Those chapters explain the basic concepts of CVS and how to use it effectively.

This chapter contains the following sections:

"Administrative Files"
> Describes CVS administrative files in the sandbox on the client computer or in the user's home directory on the server.

"CVSROOT Files"
> Describes CVS administrative files in the repository's *CVSROOT* directory.

"CVSROOT Variables"
> Describes variables that you can use in the administrative files in the *CVSROOT* directory.

"Dates"
> Describes date and time formats that you can use with CVS.

"Environment Variables"
> Describes environment variables on the server or the client that affect CVS.

"Keywords and Keyword Modes"
> Describes the keywords that CVS uses, the expansion modes that affect how CVS processes the keywords, and how CVS processes line endings.

"Pattern Matching"
> Describes regular expression and wildcard pattern matching in CVS.

"Repository Access Methods"
> Describes methods used to access local and remote CVS repositories.

Administrative Files

CVS needs to keep track of what it's doing, so it maintains a number of administrative files. Most of the files are in the *CVS* subdirectory of each sandbox directory, but there may also be hidden files in the directory itself, with filenames that start with a dot (.). In addition, the user's home directory can contain CVS administrative files that affect all of that user's sandboxes; these filenames are also prefixed with a dot.

Dot Files

In client/server mode, all the dot files other than *.rhosts* should be on the client computer. The *.rhosts* file should be in the user's home directory on the server computer.

These are the dot files in the sandbox directory:

.cvsignore
> Contains a list of files CVS should not process. This file uses the same format as *cvsignore* in the repository's *CVSROOT* directory and may be checked into CVS. See Chapter 6 for more information.

.#filename.revision
> CVS is built on the philosophy of never fully losing data. So if you get an update that overwrites a project file, and the file is not synchronized with the repository, the original file is stored as *.#filename.revision*, where *revision* is the BASE revision of the file. This way the changes you haven't saved in the repository are not lost.

These are the dot files in a user's home directory:

.cvsrc
> Contains a list of CVS commands and the options the user wants as default options for those commands. See Chapter 3 for more information.

.cvsignore
> Contains a list of files CVS should not process. This file uses the same format as *cvsignore* in the repository's *CVSROOT* directory. See Chapter 6 for more information.

.cvswrappers
> Contains a list of wrappers that affect how a file is stored. The wrappers include a pattern that CVS matches against filenames and a keyword-expansion mode that CVS applies to any file whose name matches the pattern. Wrappers are explained in Chapter 3.

.cvspass
> Used in *pserver* remote-access mode. This file contains the user's password for each repository they are logged into, stored in a simple form of encoding. Be aware that the file is human-readable and the passwords are easy to decrypt. See Chapter 8 for more information.

.rhosts

Used when connecting with RSH. This file should be in the user's home directory on the server machine, and it should contain the client's computer and username. See Chapter 8 for more information.

CVS Subdirectory Files

CVS creates a subdirectory named *CVS* in every directory of a sandbox. It stores the following sandbox administrative files in this subdirectory:

Base

A directory, not a file, that stores the pre-editing revision of any files that are being edited with *cvs edit*.

Baserev

Contains the revision information for every file in the *Base* directory, in the format `name/revision/`. Later versions of CVS may add to this format.

Baserev.tmp

Changes to the *Baserev* file are written to *Baserev.tmp*. CVS then renames *Baserev.tmp* to *Baserev*, which overwrites the original *Baserev*.

Checkin.prog

Used if the current sandbox was checked out as a module and the *modules* file in the repository's *CVSROOT* has an *-i* option for the module the sandbox was checked out as. This file stores the program to be executed when the module is checked in. *Checkin.prog* is obsolete in CVS 1.11.6 and later.

Entries

Contains a line for each file and directory in the relevant sandbox directory. Lines for files have the format:

```
/name/revision/timestamp[+conflict]/options/tagdate
```

Lines for directories have the format:

```
D/name////
```

There may be text between or after the empty slashes, but in current versions of CVS, this text is ignored. The space is reserved for future expansion.

Entries.Backup

Changes to the *Entries* file are written to *Entries.Backup*. CVS then renames *Entries.Backup* to *Entries*, which overwrites the original *Entries*.

Entries.Log

Used to record planned changes to the *Entries* file. Lines to be added start with *A*; lines to be removed start with *R*. After the *A* or *R* comes a space, followed by the line to be added or removed.

Third-party programs that read *Entries* should also check for *Entries.Log*. If *Entries.Log* exists, they should read *Entries*, apply the changes from *Entries.Log*, and then rewrite *Entries* and remove *Entries.Log*.

Entries.Static

> If this file exists, CVS did not receive a complete set of files from the repository and the sandbox directory that is the parent to the current *CVS* directory is *static* (i.e., CVS will not create new files in this directory). This setting can be cleared by using *update -d* to download a full set of files and subdirectories for the parent directory to the current *CVS* directory.

Notify

> Contains any *cvs watch* notifications that have not yet been sent to the server.

Notify.tmp

> Changes to the *Notify* file are written to *Notify.tmp*. CVS then renames *Notify. tmp* to *Notify*, which overwrites the original *Notify*.

Repository

> Contains the path from the repository root to the repository directory that the relevant sandbox directory is a reflection of. This file may contain the full path, including the path to the root of the sandbox's repository.

> If the current sandbox directory does not have a related repository directory, this file contains the string *CVSROOT/Emptydir*.

Root

> Contains the path to the root of the sandbox's repository.

Tag

> Used to store directory-specific sticky tags and dates, so that CVS can add them to new files that you add to the directory. This file is most often used when the directory is part of a branch sandbox.

> If the first character in the file is *T*, the file refers to a branch tag. *N* is a non-branch tag, and *D* is a date.

Template

> In client/server mode, this file stores the login template specified in the *rcsinfo* file in the repository's *CVSROOT* directory.

Update.prog

> Used if the *modules* file in *CVSROOT* specifies the *-u* option for the current sandbox's module. *Update.prog* stores the program to be executed when this module is updated. This file is obsolete in CVS 1.11.6 and later.

In addition, there is one file which can be stored in the CVS subdirectory in the repository:

fileattr

> Stores the settings for the *cvs watch* family of commands.

CVSROOT Files

The *CVSROOT* directory in the CVS repository contains several administrative files. Most of these files are editable by the user and are stored in both RCS format (with a *,v* suffix) and plain text to be used by CVS. With three exceptions, these files can be checked out, edited, and committed like any other CVS file.

The *history* and *val-tags* files should not be edited. The *passwd* file should never be checked out; it should be edited in place.

If your version of CVS is older than 1.12.6, see Chapter 7 for the scripting file syntax.

Between 1.12.6 and 1.12.10, there were significant changes to the *CVSROOT* files, and it's obvious that a lot of work is going into improving the features these files make possible.

If you are running a version of CVS later than 1.12.13 (the current version while I'm writing this), it's worth checking the documentation for newer nifty features.

Scripting File Syntax

As of CVS 1.12.6, the syntax for scripting files changed. If you're using an older version of CVS, please see Chapter 7 for information on the file syntax. If you have different versions of CVS in the repository and the clients, see Chapter 9 for advice on cross-version issues.

In versions later than 1.12.6, whether you use the new or old format for the scripting files is controlled by the configuration option *UseNewInfoFmtStrings*. The valid options are *yes* (to use the new format) and *no* (to use the format prior to 1.12.6). These options are set in the *config* file, normally stored in the *CVSROOT* directory.

The file syntax is as follows:

```
name-pattern action
```

The *name-pattern* is a regular expression that must match a relative path within the repository, or one of the special words *DEFAULT* and *ALL*. It is separated from the *action* by one or more spaces or tabs. Regular expressions are explained later in this chapter.

The *action* is a command-line template, or the filename (and path) of a script plus any parameters required for that script. It is good practice to use the full pathname of the script, with the *$CVSROOT* variable standing in for the repository path. You may embed one or more format strings in the template or among the script's parameters; you may also use the variables listed later in this chapter, in the section "CVSROOT Variables."

The character # at the start of a line signals a comment. Blank lines are ignored. There is no way to break a long line in current versions of CVS.

CVS processes the file by matching the current repository directory to the regular expression. It looks for the first matching line, runs the action provided on that line, and also runs the actions on any line with a name-pattern of *ALL*. Note that *DEFAULT* as a name-pattern is deemed to match everything, so ensure that it is the last name-pattern other than *ALL*.

 Even though you can call several actions with separate *ALL* lines, the actions are not guaranteed to run in sequence. If you have interdependent actions, use a script called by a single *ALL* line rather than a set of *ALL* lines.

The format strings are processed by CVS before being passed to the action's script or command. Before processing, the format string consists of a %, followed by a single variable, optionally enclosed in braces ({ }), or by a set of variables enclosed in braces. Some of the variables represent individual values, and others represent list values. Each variable in a set of variables enclosed in braces must represent a list value.

Each value represented by a format string variable is passed to its script as a single argument, irrespective of white space within the value. A list on its own is passed as a single argument for each element of the list.

A set of list values is also passed as a single argument for each element of each list, but the values are collated. For instance, *%{sVv}* in the *taginfo* file will produce a list of arguments in the format *file1 oldversion1 newversion1 file2 oldversion2 newversion2 file3 oldversion3 newversion3*.

The format string variables which are valid in all files represent single values, and are:

%   A literal percent sign (that is, %% will become %).

c   The name of the command that triggered the execution of the script. In a script run because of a *cvs commit*, for instance, the format string will be replaced with *commit*.

n   The null string.

p   The name of the directory in the repository that's currently being processed.

r   The path of the repository root directory.

R   Relevant in repositories which are involved in proxy setups. This is the referrer, or the repository which the client contacted and which referred the operation to this server.

The checkoutlist File

The *checkoutlist* file is used to designate files to be stored in the *CVSROOT* directory in both RCS and clear-text formats. Most of the CVS administrative files are stored this way automatically, and the *checkoutlist* file allows you to store user-created files in the same way. The most common files to be stored like this are scripts executed by the scripting files (*commitinfo*, *loginfo*, *rcsinfo*, *taginfo*, and *verifymsg*; and after CVS 1.12.10, *postadmin*, *postproxy*, *posttag*, *postwatch*, and *preproxy*).

The file format is to list the names of the files, one file per line. All files must be in the *CVSROOT* directory.

To display an error message if the file cannot be checked out into *CVSROOT*, add whitespace, followed by the message, to the line the file is listed on. See Example 11-1.

Example 11-1. Adding whitespace to the message

```
distribute.pl      ERROR: could not record CVSROOT/distribute.pl.
```

The commitinfo File

The *commitinfo* file defines programs to run before a file is committed. If any of the programs exit with a nonzero exit status, the commit does not proceed. These programs run on the repository computer.

This file uses the standard scripting file syntax, and supports *DEFAULT* but not *ALL*. In addition to the usual format string variables, it allows s, a list variable containing the names of the files to be committed.

For backwards compatibility, the format string *%r/%p %{s}* is appended to the *action* if there is no format string in the action. This behavior should not be relied on, as it will probably be removed in a later version of CVS.

The *commitinfo* file is usually used to enforce project standards.

The config File

The *config* file contains CVS configuration options. It is normally found in the *CVSROOT*, but from CVS 1.12.13, you can use the *-c* option to *pserver* or *server* to specify a different *config* path.

Lines that start with a # are comments. All other lines are in the form:

```
keyword=value
```

There is one keyword/value pair per line. Each keyword/value pair represents a configuration option. Whitespace is significant, including carriage returns, tabs, and extra spaces.

From CVS 1.12.13, as well as specifying which *config* path the repository should use, you can also define which repository (or repositories) specific configurations apply to. The first section of the file contains default configurations. Later sections are defined by a string of the form [*repository-path*] on a line of its own. Each section applies to the repository path that precedes it. Multiple repository paths with no intervening configurations cause the configurations that follow them to apply to all the relevant paths.

Example 11-2 shows a configuration file. The comments explain which repositories are affected by which configurations.

Example 11-2. Multirepository configuration file

```
# Default values.
RereadLogAfterVerify=stat
SystemAuth=no

# Values for the repositories /var/cvsroot and /var/cvsbase
# Set the values for admin that ordinary users can use.
[/var/cvsroot]
[/var/cvsbase]
UserAdminOptions=klqsuc

# Values for the repository /var/public/cvs
# This is a read-only public repository, so it has a separate LockDir and there's
# no need to check for verifymsg changes.
[/var/public/cvs]
LockDir=/var/public/cvslocks
RereadLogAfterVerify=no
```

These are the available configuration options:

HistorySearchPattern=pattern
HistoryLogPath=path

These two options control the files used to store the data for the *cvs history* command. The *HistoryLogPath* controls where the information is stored; the default is the file *history* in the repository's *CVSROOT* directory. The *HistorySearchPattern* controls where CVS looks for the data, and has the same default.

Any path to a filename is a valid value for *HistoryLogPath*, and can contain the variable *$CVSROOT*, which evaluates to the repository root. You can also use the substitutions listed in *man date*, the most useful of which (for this purpose) are *%Y*, *%m*, and *%d* (four-digit year, numeric month, and numeric day).

Any path to a filename is also a valid value for *HistorySearchPattern*, and it can also use *$CVSROOT*. Instead of the % substitutions, you can use pattern matches as described later in this chapter. Any files which match the pattern will be searched, in lexicographic order.

These options are valid from CVS 1.12.12 and later.

ImportNewFilesToVendorBranchOnly=value

> This option is a repository-wide version of the *-X* command option to *cvs import*: during an import, new files are added only to the vendor branch, and not to the trunk. Valid values are *yes* or *no*. The default is *no*.
>
> This option is valid from CVS 1.12.10.

KeywordExpand=value

> This option controls which keywords may be expanded. It affects all files in all projects in the repository it's configured in. The value is in the format *i|e[keyword list]*, where *keyword list* is a comma-separated list of keywords. The keywords may be any of the standard CVS keywords, or any local keyword as defined in the *LocalKeyword* configuration option (see following entry).
>
> If the first character is *i*, the keywords in the list will be the only keywords that CVS expands. If the first character is *e*, the keywords in the list will not be expanded. A typical entry might be *KeywordExpand=iAuthor, Id, Locker*, which would limit expansion to the Author, ID, and Locker keywords.
>
> This option is valid starting with CVS 1.12.2.

LocalKeyword=value=keyword

> This option creates a keyword local to the current repository, which is an alias for one of the existing keywords. You could use *LocalKeyword=Filename=RCSfile*, for example, which would mean you could use *$Filename$* instead of *$RCSfile$* as the keyword that generates the name of the current file (or *Path=Source* to get the full path from the repository root).
>
> This option is valid from CVS 1.12.2.

LockDir=directory

> If this setting is present, CVS puts lock files in the specified *directory* rather than in the repository. You must create the *directory*, but CVS creates all the necessary subdirectories. LockDir is valid from CVS 1.11.

> Do not use *LockDir* if any of your users are running CVS 1.9 or earlier on the repository server, as users will then be putting locks in two different places and not honoring each other's locks. These versions silently ignore *LockDir*.
>
> CVS 1.10 doesn't honor the *LockDir* setting; it displays an error if you use it and does not work.

LogHistory=value

> The text in *value* controls which actions are logged to the *history* file in the repository's *CVSROOT* directory. The valid values can be any combination of the following:
>
> A   Log when a file is added to the repository.
>
> C   Log when a file would have been updated in a sandbox, but needed to be merged and there were conflicts in the merge.

E   Log when a file is exported.

F   Log when a file is released.

G   Log when a file is updated in a sandbox with a successful merge.

M   Log when a file is modified (a sandbox revision is added to the repository).

O   Log when a file is checked out.

P   Log when a file is patched.

R   Log when a file is removed from the repository.

T   Log when a file is tagged or rtagged.

U   Log when a file is updated in a sandbox with no merge required.

W   Log when a file is deleted from a sandbox during an update because it is no longer active in the repository.

MaxCommentLeaderLength=value

This option affects the processing of the *Log* keyword. The text preceding the string *Log* on its line is the *comment leader*. If the comment leader exceeds the *value*, the keyword is ignored; unless the configuration option *UseArchiveCommentLeader* is set to *yes*, in which case the keyword is expanded with the comment leader specified by the repository copy of the file.

The value defaults to 20 bytes. As a bare number, it represents a value in bytes. If suffixed with *k*, *M*, *G*, or *T*, it represents kilobytes, megabytes, gigabytes, or terabytes, respectively.

This option is valid from CVS 1.12.10.

MinCompressionLevel=value
MaxCompressionLevel=value

These control the compression level used by the CVS server, and correspond to the same levels available to clients with the *-z* global option. The values range from 0 (no compression) to 9 (maximum compression). If the client requests a compression level that is outside the ranges set with these options, the server uses the closest available compression level.

If the minimum compression level is higher than 0 and the client is older than 1.12.13, the server may exit with an error message if the client doesn't request compression. Clients later than 1.12.13 handle this more gracefully.

These options are valid starting with CVS 1.12.12.

PrimaryServer=repository-path

If the repository path is not the current repository, the server acts as a write proxy to the repository specified in *repository-path*. See Chapter 6 for more information.

This option is valid starting with CVS 1.12.10.

RCSBIN=directory

This option provides the directory in which CVS should look for the *rcs* program. This option applies only to CVS Versions 1.9.12 to 1.9.18; it is obsolete and ignored in later versions.

RereadLogAfterVerify=value

The log message saved during *cvs commit* might be changed if the *verifymsg* file is in use. This option controls whether the message is reread after the program listed in the *verifymsg* file runs.

This option is useful only if the *verifymsg* file is in use. These are the available options:

always or *yes*

Reread the log message after the *verifymsg* file has been processed. This option is the default case.

never or *no*

Do not reread the log message after the *verifymsg* file has been processed.

stat

Check whether the log message has been changed, using the filesystem's *stat( )* command. If it has changed, reread the log message. This option can take up to an extra second per directory to process than the *never* case, but it may be faster than *always* if the log messages aren't always changed by *verifymsg*.

SystemAuth=value

If *value* is *yes*, the server authenticates the connecting user with the *passwd* file. If the user fails to authenticate there, the server authenticates the user against the main user database for the operating system. If *value* is *no*, the server authenticates the user only against the *passwd* file. The default value is *yes*.

This option is useful only if you have clients connecting to CVS in *pserver* mode.

 SystemAuth=yes weakens security, because CVS transmits passwords using only trivial encryption. The encryption can easily be broken, and a password obtained. The *SystemAuth=yes* setting uses the operating system's own authentication mechanism, so the obtained password will provide access to the user's shell account.

TmpDir=path

This allows CVS to use a directory other than */tmp* for its temporary files. The path should be a full path and the directory specified in the path should exist.

This option is valid from CVS 1.12.12.

TopLevelAdmin=value

If *value* is *yes*, a *CVS* subdirectory is created in the current working directory when you check out a sandbox. If *value* is *no*, the *CVS* subdirectories are created only in the actual sandbox directory tree. The default is *no*.

UseArchiveCommentLeader=value

The value may be *true* or *false*. Setting it to *true* only has an effect if the comment leader is set in the repository copy of a particular file. The comment leader can be set with the *cvs admin* command.

If the value is set to *true*, there is a comment leader in the repository file, and the text preceding the *Log* keyword in a file is longer than the value of *MaxCommentLeaderLength*, the comment leader in the repository copy of the file will be used in place of the text preceding the *Log* keyword.

Also see *MaxCommentLeaderLength*. This option is valid from CVS 1.12.10.

UseNewInfoFmtStrings=value

The value can be set to *yes* or *no*. It controls whether the scripting files use the old or new syntax. This option will be removed in later versions of CVS, and all scripting files will use the new syntax.

UserAdminOptions=value

This option is available in CVS 1.12.1 and later. If *value* exists, any user can run *cvs admin* options listed in *value*. The contents of *value* must be a string of letters with no separators or spaces, and the letters must be the command options (without parameters) for *cvs admin*.

If the *cvsadmin* group exists on the server machine, then only members of the *cvsadmin* group are allowed to run commands not listed in *value*.

The cvsignore File

The *cvsignore* file contains a list of filenames or filename patterns that CVS should not process. The syntax for this file is a space-separated or line-ending-separated list of filenames or name patterns. *cvsignore* uses wildcard pattern matching.

The special *!* filename causes CVS to clear its ignore list. The special *** filename causes CVS to ignore everything. See Chapter 6 for additional information.

The cvswrappers File

The *cvswrappers* file contains a line-ending-separated list of wrappers that control the merge method or keyword-substitution mode of files, based on a filename pattern. The syntax of a wrapper is as follows:

```
wildcard option 'value' [option 'value'...]
```

The wildcards are matched to filenames when files are added to the repository. See Chapter 3 for more information.

These are the options and values:

-m 'mode'
> Indicates the merge methodology to use for files that match the pattern. Valid modes are *COPY* or *MERGE*.

-k 'mode'
> Indicates the keyword-expansion mode to use for files that match the pattern. The keyword-expansion modes are provided in "Keywords and Keyword Modes" later in this chapter.

-f 'path_to_filter'
> Processes the file through the *filter* program every time the file leaves the repository. This option is not available in CVS 1.10 and later.

-t 'path_to_filter'
> Processes the file through the *filter* program every time the file enters the repository. This option is not available in CVS 1.10 and later.

The editinfo File

The *editinfo* file is obsolete; it has been replaced by *verifymsg* and *rcsinfo*, and removed as of CVS 1.12.2. In CVS versions that use *editinfo*, this file enforces the use of a specific editor when entering log messages. If CVS is called from a remote client, or if the *-m* or *-F* command options are used with *cvs commit*, the *editinfo* file is not used. If the editor exits with a nonzero exit status, the commit does not proceed.

The history File

The *history* file contains the information displayed by the *cvs history* command. It must be writable by all CVS users and is created by *cvs init* to be owner-, group-, and world-writable. This file should not be edited manually; all changes should occur through CVS.

If you wish to turn history logging off, a simple way to do so is to rename the *history* file. The file can also be removed or rotated like any logfile, with no effect on any CVS command other than *cvs history*. (If you do rotate the file, consider whether to lock the repository during the process of moving the file.)

 Several options in the *config* file affect the *history* file.

The loginfo File

The *loginfo* file defines programs to run when information is recorded in the repository. It runs once per directory in a *commit*, after the files in the directory have been successfully recorded. It also runs after a successful *import*, and after a directory has been successfully added to the repository. These programs run on the repository computer.

This file uses the standard scripting file syntax, and supports both *DEFAULT* and *ALL*. In addition to the usual format string variables, it allows:

s   A list variable that expands to the names of the current files being processed.

T   A list variable that expands to the tag name of the destination, or the empty string if there is no relevant tag name.

V   A list variable that expands to the files' revision number prior to the commit.

v   A list variable that expands to the files' revision number after the commit.

For backwards compatibility, if there is no *UseNewFormatStrings* setting in the configuration file, *loginfo* is processed the old way. This behavior should not be relied on, as it will probably be removed in a later version of CVS. See Chapter 7 for information on the old format.

The modules File

The *modules* file is used to group arbitrary files or directories into a single module. Once a module is defined, the project files and directories it defines can be checked out into a sandbox by either the module name or the name of the repository directory it represents. The *modules* file can also specify programs to run when files in the module are committed, exported, updated, checked out, or tagged with *rtag*.

Each module definition needs to be on a line of its own. When adding directories to module definitions, use paths relative to the repository root directory.

An *alias module* can be used to group files and directories into a single module, regardless of where they are stored in the repository tree. The syntax for an alias module definition is as follows:

```
module_name -a path [path...]
```

A *path* may be a pathname to a file or directory or it may be another module name, and there may be any number of paths. If a path leads to a directory, all subdirectories and files are included in the module. If you wish to exclude subdirectories from an alias module, use an exclamation mark (*!*) in front of the directory name.

A *regular module* is used to define options for a project. It can also be used to define subsets of a project or group modules together. The syntax of a regular module is as follows:

```
module_name [options] [directory [files|subdirectories...]] [&modules...]
```

The directory should be a path relative to the repository root directory. If filenames or subdirectory names are included, they should be in the directory, and the module definition then applies only to those files or subdirectories. You can include a pre-defined module in a regular module by prefixing the module name with an ampersand (&) and specifying the resulting name in place of *directory* in the syntax. The module can be a regular module or an alias module.

Most of the options for a regular module define scripts to run immediately after a CVS command on the files in the module. Here is the full list of options for regular modules:

-d directory_name
> Use *directory_name* rather than the module name as the name of the sandbox root directory.

-e script
> Run the *script* when the module is exported. The script is given the module name as an argument.

-i script
> Run the *script* when the module is committed. The script is given the full path-name of the relevant repository directory as an argument. This option is obsolete in CVS 1.11.6 and later.

-o script
> Run the *script* when the module is checked out. The script is given the module name as an argument.

-s status
> Provide a *status* for the module. This option has no meaning internal to CVS, but when the *cvs checkout -s* command runs, the *status* affects the display order.
>
> CVS allocates an 11-character space for the status string when it is displayed, but the string is not truncated if it is longer than 11 characters.

-t script
> Run the *script* when *rtag* is used on the module. This option does not run when *tag* is used. The script is given two arguments: the module name and the name of the tag.

-u script
> Run the *script* when the module is updated. The script is given the full path-name of the affected repository directory as an argument. This option is obsolete in CVS 1.11.6 and later.

Each script designated in the *modules* file runs immediately after its associated CVS command completes. For example, the *-o* script runs after a *checkout* command for the module completes.

If the repository is not on the same computer as the client, the scripts for the *-i* and *-u* options are copied from their original location in the repository to the client computer and stored in the *Checkin.prog* and *Update.prog* files in the *CVS* subdirectories in the sandbox. These scripts are later copied back to the server computer, where they run. For security reasons, this behavior is changed in CVS 1.11.6 and later.

All other scripts called from the *modules* file run on the repository server computer.

The sandbox copies of the *Checkin.prog* and *Update.prog* files are not changed when the *modules* file or the repository computer's copies of the scripts are changed. To change *Checkin.prog* and *Update.prog*, *commit* and *release* the sandbox and check out a new sandbox. (This step is not relevant if you're using 1.11.6 or later.)

The notify File

The *notify* file contains the commands to run when conditions exist for *cvs watch* to notify a user of a change to a watched file.

The syntax of the *notify* file is a series of lines, each line in the following format:

```
filename_pattern command
```

The `filename_pattern` can be *ALL* or any wildcard pattern. The command can be any *sh* shell command, but it must contain *%s*, which is replaced by the name of the user to notify. The rest of the notification information is provided to the command through standard input (*stdin*).

 CVS does not notify you of your own changes to a file.

The passwd File

The *passwd* file contains the usernames and passwords for the *pserver* repository method. This file is usually edited in place, not checked out like the other administrative files. If you wish to check it out, add it to the *commitinfo* file, but be aware of the security risks explained in Chapter 8.

The format for entries in the *passwd* file is:

```
CVS_username:password:system_username
```

The `CVS_username` is the name the user sends to CVS. The `system_username` is the name the CVS programs run under. If these names are the same, you don't need to include the `system_username`. The `system_username` must be a valid username on the server; if the *system_username* does not exist on the server, CVS commands will fail even if the user authenticates with CVS.

The passwords need to be encrypted with the standard Unix *crypt()* function. CVS does not provide a tool to encrypt passwords, so they need to be encrypted elsewhere and then pasted into the file. If the *password* field is empty, the user automatically authenticates. You can use the Unix and Linux program *mkpasswd* to encrypt a string for use as a password.

A single system username can be shared by multiple users with different CVS usernames. This feature allows several people to work on a project, while recording the changes across multiple users.

The postadmin File

The *postadmin* file defines programs to run after any *cvs admin* command that modifies a file is run. These programs run on the repository computer.

This file uses the standard scripting file syntax, and supports both *DEFAULT* and *ALL*.

The postproxy File

The *postproxy* file defines programs to run after a secondary server has completed a connection to a primary server, and before the secondary server releases the connection to the client. These programs run on the secondary server, and are called once per directory. It is recommended that the postproxy include a command to update the secondary server's copy of the repository.

This file uses the standard scripting file syntax, and supports both *DEFAULT* and *ALL*. It has the additional format variable *P*, the repository path of the primary server.

The posttag File

The *posttag* file defines programs to run after any *cvs tag* or *rtag* command that modifies a file is run. These programs run on the repository computer.

This file uses the standard scripting file syntax, and supports both *DEFAULT* and *ALL*. It permits the same format string attributes as the *taginfo* file: see the section on the *taginfo* file for more information.

The postwatch File

The *postwatch* file defines programs to run after any *cvs watch*, *edit*, or *unedit* command that modifies the repository's watch administrative file, *fileattr*. See Chapter 6 (specifically, information on *fileattr*) for more information on which commands are affected. These programs run on the repository computer.

This file uses the standard scripting file syntax, and supports both *DEFAULT* and *ALL*.

Note that *edit* and *unedit* do not always contact the server, and sometimes cache their notification to be run later.

The preproxy File

The *preproxy* file defines programs to run before a secondary server connects to a primary server, and after the client has contacted the secondary server. These programs run on the secondary server, and are called once, from the top directory specified by the client's request.

This file uses the standard scripting file syntax, and supports both *DEFAULT* and *ALL*. It has the additional format variable *P*, the repository path of the primary server.

The rcsinfo File

The *rcsinfo* file defines forms to display as the templates for commit log messages. The *rcsinfo* file is processed before a file is committed.

This file uses the standard scripting file syntax, and supports both *DEFAULT* and *ALL*. The action in the case of the *rcsinfo* file must be a pathname to a template file.

 The action is not processed as a command.

If the repository is not on the same computer as the client, CVS stores a copy of the template (or templates) that matches each sandbox directory in the appropriate *CVS* subdirectory of each sandbox. In versions prior to 1.12.1, this file is not updated with other sandbox files, so if the *rcsinfo* file or the main template changes, your users should release and recreate their sandboxes. (In 1.12.1 and later, the file is updated with the other sandbox files.)

The readers File

The *readers* file contains the usernames of people who have read-only access to the repository via the *pserver* remote-access method. The *readers* and *writers* files use the *CVS_username*, not the *system_username*, to determine whether a user has access. The file should contain one name per line. The newline character after the last username is significant.

If a user is listed in the *readers* file, he has read-only access to the repository, even if he is also listed in the *writers* file.

The taginfo File

The *taginfo* file defines programs to run before a file is tagged. If any of the programs exit with a nonzero exit status, the tag does not proceed.

This file uses the standard scripting file syntax, and supports both *DEFAULT* and *ALL*. In addition to the usual format string variables, it allows these:

b   Tag type. This is a single-element variable, and evaluates to *T* for a branch, *N* for a nonbranch, or *?* for unknown.

o   Operation. This is a single-element variable, and evaluates to *add*, *del*, or *mov*, for additions, deletions, or moving of a tag.

s   This is a list variable, and evaluates to the current filename(s).

T   This is a list variable, and evaluates to the tag name of the destination, or the empty string if there is no such tag name.

t   This is a single-element variable, and evaluates to the new tag name.

V   This is a list variable, and evaluates to the old version number (as for a move or delete operation).

v   This is a list variable, and evaluates to the new version number (as for an add or move operation).

For backwards compatibility, the format string *%t %o %p %{sv}* is appended to the *action* if there is no format string in the action. This behavior should not be relied on, as it will probably be removed in a later version of CVS.

The users File

The *users* file provides a list of email addresses for users whose mailboxes are not on the same machine as the CVS repository. This file is used by the command given in the *notify* file, and it becomes the input represented by the *%s* string.

The format of this file is a separate line for each user, consisting of the username and the email address to send notifications to, in the following format:

```
username:email
```

 If you are using the *pserver* access method, use the system usernames in the *users* file.

The val-tags File

The *val-tags* file contains a list of valid tag names, acting as an internal cache for CVS. It must be writable by all CVS users, and is created by *cvs init* to be owner- and group-writable. This file should not be edited manually; all changes should occur through CVS.

The verifymsg File

The *verifymsg* file defines programs to run after a log message has been entered, but before the commit takes place. The programs are passed the log message, which they can modify or parse to ensure that all essential fields have been filled in. The *verifymsg* file is usually used with the *rcsinfo* file to manage log messages. If a program called from *verifymsg* exits with a nonzero error status, the commit is aborted.

The file syntax for *verifymsg* is as follows:

```
name_pattern action
```

The *name_pattern* is a regular expression that must match a relative path within the repository. The *action* is a command-line template or the address of a script, plus any parameters required for that script or template. The log message is passed to the script or template on the standard input (*stdin*), as is the path to a temporary file containing the log message.

Lines starting with the hash symbol (#) are comments and are ignored. The special *DEFAULT* pattern matches directories that do not match any other pattern. CVS uses the script on the first line with a directory-name pattern that matches the directory tree a file is in.

A script invoked through *verifymsg* can modify the log message, and the *config* file in the *CVSROOT* directory then determines whether CVS reads and uses the modified log message or the original one for the rest of the *commit* process.

The writers File

The *writers* file contains the usernames of people who have read-write access to the repository via the *pserver* remote-access method. The *readers* and *writers* files use the CVS username, not the system username, to determine whether a user has access. The file should contain one username per line. The newline character after the last user is significant.

If a user is listed in the *writers* file but not the *readers* file, she has read-write access to the repository.

 Being listed in the *readers* file is enough to consign a user to read-only access, regardless of whether that user is also listed in the *writers* file.

CVSROOT Variables

The administrative files in *CVSROOT* can use several types of variables: internal, environment, and shell variables. You can use these variables to pass parameters to the scripts in the scripting files, or you can use them as part of command-line templates.

The internal variables allow you to use information CVS stores about the currently running command. The environment variables are used to access information from the environment the command is running in, and the shell variables are used to access information about the shell.

Environment Variables in CVSROOT Files

Three environment variables are set when CVS runs commands or scripts from CVS administrative files:

CVS_USER
> This variable is meaningful only with the *pserver* access method. It refers to the CVS username provided in the leftmost field of the appropriate line in *CVSROOT/passwd*. If this username does not exist, the variable expands to an empty string.

LOGNAME and *USER*
> Both of these variables contain the username of the user calling the CVS process.
>
> In the *pserver* access method, the username is the third field of the line in *passwd*. If no username is there, the *CVS_USER* value is used.

Internal Variables in CVSROOT Files

The syntax for referencing a CVS internal variable is *${VARIABLE}*. The *$VARIABLE* syntax can also be used if the character immediately following the variable is neither alphanumeric nor an underscore (_).

These are the internal CVS variables:

COMMITID
> The session ID of the CVS process. This is a unique ID for each commit session, and is between 16 and 256 characters in length.

CVSROOT
> The path to the repository root directory (not the path to the *CVSROOT* directory within the repository). This variable contains the path only, not any access method or host information.

CVSEDITOR or *EDITOR* or *VISUAL*
> The editor CVS is using. If you use the *-e editor* CVS option, CVS uses the editor that you specify on the command line. If you don't use *-e*, CVS reads the environment variables and uses the first editor it finds. CVS uses *CVSEDITOR* by preference, then *EDITOR*, then *VISUAL*.

USER

The username (on the server machine in client/server mode) of the user running CVS. With the *pserver* access method, this is the third field of the appropriate line in *passwd*. If no username is there, it is the name in the leftmost field.

RCSBIN

This variable applies only to CVS 1.9.18 or earlier. It contains the path to the *rcs* executable.

SESSIONID

The session ID of the CVS process. This is a unique ID for each commit session, and is between 16 and 256 characters in length.

CVS permits user-defined variables that can be passed to administrative files from the client. In the administrative files, reference such a variable with the syntax *${=VARIABLE}*. On the command line, use the *-s variable=value* CVS option to pass the variable to CVS. All strings that contain the *$* symbol, other than the variable references, are reserved for CVS internal use. There is no way to escape the *$* symbol.

Shell Variables in CVSROOT Files

Two shell variables are also used in the administrative files. These variables are expanded on the server, so if you are using the *pserver* connection method, you may get results based on the username on the server rather than the CVS username.

~/   The home directory of the user calling the CVS process

~username

The home directory of the user identified as *username*

Dates

In CVS, all dates and times are processed by a version of the GNU *getdate* function, which can translate dates and times given in several different formats. Case is always irrelevant when interpreting dates. Spaces are permitted in date strings, but in the command-line client, a string with spaces should be surrounded by quotes. If the year is 0 to 99, it is considered to be in the twentieth century.

If a time is not given, midnight at the start of the date is assumed. If a time zone is not specified, the date is interpreted as being in the client's local time zone.

For the canonical information on CVS and dates, see the information on *getdate* at *http://www.gnu.org/software/shishi/manual/html_node/Date-input-formats.html*.

Legal Date Formats

The legal time and date formats for CVS are defined by the ISO 8601 standard and RFC 822 as amended by RFC 1123. Other formats can be interpreted, but CVS is designed to handle only these standards.

ISO 8601

The basic ISO 8601 date format is as follows:

```
year-month-day hours:minutes:seconds
```

All values are numbers with leading zeros to ensure that the correct number of digits are used. Hours are given in 24-hour time. This produces the structure *YYYY-MM-DD HH:MM:SS*, which is internationally acceptable and can be sorted easily. You can use a date, a time, or both.

If you're using ISO 8601 format with the hyphens, the full date is required in CVS. The *YYYYMMDD* date format is also acceptable and can be abbreviated to *YYYYMM* or *YYYY*.

The *HH* and *HH:MM* time formats are acceptable. Times can also be specified without the colon, so *HHMMSS* or *HHMM* are usable.

 Be aware that *HHMM* may be misinterpreted as *YYYY*. Get into the habit of using separators.

In strict ISO 8601 format, a *T* is required between the date and the time, but CVS understands this format with or without the *T*. The ISO 8601 standard also states that a *Z* at the end of the string designates UTC (Universal Coordinated Time), but CVS does not recognize the use of *Z*.

RFC 822 and RFC 1123

RFCs 822 and 1123 define a precise time format:

```
[DDD ,] DD MMM YYYY HH:MM[:SS] ZZZ
```

These are the terms in the format:

DDD
    A three-letter day of the week

DD
    A two-digit date of the month

MMM
    A three-letter month

YYYY
    The year (it must be a four-digit year)

HH
    Hours

MM
    Minutes

SS

Seconds

ZZZ

The time zone (can be the text abbreviation, a military time zone, or an offset from UTC in hours and minutes)

Legal Date Keywords

CVS also allows short English phrases such as "last Wednesday" and "a month ago" to be used in placed of actual dates. Case is not significant, and CVS can understand plurals. These are the keywords it understands:

Month names

January, February, March, April, May, June, July, August, September, October, November, and *December*

Month abbreviations

Jan, Feb, Mar, Apr, Jun, Jul, Aug, Sep, Sept, Oct, Nov, and *Dec*

Days of the week

Sunday, Monday, Tuesday, Wednesday, Thursday, Friday, and *Saturday*

Day abbreviations

Sun, Mon, Tue, Tues, Wed, Wednes, Thu, Thur, Thurs, Fri, and *Sat*

Units of time

year, month, fortnight, week, day, hour, minute, min, second, and *sec*

Relative times

tomorrow, yesterday, today, and *now*

Meridian qualifiers

am, pm, a.m., and *p.m.*

Modifiers

a, last, this, next, and *ago*

Sequences

first, third, fourth, fifth, sixth, seventh, eighth, ninth, tenth, eleventh, and *twelfth* (*second* can't be used as a sequence term, because it is used as a time unit)

Time Zones

CVS understands time zones expressed in offsets from UTC, such as *+0700* (7 hours ahead) and *-1130* (11 hours, 30 minutes behind). The format for these time zones is *+HHMM* or *-HHMM*, where + means ahead of UTC and - means behind UTC. CVS also understands time-zone abbreviations such as EST and ignores case and punctuation when interpreting them, but it is not recommended that you use them, as they can be ambiguous.

One source of information on time zones is at *http://www.timeanddate.com/library/ abbreviations/timezones/*.

Environment Variables

Several environment variables affect CVS. Some are used only when CVS is the client, and some are used only when CVS is the server. In *local* or *fork* modes, both sets are used.

Client Environment Variables

The environment variables in the following list are read and used by the process that runs on the client computer and must be in the calling user's environment:

COMSPEC
> OS/2 only. This variable sets the command interpreter and defaults to *CMD.EXE*.

CVS_CLIENT_LOG
> Used for debugging CVS in client/server mode. If set, everything sent to the server is stored in the *CVS_CLIENT_LOG.in* file, and everything received by the client is stored in *CVS_CLIENT_LOG.out*.

CVS_CLIENT_PORT
> Used to set the port the client uses to connect to the CVS server in *kserver*, *gserver*, and *pserver* modes. By default, the client uses port 2401 (*gserver* and *pserver*) or port 1999 (*kserver*) to connect to the server.

CVSIGNORE
> A whitespace-separated list of filename patterns that should be ignored. See "The cvsignore File," earlier in this chapter.

CVS_IGNORE_REMOTE_ROOT
> Obsolete since CVS 1.10. When set, it prevented CVS from overwriting the *CVS/ Root* file if the *-d repository_path* option was set. CVS no longer overwrites the file.

CVSEDITOR or *EDITOR* or *VISUAL*
> Used to set the editor CVS calls when it opens an editor for log messages. On Unix and Linux systems, the default editor is *vi*. *CVSEDITOR* is preferred over *EDITOR* and *VISUAL*, because other variables may be used by other programs.

CVS_PASSFILE
> Used to change the file CVS uses to store and retrieve the password in *pserver* remote-access mode. The default file is *HOME/.cvspass*.

CVS_PROXY_PORT
> Used to define the port used in client-server mode, if working through a web proxy. This works with the GSSAPI or pserver connection methods.

CVS_RCMD_PORT

Not currently in use. It used to be set to the port number for the server's *rcmd* (remote command) daemon if the port was nonstandard.

CVSREAD

If set to *1*, CVS tries to check out your sandbox in read-only mode. (CVS actually checks whether this variable is nonnull, so it works regardless of the setting. This behavior may change in the future.)

CVSREADONLYFS

Enables CVS to work with limited functionality on read-only filesystems. Identical to the *-R* CVS option. (CVS 1.12.1 and later.)

CVSROOT

Contains the full pathname of the CVS repository, as described in Chapter 3. When you're working in a sandbox, this variable is not needed. If you're working outside a sandbox, either this variable must be present or the *-d repository_ path* option must be used.

CVS_RSH

Used to set the program CVS calls to connect to a remote repository in *ext* mode. The default program is *rsh*.

CVS_SERVER

If connecting to a CVS server using *rsh*, this variable is used to determine which program is started on the server side. In *ext* and *server* modes, this defaults to *cvs*. In fork mode, this defaults to the path to the CVS client program.

CVSWRAPPERS

May contain one *wrapper* but no more than one, as explained in Chapter 3.

HOME or *HOMEPATH* or *HOMEDRIVE*

Used to determine where the user's home directory is, to enable CVS to locate its files. On Unix, Linux, and related systems, only *HOME* is used. On Windows systems, *HOMEDRIVE* and *HOMEPATH* are used. Some Windows operating systems (Windows NT, 2000, and XP) set these variables automatically. If yours doesn't, *HOMEDRIVE* should be set to the drive letter (e.g., *C:*) and *HOMEPATH* should be set to the path (e.g., *\home\jenn*).

PATH

Used to locate any programs whose path is not compiled with the CVS program. This variable is still used, but it is less important now that the *rcs*, *diff*, and *patch* programs CVS uses are all distributed with CVS.

RCSBIN

Obsolete in CVS 1.9.20 and later. It was used for the path to the external *rcs* executable, before *rcs* was added to the CVS distribution.

Server Environment Variables

The following variables are read when CVS is operating as the server (or in local or fork modes). They must be in the calling user's environment on the server computer.

CVS_PID

Contains the process ID of the current CVS process.

CVS_SERVER_SLEEP

Used only when debugging the server in client/server mode. This variable delays the start of the server client process by *CVS_SERVER_SLEEP* seconds to allow the debugger to be attached to it.

CVSUMASK

Used to set the default permissions of files in the repository. See Chapter 6 for information on securing your projects.

This variable may be added to the client code in a later version of CVS.

PATH

Used to locate any programs whose path is not compiled with the CVS program. This variable is still used, but it is less important now that the *rcs*, *diff*, and *patch* programs CVS uses are all distributed with CVS.

TMPDIR

Sets the temporary directory CVS stores data in. This variable defaults to */tmp*.

CVS creates temporary files with *mkstemp* (BSD 4.3), if possible. If *mkstemp* is not available when CVS is compiled, it tries *tempnam* (SVID 3), *mktemp* (BSD 4.3), or *tmpnam* (POSIX), in that order. If it uses *tmpnam*, it cannot use the *TMPDIR* environment variable, and files are created in */tmp*.

Keywords and Keyword Modes

CVS contains keywords that can be included in nonbinary project files. When CVS finds a keyword in a file that it is checking out, it expands the keyword to provide metadata about the latest revision of the file. You can set keyword-expansion modes on a file to tell CVS whether (and how) to expand the keywords it finds.

Keyword-expansion modes also control line-ending conversion. Unix, Macintosh, and Windows operating systems use different sets of codes to signal the ends of lines. (Linux uses the same codes as Unix.) When you commit a file from an operating system that doesn't use Unix line endings, CVS converts the line endings to Unix style. If you are storing binary files, this conversion can corrupt the file. Use the *-kb* keyword-expansion mode to tell CVS not to convert line endings.

CVS keywords take the form:

```
$Keyword$
```

All keywords except *Log* expand to the format:

```
$Keyword: value$
```

In addition to the keywords shown here, you can configure your own keywords using the *LocalKeyword* configuration option. These are the keywords and the information they show about the file they are in:

Author

The username of the user who committed the last revision.

CVSHeader

Similar to the *Header* keyword, this contains the pathname relative to the repository root directory, rather than the full pathname. Otherwise, it has the same information as the *Header* keyword.

This is new as of version 1.12.2. If it conflicts with existing information in your files, you can exclude it using the *KeywordExpand* configuration option.

Date

The date on which the last revision was committed, in UTC.

Header

A header containing information about the file, including the author, date and revision number, path and filename of the RCS file (project file in the repository), file status, and whether the file is locked. See Chapter 5 for information about file locking.

Id

A header like the one given by the *Header* keyword, without the path of the RCS file.

Name

The tag name the file was checked out with. This keyword can display a branch or provide a more meaningful identification of a revision than the revision number alone. See Chapter 4 for more information about tags and branches.

Locker

The username of the user who locked the file with *cvs admin -l* (empty if the file is not locked).

Log

The commit messages, dates, and authors for the file. This keyword instructs CVS to store this information in the file itself. Any characters that prefix the keyword are also used to prefix log lines; this enables comment markers to be included automatically. Unlike most keywords, existing log expansions are not overwritten with the new ones; the new log expansions are merely prepended to the list.

The *cvs log* command displays all the information that the *Log* keyword provides.

The *Log* keyword is best used at the end of a file, to avoid users having to go through all the log messages to get to the important parts of the file.

The log created by the *Log* keyword does not merge neatly when CVS merges a branch back to the trunk. If your file is likely to be branched and remerged, it is better to use the *cvs log* command than to store a log within the file.

Note that several configuration options affect the processing of the Log keyword.

RCSfile
: The name of the RCS file (the project file in the repository).

Revision
: The CVS internal revision number of the file. This number is specific to the individual file and does not identify a stage within the project.

Source
: The name and path of the RCS file (the project file in the repository).

State
: The current state assigned to the current revision, set with *cvs admin -s*. See Chapter 7.

The keyword-expansion modes in the following list are used in commands and CVS wrappers to control keyword expansion and line-ending conversion. The syntax differs slightly for each use. In commands, you use the mode without a space between the option and the mode (*-kb*). In wrappers, you need a space and may need to quote (*-k 'b'*).

b
: Inhibit keyword expansion and line-ending conversion. Use this keyword-expansion mode to signal that a file is binary.

    CVS can convert line endings from the form appropriate to the server to the form appropriate to the client. This causes obvious problems when working with binary files.

k
: Generate only a keyword name, not a name and value. Use this option when merging different (nonbinary) versions of a file, to prevent keyword substitution from creating spurious merge errors. This option can corrupt binary files.

o
: Generate the version of a keyword string that was present just before the current file was last committed, rather than generating a version with the modifications of the last commit. This option is similar to *-kb*, but with line-ending conversion.

v
: Generate only the value of a keyword, rather than the name and value. This is most useful with *cvs export*, but do not use it for binary files. Once any keyword is removed from a file, further expansions are not possible unless the word is replaced.

kv

Generate the name and value of a keyword. This is the default mode.

kvl

Generate the name and value of a keyword and add the name of the locking user if the revision is locked with *cvs admin -l.*

Pattern Matching

CVS uses two different forms of pattern matching, depending on which aspect of CVS is attempting to match the pattern. Most CVS functions use *sh*-style wildcards, but the scripting files in the *CVSROOT* directory use regular expressions.

This section is not a comprehensive study of regular expressions or wildcards. For a more complete discussion of regular expressions, I recommend *Mastering Regular Expressions*, by Jeffrey E.F. Friedl (O'Reilly).

Wildcards

Wildcards are used by most CVS functions, including wrappers and ignore files. The wildcards are evaluated by a version of the *fnmatch* standard function library distributed with CVS.

The wildcards are *sh*-style, and the symbols used in CVS include:

?   Matches any single character.

\   Escapes the special symbols, so they can be used as literals.

*   Matches any string, including the empty string.

[ ]

Matches any one of the enclosed characters. Within the brackets, the following symbols are used:

! or ^

If either of these characters is the first character after the open bracket, the brackets match anything that is not included in the brackets.

char1-char2

Denotes the range of characters between *char1* and *char2*.

Regular Expressions

CVS supports regular expressions in the scripting files in the *CVSROOT* directory. In CVS 1.11.5, the scripting files are the only files that support regular expressions; all other files and functions use pattern matching. The scripting files are *commitinfo*, *editinfo*, *loginfo*, *rcsinfo*, *taginfo*, and *verifymsg*.

CVS regular expressions are based on the GNU Emacs regular expression syntax, but they do not implement all of the Emacs operators. The regular expressions are parsed by a version of the *regex* standard function library distributed with CVS.

The CVS regular-expression operators include:

^   Matches the beginning of a line. Use *^foo* to match *foo* at the beginning of a line.

$ Matches the end of a line. Use *foo$* to match *foo* at the end of a line.

.   Matches any single character, except a newline character. The expression *foo.bar* matches *foosbar* and *foo:bar*, but not *foodiebar*.

*   Repeats the previous element zero or more times. The expression *fo*bar* matches *fobar*, *foobar*, *fooobar*, and any other string in that pattern.

    The pattern matcher tries to match the longest string possible. If the next part of the expression fails to match, the pattern matcher rolls back one character at a time in an attempt to match the string. If it is parsing the regular expression *fo*obar* against the string *fooobar*, it initially matches the expression *fo** against *fooo*. It then rolls back to match *fo** against *foo*, thus freeing the *obar* in the string to match the *obar* in the expression.

+   Repeat the previous element one or more times. This operator is similar to the * operator and is processed the same way.

?   Repeat the previous element zero times or one time. The expression *fo?bar* matches *fobar* or *foobar*, but nothing else.

\   Escape the next character (\^ is a literal caret). Also used as part of some operators.

\| The OR operator. Match the element on the left or the element on the right to the end of the string, enclosing parenthesis, or another OR operator.

+? or *? or ??
    The same as the +, *, and ? operators, except that they attempt to match the shortest string possible rather than the longest.

[...]
    A character set. Any of the characters in the character set can be matched. The *[fba]* character set matches any one (and only one) of *f*, *b*, or *a*. With the * operator, the expression *[fba]** matches any sequences composed of zero or more *f*, *b*, or *a* characters.

    The only special characters or operators inside a character set are -,], and ^. To include a] in a character set, use it as the first character. To include a -, use it as the last character or just after a range. To use a ^, use it anywhere except as the first character.

    A character range can be specified inside a character set. Create a range by using a hyphen between the start and end of the range. *a–z* and *0–9* are common ranges. Note that the behavior of a mixed-case range such as *A–z* is undefined; use *[a–zA–Z]* instead.

[^...]

A complemented character set. This operator matches everything except the characters or ranges inside the set.

A] or - that immediately follows the ^ is treated as the literal character.

\(...\)

Group expressions together so that an operation works on the set. The expression *ba\(na\)+* matches *bana*, *banana*, *bananana*, and similar sequences.

Repository Access Methods

CVS provides a variety of ways to access the repository. These methods are briefly described in the following sections, and Chapter 8 explains them in more detail.

Client Side

On the client side, you specify the access method as part of the repository path. If you don't declare one of the following methods, CVS assumes either the *local* or *ext* method:

local

Connect to a repository on the same computer as the sandbox, but do not use client/server mode.

ext

Connect with an externally defined *rsh* or *rsh*-like connection method (such as *ssh*). If you use anything other than *rsh*, the *CVS_RSH* environment variable must be set on the client computer.

In CVS 1.11.22 and later, *extssh* is an alias for *ext*.

fork

Connect to a repository on the same computer as the sandbox as if it were a remote machine. This method is useful if you are trying to diagnose problems with client/server mode.

gserver

Connect to the repository using the GSS-API and Kerberos 5.

kserver

Connect to the repository using Kerberos 4.

local

Connect to a repository on the same computer as the sandbox, but do not use client/server mode.

pserver

Connect to the repository using CVS's internal password server.

server

Connect to the repository using CVS's internal *rsh* server (not always available).

Server Side

The *kserver*, *gserver*, and *pserver* access modes require a server to run on the repository computer. For these modes, the server is started with *inetd* or *xinetd*. The *inetd* configuration must be on one line and should call CVS with the *--allow-root* and *-f* options and the *pserver* or *kserver* command.

The parameter to the *--allow-root* option is the path to the repository root directory. If you intend to have several repository root directories, add more *--allow-root* options.

If your version of *inetd* doesn't allow you to use port numbers in *inetd.conf*, add appropriate lines to */etc/services* and use those service names instead of the port number in *inetd.conf*.

These are the two commands the server can use:

kserver

Accept Kerberos 4 connections.

pserver

Accept *pserver* (password server) and *gserver* (GSS-API) connections.

PAM Support

In CVS 1.12.2, experimental PAM support was added. I strongly recommend reading the official documentation for your current version of CVS. The information provided here is accurate as of CVS 1.12.13.

PAM, as mentioned earlier in the book, stands for Pluggable Authentication Modules, and I think modular authentication is the neatest thing to happen to security since the shadow password file. I'm very enthusiastic about this being added to CVS, as it puts security in the hands of the system administrator. However, until standards have been established for the CVS use of PAM, please be very careful with it. Don't use it yet if your project requires rigorous security.

Unfortunately, PAM is currently available only with the *pserver* access method, and the authentication tokens are transmitted with only trivial encryption, and stored on the client machine also with trivial encryption.

For more detail on the current implementation of PAM in CVS, see Chapter 8. I have an introductory essay on PAM at the O'Reilly web site, at *http://www.linuxdevcenter.com/pub/a/linux/2001/09/27/pamintro.html*.

## PART V

Appendixes

The following appendixes contain brief information on, and pointers to, various third-party tools that work with CVS, and also answers some common questions:

Appendix A, *Clients and Operating Systems*

This appendix discusses third-party CVS clients for Windows, Unix, GNU/Linux, and Macintosh operating systems. It also discusses the tools that integrate CVS with programmers' integrated development environments (IDEs).

Appendix B, *Administrators' Tools*

Because CVS is a useful open source tool, people have written third-party tools for it. This appendix explains some of the useful third-party tools available for CVS.

Appendix C, *Frequently Asked Questions*

The info-cvs mailing list is a good way to learn what problems people have with CVS. This appendix contains the most common questions about CVS from that mailing list, and their answers.

Clients and Operating Systems

Some people like using the command line during development; others prefer graphical interfaces. Graphical user interfaces (GUIs) also use colors and shapes to make output clearer or make the sandbox easier to work with.

Graphical CVS interfaces are available for Windows, Macintosh, Unix, and Linux systems, and there are also two Java graphical interfaces that run on any operating system with a Java Runtime Environment. These GUIs were written by third-party developers and do not come with CVS.

Third-party developers have also written tools to provide an interface between CVS and several of the common integrated development environments (IDEs). These interfaces are most useful to programmers and are available for Microsoft Visual Studio, MetroWerks CodeWarrior, NetBeans, GNU Emacs, and anything that uses the SCC-API (Common Source Code Control Application Programming Interface). IDEs that support the SCC-API include Macromedia ColdFusion, Sybase PowerBuilder, and Microsoft Visual Studio.

CVS is designed for the Unix and Linux operating systems, and it relies on the features of those operating systems. It can behave in unexpected ways when used from a different operating system. The most obvious problem is that Windows operating systems use a different character for line endings than Unix-based systems do. CVS corrects for that particular problem, but other problems are explained in this appendix.

Multi-Operating-System Clients

If your development team is not familiar with CVS, you may want to ensure that everyone is using the same CVS client. This step helps minimize support problems; if someone has a problem, his fellow developers are familiar with the tools he's using and can offer helpful advice.

The clients described in this section look and operate the same across several different environments. The first three represent a set of clients that are designed for all three major operating systems—Unix/Linux, Macintosh, and Windows—and work from the same base code. The other GUI clients are Java clients that work on any operating system with a Java Runtime Environment, and a client called Concurrent Versions Librarian.

gCVS, WinCVS, and MacCVS

Three GUI clients—gCVS, MacCVS, and WinCVS—represent a set of clients available from the same development team that work identically across Unix/Linux, Macintosh, and Windows operating systems. The clients are detailed and implement most of the functions available from the CVS command line. Using these clients, you can create a new repository, tag files, create watches, and report on the differences between files. These clients are available from *http://www.wincvs.org* and *http://cvsgui.sourceforge.net*.

gCVS is for Linux and Unix (including Mac OS X), WinCVS is for Windows, and MacCVS is for Macintosh (both pre-OS X and post-OS X versions exist). Because their interfaces are so similar, these clients are good for groups that develop software across different operating systems.

These clients are laid out with three main windows, as shown in Figure A-1 (gCVS) and Figure A-2 (WinCVS). The leftmost window contains a directory tree, the base directory of which is configurable. The upper-right window shows the contents of the current directory, and the lower-right window shows the output of the CVS commands that you execute using the GUI.

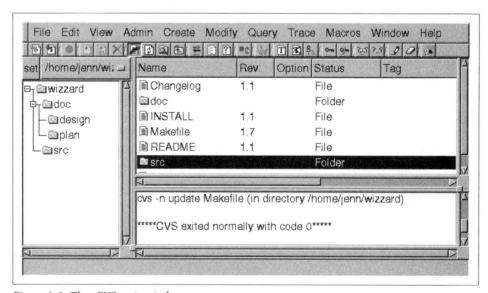

Figure A-1. The gCVS main window

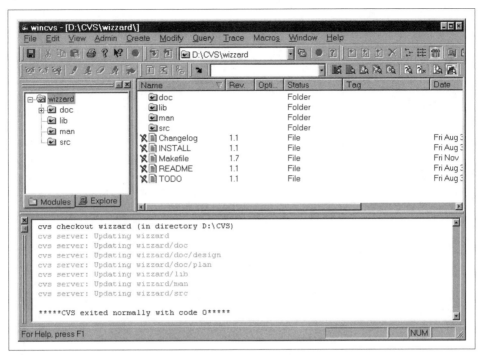

Figure A-2. The WinCVS main window

Using these GUI clients, you execute CVS commands by choosing a menu option and then filling out some fields in a dialog. The output of most commands is displayed in the lower-right window. This display can be irritating if the output from a given command is particularly large or complex to read. Fortunately, you can resize the output window to accommodate large and complex output. If you need to use options that are not available in the menus and dialogs, you can run command-line commands in these clients using the Command Line option in the Admin menu.

Figure A-3 shows a sandbox open in MacCVS.

In Chapter 2, I recommended gCVS, WinCVS, and MacCVS as CVS clients for a development team because they are popular and have a common interface. Installation is similar for all CVS clients on the same operating system, so I've chosen these three to give an example for each operating system.

Installing gCVS

gCVS is a Linux and Unix client available from *http://www.wincvs.org* and *http://cvsgui.sourceforge.net*. You can install it from source, or you can use a package manager. To use a package manager, follow the procedures given in the section "Installing CVS" in Chapter 2.

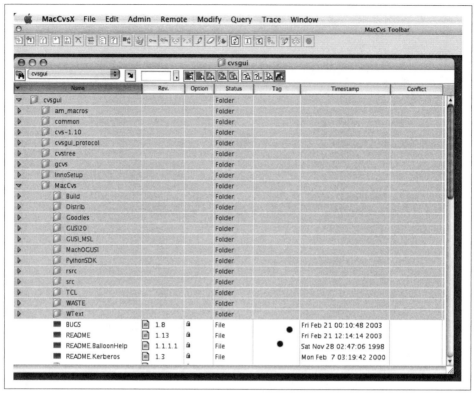

Figure A-3. MacCVS

To install CVS from source, read the detailed instructions in the section "Installing CVS" in Chapter 2. The procedure for installing gCVS is similar to the procedure for installing CVS, though some of the commands differ slightly:

1. Decompress and expand the *.tar.gz* file using *tar -zxf filename*.

2. Read the *INSTALL* file in the top directory of the source tree. If the instructions in the *INSTALL* file differ from the instructions here, use the instructions in the *INSTALL* file.

3. Check whether the *gtk* development libraries are available. gCVS needs to link to these libraries when it compiles. They are available from *http://www.gtk.org*.

4. Change directories into the top directory of the source tree.

5. Run *./make-configure --prefix=directory*, where *directory* is the location into which you want to install gCVS.

6. Run *make*.

7. Change user to *root*, then run *make install*.

8. Add the installation directory to the path for your gCVS users.

9. Run gCVS with the *gcvs* command.

Whether you install gCVS as a package or from source, you may also need to install or configure SSH or Kerberos. If you intend to use SSH and have not used it before, you need to generate keys. If you are currently using SSH, you should already have keys. As an SSH client is often installed by default in Unix and Linux systems, you may only need to configure it.

Installing WinCVS

WinCVS requires Python. If you intend to connect with SSH, it requires you to install SSH as well. These instructions assume that you will run WinCVS with SSH. Older versions of WinCVS used Cygwin instead of Python.

1. Install Python 2.1 or later from *http://www.python.org*.

2. Install an SSH client such as Putty. Putty is available at *http://www.chiark.greenend.org.uk/~sgtatham/putty/*. Ensure that you get the *plink* program as well as the basic Putty.

3. Use the key-generation program for your SSH client. Store both private and public keys in files. If the key generator gives you a public key to cut and paste, use Notepad or another text editor to store the key in a file. Generate an *ssh1* or *ssh2* key, depending on your server's SSH protocol.

4. Put a copy of the public key on the server, in your *~/.ssh/authorizedkeys* file or whichever file your server's SSH program expects public keys to be in.

5. If your SSH client runs a key agent, use it. Putty runs Pageant, which has an icon in the system tray. Add your private key to the key agent; to do this in Pageant, right-click on the icon and select View Keys, then Add Key.

6. Download WinCVS from *http://www.wincvs.org*.

7. Extract WinCVS using the extractor provided; it's distributed in a self-extracting archive.

8. Run *setup.exe*.

9. Run WinCVS.

10. Set *ssh* as the connection method. Use the following procedure:

    a. Select Preferences from the Admin menu.

    b. Open the General tab. Set the authentication option to *ssh*.

    c. Open the Settings button, and then fill in the path to your SSH client. For Putty, the executable is *plink.exe*. Also set any options necessary for your SSH client. If you are using Putty, set the *-ssh* option.

Installing MacCVS

MacCVS is distributed as a compressed image and needs to be opened with StuffIt, which is available for both OS X and pre-OS X systems. Most Macintosh systems have StuffIt installed; if yours doesn't, you can get StuffIt Expander (the free version) from *http://www.stuffit.com/mac/index.html*. Once you've downloaded the compressed archive, just double-click it to open and install the program. That's it! You're done with the installation. To run MacCVS, open the MacCVS icon from the directory in which you installed it.

MacCVS and clients written for Macintosh systems older than OS X do not support SSH through the usual access method, where the repository path is *:ext:hostname:/path* and the *CVS_RSH* environment variable is used. To work around this limitation, install an SSH client that supports port tunneling and use an SSH tunnel to connect to the CVS repository securely. Choose an alternate access method such as *pserver* or *kserver* and configure MacCVS to connect to the *localhost* on the port at the local end of the tunnel.

If you have OS X and want SSH support, try using the OS X-specific client, or use a Unix or Linux client.

CVL

CVL (Concurrent Versions Librarian) is an open source GUI frontend to CVS, available for Mac OS X and systems in the OPENSTEP family. It supports many commonly used CVS commands and multiple repositories, and it integrates with FileMerge (shipped with Mac OS X Developer Tools) to resolve merges and conflicts.

The Concurrent Versions Librarian is available from *http://sente.epfl.ch/software/cvl/*. Figure A-4 shows a CVL sandbox.

CrossVC

CrossVC, formerly LinCVS, is available from *http://www.lincvs.org*. It supports Linux/Unix, Mac OS X, and Windows environments. On Linux/Unix, it requires the QT toolkit, but it runs in most graphic environments.

Start using CrossVC by selecting the "Add to workbench" option under the Projects menu and choosing a top-level directory above at least one of your sandboxes. CrossVC searches the directory and determines which files are controlled by CVS. It then adds those files to the *workbench*, which is a directory tree in the left window. The workbench is updated automatically on a periodic basis with a configurable timeout. You can add multiple directories to your workbench.

jCVS

jCVS is a Java-based CVS client (available from *http://www.jcvs.org*) that is useful for development teams who need to work over a variety of operating systems. The tabs in the main window (shown in Figure A-5) control project administration, and the menus in the project window control the commands for the files.

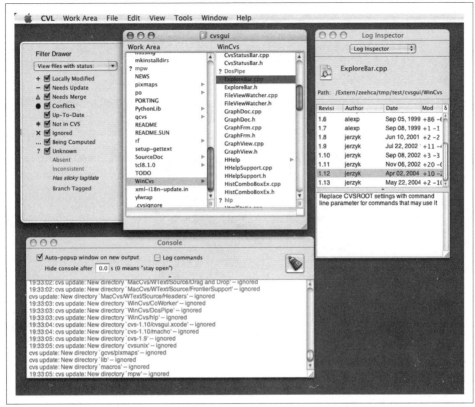

Figure A-4. Concurrent Versions Librarian

The project window displays the files' hierarchy and the status of each file currently in the sandbox. Output from *log*, *diff*, and other commands is shown in a separate window.

SmartCVS

SmartCVS is a Java-based client that runs on any operating system with a Java Runtime Environment. SmartCVS is available from *http://www.syntevo.com*.

There are two versions of SmartCVS: a free version and a professional version. Both implement the basic CVS commands and connections with both *pserver* and SSH. The professional version supports the *watch* suite of commands, and has extended conflict resolution and file comparison tools.

The main window has three parts: the folder hierarchy to the left, the files in the current sandbox in the right window, and CVS command output in the bottom window. SmartCVS provides side-by-side, color-coded displays of the differences between revisions, and a log display that includes graphical representation of branches.

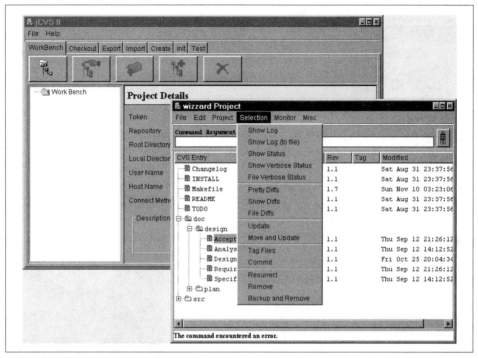

Figure A-5. The jCVS main window

Figure A-6 shows the SmartCVS main window in the background and the graphical log display in the foreground. The log display shows a branched file.

Macintosh Clients

There are three clients available specifically for the Macintosh operating system: MacCVS (described earlier in "Multi-Operating-System Clients"), MacCVSClient, and MacCVS Pro.

If you are running Mac OS 9 or earlier, be aware of two issues:

- The Macintosh CVS clients for OS 9 and earlier don't have built-in SSH support. You can use SSH by following the tunnel workaround in "Installing MacCVS."

- CVS clients in Mac OS 9 and earlier may have line-ending issues, as described in "Windows Clients," later in this chapter.

OS X does not have either of these problems, as it has a built-in SSH client and both OS X and CVS use Unix-style line endings.

 If you are running Mac OS X, in addition to using the Macintosh-specific clients that are mentioned in this chapter, you can use the CVS command-line client, as well as the Unix and Linux graphical clients.

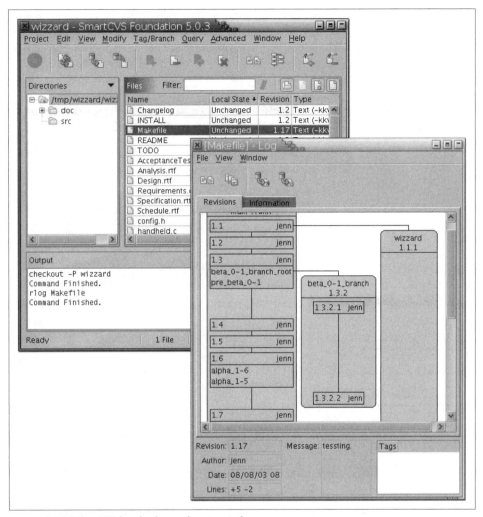

Figure A-6. SmartCVS log display and main window

MacCVSClient

MacCVSClient is available for OS X and earlier versions from *http://www.heilancoo.net/ MacCVSClient/*.

The main display of MacCVSClient is a modules window, which provides a hierarchical list of files that includes status information. Output from commands such as *diff* or *log* is stored and can be retrieved from this window later in the session, as well as immediately after you run a command. If you switch to another application, then return, MacCVSClient attempts to refresh the cached states and modification times of any open folders.

MacCVSClient for Mac OS X supports SSH. MacCVSClient for earlier versions supports the *pserver* and *ext* (*rsh*-only) repository-access methods. You can configure the repository path in the Preferences dialog from the Edit menu, shown in Figure A-7. Conflicts and the results of the *diff* command are color-coded to improve readability.

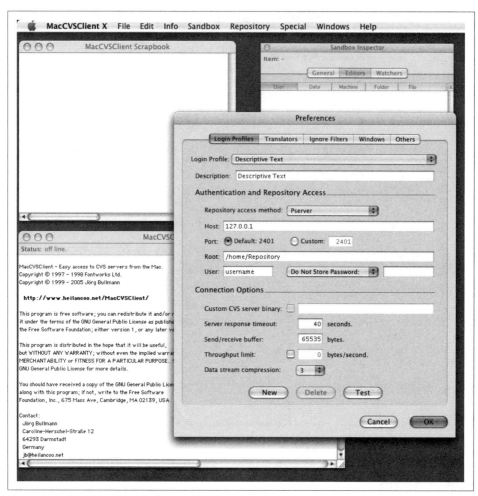

Figure A-7. MacCVSClient Preferences dialog

MacCVS Pro

MacCVS Pro is a graphical client for the Macintosh, available at *http://www.maccvs.org*. It has versions for OS X, OS 9, and earlier.

MacCVS Pro supports the Kerberos, *pserver,* and *ext* (*rsh*-only) access methods. The main display is a session window, which contains a hierarchical list of available folders and files. Files are shown with status information. Output from commands such as *log* and *diff* is displayed in a separate window. *diff* output is color-coded.

MacCVS Pro is fully multithreaded, enabling you to run several commands simultaneously. Commands that take time, such as *update* and *commit*, have a progress bar. A *find lurkers* command is a useful tool for locating files that have been left uncommitted.

Figure A-8 shows the MacCVS Pro Preferences dialog in the foreground and the main display window in the background.

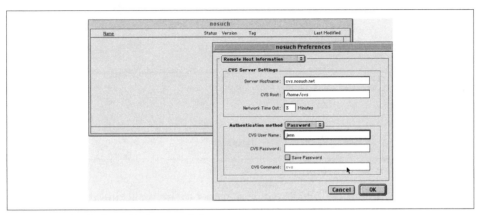

Figure A-8. MacCVS Pro Preferences dialog

Unix and Linux Clients

CVS is native to the Unix and Linux operating systems; consequently, there are no line-ending or capitalization issues. The standard, command-line client is intended for use with Unix and Linux, but there is also a wide variety of graphical CVS clients available for Unix and Linux systems.

Cervisia

Cervisia is available from *http://cervisia.kde.org*. It requires the QT and KDE libraries, but it runs on Gnome and other graphical environments if the QT and KDE libraries are available.

Cervisia provides a configurable list of frequently used CVS repositories, and configurable key bindings for common commands. Cervisia supports the *commit, import,* and *update* commands, as well as the tagging and watching sets of commands. One particularly useful setting is the option to run *cvs edit* automatically, in order to notify other developers when you intend to edit a file.

Cervisia has two main sections in its display screen, shown in Figure A-9. The upper section lists files and directories, and the lower section displays the output of the CVS commands that Cervisia executes for you. Right-click on a file in the upper section to open a menu with options to open the file in an editor, commit a changed file, add a file, remove a file, or run a *diff* over two revisions of a file.

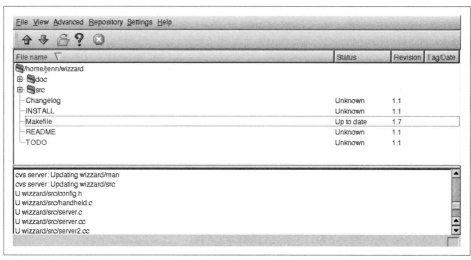

Figure A-9. The Cervisia CVS client

The Resolve menu option, which you can access by right-clicking the mouse, supports automatic conflict resolution. When you invoke automatic conflict resolution, Cervisia displays both files, as well as the merged version of the two files. Cervisia then allows you to choose from several methods for handling any conflicts that resulted from the merge.

Pharmacy

Pharmacy is available from *http://pharmacy.sourceforge.net*. It requires the Gnome libraries but runs in almost any graphic environment.

The upper-left window is a directory tree that supports multiple repositories. The upper-right window displays files. The lower window is a console that also provides other tools. The console is a full command-line system, and it also displays command output. Figure A-10 shows the Pharmacy windows.

tkCVS

tkCVS is available from *http://www.twobarleycorns.net/tkcvs.html*. It requires the Tcl/Tk libraries and works in most graphic environments.

tkCVS provides most CVS commands. It opens in your home directory and displays files and directories in the main window, with the last modification date to the right if a file or directory is not part of a sandbox. When the current working directory is a

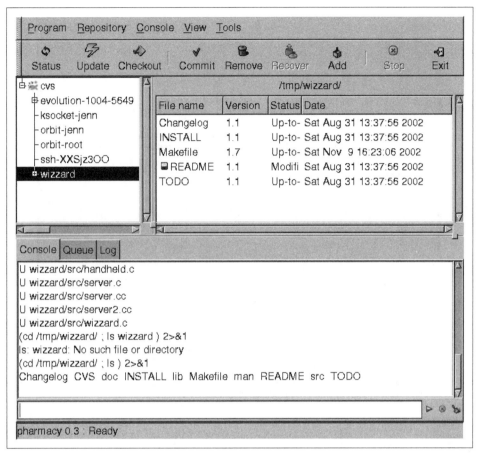

Figure A-10. The Pharmacy CVS client

sandbox, the date, status, revision, and editors are displayed to the right of the file-names. Sandbox directories have a red "CVS" label on their folders.

Double-clicking on a filename opens an editor, as does selecting the file and clicking the Edit button. Double-clicking on a directory moves you into that directory. Clicking the "go up" button takes you back to the parent directory.

Commands are available from buttons at the bottom of the window or menus in the menu bar at the top. Some commands display a dialog and have additional options within the dialog.The results of a *diff* command are displayed side-by-side in a dialog window. *diff, annotate,* and *log* dialogs are searchable, and the color-coded annotation screen is helpful. Figure A-11 shows the tkCVS main window.

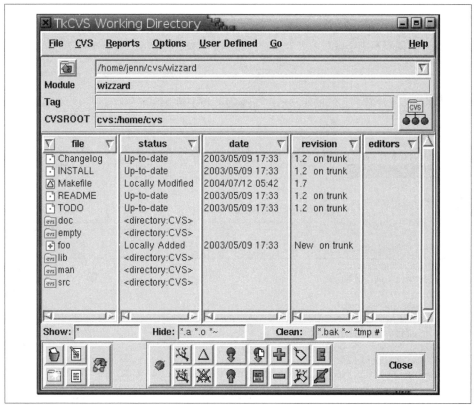

Figure A-11. The tkCVS main window

Windows Clients

There are two graphical CVS clients available specifically for Windows. One is WinCVS, which is described in "Multi-Operating-System Clients" earlier in this chapter. The other is TortoiseCVS, which modifies the way Windows Explorer presents files.

Following are some issues you might encounter when using CVS from Windows. These issues apply equally to WinCVS and TortoiseCVS.

Line endings differ between Windows and Unix

CVS automatically attempts to convert the line endings of text files to Unix format. This feature is helpful in text files, but it causes problems in binary files that are committed accidentally as text files. When a binary file is corrupted because CVS tried to "fix" the line endings, often you can recover with the following procedure:

1. Back up the current sandbox copy of the file.

2. Update the file with *cvs update* to bring the repository version into the sandbox and reconvert the line endings.

3. Check the file to ensure that it is no longer corrupt. If it is still corrupt, roll back to the most recent uncorrupted version (hopefully, the backup).

4. Use *cvs admin -kb filename* to convert the default keyword-expansion mode of the file to binary.

5. Recommit the file to the repository with *cvs commit -f*.

SSH may attempt to convert line endings
Because CVS performs its own line-ending conversion, you cannot use an SSH client that converts line endings as the client for CVS.

Filename capitalization matters under Unix
In Unix operating systems, file capitalization matters. *NoSuchFile* and *nosuchfile* are completely different files. If your repository contains two files whose names differ only in case and you are running an operating system that ignores case, the second file to download may overwrite the first when you check out or update a sandbox.

Directory separators are different under Unix and Windows
CVS uses the forward-slash character (/) as the directory separator. In most cases, internal CVS files use a forward slash wherever Windows uses the back-slash character (\). This difference should not cause problems, but it may cause confusion.

Universal time
CVS stores times in UTC (Coordinated Universal Time). This feature may also cause confusion, but it should not cause any problems if the time on the client is configured correctly.

File permissions problems
If you are running the repository on a networked filesystem accessed through a Samba server, you may have permissions problems if you are using CVS from a Windows system with the local access method. These problems can usually be fixed by enabling *WRITE=YES* in the Samba configuration.

CS-CVS

Component Software's CVS client is free for open source use and proprietary for commercial use. There is a suite of related tools, including a web-based repository browser and an RCS client. The CVS client integrates with Microsoft Word and Microsoft Excel, adding a new menu to the applications' menu bar. Among the features CS-CVS provides are colored *diff* comparisons, reserved checkout support, and a merge editor. CVS-CVS is available from *http://www.componentsoftware.com/ products/cvs/index.htm*.

TortoiseCVS

TortoiseCVS is a simple CVS client for Windows that allows you to manage CVS files from within Windows Explorer (not Internet Explorer). The standard right-click menu for files is expanded to include the CVS commands that apply to a given file. TortoiseCVS is available from *http://www.tortoisecvs.org*.

For files, the menu is changed only in an active sandbox. The right-click menu for folders that are not sandboxes is changed to include a Checkout option and a CVS submenu. You can import a new project with the Make New Module option in the submenu.

TortoiseCVS also works within the standard Windows File → Open dialog.

Figure A-12 shows a Tortoise CVS sandbox directory and the right-click menu for a CVS file.

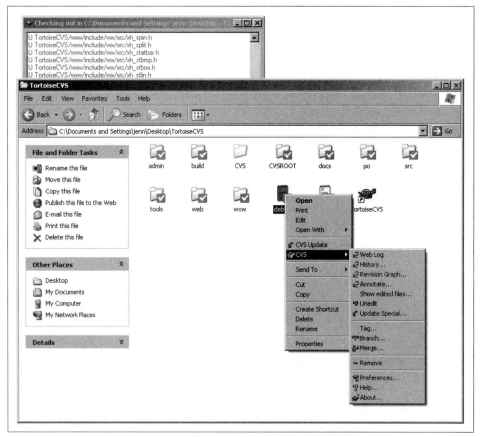

Figure A-12. TortoiseCVS right-click menu

Integration Tools

Developers rarely use CVS in isolation. The tools described in this section coordinate CVS with other programs. Some integrate CVS into IDEs; others are used in separate windows but ensure CVS can manage an IDE's files properly.

abCVS

abCVS is a plugin for CodeWarrior that allows you to use CVS without leaving the CodeWarrior IDE. It requires CodeWarrior and a command-line CVS implementation such as CVSNT (explained in Appendix B). The developers of abCVS also recommend that you have a CVS client such as WinCVS.

abCVS implements the standard suite of necessary CVS commands, along with some of the additional features. Most commands can run on a single file, or they can run recursively down a directory tree. abCVS is available from *http://www.iaanus.com/abCVS/*.

Anjuta

Anjuta is an IDE for the Linux and Unix operating systems that relies on the Gnome libraries. It supports more than a dozen languages (including C/C++, Java, Python, Perl, and ADA) and provides an integrated debugging facility, syntax highlighting, context-sensitive help, and support for *autoconf* and *automake*.

Anjuta provides simple, clean access to CVS commands on files in CVS sandboxes, including an intuitive interface to *cvs diff*. Anjuta is available from *http://anjuta.org*.

BBEdit

BBEdit is an HTML and text editor for the Macintosh that includes an integrated CVS and Subversion client that supports multiple repositories. BBEdit is available from *http://www.barebones.com/products/bbedit.html*.

CVSIn

CVSIn is an add-in for Microsoft Visual Studio that integrates Microsoft Visual Studio and WinCVS. It permits most simple CVS commands to operate directly from Microsoft Visual Studio and relies on WinCVS for more complex CVS commands and commands that operate on directories rather than individual files.

Once CVSIn is installed, new toolbar options are available in Microsoft Visual Studio. Most of the following options operate on the selected file: *update*, *commit*, *diff*, *log*, *status*, *edit*, *watch*, *tag*, and *branch*. There is also an option to launch WinCVS. Output from commands is displayed in a screen at the bottom of the window. CVSIn is available from *http://www.geocities.com/kaczoroj/CvsIn/*.

CWCVS

CWCVS is a plugin for CodeWarrior that allows you to use MacCVS without leaving the CodeWarrior IDE. It is available for the Macintosh and requires CodeWarrior Gold 11 or later, MacCVS, and a CVS repository.

CWCVS is implemented in CodeWarrior as an additional menu and provides most of the CVS functions, though you need to use MacCVS for *checkout* and some of the administrative or advanced functions. CWCVS provides dialogs for the commands that take parameters, and it displays command output in separate windows. CWCVS is available from *http://www.electricfish.com/products/CWCVS/*.

Eclipse

Eclipse is an open source development environment that runs on Windows, Linux, and Unix systems and is designed to support Java developers. It is extensible, and the developers encourage plugin support for other systems and languages. A CVS client is built in, and can be found in the Window and Projects menus. Eclipse is available from *http://wiki.eclipse.org/index.php/Development_Resources*.

Jalindi Igloo

Jalindi Igloo works with any SCC-API-compliant environment and should work with the programs listed at *http://www.jalindi.com/igloo/Compatibility/compatibility.html*. Examples of SCC-API-compliant environments include: Microsoft Visual Studio, Macromedia ColdFusion, and IBM VisualAge for Java.

Igloo provides the usual set of CVS commands and an optional auto-commit mode that automatically commits added or deleted files to the repository and automatically updates files when they are edited in the IDE. Jalindi Igloo is available from *http://www.jalindi.com/igloo/*.

NetBeans

NetBeans is an IDE that includes a built-in CVS client, as well as clients for other version control systems. CVS integration is implemented as a plugin, in which the CVS sandbox is represented within the IDE as a filesystem and the CVS commands are available through a right-click menu. NetBeans also provides a command line to use for more complex CVS tasks.

The NetBeans system (platform and IDE) is open source. NetBeans is available from *http://www.netbeans.org*.

VC

VC is the Emacs version control interface, and it provides a consistent user interface regardless of which version control system is actually recording changes.

VC is part of the Emacs editor. The relevant part of the Emacs manual is at *http://www.gnu.org/software/emacs/manual/html_node/Version-Control.html*. You need to configure VC to use CVS; the instructions for doing so are in the "Customizing VC" section of the Emacs manual.

Vim

Vim is a popular editor for Unix and Linux. The graphical version of Vim offers a choice of scripts that add a CVS menu. The more recent script is *vcscommand.vim*, and is available at *http://vim.sourceforge.net/scripts/script.php?script_id=90*.

It's also worth searching the scripts database for other CVS scripts that integrate with Vim: there are several different scripts for viewing differences between file versions, a CVSNT menu, and a script that logs your CVS commands.

Zeus SCC-CVS

Zeus SCC-CVS uses the SCC-API to connect the Zeus development environment to CVS. It should also work with any editor or development environment that uses the SCC-API.

With Zeus SCC-CVS, all CVS commands are accessed under the Workspace menu, but only a limited number of commands are available within the editor. By default, Zeus SCC-CVS automatically updates the sandbox, retrieving the most current revision from the repository when Zeus is opened. Zeus SCC-CVS is available at *http://www.zeusedit.com/index.html*.

Administrators' Tools

CVS is an open source program, and all the information necessary to interface to it or change it is freely available. It is also a very popular system. The combination of these two factors means that a wide variety of programs and tools have been written for CVS.

The tools in this appendix range from a port of CVS to the Windows family of operating systems, to a small tool to mail log messages automatically. Other programs include several different viewers to display the contents of the repository with an HTTP server and a useful program that implements access-control lists.

CVS Variants

The CVS license allows you to modify the CVS code and distribute the modified code (read the license for the exact requirements). Several variants, described in the following sections, are provided by developers who have produced expansions of CVS for specific purposes.

CVS/MVS

CVS/MVS is a port of CVS for the MVS (Multiple Virtual Storage) mainframe operating system, also known as OS/390 and zOS. CVS/MVS requires MVS with POSIX configured, and the HFS (Heirarchical File System).

CVS/MVS is a port of both the server and the command-line client.

CVS/MVS is available at *http://dccmn.com/cvsmvs/*.

cvs-nserver

cvs-nserver is a rewrite of the CVS network code, to allow support for SSL (Secure Sockets Layer) tunneling and ACLs (Access Control Lists), among other features.

ACLs are available in CVS as an added piece of code (see "cvs_acls" later in this chapter) but are native to *cvs-nserver*. The authentication is also separated out from the main code in *cvs-nserver*, to make security audits easier and to include PAM (Pluggable Authentication Modules) availability in the code. cvs-nserver is available at *http://cvs-nserver.sourceforge.net/*.

CVSNT

CVSNT is an alternative CVS server for Windows (NT, 2000, XP, and 2003), Unix, Linux, OS/400, and Mac OS X. It includes a graphic client as well as the server, and can be used with some of the integration tools described in Appendix A.

As well as running on Windows operating systems, CVSNT provides an additional access method, *sspi*, that authenticates using Windows domain passwords. The company which makes it provides a free open source version, and also provides packages which contain the free code, additional code and documentation, and commercial support. CVSNT is available at *http://www.march-hare.com/cvspro/*.

DCVS

The developers of DCVS wanted to create a CVS with distributed repositories native to the code. They released version 1.0 in November last year (2005), and included the main CVS code and features up to version 1.12.12.

The distribution system makes DCVS special—it relies on change sets, and each change set is maintained on a particular repository. Read operations are performed on the local repository, write operations on the repository responsible for the particular change set. DCVS automatically synchronizes the repositories. DCVS is available from *http://dcvs.elegosoft.com*.

Meta-CVS

Meta-CVS is an expansion of CVS that adds versioning for directories, supports symbolic links and file metadata, automatically sets the keyword-expansion mode for certain file types (such as *.png* files) to binary, and improves the user interface for branching and merging. It also improves the way CVS handles file addition and removal conflicts and changes the way vendor branches are used.

Meta-CVS is a variation of the client code and operates from a standard CVS repository. It changes the data stored in the repository, so you can't have a team on the same project with a mixture of Meta-CVS and standard CVS users. Meta-CVS is available from *http://users.footprints.net/~kaz/mcvs.html*.

OpenCVS

The OpenCVS development team states as its goals to maintain files as compatible as possible to the main CVS development stream, to be as secure as possible, and to improve access control to repository files. OpenCVS is available from *http://www.opencvs.org*.

RISC OS CVS ports

There are two ports of CVS to the RISC OS. These are available from *http://acorn.cybervillage.co.uk/cvs/* and *http://home.student.utwente.nl/m.m.bezemer/cvsuk.html*.

Distribution Tools

Often, you may want to develop a CVS project and publish the files for display or download. You can publish the resulting files with a build script or a script in one of the *CVSROOT* files. Alternatively, you can use one of the tools in this section, all of which display CVS project files.

Some of the tools in this section display the repository; others export files from the repository for publication. Some retrieve the difference between the revision they have and the latest revision in the repository, then patch the revision they have and display the final files.

Chora

Chora provides the ability to view or download the files in a CVS repository using a web browser. It integrates with the other web tools available at *http://www.horde.org*. The CVS integration is stored in a single library, so you can customize the rest of the display.

In file mode, every revision of a file is displayed along with log messages, and you also have the ability to display the differences between revisions. Chora has a nifty branch visualization tool, as well. Chora is available from *http://www.horde.org/chora/*.

CVSup

CVSup is a tool for distributing files across a network. It can be used with most file types and understands CVS project files. If desired, it can use *zlib* compression to reduce network load.

If CVSup is working from CVS files, it distributes the differences rather than the files as a whole, saving bandwidth and minimizing the network load. It also understands tags and distributes specific tagged versions if configured to do so.

Note that in CVS 1.12.1 and later, the environment variable *$CVS_LOCAL_BRANCH_NUM* is available to support local branching. CVSup is available from *http://www.cvsup.org*.

CVSviaFTP

This tool publishes CVS files using FTP. It was developed for web sites that use CVS for content management, but for which the administrator of the server requires that updates be made using the FTP protocol.

CVSviaFTP does not start an FTP session automatically; it needs to be wrapped in a script that manages login and other specifics of your FTP site. However, it is useful when you are managing content across an FTP link. CVSviaFTP is available from *http://www.siber.org/cvs-via-ftp/*.

CVSweb

CVSweb is one of several tools that allow a CVS repository to be accessed using a web browser. It allows only viewing or downloading, not the ability to change files.

CVSweb allows you to view a directory, an individual file, any revision of a file, the difference (as reported by the *diff* command) between the current and previous revisions, or an annotated view of a file. CVSweb is available from *http://www.freebsd.org/projects/cvsweb.html*.

jCVS Web (Formerly jCVS Servlet)

jCVS Web is a configurable Java implementation of the CVS protocol, and comes with several client applications as well as a Java API (application program interface). For Java programmers, it provides access to a CVS repository within Java. For others, it includes a Java-based graphic client, and a CVS repository browser that operates from a web browser. jCVS Web is available from *http://www.jcvs.org*.

SandWeb

SandWeb is one of several tools that allow a CVS repository to be accessed using a web browser. It currently works with CVS, but Subversion support is intended in the future.

SandWeb is more than a viewer; it provides the ability to add, delete, and edit text files, and it commits the changes automatically. In time, it may become an effective HTML client for CVS. SandWeb is available from *http://sandweb.sourceforge.net*.

ViewVC

ViewVC started out as a modification of CVSweb, and is another web-based repository browser. It has since been developed into quite a sophisticated tool, and supports both CVS and Subversion.

ViewCVS requires Python, and can require other programs, depending on what additional features you want (MySQL, GNU enscript, CvsGraph and the Apache HTTP Server at present). ViewCVS is available from *http://www.viewvc.org*.

Wandisco

Wandisco is more than a distribution tool—it's a mirroring tool, a proxying system, and a backup system. It provides the ability to use local repositories as if they were one connected global repository—and one (or more) of those repositories can be designated as a backup. Wandisco is available from *http://www.wandisco.com*.

Logging Tools

CVS log messages often contain useful information for project managers, programmers, and other CVS users. There are many tools that manipulate log messages, including tools to create a change log automatically, mail log messages, and change the format of log messages. These tools are most useful if you and your development team enter meaningful log messages.

CHalogen

CHalogen is a change-log generator that relies on the CVS project files being tagged at each significant stage of the project. It generates a change log that displays the changes between tag points. The generated change log is in HTML format.

CHalogen can run as a CGI script or from the command line. It is available from *http://www.softwarebee.de/products/chalogen/*.

clmerge

clmerge is a script that merges conflicts in a GNU-style change log. The change log is sent to the standard output, so the script output should usually be redirected to a file. This script is useful as a postprocessor to change log generation programs. *clmerge* is available from the *contrib* directory in the CVS source code.

commit_prep and log_accum

These scripts are designed to work together. *commit_prep* ensures that the *Id* keyword is present in the file and checks the version number of the keyword. It prevents older revisions from being copied into the sandbox and replacing an existing revision. It also records information for *log_accum*.

log_accum consolidates the log messages from a single commit of multiple directories and mails the resulting consolidated log messages—including a consolidated list of which files were added, removed, and modified—to a specified address.

These scripts should be called from the scripting files in the *CVSROOT* directory. *commit_prep* and *log_accum* are available from the *contrib* directory in the CVS source code.

cvs2cl.pl

cvs2cl.pl runs *cvs log* and converts the output to a GNU-style change log. Duplicate messages on the same date are merged. *cvs2cl.pl* runs from the command line and can be included in automated scripts. There are many configuration arguments, producing a variety of output formats. *cvs2cl.pl* is available from *http://www.red-bean.com/cvs2cl/*.

cvs-exp

cvs-exp is a *cvs log* postprocessor that creates a chronological logfile across a project. It also displays a tree structure of the branches and tags in a format more easily readable than the one *cvs log*. *cvs-exp* is available from *http://www.cs.rice.edu/~ssiyer/code/cvs-exp/*.

log

This script mails the log information provided with a CVS commit to a specified address. It includes status information for each changed file, as well as the log message and information on which files were changed. The *log* script should be called from the *loginfo* file in the *CVSROOT* directory. *log* is available from the *contrib* directory in the CVS source code.

mfpipe

mfpipe either mails log information to a specified address or pipes the mail information into a file. This script should be called from the *loginfo* file in the *CVSROOT* directory. *mfpipe* is available from the *contrib* directory in the CVS source code.

rcs2log

rcs2log is a script that creates a GNU change log from the RCS project files in the CVS repository. It has a variety of formatting arguments and recurses through the local directories. It was originally written for RCS. *rcs2log* is available from the *contrib* directory in the CVS source code.

Metadata Tools

The tools described in this section provide metadata about the CVS project files or use existing file metadata to provide additional functionality. Using these tools, you can search your log comments or your repository, see a graph showing the rate of file accesses over the past week, or find out who changed which files most recently.

CVS Monitor

CVS Monitor is a specialized CVS client that displays module and file information, graphic summaries of user activity within modules, change logs, file histories, and other information. It runs as a CGI script and presents its output in a web browser. CVS Monitor is available from *http://ali.as/devel/cvsmonitor/*.

CVSPlot

CVSPlot is a Perl script that plots statistics from a CVS project, such as the number of lines of data or the number of files in a module. It generates the results as a text file or as a *.png* graph that models the change over time.

CVSPlot is called from the command line and can be used in a script. It allows you to specify the period of time and the file types you are interested in. It requires Perl, and to plot graphically it also requires *gnuplot*. CVSPlot is available from *http://cvsplot.sourceforge.net*.

CVSSearch

CVSSearch runs keyword searches on the comments stored as a result of file commits, and can do keyword searches in the code as well. Its output includes not only every comment that contains keywords you specify, but also filenames and links to the code that matches the comment.

CVSSearch requires a web server and operates as CGI code. It is available from *http://cvssearch.sourceforge.net*.

CVSTrac

CVSTrac is a combination of repository browser, bug-tracking system, patch-set tracking system, and log manipulator. It can be run as a CGI script, or as a standalone web server, and has several security measures built in, including the ability to have anonymous users with limited permissions. CVSTrac is available from *http://www.cvstrac.org*.

Converters

If you want to use CVS with a project that is currently being stored in a version control system other than CVS, you need to convert the files from the other system to CVS. Fortunately, scripts to do just that are available on the Internet and in the CVS source distribution.

rcs-to-cvs

The *rcs-to-cvs* script checks RCS files in to CVS. It also checks in files that didn't previously have source control. It starts by checking whether the current directory's subdirectories exist in the repository; then it commits the files. Files that do not already exist in the repository are checked in as revision 1.1. *rcs-to-cvs* is available from the *contrib* directory in the CVS source code.

rcs2sccs and sccs2rcs

These scripts convert between RCS and SCCS version control. Note that *rcs2sccs* supports only one level of branching. Both scripts retain as much of the file metadata as possible. *rcs2sccs* and *sccs2rcs* are available from the *contrib* directory in the CVS source code.

VSSExtractor

VSSExtractor converts files stored under Visual Source Safe to files in a CVS repository. At the time of writing, it is still under development and hasn't reached its 1.0 milestone yet. VSSExtractor is available from *http://sourceforge.net/projects/vssextractor/*.

pvcs2rcs

pvcs2rcs reads files from Merant PVCS version control and writes a copy of those files using RCS version control. It acts recursively and leaves the PVCS archive unchanged. *pvcs2rcs* is available from the *contrib* directory in the CVS source code.

Miscellaneous

The tools described in this section are too unique to be categorized easily. However, they are very useful. They range from a tool to clear out old data from the *history* file, to a tool to mount the repository as a filesystem.

activitymail

This Perl program sends email when the CVS repository is changed. You can configure when to send the mail, and what to put in the mail message. It's intended to be used in the *loginfo* or *commitinfo* scripting files. *activitymail* is available from *http:// search.cpan.org/~dwheeler/activitymail/*.

cln_hist

This script removes most of the old records from the *history* file in the *CVSROOT* directory in the repository. It keeps records of file modification, addition, and removal, keeps the last change to each tag, and removes everything else. This effectively compresses the *history* file by removing most of the outdated data. *cln_hist* is available from the *contrib* directory in the CVS source code.

CPAN VCS::CVS

VCS is an abstracting library for Perl—it allows programmers to write applications which use version control, but which are somewhat independent of the actual version control system in use. One of the version control systems that VCS supports is CVS. The CPAN VCS libraries are available from *http://search.cpan.org/~gmccar/VCS-0.14/ VCS.pm* or from *http://sourceforge.net/projects/vcs/*.

cvs_acls

This script implements access-control lists within CVS. It must be the only script in the *commitinfo* file in the *CVSROOT* directory and should be set as *DEFAULT* so that it is called by all files. The script permits access control based on the username, project directories, and branches within the projects. *cvs_acls* is available from the *contrib* directory in the CVS source code.

CVSCheck

CVSCheck provides status information for files in the current sandbox. Its output is more concise than the output of *cvs status* or *cvs log*, so it's a handy tool for checking status in large sandbox directories. CVSCheck is available from the *contrib* directory in the CVS source code. In 1.12.7 and later, this is called *sandbox_status*.

CVSFS

CVSFS is a tool for mounting a CVS repository as a filesystem. It works only with the *pserver* access method (as of CVS 1.1.9). By default, it displays the current (*HEAD*) revision of the trunk of any file. Its main use is reading a repository, and it can be useful as a build tool. CVSFS is available from *http://sourceforge.net/projects/cvsfs/*.

CVSlib

CVSlib is another library to insulate an application from the CVS commands. Each function in the library returns the data from CVS, already parsed and ready for use by the application. CVSlib is available at *http://cvslib.tigris.org*.

CVS Utilities

This is a collection of small utilities, mostly to help manage sandboxes. It includes a tool to change the stored repository path in a sandbox; a tool to perform tasks such as file addition or deletion while disconnected from the repository; and a tool to remove all derived files from a sandbox, leaving only the core files. CVS Utilities is available at *http://www.red-bean.com/cvsutils/*.

CVS2vendor

CVS2vendor allows you to add a vendor branch to a project you created without using *cvs import* to make a vendor branch. It moves the project to a new repository directory, but it preserves tags and change records. The branch revision of each file on the vendor branch is given the same timestamp as revision 1.1 of that file. CVS2vendor is available from the *contrib* directory in the CVS source code.

descend

The *descend* script is obsolete for use with most CVS commands, but it may be useful in obscure situations. It permits you to descend through a directory tree recursively, running an arbitrary command at each point. *descend* is available from the *contrib* directory in the CVS source code.

newcvsroot

newcvsroot changes the repository path for a whole sandbox—very handy when you need to move a repository and you have users who haven't released their sandboxes. They'll need to use a tool like this (or manual editing) to reuse their existing sandbox. *newcvsroot* is available from the *contrib* directory in the CVS source code.

rcslock

rcslock is described in Chapter 5. It enables you to lock files so that only the developer who holds the file lock can commit a file. This tool is especially useful when you have binary files or other files that cannot be merged. *rcslock* is available from the *contrib* directory in the CVS source code.

sandbox_status

This script, run from within a sandbox directory, provides a list of files and their status. It reports on files which have been added, changed, or removed, but not committed. *sandbox_status* is available from the *contrib* directory in the CVS source code.

validate_repo

validate_repo checks a repository for file corruption. It doesn't actually fix the corruption, but it provides a report on its results. *validate_repo* is available from the *contrib* directory in the CVS source code.

Frequently Asked Questions

Creating this appendix was a good test of this book! You'll find that almost all of the answers refer to sections in the book, and that the ones that don't are still answered in the book, they're just really short answers.

These questions are taken from the *info-cvs@nongnu.org* mailing list, from the start of 2004 through the time of writing (August 2006), and were all asked at least twice. Some questions from early in that period haven't been answered here, because CVS has since changed.

If you have a question you think I should answer in this FAQ, please send email to *bookquestions@oreilly.com*.

Usage Questions

These are the everyday questions about the basic use of CVS, collected in one small section for easy reference. These are not "how do I use CVS at all" questions—those are answered in the quickstart guide. Rather, these answers provide useful combinations of commands, or CVS tips and tricks.

Creating Projects and Sandboxes

The very first step to successfully using a tool such as CVS is putting your files in it. So the questions about that are answered first.

How do I start a new project?

See "Importing Projects" in Chapter 2 (the quickstart guide) or "Creating a Project" in Chapter 7.

How do I avoid using a vendor tag and a release tag when I import?

There's no need to do so. When I know I won't be using them, I use *a1* and *b2* for the tagnames, and ignore them once I've finished using the import command. There's nothing special about *a1* and *b2*, by the way—they're simply legal and meaningless names. You can use *fred* and *ginger*, or *bert* and *ernie* if you want.

How do I list all the projects in a repository?

If you have CVS 1.12.8 or later, you can use the easy method to see which directories are in the top level of the repository:

```
cvs -d repository-path rls .
```

If there are any *modules* defined, you can list those with:

```
cvs -d repository-path checkout -c
```

There's a discussion of this topic at the end of "Creating a Sandbox," in the "Sandboxes and Repositories" section of Chapter 3.

How do I check out all the projects in a repository?

You can check out all the projects in the repository with:

```
cvs -d repository_path checkout -d whatever .
```

You'll need patience, particularly if it's a large repository. This command will install sandboxes for all the projects in the local directory *whatever*. If you have modules defined, you must check them out separately.

How do I get a checkout that doesn't have all that CVS administrative stuff?

The command you're after is *cvs export*. It's explained in "Exporting Files" in Chapter 7.

How do I check out only one file?

The *checkout* command takes, as parameters, a module name or the name (relative to repository root) of any file or directory in the repository. So you just need to specify the file name and path—for example, *cvs -d repository_path checkout /path/to/ file/filename*.

Using Sandboxes

Sandboxes are the most visible aspect of CVS, so there are quite a few questions about them. Answers here include an explanation of locks, and quite a few tips and tricks.

How do I tell whether there are files in the repository that I haven't checked out? How do I tell which files in my sandbox I haven't committed?

The least spammy method that I know of is to use *cvs update* with the *-n* CVS option and the *-d* command option, as in *cvs -n update -d*. The *-n* prevents CVS from actually modifying your sandbox, and the *-d* tells update to check for directories that are new to the sandbox.

You can also use *cvs status*, or in newer versions, *cvs ls* or *rls*. All of these commands are explained in Chapter 3.

How do I clear stickiness?

Stickiness, what it is, and how to clear it is explained in the section "Stickiness" in Chapter 4.

What does "move away (file), it is in the way" mean?

You see this message when CVS is trying to modify your sandbox. It happens when CVS needs to add a file with a particular name, but there's already a file of that name in the sandbox.

How do I rollback or uncommit?

This is explained in Chapter 3 in the section "Retrieving Past Revisions of a File." Take special note of the subsection "Reverting changes."

How do I recover deleted files?

This is also explained in Chapter 3, in the sections "Retrieving Past Revisions of a File" and "Retrieving Removed Files."

What is the Attic?

The most complete explanation of the *Attic* is in "Repository Structure," in Chapter 6. There is also a brief explanation in the section "Removing Files from the Repository" of Chapter 6.

How do I view changes since a particular date? What about between two dates?

Depending on what sorts of changes you want to see, you can use the commands *cvs diff*, *cvs log*, or *cvs history*. The *diff* and *log* commands are explained in "Comparing File Revisions" and "Displaying File History" in Chapter 5, and the *history* command is explained in the "Tools" section of Chapter 7.

These commands also permit you to specify two dates and see the changes that occurred between those dates.

How do I view a list of all the files with a given tag?

Use the cvs option *-n* in combination with *update* (or *checkout*) to produce a list but not actually change your sandbox. Then use *-r tagname* to specify the files with that tag. Your command would be something like *cvs -n update -r tagname*.

How do I find out which tag was set on a given date, or on what date a given tag was created?

The *cvs log* command provides both the tagname and the date for each revision of a file. It is explained in "Retrieving Past Revisions of a File" in Chapter 3, and "Displaying File History" in Chapter 4. For this purpose, you probably want to restrict its output to certain dates or certain revisions.

How do I retrieve a particular revision when I only know which date the revision was on?

This looks like a job for *cvs log*! Retrieve the log information for the date you want, and browse the log messages, tagnames, and other information until you've found the revision number or tagname you need. For further information on *cvs log*, see "Retrieving Past Revisions of a File" in Chapter 3, and "Displaying File History" in Chapter 4.

What is locking all about?

There are three different types of locking that are relevant to CVS. The first, repository locks, are internal to CVS and usually won't affect users. The other two forms are ways to help multiple developers work on the same file. The three methods of collaboration that CVS supports are explained in Chapter 5, in "Using Simultaneous Development," "Watching a File," and "Reserving Files."

Repository locks

> These are internal to CVS, and are how CVS prevents itself from trying to read a file which is being changed, or worse, write to it while it's being changed. Users should only ever see the message explained in "Lock Files" in Chapter 3. Repository administrators may need to read the section on "Clearing Locks" in Chapter 6. These locks are fully explained in "Locks" in Chapter 6.

Locks in the advisory exclusive development model

> The section "Watching a File" in Chapter 5 explains how to signal that a file is yours to edit, and that everyone else should leave it alone. It also explains how to be notified when someone else has signaled that a file is theirs: by *watching* it. A *lock* in this sense doesn't really lock the file; it simply puts a metaphorical bright red sticker on it saying "this is mine, go away."

Locks in the exclusive development model

> Instead of a metaphorical red sticker, it's possible to actually prohibit another person from committing a file you've claimed as yours. This is the third sense of *locking* and is explained in "Reserving Files" in Chapter 5.

How do I lock files so that only I can commit them?

This is the exclusive development model, which is not CVS's native method of working. CVS can do it, however, and it's explained in "Reserving Files" in Chapter 5.

Using Branches

No aspect of CVS seems to cause as much confusion as branches. The questions in this section range from how to merge, to how to resurrect a deleted branch.

How do I lock a particular branch so no one can commit to it?

Write a script that takes the *commitinfo* parameters, tests whether the attempted commit is to the branch in question, and returns a nonzero value if it is. You then add this script to the *commitinfo* scripting file. You can find examples of *commitinfo* scripting files that affect permissions in the *cvs_acls* or *rcslock* scripts described in Appendix B. The scripting files are explained in Chapter 7.

How do I get the history of all files in a particular branch?

Use *cvs log* or *cvs diff* for this purpose. Try using *cvs log* with the *-r branch-base-tag::* option, or *diff -s* or *diff --brief* with *-r branch-base-tag -r branch-tag*.

How do I check out multiple branches of a project?

Use a different sandbox for each branch. You can create a sandbox with a sandbox root name different from the project name by using the *-d* command option:

```
cvs -d repository_path checkout -r branch-tag -d new-sandbox-root-name
```

How do I merge from branch to trunk, or trunk to branch?

See the section "Merging Branches" in Chapter 4.

How do I avoid fixing the same conflicts over and over when I merge branches?

In "Merging Branches" in Chapter 4, I mention that it's good practice to tag when you've merged, and to do the next merge from that tag rather than from the root of the branch. The reason for this is to avoid fixing the same conflicts multiple times.

How do I remove a branch?

Please don't! But if you feel you must, see the section "Deleting or Moving a Branch" in Chapter 4.

How do I branch a branch? Why would I want to?

See the section "Nested branches" in Chapter 4.

How do I recreate a deleted branch tag?

Very, very painfully. Larry Jones describes the process in this archived email: *http://lists.gnu.org/archive/html/info-cvs/2004-02/msg00306.html*. Derek Price has suggestions as well, in the email: *http://lists.gnu.org/archive/html/info-cvs/2004-02/msg00309.html*.

The essence of their method requires you to follow this process for each file in the tagless branch:

1. Run *cvs log* on the file to get a list of revision numbers.
2. Identify which revision number should have the deleted branch tag.
3. Use *cvs admin -n* to relink the tagname to the branch.

The section "Branch Revision Numbers" in Chapter 4 will help you identify the revision number for your branch.

Managing Projects

Project managers have problems all their own. From managing common files for multiple projects to sending emails automatically on commit, there are always issues which make a given project unique.

How do I make a patch?

This is explained in "Making Patchfiles" in Chapter 7.

How do I make CVS support symbolic links?

You don't. CVS isn't designed to store pseudofiles such as symbolic links. Instead, put the creation of the symbolic links into your build script.

How do I import vendor upgrades directly to a branch?

This is explained in "Vendor Branches" in Chapter 7.

How can I share common files between projects?

The best way I'm aware of is to use modules. See "Project Structure and Sandboxes" and "The modules File" in Chapter 7.

How do I send emails automatically?

Use a script in one or more of the scripting files to send the mail. Choose the scripting file that runs at the time you want the mail sent: for example, use *commitinfo* or *loginfo* for commits, or *postwatch* for watch notifications. See "Scripting Files" in Chapter 7 and the *activitymail* script in Appendix B.

You can also use the *watch* family of commands for some emails if you want to allow your users to determine which files they are emailed for. See "Watching a File" in Chapter 5.

Administration Questions

The repository administrator has a range of problems, from installation and configuration, to security, to ensuring the distribution of committed files. Answers here range from upgrade problems to moving a repository.

General Administration

The fundamentals of administration include installation, configuration, and upgrades. If you don't get those right, you won't get anywhere.

How do I install and configure CVS?

There are instructions and examples in Chapters 2 and 6. If you're after a quick and easy installation, use Chapter 2.

Will upgrading cause me any problems?

In most cases, no. If you are upgrading across the changeover in the scripting files (version 1.12.6), you will start to get deprecation warnings about the change in the scripting files. See the section "Running Scripts" in Chapter 7 for information on getting rid of those warnings.

How can I automatically create a changelog from CVS?

There are a variety of changelog generators in Appendix B in the section "Logging Tools."

How do I export a current copy automatically when files are committed?

The section in Chapter 7 titled "The loginfo File," has an example of exporting automatically. The process involves including the *export* command in the *loginfo* file, making sure it runs in the background.

Permissions and Security

Permissions are one thing you must get right, especially if you're protecting important secrets, or are a target for the immature or the criminal. This section answers issues from access control lists to *pserver* passwords.

How can I manage CVS file permissions?

See "Securing Your Projects" in Chapter 6.

How do I get access control for CVS?

There is a *cvs_acls* plugin explained in Appendix B that provides this.

How do I prevent my users from deleting my repository?

See "Securing Your Projects" in Chapter 6, but be aware that ideally the only access that untrusted users have to the server is via the connection that leads straight to CVS.

How do I let multiple users use the same files?

The trick is to use group ownership of the relevant files, which is explained in "Securing Your Projects" in Chapter 6.

How do I fix permission denied problems?

Either the permissions are incorrect (see "Securing Your Projects" in Chapter 6), or there is a stale lock file (see "Clearing Locks" in Chapter 6).

How do I clear file locks?

See "Clearing Locks" in Chapter 6, or, if that is the wrong type of lock, read "Reserving a File" in Chapter 5.

How do I set up pserver?

There is an explanation and examples in Chapter 8. Be sure to read both "The pserver Access Method" and "Using inetd with gserver, kserver, and pserver."

How do I change pserver passwords?

The *pserver* passwords can be set or changed only by the repository administrator. The method is explained in "The pserver Access Method," in Chapter 8.

Repositories

The repository is the most important element of CVS, and the simplest way to handle it is to have a single repository that never changes and is never moved. But that's boring. Here are some answers for those of us with interesting repositories.

How do I rename a repository?

Just use the Unix *mv* command to rename the repository, and check your *inetd* configuration for references to the old repository. All your users must commit and release beforehand and check out again afterwards, or edit their *CVS/Root* files in their sandboxes.

How do I maintain a repository on Samba/NTFS/etc.?

The experience of most people seems to be that it doesn't work reliably, and it's almost certain to fail if the filesystem is a caching filesystem. If you choose to try, check the archives of the *info-cvs* mailing list at *http://lists.gnu.org/archive/html/info-cvs/* for the experiences of others who've tried.

How do I run multiple repositories from one pserver/kserver/gserver invocation?

Call the server with multiple *--allow-root* options. See "Using inetd with gserver, kserver, and pserver" in Chapter 8.

How do I make an anonymous, read-only repository?

See the note on read-only anonymous access in "Project Directories" in Chapter 6.

How do I make several anonymous, read-only repositories?

Combine the information in the section "Using inetd with gserver, kserver, and pserver" in Chapter 8 with the information in the note in "Project Directories" in Chapter 6.

How do I run multiple projects from one repository?

This is answered in "Project Directories" in Chapter 6.

How do I make multiple repositories with the same project information? How do I synchronize multiple CVS repositories?

These are answered in "Distributed Repositories" in Chapter 6.

How do I move a repository from one server to another?

The repository is a collection of ordinary files, and can be moved with your favorite copy program—*rsync* or *scp* are the ones I would normally use. Also read "Backing Up a Repository" in Chapter 6.

You must first find a way to prevent your users from connecting to the repository while you move it (freezing the repository will work, as will disabling connections). If the hostname will be changing, you should probably have your users release their sandboxes before the move and check out fresh ones afterward.

Final Questions

These are the last two questions in the book. One is answered, the other—well, you'll see.

How do I get off the mailing list?

Go to the list information page at *http://lists.nongnu.org/mailman/listinfo/info-cvs* and follow the instructions at the bottom of the page.

How do I make money fast?

For an answer to this question, send $100 or the equivalent in local currency, in cash, no cheques or money orders, to....

Index

Symbols

* (asterisk), 351
\ (backslash), 351, 371
! (bang), 351
{ } (braces), xiv, 209, 217, 327
[ ] (brackets), xiv, 351
^ (caret), 351
. . . (ellipses), xiv
(hash mark), 209, 212
  .#file.revision, 36, 317
  filename prefixes, 263
  lock files, 189
% (percent), 209, 216, 217, 287, 327
  loginfo, format string for, 327
%s (percents), 164
_ (underscores), 155
| (vertical bars), xiv
? (wildcard), 351

A

abCVS, 373
access methods, 48
  remote repositories, 234–255
    anonymous, read-only access, 248
    client ports, 252
    ext, 237, 240
    fork, 241
    gserver, 242
    inetd, 251
    kserver, 244
    login and logout commands, 249
    misconfiguration, 260
    options, 235
    PAM, 253–255
    server access methods, 237, 239
    SSH, 239
  repositories, 234, 353
    client side, 353
    ext, 237
    local access method, 236
    options, 235
    pserver (see pserver access method)
    server access methods, 237, 354
action, 209, 326
activitymail, 384
add command, 36, 70, 108, 273
  -kb option, 83
  projects, creating with, 201
admin command, 133, 134, 225, 274–277
  postadmin file, 217
administrative files, 148, 154, 323–325
  CVS subdirectory files, 324
  CVSROOT copies of, 158
  dot files, 323
  location, 154
  ownership, 148
administrative tools, 225
alias modules, 211, 335
Anjuta, 373
annotate command, 124, 140, 278
apt package manager, 17
asterisk (*), 351
atomic commits, 7
Attic subdirectory, 38, 97, 154
  files, 97
    moving or removing tags from, 97

We'd like to hear your suggestions for improving our indexes. Send email to *index@oreilly.com*.

R

rannotate command, 303
RCS (Revision Control System), 3
RCS files, editing, 186
rcs2log script, 381
rcs2sccs, 383
RCSBIN, 194, 343
RCS-format files, 158
rcsinfo file, 166, 218, 339
rcslock script, 132–136, 385
    committing of files, 135
    installing and configuring, 133
    releasing of files, 135
    reserving of files, 134
rcs-to-cvs script, 383
rdiff command, 99, 124, 136, 304–306
    options, 139
readers file, 168, 249, 339
read-only access, providing for, 152
regular expressions, 351
regular modules, 213, 336
    options, 336
release command, 52, 78, 307
remote repositories, 233, 246
    access methods (see access methods)
    repository paths, 233
    rsh and security, 238
    security, 250
    (see also repositories)
remove command, 70, 71–73, 108, 307
repositories, 20–23
    access methods (see access methods)
    adding files, 36, 70
    administration FAQs, 393
    Attic subdirectory, 38
    backing up, 171–177
        freezing, 172
        restores, 177
    changing, 52
    creating, 148
    deleting, 149
    directories, removing, 76
    distributed (see distributed repositories)
    editing, 180–190, 202
        clearing locks, 189
        deleting files and directories, 185
        deleting projects, 186
        moving files and directories, 181
        RCS files, editing, 186
    email notification of change via
          activitymail, 384

FAQs, 394
files
    checking out, 28
    executable files, importation of, 153
    permissions and ownership, 47
    removing, 38, 71–73
    retrieving removed files, 73–76
    sandbox files, updating, 59
    host name changes and, 259
locking, 156
managing, 147
paths, 47
permissions errors, 256
projects, checking out all, 388
projects, listing, 388
remote (see remote repositories)
remote repositories, accessing, 27
repository locks, 390
repository paths, 233
repository root and path, 13
sandboxes and, 46
storage locations, 149
structure, 154
subdirectories, 154
UTC (Coordinated Universal Time), 67
Repository file, 191, 325
reserved attribute names, 155
retroactive branching, 105
reverting changes, 64
Revision Control System (RCS), 3
Revision keyword, 112
revision numbers, 55
revisions, retrieving, 390
RFC 822 and 1123 time format, 344
.rhosts file, 192
RISC OS CVS ports, 378
rlog command, 308–310
rls command, 49, 310
rollbacks, 389
root directories
    permissions, 150
    repositories, creating, 148
Root file, 50, 191, 325
rsh (remote shell), 238
    substitutes, problems with, 262
rsync program, 178
rtag command, 88, 91, 311–313
    making branches, 103
    moving tags, 96
    removing tags, 95
    syntax, 91

version control systems, 3
    comparing, 7–10
    converting between, 383
version tracking, 3
vertical bars (|), xiv
vi text editor, 24
ViewVC, 380
Vim, 375
Visual Source Safe file conversions, 383
VISUAL variable, 193, 342
VSSExtractor, 383

W

Wandisco, 380
watch command, 12, 124, 319
    incompatible CVS versions, 130
    watch add, 125
    watch off, 128
    watch on, 125, 126, 128
watch method (exclusive development), 124
watchers command, 132, 320
watches, 126
    marking a file for watching, 128
    setting, 128
web page for this book, xvi

web searches for CVS information, 257
web-viewable repositories, 180
wildcards, 351
WinCVS, 15, 358
    installing, 361
Windows
    CVSNT server, and, 377
    WinCVS (see WinCVS)
Windows CVS clients, 370–372
wrappers, 83–85
wrappers command, 84
wrappers for binary files
    incompatible CVS versions, 85
    options, 84
write proxies, 179
writers file, 169, 249, 341

Y

yum package manager, 17

Z

Zeus SCC-CVS, 375
zOS, 376

About the Author

Jennifer Vesperman has been working with computers since the late 1980s. She began by learning to use Unix and Macintosh systems at Griffith University in Queensland, Australia. She is a programmer, system administrator, and technical writer. In the mid-1990s, she switched to using Minix on her personal machines, and in the late 1990s, she switched to Linux.

She has worked on projects both with and without version control and greatly prefers to have version control. CVS is her first choice for a version control system because she knows it well, it serves all the needs she's found so far, and it's very commonly used by colleagues and clients.

Jennifer currently works as a contractor for Cybersource, a programming, system administration, and training company in Melbourne, Australia. She also writes for the O'Reilly Network and is the current coordinator for LinuxChix (*http://www.linuxchix.org*), a Linux advocacy and support group for women.

Colophon

The animals on the cover of *Essential CVS*, Second Edition, are bobacs (*Marmota bobak*). Also known as "steppe marmots" because of their wide distribution in the *steppes* (vast, grass-covered plains) of southern Russia and Kazakhstan, bobacs range as far west as central Europe. Though they are slightly larger than black-tailed prairie dogs, bobacs are otherwise quite similar to their North American counterparts.

Unlike most marmots, which live primarily in mountain environments, bobacs prefer to build their sprawling burrows in open, rolling grasslands or on the edges of cultivated fields. Bobacs are strictly diurnal and are most active during the cooler hours of the day. When they are outside of their burrows, it is common for a sentry to stand erect and alert on its hind legs, ready to bark an alert at the first sign of a predator or other danger. After running to their burrows, bobacs will then await an "all clear" call before returning to the surface. During the summer, bobacs eat enough lush vegetation to double their weight. The added fat reserve nourishes them throughout their winter hibernation.

Like other marmots, bobacs are very social animals that live in large groups, or "towns," which may range from a single acre to over 1,000 acres. Towns are subdivided further into "wards" and even smaller "coteries," which are usually made up of a single adult male, one to four adult females, and any number of offspring under two years old. Young bobacs, born in litters of about five or six, leave their natal coterie after their second hibernation. Because their coats can be used as imitation marten fur in hats, coats, and other apparel, bobacs are greatly threatened by fur hunting.

The cover image is a 19th-century engraving from the Dover Pictorial Archive. The cover font is Adobe ITC Garamond. The text font is Linotype Birka; the heading font is Adobe Myriad Condensed; and the code font is LucasFont's TheSans Mono Condensed.

Better than e-books

Buy *Essential CVS*, 2nd Edition, and access
the digital edition FREE on Safari for 45 days.

Go to www.oreilly.com/go/safarienabled
and type in coupon code W5JT-7JRK-WWPP-T9KH-TYZV

Search
thousands of
top tech books

Download
whole chapters

Cut and Paste
code examples

Find
answers fast

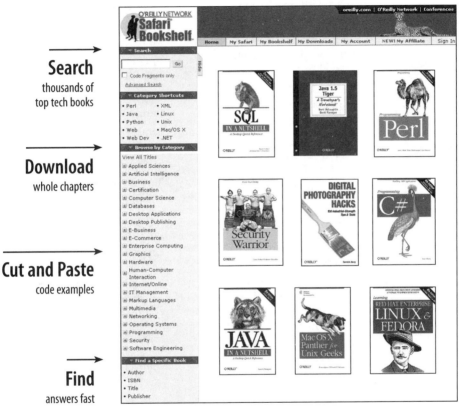

Search Safari! The premier electronic reference
library for programmers and IT professionals.

Related Titles from O'Reilly

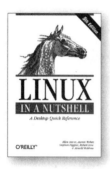

Linux

Building Embedded Linux Systems

Building Secure Servers with Linux

The Complete FreeBSD, *4th Edition*

Even Grues Get Full

Exploring the JDS Linux Desktop

Extreme Programming Pocket Guide

GDB Pocket Reference

Knoppix Hacks

Knoppix Pocket Guide

Learning Red Hat Enterprise Linux and Fedora, *4th Edition*

Linux Annoyances for Geeks

Linux Cookbook

Linux Desktop Hacks

Linux Desktop Pocket Guide

Linux Device Drivers, *3rd Edition*

Linux in a Nutshell, *5th Edition*

Linux in a Windows World

Linux iptables Pocket Reference

Linux Multimedia Hacks

Linux Network Administrator's Guide, *3rd Edition*

Linux Pocket Guide

Linux Security Cookbook

Linux Server Hacks, *Volume 2*

Linux Unwired

Linux Web Server CD Bookshelf, *Version 2.0*

LPI Linux Certification in a Nutshell

Managing RAID on Linux

More Linux Server Hacks

OpenOffice.org Writer

Producing Open Source Software

Programming with Qt, *2nd Edition*

Root of all Evil

Running Linux, *5th Edition*

Samba Pocket Reference, *2nd Edition*

SUSE Linux

Test Driving Linux

Ubuntu Hacks

Understanding Linux Network Intervals

Understanding the Linux Kernel, *3rd Edition*

Understanding Open Source & Free Software Licensing

User Friendly

Using Samba, *2nd Edition*

Version Control with Subversion